CRITICAL SURVEY
OF
LONG FICTION

Irish Novelists

Editor

Carl Rollyson
Baruch College, City University of New York

SALEM PRESS
Ipswich, Massachusetts • Hackensack, New Jersey

Cover photo:
Edna O'Brien (© Julian Calder/Corbis)

ISBN 978-1-4298-3692-0

CONTENTS

CONTRIBUTORS

Robert Becker
Original Contributor

Cynthia A. Bily
Adrian, Michigan

Steve D. Boilard
Legislative Analyst's Office

James S. Brown
*Bloomsburg University of
Pennsylvania*

John R. Clark
Original Contributor

Diane D'Amico
Original Contributor

M. Casey Diana
Arizona State University

Grace Eckley
Original Contributor

Richard A. Spurgeon Hall
Methodist College

John P. Harrington
Original Contributor

William J. Heim
Original Contributor

Greig E. Henderson
Original Contributor

Archibald E. Irwin
Original Contributor

Rebecca Kuzins
Pasadena, California

Joanne McCarthy
Tacoma, Washington

Fred B. McEwen
Original Contributor

David W. Madden
*California State University,
Sacramento*

Charles E. May
*California State University,
Long Beach*

Laurence W. Mazzeno
Alvernia College

William Nelles
*University of Massachusetts
Dartmouth*

George O'Brien
Original Contributor

Cóilín Owens
Original Contributor

K. Bhaskara Rao
Original Contributor

Dorothy Dodge Robbins
Louisiana Tech University

Marjorie Smelstor
Kauffman Foundation

Jaquelyn W. Walsh
McNeese State University

Michele Wender Zak
Original Contributor

IRISH LONG FICTION

Irish literature falls into two distinct categories. Written in the Irish language, the first category includes bardic poems and Celtic sagas. The second category, Irish literature written in English, includes what is often called Anglo-Irish literature because it was created by Protestants of English extraction. This phenomenon can be explained by England's historical colonization of Ireland and the acceptance of Irish writers within the British literary tradition.

THE EIGHTEENTH CENTURY

Although Irish writers are recognized for their contributions to poetry and drama, Irish writers beginning in the eighteenth century contributed also to the rise of the English novel. Irish writers also played a large role in the evolution of the English novel throughout the nineteenth and twentieth centuries. Very little eighteenth century Irish fiction deals with Irish subject matter. On the contrary, Irish fiction deals with humor, the sense of the grotesque and fantasy, the significance of anecdote, and the importance of the storyteller, all of which categorize the constructs of the Irish novel.

Irish long fiction took root in the eighteenth century with the writings of Jonathan Swift (1667-1745). His exuberant use of humor and fantasy, as well as his expansive imagination, demonstrates the deep influence of Ireland on his psyche and firmly distinguishes him as an Irish writer. Recognized as the foremost prose satirist in the English language, Swift spent much of his life trying to escape Ireland, which was considered then as a place of exile from England. However, politics dictated that he spend the bulk of his life as dean of St. Patrick's Anglican cathedral in Dublin.

Although Swift penned verse early in his life, his true genius did not surface until he turned to prose satire. His *A Tale of a Tub*, published anonymously in 1704, is a satire against religion and education. The book isolated Swift as a genius of satiric wit. His greatest novel, *Gulliver's Travels* (1726), assured his permanent place in literary history. The ironic tension Swift creates prompts questions about the author's views on humankind. In each of the novel's four books, Lemuel Gulliver sets sail on a voyage and ends up in a strange land. In book 1, Gulliver finds himself a giant prisoner of the six-inch-high Lilliputians, whom he saves from invasion from the neighboring Blefuscu. He escapes when he is charged with treason.

In book 2, the hero travels to Brobdingnag, where he finds himself as tiny as a toy in a world of giants. Although loved and pampered as a pet, in fear for his life he manages to escape in the talons of a large bird. In book 3, Gulliver visits the floating island of Laputa, where the islanders are so obsessed with scientific activity, particularly those in the Academy of Lagado (a parody of England's Royal Society), that they are blind to commonplace hazards. Book 4 finds Gulliver in the utopian land of the admirable, enlightened, rational horses, the Houyhnhnms, and the degraded, filthy humans, the Yahoos. Although first accepted as a curiosity by the gentle creatures, Gulliver is soon ousted as despicable because of his human physical characteristics. Although, at the end of his fourth voyage, he returns to England, he finds himself no longer able to tolerate human company and lives out his days in the company of horses.

Swift's ironic novel has no clear-cut explanation. Swift utilizes the various places his hero visits to satirize the folly of humankind. Of the human beings he encounters, the Lilliputians and the Brobdingnagians are impractical and mean-spirited, and the intellectuals in book 3 lack any wisdom, if they are not outright mad. The humanlike Yahoos are contemptible and powerless to express any reason whatsoever, but the Houyhnhnms, the horses, are reasonable and kind.

Swift was certainly not the only esteemed eighteenth century Irish writer. In *Tristram Shandy* (1759-1767), humorist Laurence Sterne (1713-1768) made a critical contribution to English literature, which secured him the reputation of a major novelist. The book is generally considered the progenitor of the psychological novel and the twentieth century stream-of-consciousness novel popularized by James Joyce and Virginia Woolf.

In the novel, the narrator, Tristram, sets out to do the seemingly impossible: to tell the story of his own life. Beginning at the narrator's moment of conception, Sterne parodies the emerging novelistic form by exploring the relativity of time in human experience. Throughout, the author disorders experiences and mocks the development of narrative by providing no consistent plot or conclusion and by inserting outrageous and lengthy digressions. Ultimately, Tristram realizes the telling of his life's story takes longer than the living of it.

Sterne also penned *A Sentimental Journey Through France and Italy* (1768) in an attempt to teach humans to love their fellow creatures. The novel, which parodies the era's wide range of travel books, had a major impact on the campaign toward sentimentalism prevalent in the second half of the eighteenth century. This movement associated acute sensibility and a sympathetic, tender heart with true virtue. In the novel, the narrator, Parson Yorick, who is frequently moved to tears, sets out to travel through France and Italy in search of "sentimental commerce," or genuine human contact.

Frances Sheridan (1724-1766), mother of the famous Irish dramatist Richard Brinsley Sheridan and much influenced by Samuel Richardson, author of *Pamela: Or, Virtue Rewarded* (1740-1741) and *Clarissa: Or, The History of a Young Lady* (1747-1748), wrote the popular sentimental *Memoirs of Miss Sidney Bidulph* (1761), which considers the effect of extreme suffering on ideal virtue by focusing on the social role assigned to women in eighteenth century society. She also wrote the highly acclaimed and didactic Eastern-themed novel, *The History of Nurjahad, by the Editor of Sidney Bidulph* (1767), much in keeping with Samuel Johnson's *Rasselas, Prince of Abyssinia: A Tale by S. Johnson* (1759).

Although Oliver Goldsmith (1728 or 1730-1774) achieved eminence as an essayist (*The Citizen of the World*, 1762), a poet (*The Deserted Village*, 1770), and a dramatist (*She*

Stoops to Conquer: Or, The Mistakes of a Night, pr., pb. 1773), he is also well recognized as a novelist for his pastoral novel *The Vicar of Wakefield* (1766). Early in his life, his first calling as a physician was soon submerged by his writing talent, which gained him much literary renown. He was one of the founding members of the famous Literary Club, which included Samuel Johnson, Sir Joshua Reynolds, David Garrick, Edmund Burke, and James Boswell.

The melodramatic *The Vicar of Wakefield* presents a picture of idealized rural village life and the unforgettable vicar, Dr. Charles Primrose. The family's troubles begin when the vicar loses his income and is forced to move the family near the estate of Squire Thornhill, who abducts his daughter Olivia. Next, the vicar's son George is imprisoned after his attempt to avenge his sister. The vicar's troubles continue when his other daughter, Sophia, is also abducted. After the family's house burns down, the vicar is imprisoned for debt. Despite such hardship, the vicar remains unfailingly charitable throughout. Goldsmith, who had the ability to crystallize the human personality, provides a comic look at the human predicament.

Maria Edgeworth (1768-1849) authentically captures eighteenth and nineteenth century rural Irish life in her popular novels and children's stories. Deeply involved with issues of nationality and cultural identity, Edgeworth is known for presenting the first believable children in the English novel form in the collection *The Parent's Assistant: Or, Stories for Children* (1796, 1800). Her actual involvement in running her father's estate in Ireland provided her with the knowledge necessary to authentically characterize rural Irish society in her first novel, *Castle Rackrent* (1800), said to be the first fully developed regional novel and the first true historical novel in English. Edgeworth focused attention on the much-maligned practice of absentee English landowning in *The Absentee* (1812), said to influence Sir Walter Scott (1771-1832) to finish his novel *Waverley: Or, 'Tis Sixty Years Since* (1814). *Patronage* (1814) and *Ormond* (1817) explore the relationship between culture and politics and heightened Edgeworth's literary reputation. During the Irish famine in 1846, Edgeworth became a spokesperson for Irish relief.

William Chaigneau (1709-1781) contributed one of the earliest Irish novels, *The History of Jack Connor* (1752). A picaresque novel in the tradition of Miguel de Cervantes's *Don Quixote de la Mancha* (1605, 1615) and later Henry Fielding's *The History of Tom Jones, a Foundling* (1749; commonly known as *Tom Jones*), *The History of Jack Connor* concerns the cultural identity of a young Irish man forced to become an English soldier.

THE NINETEENTH CENTURY

The nineteenth century saw progress from sentimentalism to sensationalism with the development of the Irish gothic tradition, which made use of gothic architecture, convoluted plot, emotional intensity, and supernatural agency. The Irish gothic was popularized by Charles Robert Maturin (1780-1824), author of *Melmoth the Wanderer* (1820), which was set inside seventeenth century madhouses, and by Joseph Sheridan Le Fanu (1814-

1873), author of *The House by the Churchyard* (1863), a tale of a ghostly hand that taps on windows.

Undoubtedly, however, the most popular Irish gothic writer is Bram Stoker (1847-1912), the author of the horror tale *Dracula* (1897), the subject of many films. Told principally through multiple diary entries, the tale features the unforgettable undead vampire Count Dracula, who travels to England and victimizes young Lucy Westerna. Dr. Van Helsing and the young solicitor Jonathan Harker attempt to overpower Dracula and keep him from Mina, Harker's fiancé. After his return to Transylvania, Dracula crumbles to dust after he is beheaded and stabbed through the heart by his captors. Stoker is also the author of the lesser-known *The Snake's Pass* (1890), *The Mystery of the Sea* (1902), *The Jewel of Seven Stars* (1903), and *The Lady of the Shroud* (1909).

Oscar Wilde (1854-1900), another renowned Irish writer better known as a dramatist (*Lady Windermere's Fan*, pr. 1892, and *The Importance of Being Earnest: A Trivial Comedy for Serious People*, pr. 1895) contributed to the Irish gothic tradition by creating one of the most popular nineteenth century novels. *The Picture of Dorian Gray* (serial 1890, expanded 1891) blends supernatural elements with French decadence. The novel caused a great deal of scandal: Wilde declared in the preface that there was no such thing as a moral or immoral book.

In the novel, the beautiful youth Dorian Gray has his portrait painted before he turns to a life of vice and corruption. However, the painting has supernatural powers and grows more and more degenerate and corrupted, reflecting the actual appearance of Gray, who maintains his youthful appearance. At the end, Gray kills the artist and stabs the painting; he is discovered as the very image of depravity, a knife through his heart, while the painting depicts an innocent youth. Wilde, a leader of the aesthetic movement in England and a well-known and flamboyant social wit, was greatly influenced by Walter Pater (1839-1894), who advocated art for art's sake.

Although not as popular, George Moore (1852-1933) nevertheless deserves consideration for his innovations in fiction. In his first novels, *A Modern Lover* (1883), set in artistic bohemian society, and *A Mummer's Wife* (1884), he introduced French naturalism into English literature, coming later to utilize the realistic techniques of Gustave Flaubert and Honoré de Balzac. Moore counted among his friends Irish poet and dramatist William Butler Yeats and played a role in the development of the Abbey Theatre. Moore is best known for *Hail and Farewell: A Trilogy* (1911-1914), a comic, autobiographical satire in monologue form that features Yeats and Irish dramatist Lady Augusta Gregory and records the history of the Irish Literary Revival.

THE TWENTIETH CENTURY

While the twentieth century Irish Literary Revival encouraged the publication of poetry, drama, and folklore, Ireland continued producing long-fiction writers. James Joyce (1882-1941), arguably one of Ireland's best novelists, is highly celebrated for his experimental use of language. In 1904, in the company of a young girl named Nora Barnacle, Joyce left his native Dublin for the European continent to begin his writing career in earnest. His early stories, and all his later works, feature the city of Dublin—socially frozen and inanimate—and deal almost exclusively with Irish subject matter. Concerned with both the Symbolist and realist literary movements, Joyce integrated both styles, utilizing every word he composed to provide meaning. His autobiographical novel, *A Portrait of the Artist as a Young Man* (serial 1914-1915, book 1916), sketches the development of young Stephen Dedalus, who ultimately leaves Dublin for Paris to dedicate his life to art.

Joyce's best-known novel, *Ulysses* (1922), parallels Homer's *Odyssey* (c. 800 B.C.E.). The action in *Ulysses* takes place in Dublin on a single day, June 16, 1904, which has popularly come to be known as Bloomsday. The novel features Dedalus, the hero of Joyce's earlier novel; Leopold Bloom, an advertising salesman; and his wife, Molly Bloom—all modern representations of the mythic Telemachus, Ulysses, and Penelope. Through interior monologue, or the stream-of-consciousness technique, their myriad thoughts, impressions, and feelings—rational and irrational—are revealed as they make their way through the day in Dublin.

Finnegans Wake (1939), written in a unique and extremely difficult but comic style, features the archetypal family, about whom everyone dreams, metaphorically falling and rising. The novel characterizes a Dublin tavern-keeper, Humphrey Chimpden Earwicker; his wife, Mrs. Anna Livia Plurabelle; and their children, Shem, Shaun, and Isabel in a dream sequence throughout the course of one night. In pervasive dreamlike fashion, Joyce utilizes puns throughout and merges various languages, mythic images, and literary and historical characters to show, albeit obscurely, how history predominates over human experience and relationships.

Although, like Goldsmith and Wilde, Samuel Beckett (1906-1989) was more popularly known as a dramatist, he also was widely recognized as a novelist. Strongly influenced by Joyce (whom he met in Paris), Beckett's popular novel *Murphy* (1938) concerns an Irishman in London who becomes a nurse in a mental institution. While hiding in France during World War II, Beckett wrote *Watt* (1953), a highly abstract novel that deals with a servant who continues to work for a master whom he never meets until he is dismissed. Between 1946 and 1949, Beckett wrote *Molloy* (1951; English translation, 1955), *Malone meurt* (1951; *Malone Dies*, 1956), and *L'Innommable* (1953; *The Unnamable*, 1958). Beckett, winner of the Nobel Prize in Literature in 1969, attempts to analyze people's social relationships with one another. His work is thick with literary, historical, and philosophical allusions and draws heavily on thirteenth century Italian poet Dante Alighieri, seventeenth century French philosopher René Descartes, and seventeenth century Dutch philosopher Arnold Geulincx, whose philosophy attempts to integrate both the physical and the spiritual sides of men and women. Beckett puzzled continuously over the human condition.

Like the work of Joyce, Edna O'Brien's (born 1930) work was banned by the Catholic Church in Ireland. Her strict Catholic convent education provided the impetus to write her popular first novel, *The Country Girls* (1960), which concerns solitary women seeking identity and a sense of belonging. This first volume of *The Country Girls Trilogy and Epilogue* (1986) features two Irish girls who leave their strict rural convent school for a more exciting, less curtailed life in Dublin. Their lives are subsequently recorded in *The Lonely Girl* (1962; also known as *Girl with Green Eyes*, 1964) and *Girls in Their Married Bliss* (1964). Disillusioned, both girls leave Dublin for London, finding neither a meaningful connection with men nor happiness in marriage.

O'Brien's novels express despair over women's repression and place in contemporary society. Lonely and empty, her female characters, although at times happy, continuously seek fulfillment in doomed erotic relationships. Her portrayals of her characters' sexuality was deemed too frank for the 1960's, and the Country Girls trilogy was banned in Ireland for a time. O'Brien's twentieth book of fiction, *The Light of Evening* (2006), uses stream of consciousness to look back on the life and relationships of an elderly widow. The novel returns to O'Brien's themes of an oppressive church and a search for female autonomy.

Although Irish writers are highly recognized for their enormous contributions to poetry and drama, the legacy of Irish long fiction is splendid and rich as well. In addition to Joyce, Beckett, and O'Brien, Forrest Reid (1875-1947), Brinsley MacNamara (1890-1963), Peadar O'Donnell (1893-1986), Joyce Cary (1888-1957), Elizabeth Bowen (1899-1973), Francis MacManus (1909-1960), Flann O'Brien (1911-1966), Mary Lavin (1912-1996), and John McGahern (1934-2006) carried on the Irish long fiction tradition in the twentieth century.

IRISH LITERATURE INTO THE TWENTY-FIRST CENTURY

Prizewinning novelists Roddy Doyle (born 1958) and Patrick McCabe (born 1955) are two of Ireland's finest contemporary novelists, following in the footprints of earlier Irish literary giants. Doyle's humorous *The Barrytown Trilogy* (1992; includes *The Commitments*, 1987; *The Snapper*, 1990; and *The Van*, 1991) centers on the irrepressible working-class Rabbitte family in Dublin.

Doyle's first novel, *The Commitments*, traces the everyday life of the Rabbitte family and their uproarious encounters with a group of working-class Irish teenagers who form a soul band, the Commitments. *The Snapper* deals hilariously with pregnancy. When nineteen-year-old Sharon Rabbitte becomes pregnant, she refuses to name the father of her "snapper." Her father, Jimmy, Sr., at first feels embarrassed and blames his daughter but eventually takes an active part in Sharon's pregnancy, coming to wonder at the marvels of life and loving. *The Van* examines male friendship. When Jimmy, Sr., loses his job, what he misses most are his evenings out at the pub with his friends. Although he joins the library and cares for his baby granddaughter, it is not until he and his best pal, Bimbo, buy a beat-up fish-and-chips van that he gains back his enthusiasm for life. All sections of the trilogy were made into successful films.

One of Doyle's strengths is his ability to give voice to a range of characters. In his Booker Prize-winning comic novel, *Paddy Clarke, Ha-Ha-Ha* (1993), Doyle captures the wonder and carefree days of youth through the speech patterns of childhood. Ten-year-old Padraic Clarke, or Paddy, runs wild through the streets of Barrytown with his gang of bullying friends, setting fires, playing "cowboys and Indians," and generally having a good time. *The Woman Who Walked into Doors* (1996) and its sequel, *Paula Spencer* (2006), concern a battered wife who uses her wits and a sharp tongue to deal with substance abuse and economic hardship.

McCabe has been compared to Joyce and Beckett, yet he could easily be classified within the Irish gothic tradition. McCabe's *The Butcher Boy* (1992), acclaimed as a masterpiece of literary ventriloquism, was short-listed for the 1992 Booker Prize. This finely crafted novel tells the story of a young adolescent's descent into madness and murder. Although Francie Brady, a schoolboy in a small town in 1960's Ireland, has a drunken father and careless mother, his buddy Joe Purcell keeps him on track. When the boys con Philip Nugent out of his comic book collection, Philip's mother calls Francie's family "pigs." Francie the "pig boy" internalizes this insult and comes to hate the socially aspiring Mrs. Nugent. After his own mother enters a mental hospital, Francie runs away to Dublin. He discovers upon his return that she has committed suicide. Feeling extreme guilt, he breaks into Mrs. Nugent's house and is then sent to reform school: His best friend, Joe, befriends Francie's nemesis Philip Nugent, and Francie is lost. He continues his descent into darkness.

McCabe's *Breakfast on Pluto* (1998), part of the author's preferred humorous-macabre genre, is another tale of a youngster unable to come to terms with the conflicts of life. The emotionally overwrought Patrick "Pussy" Braden writes his outrageous memoirs for his psychiatrist, Dr. Terence. A product of the Tyreelin parish priest and his housekeeper, Patrick is abandoned and placed in a foster home with an alcoholic, Hairy Braden. The youngster finds deliverance in dreams of stardom and female fashion, winding up with a new name, Pussy, and a new life as a cross-dressing hooker in London. The protagonist soon finds himself overwhelmed, however, when he starts working for Irish Republican Army terrorists. McCabe is also known for his novels *Music on Clinton Street* (1986), *Carn* (1989), *The Dead School* (1995), *Call Me Breeze* (2004), *Winterwood* (2007), and *The Holy City* (2009).

Other important Irish writers of the early twenty-first century include Anne Enright (born 1962), whose novel *The Gathering* (2007) won the Booker Prize, Sebastian Barry (born 1955), Joseph O'Connor (born 1963), and Antonia Logue (born 1972). Novelist Eoin Colfer (born 1965) reached a massive worldwide audience with his Artemis Fowl fantasy series, intended for young adults but enjoyed by adults for their humor and wit. The series, about a ruthless teenage criminal mastermind, began in 2001 with *Artemis Fowl*.

M. Casey Diana
Updated by Cynthia A. Bily

BIBLIOGRAPHY

Cahalan, James M. *Modern Irish Literature and Culture: A Chronology.* New York: G. K. Hall, 1993. Examines events in Irish literature and culture after 1600, connecting historical and political developments with Irish fiction, poetry, and drama.

Coughlan, Patricia, and Tina O'Toole, eds. *Irish Literature: Feminist Perspectives.* Dublin: Carysfort Press, 2009. Questions traditional narratives of Irish studies and argues for a renegotiated study of the relations of feminism with nationalism. A good contribution to contemporary debates about Irish culture, gender, and identity.

Hogan, Robert Goode, and Zack R. Bowen. *Dictionary of Irish Literature.* Rev ed. Westport, Conn.: Greenwood Press, 1996. Through critical interpretation, the authors focus primarily on Anglo-Irish writers, especially major and later Irish writers. Discusses principal themes of Irish literature and the history of Irish writing in English.

Jeffares, A. Norman, and Peter Van de Kamp. *Irish Literature: The Nineteenth Century.* Dublin: Irish Academic Press, 2006-2007. Focuses on literature of the mid-nineteenth century, and on the Great Famine and the rise of cultural nationalism.

Kelleher, Margaret, and Philip O'Leary, eds. *The Cambridge History of Irish Literature.* 2 vols. New York: Cambridge University Press, 2006. First comprehensive history of Irish literature in the Irish, English, medieval Latin, and Norman languages. Includes a chronology, maps, and suggestions for further reading.

Leerssen, Joep. *Mere Irish and Fior Ghael: Studies in the Idea of Irish Nationality, Its Development, and Literary Expression Prior to the Nineteenth Century.* South Bend, Ind.: Notre Dame University Press, 1997. Examines the idea of Irish national identity, Irish historical background, and how Ireland and fictional Irish characters are represented in English literature.

Powell, Kersi Tarien. *Irish Fiction: An Introduction.* New York: Continuum, 2004. Handbook designed to introduce readers to Irish fiction, explore themes common among most Irish writers, and examine key novels that have shaped the genre.

Shaffer, Brian W., ed. *A Companion to the British and Irish Novel, 1945-2000.* Malden, Mass.: Blackwell, 2005. Collection of critical essays on the major issues, themes, writers, and works of the second half of the twentieth century.

Welch, Robert, ed. *The Oxford Companion to Irish Literature.* 1996. Reprint. New York: Clarendon Press, 2001. More than two thousand entries cover the major works and writers, literary genres, folklore, and mythology, along with articles on Protestantism, Catholicism, Northern Ireland, the Irish Republican Army, and the political and cultural background necessary to understand Irish literature.

JOHN BANVILLE

Born: Wexford, Ireland; December 8, 1945
Also known as: Benjamin Black

PRINCIPAL LONG FICTION
Nightspawn, 1971
Birchwood, 1973
Doctor Copernicus, 1976
Kepler, 1981
The Newton Letter, 1982 (novella)
Mefisto, 1986
The Book of Evidence, 1989
Ghosts, 1993
Athena, 1995
The Untouchable, 1997
Eclipse, 2000
Shroud, 2003
The Sea, 2005
Christine Falls, 2006 (as Benjamin Black)
The Silver Swan, 2007 (as Black)
The Lemur, 2008 (as Black)

OTHER LITERARY FORMS

The first book that John Banville (BAN-vihl) published was a collection of short stories, *Long Lankin* (1970), and he has written a small amount of uncollected short fiction. He has also written two plays and has collaborated in writing television adaptations of his novels *The Newton Letter* and *Birchwood*.

ACHIEVEMENTS

John Banville is one of the most original and successful Irish novelists of his generation. His work has received numerous awards, including the prestigious James Tait Black Memorial Prize, the American-Irish Foundation Award, the GPA Prize, and the Man Booker Prize. Reviewers have treated each of Banville's new works with increasing respect for the author's ambition, verbal felicity, and individuality, and Banville has inspired a sizable amount of critical commentary. The development of his career coincides with a period of restlessness and experimentation in Irish fiction.

Not the least significant of Banville's achievements is that he has availed himself of the artistic example of such postwar masters of fiction as Jorge Luis Borges, Gabriel García Márquez, and Italo Calvino. By admitting such influences, as well as those of the great

Irish modernists James Joyce and Samuel Beckett, Banville's fiction has embodied a new range of options for the Irish novel and has provided an international dimension to an often provincial literary culture.

BIOGRAPHY

John Banville was born in Wexford, the seat of Ireland's southeasternmost county, on December 8, 1945. He was educated locally, first at the Christian Brothers School and, on the secondary level, at St. Peter's College. After school, he worked for Aer Lingus, the Irish airline. Subsequently, he worked in England for the post office and, briefly, for a London publisher. Returning to Ireland, he worked as a subeditor for the *Irish Press*, a national daily, and then later went to work at the *Irish Times*, where he served as literary editor from 1988 to 1999. The recipient of numerous awards, he also spent a semester in the International Writing Program at the University of Iowa. In 2005, he received the prestigious Man Booker Prize for his novel *The Sea*.

ANALYSIS

John Banville's subject matter and methods of artistic execution form the basis of his reputation for originality. In the context of contemporary fiction, Banville is notable for his commitment, for his felicity of phrase, and for his relationship to an important fictional genre, the historical novel. He has communicated, through both his artistic strategies and his choices of material, some of the main questions faced by contemporary fiction—communicated them perhaps too conspicuously and with an ease and self-possession uncharacteristic of many contemporary writers. Some readers may find that Banville's manner is paradoxically at odds with his central themes.

Banville's short stories, his novella *The Newton Letter*, and his novels constitute a remarkably unified and consistent body of work. From the outset of his career, he has shown immense artistic self-possession and an equally assured possession of his themes. Over the years, his style, while not remaining constant, has undergone comparatively little change. It is therefore possible to speak of Banville in terms of a completeness and typicality that most novelists of his age are still in the process of discovering.

The unity and integrity that are the most striking features of Banville's career and oeuvre become more striking still by virtue of their being so thematically important in his work. Fascination with the spectacle of the mind in the act of creation is a major concern of this author, and his career may be described in terms of an increasingly deliberate and far-reaching series of attempts to articulate this subject. This preoccupation has given his work a range, ambition, and commitment to large concepts that are extremely rare in modern Irish fiction and only slightly less rare in contemporary fiction generally.

In addition, the manner in which Banville elaborates his interest in humanity's creative dimension commands more critical attention than it has received. For example, his fiction is suffused with hints suggesting links among artistic strategies, scientific inquiry, and historical actuality. From these, it is possible to detect a rudimentary, though sustained, critique of traditional epistemological procedures. To complement this critique, the typical Banville protagonist either discovers unsuspected modes of perception or believes that he has no choice but to set out deliberately to discover them.

Together with the intellectual commitment implicit in such concerns, Banville's work possesses a typically complete and essentially unchanging aesthetic apparatus through which ideas and fiction's critique may be perceived. Since it is central to Banville's artistic vision that fiction's critique of conceptual thinking be considered inevitable and unavoidable, his novels' aesthetic apparatus is largely premised on techniques of doubleness, repetition, echoes, and mirrors. Protagonists often have problematic brothers or missing twins. Personal experience finds its counterpart in historical events. The result is a paradox: The duplicitous character of experience, which renders humanity's possession of its existence so frail and tentative, impels people, precisely because of that very frailty, to anchor themselves in the presumed security of defined abstractions.

Despite the presence of these thematic concerns throughout Banville's output, and despite the fact that his treatment of them has always been marked more by an ironic playfulness than by earnest sermonizing, his first two works of fiction are somewhat callow. In particular, *Nightspawn*, the story of an Irish writer's adventures in Greece on the eve of the colonels' coup, treats the material with a kind of relentless playfulness that is both tiresome in itself and in questionable taste. Despite the author's admitted—though not uncritical—affection for this novel, and despite its containing in embryonic form the concerns that beset all of his work, *Nightspawn*, as perhaps its title suggests, is an example of a young writer allowing his wonderfully fertile imagination to run to baroque lengths.

BIRCHWOOD

It is more appropriate, therefore, to begin a detailed consideration of John Banville's fiction with his second novel, *Birchwood*. Like *Nightspawn*, this novel is written in the first person—arguably Banville's preferred narrative mode. In *Birchwood*, Gabriel Godkin, the protagonist, tells in retrospect the story of his dark heritage and his efforts to escape it. Again, as in *Nightspawn*, much of the material has baroque potential, which the novel's middle section, depicting Gabriel's adventures with the circus of a certain Prospero, accentuates rather than dispels.

The circus escapade shines in the novel like a good deed in an evil world. While Gabriel is within the protected ring of the circus troupe, he seems to be essentially immune from the troubles of his past and from the state of famine and unrest that consumes the country through which the circus travels. Thanks to Prospero, he is islanded and becalmed in the surrounding tempest. Even under such conditions of childish play, however, the world is not a safe place. Adult imperfections continually intrude. Crimes are committed in the name of love; futile and obsessive hostilities break out. Innocent Gabriel flees the disintegrating circle—it seems appropriate to think of the circus in etymological terms, since circle and ring possess strong connotations of unity and completeness.

Gabriel forsakes the circus in a state of rather paranoid distress and finds himself, still more distressingly, to have come full circle, back to where he started. Now, however, he finds himself compelled to face his origins, which lie in the house of doom that gives this novel its title. The first part of the novel gives the history of the Godkin family. Like the circus sequence, this opening section of *Birchwood* owes more to imagination than it does to actuality. Many readers will be reminded of both Edgar Allan Poe and William Faulkner by Banville's combination of brooding atmosphere and theme of cultural decay on which this section is premised. Banville's farcical tone, however, without prejudicing young Gabriel's sensitivity, prevents the heavy-handedness and extravagance to which the gothic nature of his material is in danger of giving rise. The seriousness with which the elder Godkins take their insecurities is rendered laughable by the incompetence that ensues from their transparent intensity.

Gabriel, however, for all of his alienation from his heritage's inadequacies, finds it impossible to do other than to confront them. In a novel that satirically articulates the cultural shibboleth of bad blood, Gabriel feels compelled to carry out an act of blood that will purge his house of the usurper. The usurper in question is Gabriel's twin brother, Michael. The novel ends with Gabriel in sole possession of Birchwood.

This turn of events, however, does not mean that Gabriel is able, or intends, to restore the house to its former glory, a glory in which he never participated. As a writer, he seems to have the objective of reclaiming the house as it really was rather than imagining it as something other, something that imaginative treatment would make easier to assimilate. In this objective, students of Irish literature may see a critique of the lofty status often accorded the Big House in the poetry of William Butler Yeats. An appreciation of Banville's fiction does not require that he be seen as a defacer of the cultural icons of a previous generation. Nevertheless, the status of the Big House in *Birchwood*, coupled with themes of survival, inheritance, and artistic expression, offers a sense of the oblique manner in which this author regards his own cultural heritage while at the same time situating his regard in the wider, more generic contexts of such concerns as individuality, history, the role of the artist, and the nature of the real.

Given the significant, if problematic, status of the Big House in modern Irish literature (Big House being the generic name given to the imposing mansions of the socially dominant, landowning Anglo-Irish class), the degree to which *Birchwood* avoids a specific historical context is noteworthy. The work provides a sufficient number of clues (the famine and unrest already mentioned, the frequent mention of "rebels" in the first part of the novel) to suggest that the locale is Ireland. A larger historical context is obviated, however, by the obsessive, and more psychologically archetypal, quality of Gabriel's sense of his personal history. The result is a novel that is ultimately too reflexive, private, and inward looking to be entirely satisfactory.

DOCTOR COPERNICUS

It may be that the author himself reached the same conclusion, given that in his next two novels, *Doctor Copernicus* and *Kepler*, a specific and detailed sense of history is an important dimension of events. *Doctor Copernicus* inaugurates Banville's most important and ambitious project, and the one on which his long-term international reputation will probably be based. This project consists of four books dealing with the nature of the creative personality, conceived of in terms of the scientific imagination. A subtitle for the series might be "The Scientist as Artist," meaning that Banville considers the accomplishments of Copernicus, Kepler, and Isaac Newton (subject of *The Newton Letter*) in the field of scientific inquiry to be comparable to what an artist might produce. The series concludes with *Mefisto*, which both crystallizes and challenges the assumptions of its predecessors. The most fundamental link joining the four books is chronological, *Mefisto* being set in contemporary Ireland. Although other, more sophisticated connections may be made among the four novels, each may also be read independently.

Doctor Copernicus is a fictionalized biography of the astronomer who revolutionized humanity's sense of its place in the order of creation. The biography is presented in such a way as to dramatize the crucial tensions between Copernicus and the history of his time. Beginning with the astronomer's unhappy childhood, the novel details the essentially flawed, anticlimactic, unfulfilling (and unfulfillable) nature of human existence as Copernicus experiences it. The protagonist's character is conceived in terms of his inability to give himself fully to the world of men and women and affairs, whether the affairs are those of state or of the heart.

Sojourning in Italy as a young man, Copernicus has a homosexual affair that temporarily makes him happy. He lacks the self-confidence and will to believe in his happiness, however, and rejects it in an attack of spleen and confusion. Later in his career, he is required to take a political role, negotiating with Lutheran enemies of the Catholic Church and administering Church properties. Although he discharges his obligations in a responsible manner, it is perfectly clear that, given the choice between being a man of his time or being a student of the stars in their eternal courses, Copernicus prefers the latter isolated, impersonal service. The imperfections of the world—not only in the aggregate, demonstrated by the machinations of history, but also intimately, embodied by the astronomer's syphilitic brother, Andreas—prove emotionally insupportable, philosophically unjustifiable, and morally anesthetizing. Finding no basis for unity and completeness in the sorry state of mortal humans, Copernicus takes the not particularly logical but impressively imaginative step of considering the heavens.

The astronomer's declared intention in pursuing this line of inquiry is not to bring about the revolution that history commemorates in his name. On the contrary, Copernicus sees his pursuits as conservative, intended to assert a model of order, design, and harmony where it cannot be said for certain one exists. Copernicus's efforts are fueled by his will and spirit, and the intensity of his commitment should not be underestimated because his results are stated in mathematical terms. What his conclusions provide is the fiction of order, a fiction posited on the conceit of mathematics being essentially a rhetoric—a product of mind, not an offspring of matter. Indeed, as Copernicus's career in the world of things and people suggests, his fiction elicits worldlings' assent all the more urgently for being necessarily untrue.

KEPLER

Banville's approach as a biographer in *Doctor Copernicus* is strictly chronological, which gives the novel both scope and a sense of the inevitability of the protagonist's development. Copernicus's integrity, continually challenged, is nourished by the inevitable nature of his spiritual needs and tendencies; in *Kepler*, the approach is fundamentally the same. Instead of providing a chronology of Kepler's life, however, Banville concentrates on the astronomer's productive years, using flashbacks to illuminate and enlarge aspects of the protagonist's character, as the need arises. This approach shifts the narrative emphasis from the protagonist's temperament, as it was in *Doctor Copernicus*, to the protagonist's working conditions. The effect of this modulation in authorial standpoint is to give historical circumstances greater prominence than in the earlier work and thus provide, from an aesthetic perspective, an image of humankind in the world that reverses the one provided in *Doctor Copernicus*.

Kepler is far more life-loving (which Banville communicates as far more capable of love) than his predecessor. He is far more attuned to the eddies and quicksands of the historical forces of his time, consciously aligning himself with one set of forces rather than another instead of disdainfully and brokenheartedly attempting to rise above the forces, as Copernicus tries to do. Kepler's astronomy, therefore, is presented as, in his own eyes, the opposite of Copernicus's model of conservation. Much of Kepler's achievement, in fact, is based on his critique of his predecessor's findings.

In addition, Kepler's generally worldly disposition leads him to develop practical applications of astronomical researches. When most successful in his own eyes, however, constructing his geometrical model of planetary harmony, he is unwittingly failing. His model is adequate to his own need of it but is not, by virtue of that adequacy, foolproof. The reader is given a strong sense that the model that Kepler's discoveries serve introduces as many errors as it corrects in Copernicus's model. In Copernicus's case, the model is the necessary transmutation of sorrow; in Kepler's case, it is the necessary transmutation of joy. Despite fate's cruel blows, Kepler asserts that the world should be considered part of a harmoniously integrated system. Because of fate's cruel blows, Copernicus asserts the same theory.

It would be invidious to conclude that one of these heroic figures suffers more than the others. Banville is at pains, as the dramatic structure of *Kepler* demonstrates, to point out that the astronomer's faith in the world proves to be as destructively alienating as Copernicus's skepticism. The spectacle—which concludes the novel—of this great scientific visionary spending his time and energy attempting to bring his debtors to account is a painfully ludicrous commentary on the all-too-understandable vanity of human wishes as well as a cogent expression of Banville's own perspective on his material.

THE NEWTON LETTER

In the novella *The Newton Letter* Banville changes his approach without quite changing his theme, returning once more to an ironic treatment of the Big House theme. Here the scenario is not biography but failed biography. The protagonist is not the great scientist but the apparently less-than-great modern writer attempting to recapture the scientist's life. This short work gives an inverted picture of the procedures that seem natural in the two earlier works in the series. The presupposition of expository coherence leading to insight and comprehension that is crucial, however unspoken, to the fictionalized biographies becomes a subject open to criticism in *The Newton Letter*—open, like the procedures of Copernicus and Kepler, to the charge of fiction.

In addition, the fictional biographer (the protagonist of *The Newton Letter*) is failing to complete his work because of Newton's failure to pursue his research. By this means, the interrelationship between fiction and reality, and the possibility that these terms interchangeably reflect dual perspectives on immutable phenomena, is brought yet more clearly to the forefront of Banville's concerns.

Indeed, as in the case of the earlier novels of the series, life keeps interrupting the Newton biographer. The country house to which he has retreated in order to complete his work, while not possessing the menace and uncertainty of Birchwood, distracts and ultimately ensnares him, so that he is forced to choose between the demands of completeness (his work) and the obligations of incompleteness (his life). The biographer's failed project becomes a synonym for his mortal destiny.

MEFISTO

Banville's rejection of the biographical approach to the life of the mind is completed in the final volume of the series, *Mefisto*, in which the protagonist, a mathematician named Gabriel Swan, writes his own story. With this formal development, the procedure of both *Doctor Copernicus* and *Kepler* is completely inverted, and the value of the project, both from a biographical and from a scientific point of view, is most rigorously challenged. One reason it is possible to make such a claim is that *Mefisto* reaches back beyond its three predecessors to *Birchwood*, to which it bears some strong resemblances.

The most obvious novelty of *Mefisto*, however, is that it does not deal with a historical twentieth century scientist. Most of Banville's readers were not prepared for this development, which is a tribute to Banville's own conception of his project's integrity. It is unlikely, however, that the question of integrity is the only one at issue here. On one hand, this development is typical of the sly and slapstick humor that pervades Banville's work. On the other hand, the fictitiousness of *Mefisto*'s protagonist is an obvious expression of the status of failure in Banville's oeuvre, the failure from which the artist is obliged to begin and that his work, by attempting to mask or redeem it, merely makes more obvious. In addition, given that *Mefisto* has a historical context about which it is possible to say much, and that it is a novel that brings to an end a series of works in which historical events are given a prominent and influential place, it must be considered provocative and instructive that *Mefisto* eschews explicit information of a historical nature.

Mefisto is a novel of missing parts. It lacks a specific sense of time and space, though the alert reader will find part 1 of the novel set in a market town in provincial Ireland and part 2 in an Irish city that is presumably Dublin. The hero, Gabriel (a name that, in a novelist as self-conscious as Banville, must be an echo of the protagonist of *Birchwood*, particularly since in part 1 there is a dilapidated, Birchwood-like house), is a mathematician of genius, but it is difficult to deduce what his branch of mathematics is.

It is Gabriel's misfortune to believe that there can be a redemptive function in his symbols and abstractions. He mistakenly believes that, because of the light he finds shining in the purity of math, he can rescue damsels in distress—in genuine distress, like the drug-besotted Adele in part 2. This belief is cultivated by the jauntily cynical and amoral Felix, who fills the role of Mephistopheles, Gabriel's dark angel. There is enough twinning and doubling in the novel to suggest that Felix may also be Gabriel's stillborn twin brother. Events prove both the hopelessness and the inevitability of Gabriel's outlook. First, Gabriel is severely burned—the potential fate, no doubt, of all who make Mephistophelian contact. Second, he is brokenhearted by his failure to rescue Adele. The end of the novel, however, finds him rededicating himself to his vision of mathematics, to the rhetoric of perfection and security that it symbolizes.

The combination of failure and rededication on which *Mefisto* ends is an illuminating gloss on one of Banville's most crucial themes. Echoing a pronouncement of Samuel Beckett, Banville believes that the artist necessarily has failure for a theme and that the artist's work articulates that theme's pressing reality. On the other hand, Banville is still romantic enough to conceive of his theme in terms of world-changing, concept-forming figures. His work is thus also preoccupied with the meaning of success, which in turn is linked to ideas of progress, clarity, precision, and enlightenment. Failure is relativized by success, and success by failure. The sense of doubleness and unity suggested by such a conclusion is typical of Banville's outlook.

THE BOOK OF EVIDENCE

Binary interplay is very much to the fore in Banville's most commercially successful novel, *The Book of Evidence*. This work takes the form of a first-person account of a vertiginous fall from grace undertaken by a lapsed mathematician, Freddie Montgomery, while Freddie is awaiting trial. In financial straits, Freddie decided to steal a painting, and in order to do so he murdered an innocent bystander, a servant. No good comes of these actions, unless it is to reveal to the scapegrace protagonist the necessity that his nature acknowledge limits and that the limits are those enjoined by the existence of others. As Freddie perceives, his failure to imagine the lives of others leads him into reckless disregard of those lives. His crime is this failure. Through the comprehensiveness and comprehension of his narrative, Freddie arrives at a perspective on his actions that he had previously lacked, having been hitherto driven to act by cupidity, fear, and callowness.

In a reflexive turn typical of Banville, Freddie's book becomes more substantial than his life. For all its narrative discontinuities, the story remains a simple one, reminiscent of a ballad, providing *The Book of Evidence* with an unlikely kinship to *Long Lankin*, the stories in which are premised on a ballad. This formal association also suggests *The Book of Evidence*'s indebtedness to two classics of jail literature, both by Oscar Wilde: *De Profundis* (1905; a first-person attempt at vindication) and *The Ballad of Reading Gaol* (1898; with its refrain, "For each man kills the thing he loves," which is clearly the case of Freddie and the stolen painting). Such objective possibilities of order counterpoint Freddie's subjective flouting of law—not merely the law of the land, which is held at such a distance in *The Book of Evidence* as to seem beside the point, but laws more fundamentally pertaining to the viability of the project of being human, with its obligations to others, obligations that in the distorted form of financial indebtedness to hoodlums motivate Freddie's murderous actions.

While conceptually and stylistically *The Book of Evidence* is at least the equal of Banville's earlier attainments, it also articulates much more decisively than does *Mefisto* the author's sense of contemporary social reality. Its uniformly favorable critical reception suggests that it is a work that will contribute to Banville's gaining the wider readership that his originality, commitment to large questions, and aesthetic poise deserve.

ATHENA

Athena completes the trilogy begun with *The Book of Evidence* and continued with the ethereal *Ghosts*. Each novel centers on Freddie, here referred to only as Morrow, and once again Banville sets the action in another decaying house, portentously located on Rue Street. Morrow's criminal past reasserts itself as he falls in with Morden, an enigmatic figure who commissions the protagonist to catalog and evaluate eight Flemish paintings. The narrative is then punctuated by detailed descriptions of seven of these paintings, each of which is a fraud.

As he becomes more enmeshed in Morden's machinations, Morrow enters a hypnotic and masochistic relationship with another mysterious figure, a woman known only as A. Gradually the mystery evaporates—Morden and A. are siblings working for Da, their father, and Morrow is little more than a useful and available tool. Like Banville's earlier novels, *Athena* is driven by the self-conscious ruminations of the principal character, and like those other protagonists, Morrow is obsessed with the gulf between chaotic, shoddy reality and the perfection of art and the imagination. He longs for order, the model of which he finds in art, but his actions lead repeatedly to more frustration and havoc. The novel positively brims with allusions to other paintings and novels, and thus the self-conscious and ironic practices of the early novels are maintained. Along with *The Newton Letter*, *Athena* arguably ranks among Banville's best novels for its inventiveness and epistemological probity.

THE UNTOUCHABLE

In his work *The Untouchable*, Banville returns to the historical concerns that characterize so many of his earlier works. Here, Victor Maskell, narrator, art scholar, and former spy, is a thinly disguised version of Anthony Blunt, the British traitor who joined a spy ring while a student at Cambridge University in the 1930's. The novel is set in the 1970's, when Blunt was exposed, but again another subjective narrator shuttles back and forth through time in a mélange of history and personal reflection. The story takes the reader through Maskell's boyhood, years at Cambridge, and years during World War II, when his involvement with the Russians deepens in spite of his skepticism of their social project.

Like Morrow, Maskell is dedicated to art and ascends to the influential position of Keeper of the Royal Pictures, confessing that art is the only thing of any importance or stability in his life. Art in fact become a lens through which he views and evaluates himself, whereby he is alternately creator and created, forever suspended on his own perfect Grecian urn. However, the single painting around which he has organized his life, and which he purchased as a young man, French classical artist Nicolas Poussin's *The Death of Seneca*, may be a forgery, thus making his whole life a fraud. Like earlier Banville characters, Maskell is a searcher, seeking a fixed sense of identity that is forever out of reach. Once again, the subjective narrator is a self-betrayed figure, one whose most clever deceptions and stratagems rebound disastrously on him; once again readers encounter a profoundly lonely, alienated character.

THE SEA

Banville continues his consideration of old age, memory, and guilt in the Booker Prize-winning *The Sea*, which many critics consider his finest novel. After the death of his wife, Anna, from cancer, art critic Max Morden abandons his home and relocates to the Cedars, a seaside boardinghouse where, as a child many years earlier, he had encountered the affluent Grace family. Morden is working desultorily on an analysis of the French artist Pierre Bonnard. The novel moves fluidly among three time periods: Morden's present as a widower; his married life, focusing on the period leading up to his wife's death; and the summer long ago when he was befriended by the Graces.

The Graces—the ominously masculine father, the alluring mother, the uncanny twins, Chloe and Myles, and the ineffectual governess, Rose—represent a life utterly foreign and attractive to Max, an only child being raised by a single mother. He develops a passionate crush on Mrs. Grace that reaches its climax when he is afforded a voyeuristic peep up her skirt as she reclines on the ground; eventually these feelings are redirected toward Chloe, with whom he shares a first kiss and some other exploration. Looking back on his suddenly empty life, Morden replays the seminal events of that singular summer in an attempt to understand how that child has become the bitter, bereft old man he is. His entire present must be reexamined through the lens of that summer long past, including his relationship with his daughter Claire, who has sacrificed a promising career as an art historian under the influence of a suitor of whom Max disapproves. *The Sea* looks backward over Banville's earlier novels through his playful, mysterious use of character names form earlier works and the work's relentless, reluctant uncovering of a long-submerged mystery.

CHRISTINE FALLS

In *Christine Falls*, Banville—writing under the pseudonym Benjamin Black—moves firmly into the genre of mystery and detective fiction. Set in the 1950's, the novel introduces the protagonist Quirke, a pathologist in a Dublin hospital. After discovering his brother-in-law, Malachy Griffin, in the act of tampering with the death record of a young woman who has died in childbirth, Quirke begins to unravel a story that soon goes far beyond the question of the woman's death and her baby's fate. Eventually the mystery involves the Catholic Church, orphanages in both Ireland and the United States, the notorious convent laundries that employed and imprisoned young women, and Quirke's own position within his adopted family.

In this novel Banville shows a willingness to explore multiple points of view, adhering more to the conventions of the popular mystery genre than to the techniques of his earlier novels. The fallible and self-deceptive Quirke is very much a Banville protagonist, however; his alienation and his reluctant (but inevitable) pursuit of truths about himself are themes that *Christine Falls* shares with many of Banville's other novels.

George O'Brien; David W. Madden
Updated by James S. Brown

OTHER MAJOR WORKS

SHORT FICTION: *Long Lankin*, 1970 (revised 1984).

PLAYS: *The Broken Jug*, pb. 1994 (adaptation of Heinrich von Kleist's *Der zerbrochene Krug*); *God's Gift*, pb. 2000 (adaptation of Kleist's *Amphitryon*).

SCREENPLAYS: *Reflections*, 1984 (adaptation of his novel *The Newton Letter*); *Birchwood*, 1986 (adaptation of his novel); *The Last September*, 1999 (adaptation of Elizabeth Bowen's novel).

TELEPLAY: *Seaview*, 1994.

NONFICTION: *Prague Pictures: Portraits of a City*, 2003.

BIBLIOGRAPHY

Booker, M. Keith. "Cultural Crisis Then and Now: Science, Literature, and Religion in John Banville's *Doctor Copernicus* and *Kepler*." *Critique* 39, no. 2 (Winter, 1998):

176-192. Examines how Banville uses the complex parallels between science and literature as a way of exploring and representing reality in his renderings of the lives of the scientists in the two novels.

Deane, Seamus. "'Be Assured I Am Inventing': The Fiction of John Banville." In *The Irish Novel in Our Time*, edited by Patrick Rafroidi and Maurice Harmon. Lille, France: Publications de l'Université de Lille, 1975. Presents an excellent discussion of Banville's first three works of fiction. Deane, one of Ireland's leading critics, is particularly insightful concerning the reflexive elements in *Long Lankin*, *Nightspawn*, and *Birchwood*. Concludes with a challenging critique of the cultural significance of Banville's work.

D'Haen, Theo. "Irish Regionalism, Magic Realism, and Postmodernism." In *International Aspects of Irish Literature*, edited by Toshi Furomoto et al. Gerrards Cross, England: Smythe, 1996. Compares Banville's *Birchwood* and Desmond Hogan's *A Curious Street* to demonstrate the postmodern and Magical Realist qualities of each. Such features express the marginality of Ireland and of the Irish to Europe's dominant beliefs in Banville's fiction.

D'hoker, Elke. *Visions of Alterity: Representation in the Works of John Banville*. Atlanta: Rodopi, 2004. Scholarly work presents detailed readings of Banville's most important novels, focusing on their philosophical dimension. Includes bibliography and index.

Imhof, Rüdiger. *John Banville: A Critical Introduction*. Enlarged ed. Dublin, Ireland: Wolfhound Press, 1997. Early study of Banville's works discusses the novels up to and including *Mefisto*; additional material added for this enlarged edition addresses *The Book of Evidence*, *Ghosts*, and *Athena*. Provides an intellectual guide to Banville's fictional preoccupations as well as a full bibliography.

Irish University Review 11 (Spring, 1981). Special issue on Banville presents a number of critical overviews, a bibliography, a wide-ranging interview with Banville, and the transcript of a talk he gave at the University of Iowa's Writers' Workshop—a rare formal statement on fiction and authorship.

Jackson, Tony E. "Science, Art, and the Shipwreck of Knowledge: The Novels of John Banville." *Contemporary Literature* 38, no. 8 (1997): 510-533. Examines Banville's postmodern sensibility in five novels. Basing his argument on Friedrich Nietzsche's theories about the indeterminacy of truth, Jackson demonstrates that scientific truths in Banville's novels can never explain everything and that art fills the gaps for which history and science cannot account.

McIlroy, Brian. "Pattern in Chaos: John Banville's Scientific Art." *Colby Quarterly* 31, no. 1 (1995). Uses examination of *Doctor Copernicus*, *Kepler*, *The Newton Letter*, and *Mefisto* to show how Banville illustrates the similarities between scientific and artistic methods of thinking and discovery. Also discusses the ways in which history, politics, religion, and sex influence scientific inquiry and art.

McMinn, Joseph. *The Supreme Fictions of John Banville*. New York: St. Martin's Press,

1999. Presents critical commentary on all of Banville's works of fiction through *The Untouchable*. Includes an introduction that places Banville's work within the context of American, Irish, and European writing.

Murphy, Neil. *Irish Fiction and Postmodern Doubt: An Analysis of the Epistemological Crisis in Modern Fiction*. Lewiston, N.Y.: Edwin Mellen Press, 2004. Discusses the works of Banville and two other Irish novelists, Neil Jordan and Aidan Higgins, in the context of postmodernist fiction. Relates the authors' works to Irish and international literary traditions. Includes bibliography and index.

SAMUEL BECKETT

Born: Foxrock, near Dublin, Ireland; April 13, 1906
Died: Paris, France; December 22, 1989
Also known as: Samuel Barclay Beckett

PRINCIPAL LONG FICTION

Murphy, 1938
Malone meurt, 1951 (*Malone Dies*, 1956)
Molloy, 1951 (English translation, 1955)
L'Innommable, 1953 (*The Unnamable*, 1958)
Watt, 1953
Comment c'est, 1961 (*How It Is*, 1964)
Mercier et Camier, 1970 (*Mercier and Camier*, 1974)
Le Dépeupleur, 1971 (*The Lost Ones*, 1972)
Company, 1980
Mal vu mal dit, 1981 (*Ill Seen Ill Said*, 1981)
Worstward Ho, 1983

OTHER LITERARY FORMS

Samuel Beckett produced work in every literary genre. His first book, published in 1931, was the critical study *Proust*, and during the next fifteen years, Beckett published a number of essays and book reviews that have yet to be collected in book form. After struggling with an unpublished play titled *Eleutheria* in the late 1940's (which was eventually published in 1995), he began publication of the series of plays that are as important as his novels to his current literary reputation. These include, notably, *En attendant Godot* (pb. 1952; *Waiting for Godot*, 1954), *"Fin de partie," suivi de "Acte sans paroles"* (pr., pb. 1957; music by John Beckett; *"Endgame: A Play in One Act," Followed by "Act Without Words: A Mime for One Player,"* 1958), *Krapp's Last Tape* (pr., pb. 1958), *Happy Days* (pr., pb. 1961), and many short pieces for the stage, including mimes. In addition to these works for the stage, he wrote scripts for television, such as *Eh Joe* (1966; *Dis Joe*, 1967); scripts for radio, such as *All That Fall* (1957; revised 1968); and one film script, titled *Film* (1965). Most, but not all, of Beckett's many short stories are gathered in various collections, including *More Pricks than Kicks* (1934), *Nouvelles et textes pour rien* (1955; *Stories and Texts for Nothing*, 1967), *No's Knife: Collected Shorter Prose, 1947-1966* (1967), *First Love, and Other Shorts* (1974), *Pour finir encore et autres foirades* (1976; *Fizzles*, 1976; also known as *For to Yet Again*), and *Collected Short Prose* (1991). Beckett's poetry, most of it written early in his career for periodical publication, has been made available in *Poems in English* (1961) and *Collected Poems in English and French* (1977). Many of the various collections of his short pieces mix works of different literary

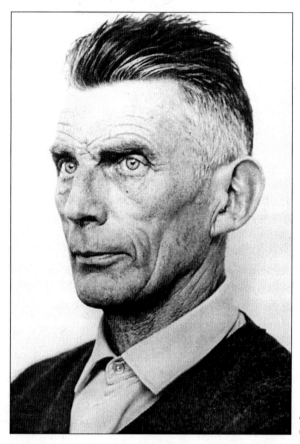

Samuel Beckett
(Nobel Foundation)

genres, and Richard Seaver has edited a general sampling of Beckett works of all sorts in an anthology titled *I Can't Go On, I'll Go On: A Selection from Samuel Beckett's Work* (1976).

ACHIEVEMENTS

Samuel Beckett did not begin to write his most important works until he was forty years of age, and he had to wait some time beyond that for widespread recognition of his literary achievements. By the time he received the Nobel Prize in Literature in 1969, however, he had established a solid reputation as one of the most important and demanding authors of plays and novels in the twentieth century.

In the 1930's, when he began to write, Beckett seemed destined for the sort of footnote fame that has overtaken most of his English and Irish literary companions of that decade. His work appeared to be highly derivative of the avant-garde coterie associated with *Tran-*

sition magazine and especially of the novels of James Joyce, who as an elder Irish expatriate in Paris befriended and encouraged the young Beckett. By the time Beckett was forty
years old and trying to salvage a literary career disrupted by World War II, his anonymity
was such that his own French translation of his first novel, *Murphy*, had sold exactly six
copies. At the same time he presented his skeptical Paris publisher with another
manuscript.

Nevertheless, it was at that time—the late 1940's—that Beckett blossomed as a writer.
He withdrew into a voluntary solitude he himself referred to as "the siege in the room," began to compose his works in French rather than in English, and shed many of the mannerisms of his earlier work. The immediate result was the trilogy of novels that constitute his
most important achievement in prose fiction: *Molloy, Malone Dies*, and *The Unnamable*.
This period also produced *Waiting for Godot*, and it was this play that first brought Beckett
fame. *Waiting for Godot*, considered a formative influence on the Theater of the Absurd,
stimulated the first serious critical treatments of Beckett's work. Although Beckett himself attached more importance to his novels than to his plays, it was not until the 1960's
that critics went beyond his plays and began to bring his prose works under close scrutiny.
Then, as now, most criticism of Beckett's fiction focused on the trilogy and the austere
prose fiction in French that followed it.

In the years since then, Beckett's novels have risen in critical estimation from essentially eccentric if interesting experiments to exemplars of self-referential "postmodern"
fiction commonly cited by literary theorists. Disagreements about the nature of particular
works and skepticism about the bulk of commentary generated by very brief prose fragments have also inevitably accompanied this rather sudden enshrinement of a difficult and
extremely idiosyncratic body of work. However, even the most antagonistic later analyses
of Beckett's novels grant them a position of importance and influence in the development
of prose fiction since World War II, and they also accept Beckett's stature as one of the
most important novelists since his friend and Irish compatriot James Joyce.

BIOGRAPHY

Samuel Barclay Beckett was born in Foxrock, a modestly affluent suburb of Dublin,
Ireland. He gave Good Friday, April 13, 1906, as his birth date, but some convincing contrary evidence suggests that this particular day may have been chosen more for its significance than for its accuracy. His parents, William and Mary (May) Jones Roe, belonged to
the Protestant middle class known as Anglo-Irish in Ireland. Beckett's childhood, in contrast to the unpleasant imagery of many of his novels, was a relatively cheery one of genteel entertainment at the family home, Cooldrinagh, private education at Portora Royal
School in county Fermanagh, and greater success on the cricket green than in the
classroom.

Beckett matriculated to Trinity College, Dublin, in 1923, and there he developed his
first literary interests. He completed a curriculum in Romance languages at Trinity, and

this led to an appointment as lecturer at the École Normale Supérieure in Paris after graduation in 1927. In Paris, Beckett began to associate with the bohemian intellectual circles of French, English, and American writers for which the city was then famous. Beckett returned to Dublin for a brief time in 1930 for graduate work and a teaching position at Trinity, but within a few months he returned to the Continent for travel throughout Germany and France and an extended reunion with his friends in Paris, including James Joyce. His first works of fiction, the stories in *More Pricks than Kicks* and the novel *Murphy*, are set in Dublin and its environs, but their intellectual preoccupations and bohemian antagonism toward middle-class complacency derive more from the environment of Paris than that of Ireland.

At the outbreak of World War II, Beckett was a permanent resident of Paris. As an Irish citizen, he could have returned home, but instead he took refuge in the French countryside from the Nazi occupation of Paris. There, he assisted the Resistance and began to write the novel *Watt*, which marks a movement toward the style of his major fiction in its strangely dislocated senses of time and place. After the war, Beckett was decorated with the Croix de Guerre for his assistance to the French underground, and this award is generally cited as evidence of an essential humanism underlying the frequently misanthropic tenor of his novels. All evidence suggests, however, that the experience of the war increased Beckett's antagonism toward social affiliations and his skepticism about humanistic values.

Beckett returned to Paris after the war, and from 1946 to 1950, he retired into the "siege in the room," his most fertile period in a long literary career. By the time *Waiting for Godot* established his reputation, he had already developed the reclusive lifestyle that he maintained in his years of fame despite persistent media attention. He was married to longtime companion Suzanne Deschevaux-Dumesnil in secrecy in London in 1961, and he refused to attend the award ceremony for his Nobel Prize in Literature in 1969. He died in Paris on December 22, 1989.

ANALYSIS

It was a matter of some pleasure to Samuel Beckett that his work resists explication. His most important novels and plays are artfully constructed contemplations on their own form rather than commentaries on the familiar world of causal relationships and social contingencies. His most important novels abandon progressive narrative for the more difficult and subtle suggestiveness of haunting images, deliberate enigmas, and complexly ironic epigrams.

Although Beckett's work defies criticism, the author issued critical statements and congenially submitted to interviews with critics, managing to transform both sorts of critical occasions into intellectual performances as provocative, and occasionally as humorous, as his fiction. Two particular comments by Beckett, out of many stimulating ones, may serve as instructive introductions to the body of his prose works. In his first published book, *Proust*, Beckett wrote that artistic creation is essentially an excavatory process, comparable to an attempt to reach an ideal, impossibly minuscule, core of an onion. Beckett's novels relentlessly pursue this sort of process, stripping away layers of assumptions about the self and the world, peeling away conventional modes of thought to reach a pure essence of existence free of the inevitably distorting effects of intellect, logical structure, and analytic order. This image of the onion is a rich one because it communicates the sense in Beckett's work that this excavatory process is unending, that disposal of each mode of thought reveals yet another, even more resistant, habit of mind. Beckett himself often spoke of his novels as a series, and it is this progressive penetration through one form of thought to another that marks the stages in the series.

Thirty years after *Proust*, Beckett submitted to an unusually provocative interview with Tom Driver that was published in *Columbia University Forum* in the summer of 1961. In this interview, he dwelled specifically on form. After contrasting the orderly form of most art to the intransigently chaotic nature of existence, he said: "The Form and the chaos remain separate. The latter is not reduced to the former. . . . to find a form that accommodates the mess, that is the task of the artist now." Beckett's novels reveal three stages in this attempt to discover a literary form that will accommodate the chaotic nature of existence. In the first stage, represented by *Murphy* and *Watt*, the process is a destructive one of ridiculing literary convention by parody and satire to suggest an as yet undiscovered alternative form of expression. In the second stage, represented by the trilogy, the attempt to give voice to that alternative takes the form of the disordered and at times deliberately incoherent monologues of individual narrators. In the third stage, represented by *How It Is* and the subsequent short prose pieces, the process takes the form of presenting metaphorical worlds that accommodate their own chaos.

This last stage, especially, is marked by the unpleasant emphasis on miserable degradation and the recurring private images that have given Beckett an undeserved reputation for misanthropy and deliberate obscurity. These charges are effectively rebutted by his own stated sense of "the task of the artist now." Beckett's works do not provide relaxing reading experiences. They are designed to disorient, to dislocate, and to thwart intellectual complacency. The formidable difficulties they present to the reader, however, are essential records of the intellectual ambience of advanced mid-twentieth century thought.

MURPHY

Beckett's earliest fiction, the stories in *More Pricks than Kicks*, describes the passive resistance to social conformity and death under anesthesia of a protagonist named Belacqua (an allusion to Dante). Beckett's first novel, *Murphy*, presents the same resistance and senseless death in the story of Murphy, given the most common surname in Ireland. Murphy is the first of numerous Beckett protagonists who seek to relinquish all ties to their environment and their compulsion to make sense of it. The centerpiece of *Murphy* is an analysis of the discrete zones of the character's mind in the sixth chapter. The third and last of these zones is a darkness of selflessness in which mind itself is obviated. It is this zone beyond consciousness that most Beckett protagonists seek; it is their failure to reach it that creates the tension in most of Beckett's fiction.

Murphy is surrounded by representatives of two frames of reference that prevent his withdrawal from the world. The first is nationality, represented here by character types such as the drunken Irish poet Austin Ticklepenny and monuments to national ideals such as the statue of Cuchulain in the Dublin General Post Office. The second frame of reference is erudition, represented here by a plethora of arcane references to astronomy, astrology, philosophy, and mathematics. Assaulted by these adjuncts of identity, Murphy remains unable to disengage himself fully from the world, to withdraw completely into the third zone of his mind.

The problem that Beckett confronts in *Murphy* is central to all of his novels: to define consciousness in a novel without the usual novelistic apparatus of recognizable environment, nationality, and psychology. The novel only approaches such a definition in the chapter on Murphy's mind and in the image of an eerily withdrawn character named Mr. Endon. Elsewhere, Beckett is able to suggest an alternative only by destructive means: by heaping scorn on things Irish, by deflating intellectual pretensions, and by parodying novelistic conventions. These forms of ridicule make *Murphy* Beckett's most humorous and accessible novel. The same reliance on ridicule, however, ensures that *Murphy* remains derivative of the very forms of thought and literature it intends to challenge.

WATT

Although it was not published until 1953, after *Molloy* and *Malone Dies*, *Watt* was written a decade earlier and properly belongs among Beckett's early novels. It is a transitional work, written in English, in which one can observe intimations of the central concerns of the trilogy of novels written in French.

Like Murphy, Watt is an alienated vagabond seeking succor from the complexities of existence. In the opening and closing sections of this four-part novel, Watt's world is a recognizably Irish one populated with middle-class characters with small social pretensions. In the central two sections, however, Watt works as a servant on the surreal country estate of a Mr. Knott. *Watt* most resembles Beckett's later fiction in these central sections. In them, Watt ineffectually attempts to master simpler and simpler problems without the benefit of reliable contingencies of cause and effect or even the assurance of a reliable system of language. The structure of the novel is ultimately dislocated by the gradual revelation that the four parts are not in fact presented in chronological order and that they have been narrated by a character named Sam rather than by an omniscient narrator. Sam's account proves unreliable in particulars, thus completing the process by which the novel undermines any illusion of certainty concerning the interaction of the characters Watt ("What?") and Knott ("Not!").

Watt, like *Murphy*, relies on satire of literary precedents and disruption of novelistic conventions. There are allusions in the novel to the work of William Butler Yeats and

James Jones and to the poet Æ (George William Russell), to cite only the Irish precedents. The great disruption of novelistic conventions is effected by "Addenda" of unincorporated material at the end of the text and by pedantic annotations throughout the novel. Nevertheless, *Watt* does look ahead to *Molloy* in its central sections, dominated by episodic problems such as the removal of Knott's slops and the attempt of the wretched Lynch family to have the ages of its living members total exactly one thousand. The full emergence of this sort of episodic narrative in Beckett's fiction, however, seems to have required the focus of attention on language itself (rather than on literary conventions). That was one important effect of Beckett's decision to begin to compose novels in French rather than in English.

MERCIER AND CAMIER

Mercier and Camier, although published in 1970, was written in French in 1946, soon after Beckett returned to Paris at the end of the war. Like *Watt*, it is best placed among Beckett's works by date of composition rather than publication. Written at the outset of the "siege in the room" that produced Beckett's major novels, it illuminates the process by which the style of the trilogy emerged from concentration on elements of composition rather than on the social concerns that dominate most conventional novels.

Mercier and Camier is an account of an aimless journey by two decrepit characters out of and back into a city that resembles Dublin. A witness-narrator announces his presence in the opening sentence but remains otherwise inconspicuous. The descriptions of the two characters' generally enigmatic encounters with others, however, are periodically interrupted by subtly disported tabular synopses that call attention to the arbitrary features of the narrator's accounts. The novel is thus a shrewdly self-conscious narrative performance, with the emphasis falling on the telling rather than on the meaning of the tale.

The belated publication of *Mercier and Camier* was a welcome event because the work represents what must have seemed to Beckett an unsatisfactory attempt to open the novel form to accommodate the "mess" he finds dominant in the world. His composition of the novel in French produced a spare prose style and calculated use of language that would prove essential to his later fiction. Like *Watt*, however, the novel retained a peripheral witness-narrator; this may have been one of the sources of Beckett's dissatisfaction with the novel, for immediately after *Mercier and Camier* he shifted to the monologue essential to the three works that followed.

Beckett's major accomplishment in prose fiction is the trilogy of novels begun with *Molloy*, written in French in 1947 and 1948. All three are narrative monologues, all seek to explain origins, and all expose various forms of self-knowledge as delusions. Thus, they approach that ideal core of the onion in their quest for explanations, and they assert the governing "mess" of incoherence, which continues to resist artificial, if comforting, intellectual fabrications.

MOLLOY

In structure, *Molloy*, translated into English by Beckett in collaboration with Patrick Bowles, is the most complex work in the trilogy. The first part of the novel is the narrative of the derelict Molloy, who discovers himself in his mother's room and attempts unsuccessfully to reconstruct his arrival there. The second part is the narrative of the Catholic and bourgeois detective Jacques Moran, who has been commissioned by an authority named Youdi to write a report on Molloy. As Moran's report proceeds, he gradually begins to resemble Molloy. His narrative ends with the composition of the sentence with which it began, now exposed as pure falsehood.

Molloy and Moran are counterparts whose narratives expose the alternative fallacies, respectively, of inward and outward ways of organizing experience. Molloy's self-involved preoccupations, such as his chronic flatulence, function as counterparts of Moran's more social preoccupations, such as Catholic liturgy and his profession. Both are left in unresolved confrontation with the likelihood that the ways they have attempted to make sense of their origins and present circumstances are pure sham. The special brilliance of *Molloy* is the manner in which this confrontation is brought about by the terms of each narrator's monologue. The prose style of the novel is dominated by hilarious deflations of momentary pretensions, ironic undercutting of reassuring truisms, and criticism of its own assertions. It is in this manner that *Molloy* manages to admit the "mess" Beckett seeks to accommodate in the novel form: Its compelling and humorous narratives effectively expose the limits rather than the fruits of self-knowledge.

MALONE DIES

Malone Dies is the purest of the narrative performances of Beckett's storytellers. In it, a bedridden man awaits death in his room and tells stories to pass the time. His environment is limited to the room, the view from a window, and a meager inventory of possessions he periodically recounts with inconsistent results. Beyond these, he is limited to the world of his stories about a boy named Sapo, an old man named MacMann, an employee in an insane asylum named Lemuel, and others. All are apparently fictions based on different periods in Malone's own life. At the end of the novel, Malone's narrative simply degenerates and ends inconclusively in brief phrases that may suggest death itself or simply the end of his willingness to pursue the stories further.

It is essential to the novel that Malone criticize his own stories, revise them, abandon them, and rehearse them once again. His predicament is that he knows the stories to be false in many respects, but he has no alternative approach to the truth of his own origins. Like Beckett, Malone is a compulsive composer of fictions who is perpetually dissatisfied with them. As a result, *Malone Dies* is one of the most completely self-critical and self-involved novels in the twentieth century stream of metafictions, or novels about the nature of the novel. It demonstrates, with bitter humor and relentless self-examination, the limits of fiction, the pleasure of fiction, and the lack of an acceptable substitute for fiction.

THE UNNAMABLE

In *The Unnamable*, Beckett pursues the preoccupations of *Molloy* and *Malone Dies* to an extreme that puts formidable difficulties before even the most devoted reader of the modern novel. In *Molloy* the focus is on two long narrative accounts, in *Malone Dies* it narrows to concentrate on briefer stories, and in *The Unnamable* it shrinks further to probe the limits of language itself, of words and names. As the title suggests, these smaller units of literary discourse prove to be just as false and unreliable as those longer literary units have proven to be in Beckett's previous two novels. In *The Unnamable*, there is no character in the ordinary sense of the term. Instead, there are only bursts of language, at first organized into paragraphs, then only into continuous sentences, and finally into pages of a single sentence broken only by commas.

The premise of the novel is that a paralyzed and apparently androgynous creature suspended in a jar outside a Paris restaurant speaks of himself and versions of himself labeled with temporary names such as Mahood and Worm. As he speaks, however, he is diverted from the content of his speech by disgust with its elements, its words. The names of Murphy, Molloy, and Malone are all evoked with complete disgust at the complacent acceptance of language inherent in the creation of such literary characters. *The Unnamable* thus attempts to challenge assumptions of literary discourse by diverting attention from plot and character to phrase and word. It is tortuous reading because it calls into question the means by which any reading process proceeds.

The preoccupation with speaking in the novel leads naturally to a corollary preoccupation with silence, and *The Unnamable* ends with a paradoxical assertion of the equal impossibility of either ending or continuing. At this point, Beckett had exhausted the means by which he attempted to admit the "mess" into the form of the novels in his trilogy. He managed to proceed, to extend the series of his novels, by exploring the richness of metaphorical and generally horrific environments like that of the unnamable one suspended, weeping, in his jar.

HOW IT IS

Beckett's critics commonly refer to the series of prose fictions begun with *How It Is* as "post-trilogy prose." The term is useful because it draws attention to the methods of Beckett's works as well as their chronology. Even in the midst of the incoherence of *The Unnamable*, there are references to the familiar world, such as the fact that the narrator is located in Paris. In *How It Is* and the works that followed, however, the environment is an entirely metaphorical and distinctly surreal one. Without reference to a familiar world, these works are governed by an interior system of recurrent images and memories. *How It Is* marks the beginning of this final stage in the series of Beckett's works, and so its French title, *Comment c'est*, is an appropriate phonetic pun meaning both "how it is" and *commencer*, or "to begin."

In *How It Is*, the speaker, named Bom, is a creature crawling in darkness through endless mire, dragging with him a sack of canned provisions, and torturing and being tortured by other creatures with their indispensable can openers. His narrative takes the form of brief, unpunctuated fragments separated by spaces on the page. Each fragment is of a length that can be spoken aloud, as it ideally should be, and the style may be in part a product of Beckett's experience in the production of plays. There is a second character, named Pim, against whom the narrator tends to define his own status. The novel, which many prefer to term a prose poem, is thus broken into three parts: before Pim, with Pim, and after Pim.

The Bom and Pim interaction is an excruciating account of misery in a netherworld of darkness and slime. It is related entirely in retrospect, however, and the changing relationships of domination and subordination are less important than the manner in which the language of the fragments creates its own system of repetitions and alterations of phrases. *How It Is* dramatizes, in fact, how it *was* for Bom, and in place of clear references to the familiar world, it offers a verbal model for the mechanics of memory. This remains a consistent, if extraordinarily complex, extension of Beckett's attempt to accommodate the "mess" of chaos in the novel form. Its extremely calculated prose creates a sense of the consistent, but inexplicable and ultimately uninformative, impingement of the past on the present.

THE LOST ONES

The Lost Ones is a representative example of Beckett's prose fiction immediately following *How It Is*. He composed many brief prose pieces in this period, abandoned most of them, and resurrected them for publication at the urging of enthusiastic friends. Most are published in collections of his short works. *The Lost Ones*, however, is a more sustained narrative performance (sixty-three pages in the American edition). It was abandoned in an incomplete form in 1966 but retrieved and supplemented with an effective conclusion in 1970. It has also gained greater attention than most of Beckett's works from this period because of an innovative stage adaptation by the Mabou Mines Company in New York City in 1973.

The Lost Ones is unique among Beckett's works because it focuses on a group rather than on an individual. In fifteen unnumbered passages of prose, it describes the workings of a huge cylinder populated by male and female figures who maneuver throughout its various areas by means of ladders. The prose style is remarkably understated in comparison to the painful, if metaphorical, imagery of *How It Is*, and the primary action is the continual reorganization of this closed set of persons according to an entropic process of diminishing energies. Mathematical computation, a motif in many of Beckett's novels, is a primary feature in *The Lost Ones*. As language does in so many of Beckett's earlier novels, numerical calculations prove an inadequate means of organizing experience in this work, and the crucial final paragraph added in 1970 is a fatalistic exposure of the worthlessness of these computations as indications of the past, present, or future of this surreal environment. As in many of Beckett's later prose pieces, the metaphorical environment created by the prose is open to many interpretive referents. The text is subtly allusive—the French title, for example, evokes Alphonse de Lamartine—and the viability of literature as an effective indication of past, present, or future is among the possible subjects of this spare and immensely suggestive text.

COMPANY

With the exceptions of *The Lost Ones* and other aborted works, nearly twenty years elapsed between the writing of *How It Is* and the next of Beckett's prose fictions to approach the novel in form if not in length. *Company* ended this relative silence, during which Beckett produced a variety of works in other genres. Like *How It Is* and the intervening works, *Company* presents a generally metaphorical environment and a consistent emphasis on the workings of memory. Unlike Beckett's other late works, however, it was composed in English and apparently generated out of contemplation of distinctly autobiographical images.

Company is a narrative by a figure immobilized on his back in darkness. Despite this surreal premise, it dwells on images of a familiar, suggestively Irish environment marked by features such as Connolly's store and the Ballyogan Road. It thus combines the astringency of Beckett's "post-trilogy prose" with the references to an identifiable world common in the trilogy. It is, however, far from a regression from experimental form or an abandonment of the attempt to accommodate the "mess" in a novel. Instead, it represents the fruit of Beckett's years of careful manipulation of a spare prose style in his second language. Like *How It Is*, *Company* concentrates on the inexplicable workings of memory. Unlike *How It Is*, the novel does so in a passive and restrained mixture of nostalgic and ironic images free of the vulgar and painful hostility of that earlier novel. In less flamboyant ways than Beckett's earlier works, *Company* also manages to underscore its own nature as an artificial, literary construction. Its governing metaphor of "company" manages to encompass both the memories surrounding the narrator and the meeting of author and reader of a literary text.

ILL SEEN ILL SAID

Company was followed by *Ill Seen Ill Said*, a series of paragraphs consisting primarily of sentence fragments. They describe a woman and her attempt to capture the details of her environment. The devotion to detail is such that vocabulary, rather than image, tends to capture attention, frequently because of intentional neologisms, interior rhymes, and sporadic echoes. It is more an evocation of a mood than a plotted novel, one that reveals the author, having rid himself of complacent use of language in earlier works, as a prose stylist with marked affinities to a poet. *Ill Seen Ill Said*, despite the disparagement of voice in its title, marks the emergence in Beckett's works of a devotion to pure sensation unmodulated by systems of logic or desire. It is in this respect that *Ill Seen Ill Said* is a necessary and inevitable extension of "the task of the artist now" addressed in a long series of novels. Rather than suggesting an alternative literary expression by destructive irony or subverting complacency by incoherent monologue, it attempts to present consciousness free of artificial order in a distinctly lyrical form of prose fiction.

In an early essay on the Irish poet Denis Devlin published in *Transition* in 1938, Beckett offered this dictum: "Art has always been this—pure interrogation, rhetorical question less the rhetoric." Like so many of his statements on other writers, this has a special relevance to Beckett's own literary career. Over a period of a half century, he produced fictions that relentlessly question assumptions of intellectual and literary order. He did so with a single-minded devotion to what he took to be "the task of the artist now" and so compiled an oeuvre that is unique in the twentieth century in its concentration on a central purpose and in its literary expression of the great philosophical preoccupations of its time. Beckett's work has been discussed by critics in reference to other innovative thinkers of the century as disparate as Albert Einstein, Sigmund Freud, and Jean-Paul Sartre. In addition to fueling the literary debates of his time, Beckett's work may be said to have created, in part, contemporary literary theories such as structuralism and deconstruction. Despite their formidable difficulties, then, Beckett's novels have an indisputable importance to anyone seriously interested in the intellectual climate of the twentieth century.

John P. Harrington

OTHER MAJOR WORKS

SHORT FICTION: *More Pricks than Kicks*, 1934; *Nouvelles et textes pour rien*, 1955 (*Stories and Texts for Nothing*, 1967); *No's Knife: Collected Shorter Prose, 1947-1966*, 1967; *First Love, and Other Shorts*, 1974; *Pour finir encore et autres foirades*, 1976 (*Fizzles*, 1976; also known as *For to Yet Again*); *Four Novellas*, 1977 (also known as *The Expelled, and Other Novellas*, 1980); *Collected Short Prose*, 1991.

PLAYS: *En attendant Godot*, pb. 1952 (*Waiting for Godot*, 1954); *"Fin de partie," suivi de "Acte sans paroles,"* pr., pb. 1957 (music by John Beckett; *"Endgame: A Play in One Act," Followed by "Act Without Words: A Mime for One Player,"* 1958); *Krapp's Last Tape*, pr., pb. 1958; *Act Without Words II*, pr., pb. 1960 (one-act mime); *Happy Days*, pr., pb. 1961; *Play*, pr., pb. 1963 (English translation, 1964); *Come and Go: Dramaticule*, pr., pb. 1965 (one scene; English translation, 1967); *Not I*, pr. 1972; *Ends and Odds*, pb. 1976; *Footfalls*, pr., pb. 1976; *That Time*, pr., pb. 1976; *A Piece of Monologue*, pr., pb. 1979; *Ohio Impromptu*, pr., pb. 1981; *Rockaby*, pr., pb. 1981; *Catastrophe*, pr. 1982; *Company*, pr. 1983; *Collected Shorter Plays*, 1984; *Complete Dramatic Works*, 1986; *Eleutheria*, pb. 1995.

POETRY: *Whoroscope*, 1930; *Echo's Bones and Other Precipitates*, 1935; *Poems in English*, 1961; *Collected Poems in English and French*, 1977.

SCREENPLAY: *Film*, 1965.

TELEPLAYS: *Eh Joe*, 1966 (*Dis Joe*, 1967); *Tryst*, 1976; *Shades*, 1977; *Quad*, 1981.

RADIO PLAYS: *All That Fall*, 1957 (revised 1968); *Embers*, 1959; *Words and Music*, 1962 (music by John Beckett); *Cascando*, 1963 (music by Marcel Mihalovici).

NONFICTION: *Proust*, 1931; *The Letters of Samuel Becket: Vol. 1, 1929-1940*, 2009 (Martha Dow Fehsenfeld and Lois More Overbeck, editors).

TRANSLATION: *An Anthology of Mexican Poetry*, 1958 (Octavio Paz, editor).

MISCELLANEOUS: *I Can't Go On, I'll Go On: A Selection from Samuel Beckett's Work*, 1976 (Richard Seaver, editor).

BIBLIOGRAPHY

Acheson, James. *Samuel Beckett's Artistic Theory and Practice: Criticism, Drama, and Early Fiction*. New York: St. Martin's Press, 1997. An examination of Beckett's literary viewpoint as it expressed itself in his drama and early fiction. Chapter 6 focuses on the trilogy—the novels *Molloy, Malone Dies*, and *The Unnamable*. Includes bibliography and index.

Alvarez, Alfred. *Beckett*. 2d ed. London: Fontana, 1992. A short, lively, and sometimes opinionated discussion of Beckett by a critic who does not altogether trust the author and who knows how to argue not only for his strengths but also against his limitations. Contains a good short discussion of the intellectual climate that precipitated absurd literature.

Bair, Deirdre. *Samuel Beckett: A Biography*. 1978. Reprint. New York: Simon & Schuster, 1993. Although Beckett was often reluctant to talk about himself, he cooperated with Bair. This work is among the fullest versions of a life of Beckett in print, and to know his life is to understand his art. The criticism of the specific texts is often limited, but Bair is very good at putting the work in the context of Beckett's very odd life. Contains good illustrations.

Cronin, Anthony. *Samuel Beckett: The Last Modernist*. New York: HarperCollins, 1996. Fully documented and detailed biography describes Beckett's involvement in the Paris literary scene, his response to winning the Nobel Prize, and his overall literary career.

Ellman, Richard. *Four Dubliners: Wilde, Yeats, Joyce, and Beckett*. New York: George Braziller, 1988. Examines the Irish roots in Beckett's novels and plays and their subsequent influence on Irish writing. A lively and interesting study of four Irish writers, suitable for all students.

Esslin, Martin, ed. *Samuel Beckett: A Collection of Critical Essays*. Englewood Cliffs, N.J.: Prentice Hall, 1965. Collection of major essays by some of the most widely respected Beckett critics. Includes essays on all phases of his work, not only by English-speaking critics but also by European writers, who see Beckett not as a writer in English but as a part of the European tradition.

Hill, Leslie. *Beckett's Fiction: In Different Worlds*. New York: Cambridge University Press, 1990. Focuses on Beckett's novels from *Murphy* to *Worstward Ho*. Includes a preface that briefly characterizes previous criticism as reductive. Includes notes and bibliography.

Kenner, Hugh. *A Reader's Guide to Samuel Beckett*. London: Thames and Hudson, 1973. This essential companion for anyone determined to make some kind of sense of the works of Beckett comments clearly and simply on the individual texts.

――――. *Samuel Beckett: A Critical Study*. Berkeley: University of California Press, 1968. Work by probably the best commentator on Beckett is lively, imaginative, and extremely good at placing Beckett in the Irish tradition as well as assessing his part in the movement of experimental literature.

Knowlson, James. *Damned to Fame: The Life of Samuel Beckett*. New York: Simon & Schuster, 1996. Comprehensive biography presents a great deal of material on Beckett's life that was not previously available. Includes detailed notes and bibliography.

McDonald, Rónán. *The Cambridge Introduction to Samuel Beckett*. New York: Cambridge University Press, 2006. Chapter 4 of this succinct overview of Beckett's life and works focuses on his prose fiction, including the novels *Murphy, Watt, Molloy, Malone Dies, The Unnamable*, and *How It Is*.

Pattie, David. *The Complete Critical Guide to Samuel Beckett*. New York: Routledge, 2000. Reference volume combines biographical information with critical analysis of Beckett's literary works, including the novels *Murphy, Watt, Mercier and Camier*, and *How It Is*.

Pilling, John, ed. *The Cambridge Companion to Beckett*. New York: Cambridge University Press, 1994. Comprehensive reference work provides considerable information about the life and works of Beckett, including analysis of his novels. Includes bibliography and indexes.

ELIZABETH BOWEN

Born: Dublin, Ireland; June 7, 1899
Died: London, England; February 22, 1973
Also known as: Elizabeth Dorothea Cole Bowen

<small>PRINCIPAL LONG FICTION</small>
The Hotel, 1927
The Last September, 1929
Friends and Relations, 1931
To the North, 1932
The House in Paris, 1935
The Death of the Heart, 1938
The Heat of the Day, 1949
A World of Love, 1955
The Little Girls, 1964
Eva Trout, 1968

<small>OTHER LITERARY FORMS</small>

The first seven novels that Elizabeth Bowen (BOH-uhn) produced were republished by Jonathan Cape in Cape Collected Editions between the years 1948 and 1954, when Cape also republished four of her short-story collections: *Joining Charles* (1929), *The Cat Jumps, and Other Stories* (1934), *Look at All Those Roses* (1941), and *The Demon Lover* (1945). Other collections of her short stories are *Encounters* (1923), *Ann Lee's, and Other Stories* (1926), *Stories by Elizabeth Bowen* (1959), and *A Day in the Dark, and Other Stories* (1965). *The Demon Lover* was published in New York under the title *Ivy Gripped the Steps, and Other Stories* (1946); this work, as the original title indicates, has supernatural content that scarcely appears in Bowen's novels. Bowen's nonfiction includes *Bowen's Court* (1942), a description of her family residence in Ireland; *Seven Winters* (1942), an autobiography; *English Novelists* (1946), a literary history; *Collected Impressions* (1950), essays; *The Shelbourne: A Center of Dublin Life for More than a Century* (1951), a work about the hotel in Dublin; *A Time in Rome* (1960), travel essays; and *Afterthought: Pieces About Writing* (1962), which collects transcripts of broadcasts and reviews. A play that Bowen coauthored with John Perry, *Castle Anna*, was performed in London in March, 1948.

<small>ACHIEVEMENTS</small>

Considered a great lady by those who knew her, Elizabeth Bowen draws an appreciative audience from readers who understand English gentility—the calculated gesture and the controlled response. Bowen's support has come from intellectuals who recognize the

Elizabeth Bowen
(Library of Congress)

values of the novel of manners and who liken her work to that of Jane Austen and Henry James. Her contemporaries and colleagues included members of the Bloomsbury Group and scholars of Oxford University, where the classical scholar C. M. Bowra was a close friend. Many readers know Bowen best through her novel *The Death of the Heart* and her short stories, especially "The Demon Lover," "Joining Charles," and "Look at All Those Roses," which are frequently anthologized in college texts. Bowen was made a Commander of the Order of the British Empire in 1948, and she was awarded an honorary doctor of letters degree at Trinity College, Dublin, in 1949, and at Oxford University in 1957. She was made a Companion of Literature in 1965.

BIOGRAPHY

Although born in Ireland, Elizabeth Dorothea Cole Bowen came from a pro-British family who received land in county Cork as an award for fighting with Oliver Cromwell in 1649. The family built Bowen's Court in 1776—what the Irish call a "big house"—as a

Protestant stronghold against the mainly Catholic Irish and lived there as part of the Anglo-Irish ascendancy. Bowen was educated in England and spent some summers at Bowen's Court. Not until after the Easter Rising in 1916 did she come to realize the causes of the Irish struggle for independence, and in writing *Bowen's Court* she admitted that her family "got their position and drew their power from a situation that shows an inherent wrong."

Her barrister father, when he was nineteen, had disobeyed forewarnings and carried home smallpox, which eventually killed his mother and rendered his father mad. Preoccupied with the desire for a son, Bowen's father nearly lost his wife in the attempt to have one in 1904, and, burdened with the debts of Bowen's Court, he suffered severe mental breakdowns in 1905 and 1906 and again in 1928. He was the cause of Elizabeth's removal to England, where, as an Irish outcast, her defense was to become excessively British. Living in a series of locations with her mother, she was kept uninformed of family circumstances; as an adult, her novels provided for her an outlet for her sense of guilt, the result of her feeling responsible for the unexplained events around her. Her lack of roots was intensified with the death of her mother in 1912.

Bowen studied art, traveled in Europe, and worked as an air-raid warden in London during World War II. In 1923, she married Alan Charles Cameron, who was employed in the school system near Oxford, and they lived there for twelve years. She inherited Bowen's Court in 1928 when her father died, and in 1952, she and her husband returned there to live. Bowen's husband, however, died that year. Bowen sold the home in 1960 and returned to Oxford.

Bowen's career as a novelist spanned years of drastic change, 1927 to 1968, and, except for *The Last September*, she wrote about the present; her war experiences are reflected in the short-story collection *The Demon Lover* and in the novel *The Heat of the Day*. After 1935, she also wrote reviews and articles for the *New Statesman* and other publications, for the Ministry of Information during World War II, and for *The Tatler* in the 1940's, and she helped edit *The London Magazine* in the late 1950's. Afflicted with a slight stammer, Bowen lectured infrequently but effectively; transcripts of two of her BBC broadcasts, "left as they were spoken," may be read in *Afterthought*. After a visit to Ireland in 1973, Bowen died in London, leaving an unfinished autobiographical work, *Pictures and Conversations* (1975).

ANALYSIS

Elizabeth Bowen had a special talent for writing the conversations of children around the age of nine, as is evident in *The House in Paris*. Somewhat corresponding to her personal experience, her novels often present a homeless child (usually a girl), orphaned and shunted from one residence to another, or a child with one parent who dies and leaves the adolescent in the power of outwardly concerned but mainly selfish adults. Frequently, management by others prolongs the protagonist's state of innocence into the woman's twenties, when she must begin to assert herself and learn to manage her own affairs. (At age twenty-four, for example, Eva Trout does not know how to boil water for tea.) On the other side of the relationship, the controlling adult is often a perfectly mannered woman of guile, wealthy enough to be idle and to fill the idleness with discreet exercise of power over others. The typical Bowen characters, then, are the child, the unwanted adolescent, the woman in her twenties in a prolonged state of adolescence, and the "terrible woman" of society. Young people, educated haphazardly but expensively, are culturally mature but aimless. Genteel adults, on the other hand, administer their own selfish standards of what constitutes impertinence in other persons; these judgments disguise Bowen's subtle criticism of the correct English.

Typical Bowen themes include those of loss of innocence, acceptance of the past, and expanding consciousness. The pain and helplessness attendant on these themes and the disguise of plentiful money make them unusual. Although Bowen writes about the privileged class, three of her four common character types do not feel privileged. To handle her themes, Bowen frequently orders time and space by dividing the novels into three parts, with one part set ten years in the past and with a juxtaposition of at least two locations. The ten-year lapse provides a measure of the maturity gained, and the second location, by contrast, jars the consciousness into reevaluation of the earlier experience.

THE HOTEL

The fact that the Bowen women often have nothing to do is very obvious in *The Hotel*, set in Bordighera on the Italian Riviera, but of greater interest is the fact that, like Ireland, Bordighera is another place of British occupancy. The hotel guests' activities are confined to walking, talking, taking tea, and playing tennis. Mrs. Kerr is the managing wealthy woman who feeds on the attentions of her protégé, Sydney Warren, and then abandons Sydney when her son arrives. At age twenty-two, Sydney, for lack of better purpose, studies for a doctorate at home in England. Back in Italy, she becomes engaged to a clergyman as a means of achieving an identity and popularity, but her better sense forces reconsideration, and she cancels the engagement and asserts her independence.

THE LAST SEPTEMBER

The Last September, set in 1920, when the hated British soldiers (the Black and Tans) were stationed in Ireland to quell rebellion, shows Sir Richard and Lady Myra Naylor entertaining with tennis parties at their big house. Like Bowen, who wrote in *Afterthought* that this novel was "nearest my heart," Lois Farquar is a summer visitor, aged nineteen, orphaned, asking herself what she should do. An older woman tells her that her art lacks talent. Almost engaged to a British soldier, Gerald Lesworth, she might have a career in marriage, but Lady Naylor, in the role of graceful-terrible woman, destroys the engagement in a brilliant heart-to-heart talk in which she points out to Lois that Gerald has no prospects.

As September closes the social season, Gerald is killed in ambush, and as Lois—much more aware now and less innocent—prepares to depart for France, her home, Danielstown, is burned down; this loss signals her separation from the protected past.

TO THE NORTH

After *Friends and Relations*, Bowen entered the most fruitful part of her career. Her next four novels are generally considered to be her best work. *To the North* has rather obvious symbolism in a protagonist named Emmeline Summers, whose lack of feeling makes her "icy." She runs a successful travel agency with the motto "Travel Dangerously" (altering "Live Dangerously" and "Travel Safe"); the motto reflects both her ability to understand intellectually the feelings of others through their experience and her orphan state in homelessness. Emmeline tries to compensate for her weaknesses by imposing dramatic opposites: Without a home of her own, she overvalues her home with her widowed sister-in-law, Cecilia Summers; frequently called an angel, she has a fatal attraction to the devil-like character Markie Linkwater. When Cecilia plans to remarry (breaking up the home), when Markie (bored with Emmeline) returns to his former mistress, and when Emmeline's travel business begins to fail rapidly because of her preoccupation with Markie, she smashes her car while driving Markie north; "traveling dangerously" at high speeds, she becomes the angel of death.

The cold of the North suggested by the novel's title also touches other characters. Lady Waters, who offers Emmeline weekends on her estate as a kind of second home, feeds mercilessly on the unhappiness of failed loves and gossip. Lady Waters tells Cecilia to speak to Emmeline about her affair with Markie and thereby initiates the fateful dinner party that leads to the accident. Pauline, the niece of Cecilia's fiancé, is the orphaned adolescent character on the verge of becoming aware of and embarrassed by sex. Bowen describes Emmeline as the "stepchild of her uneasy century," a century in which planes and trains have damaged the stability and book knowledge of sexual research (indicated by the reading of Havelock Ellis), thereby freeing relationships but failing to engage the heart. The travel and the lack of warmth make the title a metaphor for the new century's existence. With her tenuous hold on home, love, and career, Emmeline commits suicide.

THE HOUSE IN PARIS

The House in Paris is set in three locations that reflect different aspects of the protagonist, Karen Michaelis: England, the land of perfect society; Ireland, the land of awareness; and France, the land of passion and the dark past. Parts 1 and 3 take place in a single day in Paris; part 2 occurs ten years earlier, during four months when Karen was age twenty-three. The evils of the house in Paris become apparent in the flashback and can be appreciated only through recognition of the terrible woman who runs it, Mme Fisher, and the rootlessness of the foreign students who stay there. Among other students, Mme Fisher has had in her power Karen and her friend Naomi Fisher (Mme Fisher's daughter), and the young Max Ebhart, a Jew with no background. Ten years later, when Max wants to break his engagement with Naomi to marry another, Mme Fisher interferes, and he commits suicide.

The book begins and ends in a train station in Paris. In part 1, Leopold (age nine and the illegitimate child of Karen and Max Ebhart) and Henrietta Mountjoy (age eleven and the granddaughter of a friend of Mme Fisher) arrive on separate trains—Henrietta from England in the process of being shuttled to another relative, and Leopold from his adoptive parents in Italy to await a first acquaintance with his real mother. Leopold and Henrietta, meeting in the house in Paris, become symbolic of the possibility that, with Mme Fisher bedridden for ten years (since Max's suicide) and now dying, the future will be free of the mistakes of the past. Mme Fisher, in an interview with Leopold, tells him that the possibility of finding himself "like a young tree inside a tomb is to discover the power to crack the tomb and grow up to any height," something Max had failed to do.

Dark, egotistic, self-centered, and passionate like his father, Leopold constructs imaginatively a role for his unknown mother to play and then breaks into uncontrollable weeping when a telegram arrives canceling her visit. The mature and implacable Henrietta, orphaned like Leopold but accustomed to the vicissitudes of adult life, shows him how to crack out of the tomb of childhood. In part 3, quite unexpectedly, Ray Forrestier, who had given up diplomacy and taken up business to marry Karen in spite of her illegitimate child, urges a reunion with her son Leopold, takes matters into his own hands, and brings Leopold to Karen.

THE DEATH OF THE HEART

The three-part structure of Bowen's novels is most fully realized in *The Death of the Heart*. The parts of this novel are labeled "The World," "The Flesh," and "The Devil," and they follow the seasons of winter, spring, and summer. The world of Windsor Terrace, the Quaynes' residence in London, is advanced and sterile. Portia enters into this world at age fifteen, an orphan and stepsister to the present Thomas Quayne. Thomas's wife, Anna, who has miscarried twice and is childless, secretly reads Portia's diary and is indignant at the construction Portia puts on events in the household. Portia sees much "dissimulation" at Windsor Terrace, where doing the "right" thing does not mean making a moral choice. As one of Bowen's radical innocents who has spent her youth in hotels and temporary locations, Portia says no one in this house knows why she was born. She has only one friend in this, her first home: Matchett, the head servant, who gives Portia some religious training. Of the three male friends who wait upon Anna—St. Quentin Martin, Eddie, and Major Brutt—Portia fastens on the affections of Eddie.

Spring, in part 2, brings a much-needed vacation for the Quaynes. Thomas and Anna sail for Capri, and Portia goes to stay with Anna's former governess at Seale-on-Sea. At the governess's home, dubbed Waikiki, Portia is nearly drowned in sensuality—the sights, smells, sounds, and feelings of a vulgar and mannerless household. Portia invites

Eddie to spend a weekend with her at Seale-on-Sea, which further educates her in the ways of the flesh.

On her return to London in part 3, Portia's more open nature is immediately apparent to Matchett, who says she had been "too quiet." The Devil's works are represented both obviously and subtly in this section, and they take many identities. St. Quentin, Anna, Eddie, even the unloving atmosphere of Windsor Terrace make up the Devil's advocacy. St. Quentin, a novelist, tells Portia that Anna has been reading Portia's diary, a disloyalty and an invasion of privacy with which, after some contemplation, Portia decides she cannot live. Herein lies the death of her teenage heart, what Bowen calls a betrayal of her innocence, or a "mysterious landscape" that has perished.

Summer at Windsor Terrace brings maturity to Portia as well as to others: Anna must confront her own culpability, even her jealousy of Portia; St. Quentin, his betrayal of Anna's reading of the diary; Thomas, his neglect of his father and his father's memory. Even Matchett takes a terrified ride in the unfamiliar cab, setting out in the night to an unknown location to pick up Portia. They all share in the summer's maturation that Portia has brought to fruition.

William Shakespeare's Portia prefers mercy to justice, paralleling the Portia in this novel. Bowen's Portia observes everything with a "political seriousness." The scaffolding of this novel supports much allusion, metaphor, and drama—all artfully structured. The world, the flesh, and the Devil as medieval threats to saintliness are reinterpreted in this context; they become the locations of the heart that has been thrust outside Eden and comprise a necessary trinity, not of holiness but of wholeness. This novel earns critics' accord as Bowen's best.

THE HEAT OF THE DAY

In *The Death of the Heart*, ranked by many critics as a close second in quality to *The Heat of the Day*, Bowen uses World War II to purge the wasteland conditions that existed before and during the years from 1940 through 1945. Middle-class Robert Kelway has returned from the Battle of Dunkirk (1940) with a limp that comes and goes according to the state of his emotions. At the individual level, it reflects the psychological crippling of his youth; at the national level, it is the culmination of the condition expressed by the person who says, "Dunkirk was waiting there in us."

Upper-class Stella Rodney has retreated from the privileges of her past into a rented apartment and a war job. Having grown impassive with the century, divorced, with a son (Roderick) in the army, she has taken Robert as her lover. She has become so impassive, in fact, that in 1942, a sinister and mysterious government spy named Harrison tells her that Robert has been passing information to the enemy, and she says and does nothing.

Critics have commented frequently on this novel's analogies to William Shakespeare's *Hamlet, Prince of Denmark* (pr. c. 1600-1601), an obvious example being Holme Dene (Dane home), Robert Kelway's country home. Psychologically weak, Robert is ruled by his destructive mother, who also had stifled his father and planted the seeds of Robert's defection from English ways. While Stella visits Holme Dene and learns to understand Robert, her son visits a cousin who tells him that Stella did not divorce her husband, as was commonly thought, but rather was divorced by him while he was having an affair, although he died soon after the divorce. Roderick, however, has managed to survive Stella's homelessness with a positive and manly outlook; when he inherits an estate in Ireland, he finds that it will give him the foundation for a future.

EVA TROUT

In *Eva Trout*, the various autobiographical elements of Bowen's work come to life: Bowen's stammer in Eva's reticence, the tragic deaths of both parents, the transience and sporadic education, the delayed adolescence, the settings of hotels and train stations. Eva Trout lives with a former teacher, Iseult Arbles, and Iseult's husband, Eric, while she waits for an inheritance. She turns twenty-four and receives the inheritance, which enables her to leave their home, where the marriage is unstable, and buy a home of her own filled with used furniture. She also escapes the clutches of Constantine, her guardian, who had been her father's male lover.

Eva discovers that a woman with money is suddenly pursued by "admirers," and Eric visits her in her new home. Eva subsequently lets Iseult think that Eric has fathered her child, Jeremy, whom she adopts in the United States. After eight years in American cities, where Eva seeks help for the deaf-mute Jeremy, Eva and Jeremy return to England. From England, they flee to Paris, where a doctor and his wife begin successful training of Jeremy. Back in England, Eva attempts the next phase of reaching security and a normal life. She seeks a husband and persuades the son of Iseult's vicar to stage a wedding departure with her at Victoria Station. All her acquaintances are on hand to see the couple off, but Jeremy—brought from Paris for the occasion—playfully points a gun (which he thinks is a toy) at Eva and shoots her. In the midst of revelry, on the eve of her happiness, Eva drops dead beside the train.

Eva Trout makes a poignant and haunting last heroine for the Bowen sequence. This novel offers Bowen's final bitter statement on the elusiveness of security and happiness.

Grace Eckley

OTHER MAJOR WORKS

SHORT FICTION: *Encounters*, 1923; *Ann Lee's, and Other Stories*, 1926; *Joining Charles*, 1929; *The Cat Jumps, and Other Stories*, 1934; *Look at All Those Roses*, 1941; *The Demon Lover*, 1945 (also known as *Ivy Gripped the Steps, and Other Stories*, 1946); *The Early Stories*, 1951; *Stories by Elizabeth Bowen*, 1959; *A Day in the Dark, and Other Stories*, 1965; *Elizabeth Bowen's Irish Stories*, 1978; *The Collected Stories of Elizabeth Bowen*, 1980.

PLAYS: *Castle Anna*, pr. 1948 (with John Perry).

NONFICTION: *Bowen's Court*, 1942; *Seven Winters*, 1942; *English Novelists*, 1946; *Collected Impressions*, 1950; *The Shelbourne: A Center of Dublin Life for More than a Century*, 1951; *A Time in Rome*, 1960; *Afterthought: Pieces About Writing*, 1962; *Pictures and Conversations*, 1975; *The Mulberry Tree: Writings of Elizabeth Bowen*, 1986.

CHILDREN'S LITERATURE: *The Good Tiger*, 1965.

BIBLIOGRAPHY

Bennett, Andrew, and Nicholas Royle. *Elizabeth Bowen and the Dissolution of the Novel: Still Lives*. New York: St. Martin's Press, 1994. Asserts that Bowen was one of the most important authors in English in the twentieth century and that her work has been undervalued. A good source of information about Bowen's novels and their influence.

Bloom, Harold, ed. *Elizabeth Bowen: Modern Critical Views*. New York: Chelsea House, 1987. Collection of eleven essays surveys the range of Bowen criticism. Includes excerpts from important book-length critical works on Bowen. Supplemented by an extensive bibliography.

Corcoran, Neil. *Elizabeth Bowen: The Enforced Return*. New York: Oxford University Press, 2004. Analyzes several of Bowen's novels by showing how these and other of her works focus on three themes that are central to Bowen's writing: Ireland, children, and war.

Craig, Patricia. *Elizabeth Bowen*. Harmondsworth, England: Penguin Books, 1986. Short biographical study is indebted to Victoria Glendinning's work cited below, although it draws on later research, particularly on Bowen's Irish connections. Offers perceptive readings of Bowen's stories and novels and includes a useful chronology.

Ellmann, Maud. *Elizabeth Bowen: The Shadow Across the Page*. Edinburgh: Edinburgh University Press, 2003. Examination of Bowen's life and writings uses historical, psychoanalytical, and deconstructivist approaches to interpret her works. Focuses on analysis of Bowen's novels but also explicates some of her short stories and nonfiction.

Glendinning, Victoria. *Elizabeth Bowen*. New York: Alfred A. Knopf, 1977. Comprehensive biography by an author who is well versed in the complexities of Bowen's Irish context and details them informatively. Establishes and assesses Bowen's standing as an eminent English novelist of the 1930's. Also candidly discusses Bowen's private life, making full use of Bowen's numerous autobiographical essays.

Hoogland, Renée C. *Elizabeth Bowen: A Reputation in Writing*. New York: New York University Press, 1994. Views Bowen's work from a lesbian feminist perspective, concentrating on the ways in which Bowen's fiction explores the unstable and destabilizing effects of sexuality.

Jordan, Heather Bryant. *How Will the Heart Endure: Elizabeth Bowen and the Landscape of War*. Ann Arbor: University of Michigan Press, 1992. Focuses primarily on Bowen's novels and argues that war was the most important influence on Bowen's life and art. Discusses how two of her most common fictional motifs—of houses and ghosts—reflect war's threat to cultural values and its blurring of the lines between reality and fantasy.

Lee, Hermione. *Elizabeth Bowen: An Estimation*. London: Vision Press, 1981. Comprehensive and sophisticated study makes large claims for Bowen's work. Asserts that she is both the equal of her Bloomsbury contemporaries and an important exponent of the European modernism deriving from Gustave Flaubert and Henry James. Also incisively analyzes Bowen's concentration on the intersection of the cultural and the psychological.

Rubens, Robert. "Elizabeth Bowen: A Woman of Wisdom." *Contemporary Review* 268 (June, 1996): 304-307. Examines the complex style of Bowen's work as a reflection of her personality and background; discusses her romanticism and her rejection of the dehumanization of the twentieth century.

Walshe, Eibhear, ed. *Elizabeth Bowen Remembered*. Dublin: Four Courts Press, 1998. Collection of essays drawn from the annual lectures at the church where Bowen was buried. In addition to a brief biography, includes discussions of Bowen's use of Irish locales, motifs of gardens and gardening, and the Anglo-Irish tradition in Bowen's writing.

JOYCE CARY

Born: Londonderry, Ireland; December 7, 1888
Died: Oxford, Oxfordshire, England; March 29, 1957
Also known as: Arthur Joyce Lunel Cary; Thomas Joyce

OTHER LITERARY FORMS

All of Joyce Cary's short stories published under his own name are contained in *Spring Song, and Other Stories* (1960), edited by Winnifred Davin. Ten early stories published under the pseudonym Thomas Joyce are not included that collection. More than half a dozen of these stories, which deal with bohemian life in Paris, Cary sold to the *Saturday Evening Post* (1920) in order to support his serious writing. Cary's self-admitted formula for these "potboilers" was a little sentiment, a little incident, and surprise.

Cary also published three booklets of verse and many essays, the latter appearing in such periodicals as *Harper's Magazine*, *The New Yorker*, and the *Sunday Times*. The most significant pieces of Cary's occasional writing have been gathered by A. G. Bishop into a volume titled *Selected Essays* (1976). This collection is of interest to the literary student because it includes some samples of Cary's practical criticism and of his views on the theory and practice of writing as well as interesting material about his background and political views. *Art and Reality* (1958) is a sequence of meditations on aesthetics that Cary composed for the 1956 Clark Lectures at Cambridge University but was too ill to deliver.

Joyce Cary
(Library of Congress)

Cary's other nonfiction mainly articulates his views on the philosophy and practice of politics, concerning itself with such issues as history, imperialism, and war. These works include *Power in Men* (1939), *The Case for African Freedom* (1941; reprinted with other essays about Africa in 1962), *Process of Real Freedom* (1943), and *Memoir of the Bobotes* (1960). These works shed light on Cary's treatment of ethical and political issues in his fiction. A collection of Cary's unpublished manuscripts, papers, letters, and diaries is in the possession of the Bodleian Library at Oxford University.

ACHIEVEMENTS

Joyce Cary's major artistic achievements—the novel *Mister Johnson* and the trilogy comprising *Herself Surprised*, *To Be a Pilgrim*, and *The Horse's Mouth*—are realistic works that reflect social, moral, and historical change as well as technical performances that embody the formal and linguistic innovations of literary modernism. This distinctive mixture of traditional realism and modernist style is Cary's principal legacy as a novelist. Although he experiments with techniques such as stream of consciousness, interior monologue, disrupted chronology, shifting point of view, and present-tense narration, he consistently rivets the action—past or present—to a particular historical and social context. The continuity of exterior events never completely disintegrates, though it is sometimes difficult to reconstruct.

To be sure, the various novels offer the reader different perspectives and interpretations of social reality. The intention, however, is not to obscure that reality or to render it relative to the subjectivity of the narrator, but rather to layer it, to augment its texture. Cary's perspective, therefore, is not nihilistic. His experiments in the trilogy form enhance the reader's sense of dwelling in a shared or intersubjective reality, even though each novel in the series adroitly captures the idiosyncratic perspective of its first-person narrator. Cary refuses to endorse any sort of feckless relativism (he was repelled by the moral defeatism and philosophical pessimism of such post-World War I writers as Aldous Huxley) and yet manages to incorporate into his writing the innovations of modernism. His self-proclaimed comedy of freedom extends the range of traditional realism and offers new possibilities for the form of fiction.

Recognition of Cary's literary merit came only late in his life. Under the pseudonym Thomas Joyce, he published in the *Saturday Evening Post* several stories based on his youthful experiences of bohemian life in Paris, but he considered these efforts to be potboilers rather than serious pieces of fiction. The magazine, in fact, rejected his subsequent stories for being too "literary." Not until 1932, when Cary was forty-three, was his first novel, *Aissa Saved*, published. It was not a commercial success. He continued to produce novels, and finally, in 1941, after the publication of *A House of Children*, his seventh novel, he won his first literary award: the James Tait Black Memorial Prize for the best British novel of the year. After this award, Cary's reputation increased steadily. In 1950, the *Adam International Review* devoted a special issue to his work, and in 1953, Walter Allen's seminal study of his work, *Joyce Cary*, appeared. Cary enjoyed a successful lecture tour in the United States in 1951, and he was asked to deliver the 1956 Clark Lectures at Cambridge University. During his lifetime, he was praised by such prestigious critics as Allen, John Dover Wilson, and Barbara Hardy. Since his death in 1957, Cary scholarship has grown steadily. In 1963, *Modern Fiction Studies* devoted a special issue to his work, and numerous books and articles continue to be published that address Cary's achievements.

BIOGRAPHY

Arthur Joyce Lunel Cary was born in Londonderry, Ireland, on December 7, 1888. His ancestors had been Irish landlords since the early seventeenth century. The Arrears Act of 1882, however, plunged his grandfather into ruinous debt, and his father, Arthur Cary, a prospective civil engineer, moved the family to London shortly after Cary's birth. There the nexus of traditional family life was Cromwell House, owned by Cary's Uncle Tristam. Cary never lost contact with his Irish roots and the legacy of his family history, spending childhood vacations at his grandparents' cottages in Ireland and gaining familiarity with Devon, England, the point of his family's origin. These settings, along with the familial stability and continuity they represented, were important to Cary's fiction. *Castle Corner* deals with a half century of life in Ireland, England, and Africa, moving from the 1870's to the brink of World War I; *Charley Is My Darling* deals with the World War II evacuation of thousands of London children to Devon; *A House of Children* is a poetical evocation of childhood based on Cary's recollections of his Irish vacations; and *The Moonlight* and his two trilogies are set mainly in Devon.

A tragic note entered Cary's life when his mother died in 1898, and his sense of life's miseries was compounded when his stepmother died five years later. His performance as a student at Hurstleigh and Clifton was average at best, though he did show interest in telling stories and writing poetry. In 1904, at the age of fifteen, he went on a sketching trip with his aunt to France, which was his first exposure to Impressionist painting. Two years later, he went to Paris as an art student and experienced bohemian life. He then went to Edinburgh for formal artistic training; at the age of twenty, he decided that he was not good enough to be a first-rate painter: Writing would be his vocation and painting his hobby. *Verses by Arthur Cary*, a decidedly mediocre effort, was published in 1908.

These early experiences were later exploited in his fiction. The first fictional pieces he published were short stories that dealt with bohemian life in Paris, and *The Horse's Mouth*, his portrait of the artist, not only draws some of its material from his life in Paris and Edinburgh but also bases its style on a literary approximation of Impressionism in painting. Cary's highly developed visual imagination is evident throughout his writings.

In accordance with his choice of vocation, Cary went to Oxford University in 1909 to take a degree in law, intending to provide himself with an alternate career should his literary attempts fail. His fourth-class degree, however, the lowest one possible, barred him from pursuing a gainful career in either the civil service or the field of education. In 1912, the Balkan War erupted, and Cary decided to go to the aid of Montenegro, Yugoslavia, feeling that the firsthand experience of war would offer a writer valuable material. *Memoir of the Bobotes* is a nonfictional account of his Montenegrin sojourn. He returned to England in 1913, entered the Nigerian service in 1914, and fought against the Germans in West Africa. In 1916, in England on leave from Nigeria, he married Gertrude Ogilvie, whom he had met in Oxford. He returned to Nigeria before the end of the year.

Cary's African years (1914-1919) had a formative influence on the shape of his fiction. *Aissa Saved* deals with the collision between Western religion and African paganism; *An American Visitor* explores the difference between the Western idealization of the noble savage and the African reality of tribal life; *The African Witch* reveals the prejudices of some Britons in Africa; *Mister Johnson* depicts the vibrantly imaginative existence of a young black clerk with "civilized" aspirations and his tragicomic relationship with District Officer Rudbeck; and *Cock Jarvis* dramatizes the experience of a "Joseph Conrad character in a Rudyard Kipling role," a morally sensitive liberal whose paternalistic and imperialistic attitudes do not coincide with the historical situation in twentieth century Africa. Without his experience as an assistant district officer in Nigeria—a position that required him to work as a policeman, tax collector, judge, administrator, census taker, mapmaker, and road builder, not to mention someone capable of dealing tactfully with the mysteries of witchcraft and juju—Cary would not have developed the sympathetic imagination that allowed him to understand and record the African point of view with sensitivity and knowledge.

Not surprisingly, his long residence in Africa put some strain on his marriage; his first two children, born in England during his absence, were virtual strangers to him. Despite occasional outbreaks of tempestuous disagreement, Cary and his wife shared a love that carried them through several adversities and the birth of three more children. Gertrude died in 1949. Cary's ability to render vividly the perspectives of women is particularly evident in *Herself Surprised*, *The Moonlight*, *A Fearful Joy*, and *Prisoner of Grace*; in part, this ability derives from the depth and intensity of his relationship with his wife.

In 1920, Cary returned to England, and he, his wife, and their two sons moved to a house in Oxford, where Cary lived until his death. After the publication of his first novel, *Aissa Saved*, in 1932, he produced novels at the impressive rate of almost one a year. His literary reputation increased steadily after he won the James Tait Black Memorial Prize in 1941.

ANALYSIS

The entirety of Joyce Cary's fiction is, as the author himself suggests, about one world—the world of freedom, "the active creative freedom which maintains the world in being . . . the source of moral responsibility and of good and evil . . . of injustice and love, of a special comedy and a special tragic dilemma which can never be solved." It is "a world in everlasting conflict between the new idea and the old allegiances, new arts and new inventions against the old establishment." Cary sees human beings as condemned to be free and society as perpetually poised between the extremes of anarchy and totalitarianism. Because creative imagination is of the highest value, the individual must rebel against the forces that threaten to trammel or stultify the free expression of his imagination, whether the forces be those of the established church, the state, tribalism, nationalism, conventional morality, or whatever. Throughout his novels, Cary dramatizes the tension between the intuitive and the analytical, the imaginative and the conceptual, the concrete and the abstract, and the vital and the mechanical.

Cary's romanticism, however, is not naïve. He is acutely aware that the tension between freedom and authority is necessary, that the will to create is continually in conflict with the will to preserve. His first trilogy, for example, sympathetically portrays a survivalist, a conservative, and a rebel. Even radically different characters, however, must enact their lives and secure their salvation or damnation in the moral world of freedom, imagination, and love.

In *Joyce Cary* (1973), R. W. Noble conveniently divides Cary's novels into five categories, according to their subject matter: Africa and empire, youth and childhood, women and social change, the artist and society, and politics and the individual. The novels of Africa and empire are substantial achievements but not major novels of the twentieth century, save for *Mister Johnson*.

EARLY NOVELS

Cock Jarvis, Cary's first effort, was abandoned in 1937; it was published posthumously. The problem with the novel was that Cary could not construct a plot adequate to encompass the character of Cock Jarvis, for at this point Cary had not assimilated the modernist style. Without recourse to first-person narration or stream of consciousness, his eminently interesting character was locked into a melodramatic and conventional plot structure. Whether Jarvis was to murder his wife and her lover, forgive them, or commit suicide, Cary never decided; none of the resolutions would solve the essential problem, which is technical.

Aissa Saved, with its seventy or more characters, has so many cultural conflicts, disconnected episodes, and thematic concerns that the aesthetic experience for the reader is congested and finally diffuse. Its analysis of the transforming powers of religious conversion, however, is penetrating and ironic. The juxtaposition of Aissa, an African convert who understands the sacrifice of Christ in a dangerously literal way and ingests Him as she would a lover, and Hilda, an English convert, is effective. Though the backgrounds of the two converts are divergent, they both end by participating in gruesome blood sacrifices. The novel as a whole, however, suffers from two problems. First, its central action, which revolves around attempts to end a devastating drought, cannot unify the manifold details of the plot: the cultural, religious, and military conflicts among Christians, pagans, and Muslims. Second, its tone is somewhat ambiguous. It is not clear whether the novel is meant to be an outright attack on missionaries and thus an ironic and cynical treatment of Aissa's so-called salvation or a more moderate assessment of the transforming powers of religious conversion.

An American Visitor has more manageable intentions. The book effectively dramatizes the difference between practical and theoretical knowledge and concrete and abstract knowledge. The preconceptions of the American visitor, Marie Hasluck, are not experientially based and are contrasted with the practices of the local district officer, Monkey Bewsher, who strives to strike a balance between freedom and authority. Even though reality forces Marie to abandon some of her pseudoanthropological beliefs, utopianism is so much a part of her psychological complex that she turns to religious pacifism for compensation, a turning that has tragic consequences for the pragmatic, imaginative, and somewhat self-deluded officer.

The African Witch is more panoramic in scope. It deals with the social, political, and religious lives of both Europeans and Africans. The plot revolves around the election of a new emir: The Oxford-educated Aladai is pitted against Salé, a Muslim. Aladai's Western demeanor offends many of the Europeans; they prefer Africans to be noble savages rather than liberal rationalists. In the end, the forces of juju and political corruption prevail.

Aladai is rejected and chooses a self-sacrificial death, presumably abandoning his rationalism and lapsing into stereotype. The conclusion of the novel is not convincingly wrought.

Castle Corner is part of a projected trilogy or quartet of novels that Cary decided not to continue. Covering a half century of life in Ireland, England, and Africa, the novel moves from the 1870's to the brink of World War I. Because of its congeries of characters and variety of themes, the book resists summary. In general, however, it puts the world of individual freedom and responsibility in collision with the world of historical change, but it has too much explicit debate and attitudinizing to be dramatically effective.

Generally, Cary's novels of Africa and empire are competent but not exceptional fiction. More materially than formally satisfying, they suffer finally from a lack of cohesion and unity; the form is not adequate to the content, which is rich and detailed. Nevertheless, these novels well delineate the everlasting conflict between new ideas and the old allegiances, the necessary tension between freedom and authority, reflecting Cary's characteristic preoccupation with the struggle for imaginative freedom on personal, moral, social, religious, and political levels.

MISTER JOHNSON

Mister Johnson is an exceptional piece of fiction. The character from whom the novel takes its title, as Cary points out in the preface, is a young clerk who turns his life into a romance, a poet who creates for himself a glorious destiny. Johnson is a supreme embodiment of imaginative vitality and, as such, a prototype for the picaresque heroes in Cary's later novels. Even though Johnson's fate is ultimately tragic, his mind is full of active invention until the end.

The novel occupies a pivotal moment in the dialectic of Cary's art, for not only is the content exceptional—Mr. Johnson is an unforgettable character; his adventures indelibly impress themselves on the reader—but also the innovative form is adequate to that content. In *Mister Johnson*, Cary deploys third-person, present-tense narration. He notes in the preface that he chose this style because it carries the reader unreflectingly on the stream of events, creating an agitated rather than a contemplative mood. Because Johnson lives in the present and is completely immersed in the vibrant immediacy of his experience, he does not judge; nor does the reader judge, as the present-tense narration makes the reader swim gaily with Johnson on the surface of life.

Cary's choice of third-person narration, which he does not discuss in the preface, is equally strategic. The first-person style that he uses so effectively in some of his later novels would have been appropriate. By using the third-person style, he is able not only to give the African scene a solidity of local detail but also to enter into the mind of Rudbeck, so that the reader can empathize with his conscientious decision to shoot Johnson, a personal act, rather than hanging him, an official act. The impact of the tragic outcome is thereby intensified.

The novel traces the rise and fall of Mr. Johnson, chief clerk of Fada in Nigeria. A southerner in northern Nigeria and an African in European clothes, he has aspirations to be civilized and claims to be a friend of District Officer Rudbeck, the Wazirin Fada, the King of England, and anyone who vaguely likes him. Johnson's aspirations, however, are not in consonance with his finances, and his marriage, machinations, schemes, stories, parties, petty thefts, capital crime, and irrepressible good spirits become part of the exuberant but relentless rhythm of events that lead to his death. For Johnson, as Cary suggests, life is simply perpetual experience, which he soaks into himself through all five senses at once and produces again in the form of reflections, comments, songs, and jokes. His vitality is beyond good and evil, equally capable of expressing itself anarchistically or creatively.

Rudbeck, too, is a man of imagination, though not as liberated from constraint as Johnson. His passion for road building becomes obsessive once Johnson's imagination further fuels his own. He goes so far as to misappropriate funds in order to realize his dream. Without the infectious influence of Johnson's creativity, Rudbeck would never have rebelled against the forces of conservatism. The completed road demonstrates the power of creative imagination.

The road, however, brings crime as well as trade, and in his disillusionment, Rudbeck fires Johnson for embezzlement. In the end, Johnson murders a man and is sentenced to death by Rudbeck. Johnson wants his friend Rudbeck to kill him personally, and Rudbeck eventually complies with his clerk's wish, putting his career as district officer in jeopardy by committing this compassionate but illegal act.

CHARLEY IS MY DARLING *and* A HOUSE OF CHILDREN

After *Mister Johnson*, Cary chose domestic settings for his novels. His novels of youth and childhood, *Charley Is My Darling* and *A House of Children*, are set in Devon and Ireland. The former deals with the evacuation of thousands of London children to Devon during World War II; the latter is a poetical evocation of childhood vacations in Ireland.

In *Charley Is My Darling*, the main character, Charley, like Mr. Johnson, is thrust into an alien world, and the urban values he represents are contrasted with the rural values represented by Lina Allchin, the well-intentioned supervisor of the evacuees. Charley, whose head is shaved as part of a delousing process, is isolated from his peers and consequently channels his imaginative energies into crime and ultimately into anarchistic destruction in order to gain acceptability. Because neither school nor society offers him any outlet for his creative individuality, it expresses itself in violence, an expression that is perhaps a microcosmic commentary on the causes of war.

A House of Children is autobiographical. Technically innovative, it has no omniscient point of view and relies instead on one central consciousness, which narrates the story in the first person. This was to become Cary's characteristic narrative style. The novel has a poetic rather than a linear coherence, depending on a series of revelations or epiphanies rather than on plot. Cary obviously learned a great deal from James Joyce's *A Portrait of the Artist as a Young Man* (1916), which he had read in Africa.

THE FIRST TRILOGY

Cary's masterpiece, his first trilogy, focuses on the artist and society. Cary designed the trilogy, he said, to show three characters not only in themselves but also as seen by one another, the object being to get a three-dimensional depth and force of character. Each novel adapts its style to the perceptual, emotive, and cognitive idiosyncrasies of its first-person narrator. *Herself Surprised*, the narrative of Sara Monday, is reminiscent of Daniel Defoe's *Moll Flanders* (1722), and its autobiographical style is ideally suited to dramatize the ironic disparity between Sara's conventional moral attitudes and her "surprising," unconventional behavior. *To Be a Pilgrim*, the narrative of Tom Wilcher, is akin to a Victorian memoir, and the formal politeness of its language reflects the repressed and conservative nature of its narrator. *The Horse's Mouth*, the narrative of Gulley Jimson, uses stream of consciousness and verbally imitates the Impressionist style of painting, an imitation that strikingly reveals the dazzling power of Gulley's visual imagination. The entire trilogy is a virtuoso performance, underscoring Cary's talent for rendering characters from the inside.

Sara Monday is the eternal female—wife, mother, homemaker, mistress, and friend. In accordance with her working-class position as a cook, she consistently describes her world in domestic images and metaphors—the sky for her is as warm as new milk and as still as water in a goldfish bowl. Her desire to improve her socioeconomic lot is a major motivating factor in her life, and this desire often encourages her to operate outside the bounds of morality and law. Sara, however, is not a moral revolutionary; her values mirror her Victorian education. In her terms, she is constantly "sinning" and constantly "surprised" by sin, but in terms of the reader's understanding of her, she is a lively and sensuous being with an unconscious genius for survival who succumbs, sometimes profitably, sometimes disastrously, to immediate temptation. Her language of sin, which is vital and concrete, belies her language of repentance, which is mechanical and abstract. Nevertheless, Sara, unlike Moll Flanders, does not seem to be a conscious opportunist and manipulator.

Sara betters her socioeconomic status by securing a middle-class marriage to Matthew Monday. The marriage, however, does not prevent her from having affairs with Hickson, a millionaire, and Jimson, an artist. (The narrative description of these "surprises" is exquisitely managed.) Though she sincerely believes in conventional morality, that morality is no match for her joy of life. Cary also shows the negative aspects of Sara's mode of being. Like other characters in his fiction, she is a creative being whose imaginative vitality borders on the anarchistic and irresponsible. She virtually ruins her first husband and makes little effort to keep contact with her four daughters.

After her violent relationship with Gulley Jimson, Sara becomes a cook for the lawyer

Wilcher and is about to marry him when his niece has Sara jailed for theft. She had been stealing in order to purchase art supplies for Gulley and to pay for his son's education. Her will to live is thus an implicit critique of the conventional morality that her conscious mind mechanically endorses. She is a survivalist par excellence.

Unlike the events in *Herself Surprised*, those in *To Be a Pilgrim* are not presented chronologically. The narrative is layered, juxtaposing Wilcher's present situation of imminent death with the social, political, and religious history of his times. The disrupted chronology poignantly accentuates Wilcher's realization, which comes too late, that he ought to have been a pilgrim, that possessions have been his curse. Now his repressed energies can only counterproductively express themselves in exhibitionism and arson. Marriage to Sara Monday, which might have been a redemptive force in his life, is now impossible, for she has already been incarcerated for her crimes.

In the present time of the novel, Wilcher is a virtual prisoner at Tolbrook Manor, the family home. His niece Ann, a doctor and the daughter of his dead brother Edward, a liberal politician whose life Wilcher tried to manage, is his warden. She marries her cousin Robert, a progressive farmer devoted to the utilitarian goal of making the historic manor a viable commercial enterprise, much to Wilcher's chagrin. Ultimately, Wilcher is forced to recognize that change is the essence of life and that his conservative fixation with tradition, the family, and moral propriety has sapped him of his existential energy, of his ability to be a pilgrim.

The Horse's Mouth, a portrait of the artist as an old man, is justly celebrated as Cary's most remarkable achievement. (Although the Carfax edition of Cary's novels is complete and authoritative, the revised Rainbird edition of *The Horse's Mouth*, 1957, illustrated by the author, includes a chapter—"The Old Strife at Plant's"—that Cary had previously deleted.) Its reputation has been enhanced by the excellent film version, released in 1958, in which Alec Guinness plays the role of Gulley Jimson.

Gulley Jimson is a pilgrim; he accepts the necessity of the fall into freedom with joy and energy, conceiving of it as a challenge to his imagination and thereby seeking to impose aesthetic order on experiential chaos. For Gulley, anything that is part of the grimy reality of the contingent world—fried fish shops, straw, chicken boxes, dirt, oil, mud—can inspire a painting. The impressionist style of his narrative reflects his vocation, for he mainly construes his world in terms of physical imagery, texture, solidity, perspective, color, shape, and line, merging Blakean vision with Joycean stream of consciousness. Gulley's sensibility is perpetually open to novelty, and his life affirms the existential value of becoming, for he identifies with the creative process rather than with the finished product. His energies focus on the future, on starting new works, not on dwelling on past accomplishments. Even though he is destitute, he refuses to paint in the lucrative style of his Sara Monday period.

Gulley is also a born con artist, a streetwise survivor. He is not averse to stealing, cheating, swindling, blackmailing, or even murdering if his imaginative self-expression is at stake. He is completely comfortable in a brutal, violent, and unjust world. His vision, therefore, has limitations. His pushing Sara down the stairs to her death shows the anarchistic irresponsibility implicit in regarding life as merely spiritual fodder for the imagination. Moreover, Gulley lacks historical consciousness. Even though the novel chronicles his life before and after the beginning of World War II, Gulley seems to have no conception of who Adolf Hitler is and what he represents.

For the most part, this novel clearly champions the creative individual and criticizes the repressive society that inhibits him, although Cary is always fairminded enough to imply the limitations of his characters. Gulley Jimson remains a paradigm of energetic vitality, an imaginative visionary who blasts through generation to regeneration, redeeming the poverty of the contingent world and liberating consciousness from the malady of the quotidian. The entire trilogy is a masterpiece; the created worlds of the three narrators mutually supplement and criticize one another, stressing the difficulty of achieving a workable balance between the will to survive, to preserve, and to create.

THE SECOND TRILOGY

Cary's second trilogy—*Prisoner of Grace*, *Except the Lord*, and *Not Honour More*—deals with politics and the individual. It is a commentary on radical liberalism, evangelicalism, and crypto-fascism, moving from the 1860's to the 1930's and involving the lives of three characters (Nina Nimmo/Latter, Chester Nimmo, and Jim Latter) whose lives are inextricably enmeshed, unlike those of the characters of the first trilogy.

In *Prisoner of Grace*, Nina Nimmo (Nina Latter by the end of her narrative) tries to protect and defend both her lovers—the radical liberal politician Nimmo, maligned for his alleged opportunism and demagoguery, and the crypto-fascist Latter, a military man obsessed by a perverted notion of honor. The time span of the novel covers the Boer War, the Edwardian reform government, the World War I victory, the prosperous aftermath, and the 1926 General Strike. The action takes place mainly in Devon, where Chester Nimmo makes his mark as a politician and becomes a member of Parliament, and in London, where Nimmo eventually becomes a cabinet minister.

Nina, carrying the child of her cousin Jim Latter, marries the lower-class Chester Nimmo, who is handsomely remunerated for rescuing the fallen woman in order to secure a respectable future for the child. Nina never loves Nimmo but is converted to his cause by his political and religious rhetoric. She writes her account in order to anticipate and rebut criticism of his conduct.

Thrust into the duplicitous and morally ambiguous world of politics, she succumbs both to Chester's ideals, values, morals, and beliefs and to his lusts, lies, schemes, and maneuverings, seemingly incapable of distinguishing the one from the other, as is the reader, who has only the information available in Nina's unreliable account. Unlike the disingenuousness of Sara Monday in *Herself Surprised*, which the reader can easily disentangle—Sara's sensuous vitality gives the lie to the maxims of conventional piety she mechanically utters—Nina's disingenuousness is a fundamental part of her character. Nina, like Chester, is both sincere and hypocritical, genuinely moral and meretriciously rhetorical, an embodiment of the political personality. Even the politics of their marriage parallel in miniature the politics of the outside world.

Nina is a prisoner of grace once she has converted to the belief that Chester's being is infused with grace and that his religious and political beliefs enjoy moral rectitude by definition. Her love for Jim is also a grace that imprisons her and ultimately impels her to divorce Chester and marry Jim. The reader, too, is a prisoner of grace, unable to get outside Nina's "political" point of view and thus unable to separate truth and falsity, the authorial implication being that the two are necessarily confused and interdependent in the political personality. Like Sara, Nina is a survivalist, and after she becomes adulterously involved with Nimmo, she, like Sara, is murdered by a man whom she had helped. Survivalism has limits.

Except the Lord, the story of Nimmo's childhood and youth, takes place in the 1860's and 1870's. It is the history of a boy's mind and soul rather than one of political events. Like *To Be a Pilgrim*, it takes the form of a Victorian memoir in which the mature narrator explores the events and forces that caused him to become what he is. Nurtured in an environment of poverty, fundamentalist faith, and familial love, Nimmo becomes in turn a radical preacher, labor agitator, and liberal politician.

According to the first verse of Psalm 127, "Except the Lord build the house, they labour in vain that would build it; except the Lord keep the city, the watchman waketh but in vain." Since this novel stops before the events of *Prisoner of Grace* and *Not Honour More* begin, and since it principally induces a sympathetic response to Nimmo, the reader has a difficult time interpreting the significance of the title. The reader tends to see Nimmo differently after having read the account of the latter's youth but is still uncertain whether Nimmo is a knight of faith or an opportunistic antinomian. The trilogy as a whole seems to suggest that Chester is both.

Not Honour More is the story of a soldier, Jim Latter, who sees the world in dichotomous terms and cannot accept the necessarily ambiguous transaction between the realms of freedom and authority. The novel is a policewoman's transcript of Jim's confession; it is dictated as he awaits execution for the murder of Nina, provoked by his discovery of her adulterous relationship with Nimmo, her ex-husband. His language is a combination of clipped military prose, hysterical defensiveness, and invective against both the decadence of British society around the time of the 1926 General Strike and the corruption of politicians such as Nimmo.

Latter believes in authority, in imposing law and order on the masses. He has no sense of the moral ambiguity of human behavior, no sense of the complexity of human motivation. A self-proclaimed spiritual descendant of the Cavalier poet Richard Lovelace, Jim believes that his murder of Nina proves that he loves honor more. He conceives of the murder as an execution, a moral act, whereas it is in reality a perversion of honor, a parody of the code that Lovelace represents. District Officer Rudbeck, of *Mister Johnson*, is by comparison a truly honorable man: He personalizes rather than ritualizes Mr. Johnson's death. Because Jim believes in the rectitude of authoritarians with superior gifts, he is a cryptofascist. The best that can be said of him is that he has the courage of his misplaced convictions.

Throughout his novels, Cary focused his creative energies on human beings who are condemned to be free, to enact their lives somewhere between the extremes of anarchism and conformity. His achievement demonstrates that it is possible for a novelist to be at once stylistically sophisticated, realistically oriented, and ethically involved.

Greig E. Henderson

OTHER MAJOR WORKS

SHORT FICTION: *Spring Song, and Other Stories*, 1960 (Winnifred Davin, editor).

POETRY: *Verses by Arthur Cary*, 1908; *Marching Soldier*, 1945; *The Drunken Sailor*, 1947.

NONFICTION: *Power in Men*, 1939; *The Case for African Freedom*, 1941 (revised 1944); *Process of Real Freedom*, 1943; *Britain and West Africa*, 1946; *Art and Reality*, 1958; *Memoir of the Bobotes*, 1960; *Selected Essays*, 1976 (A. G. Bishop, editor).

BIBLIOGRAPHY

Adams, Hazard. *Joyce Cary's Trilogies: Pursuit of the Particular Real.* Tallahassee, Fla.: University Presses of Florida, 1983. Adams attempts to rescue Cary from what he views as misplaced critical emphasis by focusing on the particularity of Cary's two trilogies. Includes two appendixes devoted to chronologies of the trilogies.

Christian, Edwin Ernest. *Joyce Cary's Creative Imagination.* New York: Peter Lang, 1988. Analyzes Cary's work to demonstrate the truth of Cary's statement that "all my books are part of one expression: that is, they are like different chapters in one work, showing different angles of a single reality." Includes bibliography and index.

Echeruo, Michael J. *Joyce Cary and the Novel of Africa.* London: Longman, 1973. Places Cary's African novels in the tradition of the foreign novel and argues that they have a special place in this genre. Provides new insights into the growth of Cary's art as well as valuable criticism of Cary's African novels.

Erskine-Hill, Howard. "The Novel Sequences of Joyce Cary." In *The Fiction of the 1940's: Stories of Survival*, edited by Rod Mengham and N. H. Reeve. New York: Palgrave, 2001. Examines Cary's two trilogies and describes how the six novels share a number of special features that distinguish them from other novel sequences.

Foster, Malcolm. *Joyce Cary: A Biography.* London: Michael Joseph, 1969. Exhaustive, informative study of Cary presents only brief discussion of each novel but offers some interesting insights into the author's works. Foster had access to the Cary collection at the Bodleian Library in Oxford, England.

Hall, Dennis. *Joyce Cary: A Reappraisal.* London: Macmillan, 1983. Discusses all of Cary's novels with conscientious thoroughness and makes the point that there are two Carys: the thinker and the artist. Hall is sympathetic to Cary but notes the unevenness of his work and concludes that Cary is "his own worst enemy." Includes bibliography.

Levitt, Annette S. *The Intertextuality of Joyce Cary's "The Horse's Mouth."* Lewiston, N.Y.: Edwin Mellen Press, 1993. Study of *The Horse's Mouth* analyzes the influence of William Blake and the other sources on which Cary drew in creating the novel. Includes bibliographical references and index.

Majumdar, Bimalendu. *Joyce Cary: An Existentialist Approach.* Atlantic Highlands, N.J.: Humanities Press, 1982. Scholarly study of Cary is devoted to critical appraisal of his work. Focuses on the central existential theme in Cary's novels: the uniqueness of the individual who "refuses to fit into some system constructed by rational thought."

Roby, Kinley E. *Joyce Cary.* Boston: Twayne, 1984. After providing an overview of Cary's biography, this brief volume surveys Cary's fiction—all of which, according to Roby, is concerned with the "unchangeable changeableness of life." Also gives glancing attention to Cary's literary criticism and journalism. Includes chronology and select bibliography.

Ross, Michael L. "Joyce Cary's Tragic African Clown." In *Race Riots: Comedy and Ethnicity in Modern British Fiction.* Montreal: McGill-Queen's University Press, 2006. Discusses how the racial humor in Cary's works reflects Great Britain's disdain for non-Europeans in the period before World War II.

J. P. DONLEAVY

Born: Brooklyn, New York; April 23, 1926
Also known as: James Patrick Donleavy

PRINCIPAL LONG FICTION

The Ginger Man, 1955, 1965
A Singular Man, 1963
The Saddest Summer of Samuel S, 1966
The Beastly Beatitudes of Balthazar B, 1968
The Onion Eaters, 1971
A Fairy Tale of New York, 1973
The Destinies of Darcy Dancer, Gentleman, 1977
Schultz, 1979
Leila: Further in the Destinies of Darcy Dancer, Gentleman, 1983
*De Alfonce Tennis, the Superlative Game of Eccentric Champions: Its History,
    Accoutrements, Rules, Conduct, and Regimen*, 1984
Are You Listening, Rabbi Löw?, 1987
That Darcy, That Dancer, That Gentleman, 1990
*The Lady Who Liked Clean Rest Rooms: The Chronicle of One of the Strangest
    Stories Ever to Be Rumoured About Around New York*, 1995
Wrong Information Is Being Given out at Princeton, 1998

OTHER LITERARY FORMS

All of the principal works produced by J. P. Donleavy (DUHN-lee-vee) are novels, but some of the protagonists and central situations of these novels are explored in other literary forms. *A Fairy Tale of New York* is derived from the play *Fairy Tales of New York* (pb. 1961) and the short story "A Fairy Tale of New York" (1961), later collected in Donleavy's volume of short stories *Meet My Maker the Mad Molecule* (1964). Donleavy adapted several of his published novels for the stage: *The Ginger Man* (pr. 1959), *A Singular Man* (pb. 1965), *The Saddest Summer of Samuel S* (pb. 1972), and *The Beastly Beatitudes of Balthazar B* (pr. 1981). He also wrote a book of satiric nonfiction, *The Unexpurgated Code: A Complete Manual of Survival and Manners* (1975). Among Donleavy's limited production of occasional pieces are two important autobiographical essays: "What They Did in Dublin," an introduction to his play *The Ginger Man*, and "An Expatriate Looks at America," which appeared in *The Atlantic Monthly* in 1976. He explored his Irish heritage in *J. P. Donleavy's Ireland: In All Her Sins and Some of Her Graces* (1986), *A Singular Country* (1990), and *The History of the Ginger Man* (1994).

J. P. Donleavy
(Library of Congress)

ACHIEVEMENTS

The prevailing literary image of J. P. Donleavy is that of the one-book author: He gained celebrity status of a notorious sort with his first novel, *The Ginger Man*, but his subsequent novels failed to generate equal interest. Reactions to *The Ginger Man*, a book that did not appear in an unexpurgated American edition until ten years after its first publication, ranged from outraged condemnations of it as obscene in language and immoral in content to later appreciations of it as a comic masterpiece. The later novels have been received with moderate praise for their style and humor and with slight dismay for their lack of structure or apparent intent. Donleavy himself remained confidently aloof from all critical condemnation, exaltation, and condescension. He continued to pursue his private interests in fiction, to discourage academic interest in his work, and to express, when pressed, bemusement at literary frays of any sort. His work is difficult to place in standard literary traditions: His residency in Ireland and fondness for Irish settings seem to place his work outside American literature, but his birth and use of American protagonists seem to place it outside Anglo-Irish literature as well.

BIOGRAPHY

James Patrick Donleavy was born of Irish parents in Brooklyn, New York, on April 23, 1926. He served in the U.S. Navy during World War II, and though he saw no action in the service, he did encounter the work of James Joyce through an English instructor at the Naval Preparatory School in Maryland. This combination of family background and reading interests led to his enrollment in Dublin's Trinity College from 1946 to 1949, on funds provided by the American G.I. Bill. There he was registered to read natural sciences, but he has readily admitted that most of his energies were devoted to pub crawls with fellow American students such as Gainor Crist, the model for Sebastian Dangerfield in *The Ginger Man*, and A. K. O'Donoghue, the model for O'Keefe in the same novel.

Donleavy married Valerie Heron after leaving Trinity and briefly considered pursuing a career as a painter. He returned to the United States, where he finished *The Ginger Man* in 1951, but the novel was rejected by one publisher after another on the basis of its supposed obscenity. On his return to Dublin in 1954, he became friends with playwright and man-about-town Brendan Behan. Through Behan's efforts, *The Ginger Man*, having been refused by some thirty-five American and British publishers, was accepted for publication in 1955 by the Olympia Press of Paris, a house whose main list of pornography enabled it to gamble on unusual literary properties such as Behan's works and Samuel Beckett's novel *Watt* (1953). Donleavy's book was greeted rudely by the British press and by the British courts, where it was prosecuted for censorship violations, but the ensuing publicity, combined with the enthusiasm of early critics and readers, led to the publication of expurgated English (1956) and American (1958) editions that brought Donleavy financial stability and an enviable literary reputation for a first novelist. These editions also marked the beginning of a series of lawsuits filed against Donleavy by Olympia Press over the rights to republish the novel. The litigation ended with appropriate irony when Donleavy acquired the ownership of Olympia Press after decades of legal maneuvering, a story told in his *The History of the Ginger Man*. After that time, he made his home in Ireland, on Lough Owel in Westmeath, in rather baronial circumstances that resembled the affluence of his later characters rather than the student poverty of *The Ginger Man*.

After his marriage to Valerie Heron ended in divorce in 1969, Donleavy married Mary Wilson Price. Each of his marriages produced one son and one daughter. He became an Irish citizen in 1967 and settled in a twenty-five-room mansion on a 180-acre estate near Mullingar, about sixty miles from Dublin. Fittingly, descriptions of his house appear in James Joyce's early *Stephen Hero* (1944), providing yet another link to the writer with whom Donleavy is most frequently compared. Donleavy is also known as a serious artist whose numerous paintings have appeared at many exhibitions.

ANALYSIS

In an interview published in the *Journal of Irish Literature* in 1979, J. P. Donleavy said: "I suppose one has been influenced by people like Joyce. But also possibly—and this is not too apparent in my work—by Henry Miller who was then literally a private god." Appreciation of Donleavy's work is indeed improved by cognizance of these two acknowledged predecessors, and it is entirely appropriate that the former is Irish and the latter American and that all three expatriates have been subject to censorship litigation.

The influence of James Joyce is most apparent in Donleavy's style, and it should be noted that the Ireland of Donleavy's work scarcely overlaps with that of Joyce's work. Joyce made self-conscious and even self-indulgent style a necessity for the serious modern novelist, and Donleavy creates his own evocation of Dublin and other Irish environs in an intricate prose style characterized by minimal punctuation, strings of sentence fragments, frequent shifts of tense, and lapses from standard third-person narration into first-person stream of consciousness. The single most obvious indication of Donleavy's stylistic ambitions is his habit of ending his chapters with brief poems.

The influence of Miller is most apparent in the fact that Donleavy's novels, for all their supposedly "graphic" language and sexual encounters, create a world that is a patent fantasy. As in Miller's case, the primary aspect of the fantasy is a distinctly male fabrication based on unending sexual potency and invariably satisfying liaisons with uniformly passionate and voluptuous women. To this, Donleavy adds fantasies about immense wealth, requited infantile eroticism, Dionysian thirst, and spectacular barroom brawls. Because of this comic freedom from actual contingencies, his work satirizes absurd caricatures of recognizable social evils.

The central concern of all of Donleavy's novels is the fortune of a single male protagonist isolated from family and country and pursuing a lifestyle that is improvised and erratic. The great exemplar of this essential situation is *The Ginger Man*, a novel that weighs the joys of decadent drunkenness and ecstatic sex against spiritual fears of loneliness and death. After that first novel, which left the future of its protagonist ambiguous, Donleavy went through a period of bleak despair over the viability of a free lifestyle and emerged from it into a period of wholehearted endorsement of its pleasures. In the process, his view of the world changed from a belief in its essential malevolence to an assertion of its essential benevolence. He thus confronted the problem of the value of independence from social conformity from two wholly different perspectives.

THE GINGER MAN

The Ginger Man, Donleavy's famous first novel, opens with a pair of subordinate clauses; the first celebrates the spring sun, and the second laments Dublin's workaday horse carts and wretched child beggars. It is between these two emotional poles that the Ginger Man, Sebastian Dangerfield, vacillates throughout the novel. He will be exalted by visions of freedom and possibility, but he will also be crushed by fears and depressions. In *The Ginger Man*, freedom is revolt against the forces of social conformity and rigidity, a casting over of the bulwark virtues of thrift, reverence, and self-discipline. The fear, however, is of the ultimate victory of those same forces and values. The novel refuses to resolve these oppositions neatly. Dangerfield, subject to reckless extremes throughout, finally remains both the Ginger Man, an alias suggestive of spirit and mettle, and Sebastian, the namesake of a betrayed and martyred saint.

One of the novel's achievements is its candid admission of the most deplorable aspects of a quest for freedom such as Dangerfield's. It is appropriate and commonplace in contemporary fiction that an alienated protagonist should court his wife for her dowry and run into debt with landlords, shopkeepers, and other pillars of middle-class society. Donleavy, however, proceeds beyond this comfortable degree of roguery to a proposal of a more complete anarchy that is the novel's most compelling and disturbing quality. Dangerfield also beats his wife, abuses his child, senselessly vandalizes the property of strangers, and is otherwise selfishly destructive because of a self-proclaimed natural aristocracy, a phrase crucial to Donleavy's later novels. In this respect, he sins far more than he is sinned against, and one measure of the novel's complexity is the fact that its most sympathetic character is a matronly Miss Frost, who is devoted to Sebastian but is abandoned by him when her finances have been consumed. *The Ginger Man* is superior to many contemporary novels contemptuous of society because of this admission of the sheer egotism and selfishness underlying such contempt.

Dangerfield's redeeming features, which make him an antihero rather than a villain, are his invigorating bohemian bravura and his true appreciation of life's quiet beauties. The novel is appropriately set in Dublin, mirroring a fine appetite for great talk and plentiful drink. On one level, the novel is about the meeting of the vital New World with the stagnant Old World, for Dangerfield and his Irish American cronies flamboyantly outtalk and outdrink the Irish, who are portrayed as a mean and frugal people who can only be bettered by insult. Dangerfield's appreciation of subtler sensual delights, however, is as essential to his character as those more raucous tastes. His love of the smell of freshly ground coffee wafting from Bewley's in Grafton Street is as important to this novel as its more notorious adventures with whiskey and women. In these aesthetic moments, including the appreciation of the rising sun in the opening of the novel, Sebastian provisionally justifies his sense of aristocracy and demonstrates a kind of moral purity not shared by the novel's other characters.

In conjunction with the picaresque comedy and titillation of Dangerfield's more preposterous adventures, there remains the essentially naïve and ultimately unfulfilled desire for a simpler, solitary bliss. *The Ginger Man* is Donleavy's salient novel because it manages this balance between frivolity and remorse, between freedom and surrender, an opposition resolved in different ways in all of his subsequent novels.

A SINGULAR MAN

His second novel, *A Singular Man*, was also held up by worries about censorship, and it was published only after Donleavy threatened to sue his own publisher. Donleavy left the bohemian lifestyle that gave Sebastian Dangerfield vitality for the opulent but gloomy existence of George Smith, whose freedoms have been lost to the encroachments of great wealth. The premise of the novel has obvious autobiographical relevance to the success of *The Ginger Man*; George Smith is accused by his estranged wife of sneaking into society, and he is in fact bewildered by his inexplicable attainment of sudden wealth and fame. The novel frustrates autobiographical interpretation, however, because it represents the emergence in Donleavy's work of the caricatured environment common in his later novels. The nature of Smith's industrial empire is mysterious, but he travels through surroundings with names such as Dynamo House, Electricity Street, and Cinder Village, and makes his home in Merry Mansions.

Smith's only obvious claim to singularity is his solitary appreciation of the hollowness of material wealth, and the novel records his increasing disillusionment and despair. The only satisfying one of his several love affairs is with the sassy Sally Thompson, doomed by the sorrowful machinations of the plot to death in an automobile accident. Smith's only respite from the responsibilities of his financial empire is the construction of a fabulous mausoleum under the pseudonym "Doctor Fear." *A Singular Man* is controlled completely by the obsession with death that was always counterpointed in *The Ginger Man* with a potential for sudden joy, and its style reflects this severe introversion in its reliance on more extended passages of stream-of-consciousness narration than is common in Donleavy's novels.

THE SADDEST SUMMER OF SAMUEL S

While *A Singular Man* explored the despair of wealth, *The Saddest Summer of Samuel S* broadened the gloom of Donleavy's post-*Ginger Man* novels by exploring the despair of a vagrant lifestyle. An expatriate American living in Vienna, Samuel S is an overage Ginger Man whose misery is caused by the stubborn isolation from society that was at least a mixed virtue in Donleavy's first novel. In this novel, the only humor is provided by Samuel's bleak confessions to his shocked psychoanalyst Herr S, who functions as a socially acclimated if complacent foil to the alienated but determined Samuel S. The comedy is, however, completely overwhelmed by Samuel's inability to accept the apparent happiness of a relationship with an invigorating American student named Abigail. It is as if Donleavy set out to correct simplistic praise for *The Ginger Man* as an unambiguous paean to rootlessness by stressing in *The Saddest Summer of Samuel S* the costs of bohemian disregard for domestic and social comforts. The novel presents no acceptable alternative to Samuel's self-destructive insistence on alienation for its own sake, none of the moments of happy appreciation of life that redeemed Sebastian Dangerfield.

THE BEASTLY BEATITUDES OF BALTHAZAR B

Balthazar B is Donleavy's most withdrawn and morbid protagonist, and the novel named for him represents the author's most consistent use of religious resignation as a metaphor for a passive secular disengagement from a malevolent world. The presence of his prep school and college classmate Beefy adds a raucous dimension reminiscent of *The Ginger Man*, however, and *The Beastly Beatitudes of Balthazar B* resuscitates the power of outrageous farce in Donleavy's work. Balthazar, another Donleavy protagonist who is fatherless and without a surname, progresses only from childhood fantasies about African pythons to more adult but equally futile ones about sex in aristocratic surroundings. Throughout the novel, he provides naïve perspective that enables Donleavy to satirize social pretensions and rampant materialism. The beatitudes that govern most of the novel are Beefy's, which bless the beastly virtues of complete decadence and joyful carnality but prove inadequate in the face of repressive social conformity. The ultimate beatitudes of the novel, however, are Balthazar's, which emerge late in the work and resemble those delivered in the Sermon on the Mount. Having accompanied Beefy on his salacious adventures and seen his companion undone, Balthazar—who, like Donleavy's other early protagonists, identifies with martyrs—is left only with a saintly hope for later rewards such as those in the beatitudes recorded in Matthew's gospel.

THE ONION EATERS

Like Balthazar B, Clementine of *The Onion Eaters* is a protagonist plagued by lonely remorse and surrounded by a dynamism in others that he is unable to emulate. He is a young American heir to a medieval British estate, a situation whose effect is that of placing an introspective and morose modern sensibility in the raucous world of the eighteenth century novel. As in most of Donleavy's novels, the central theme is the vicissitudes of a natural aristocracy, here represented by the fortunes of Clementine of the Three Glands in a chaotic world of eccentric hangers-on and orgiastic British nobility. The emotional tension of the novel is based on a deep desire for the freedom of complete decadence in conflict with a more romantic yearning for quieter satisfactions. That conflict enables Donleavy, as in parts of *The Ginger Man*, to create a titillating fantasy while concurrently insisting on a sort of innocence, for Clementine survives his picaresque adventures with his essential purity intact. The significant contemporary revision of an older morality, however, lies in the fact that in Donleavy's fiction such virtue goes unrewarded.

A FAIRY TALE OF NEW YORK

In Donleavy's later work, fantasy is allowed to prevail over remorse, and this new direction emerges first in *A Fairy Tale of New York*, in which a protagonist named Christian is tempted by the evils of the modern metropolis much as the traveler Christian is tempted in John Bunyan's *The Pilgrim's Progress* (1678, 1684). This novel has a special interest within Donleavy's work for its description of a return from Ireland to New York City, which is characterized in the novel by gross consumerism. In *A Fairy Tale of New York*, Christian is more a protector of real virtues than a seeker of them, and the novel ends with a comment on life's minor and earthy beauties rather than the plea for mercy that is common in Donleavy's earlier works. A brief vignette of the same title published a decade earlier provided the opening of *A Fairy Tale of New York*, and the intervening years saw a change in Donleavy's literary interests that enabled him to pursue a fulfilling fantasy beyond the limits of vignette. The result, however it may finally be judged, is a sacrifice of the emotional tension of his finest earlier work in favor of the pleasure of unconstrained fabrication, a surrender of psychological depth for a freer play of literary imagination.

THE DESTINIES OF DARCY DANCER, GENTLEMAN

Returning to the spirit of the eighteenth century novel that animated *The Onion Eaters*, *The Destinies of Darcy Dancer, Gentleman* evokes a world of baronial splendor, earthy servants, seductive governesses, and naïve tutors without apparent concern for the forces of modern technology and consequential social ills common to the contemporary novel. It is a stylish and literate entertainment without moral pretensions, a vein of fiction entirely appropriate to the alliance with freedom of imagination arduously explored in the course of Donleavy's work.

There are allusions to a darker world beyond the novel's immediate environs, such as housekeeper Miss von B.'s wartime experiences in Europe, but these serve only to stress the value of the free lifestyle pursued by Darcy Dancer without guilt and without controls beyond a decent sense of chivalry. One indication of the shift from morbidity to frivolity apparent in Donleavy's work is the fact that the setting here is Andromeda Park, named for a goddess whose miseries were relieved rather than for a saint who was martyred. Yet *Leila*, sequel to *The Destinies of Darcy Dancer, Gentleman*, retains the tone of upper-class superficiality while reintroducing a darker view: In this novel, Dancer becomes enamored of a woman but is left helpless when his love is married to another.

SCHULTZ

Schultz is similar to *The Ginger Man* but expresses no remorse or recrimination. Its operative assumption and central motif is a concept of the world as a pointless Jewish joke, and this permits the London theatrical impresario Sigmund Schultz to exploit materialism without moral doubts and Donleavy to create a world in which even the sinfully rich prove ultimately benevolent. Class consciousness and privilege are a matter for comedy rather than bitterness in this novel, and the foul-mouthed American social climber Schultz is accepted with amusement rather than repelled with horror by English royalty.

The perspective of the novel is so completely comic that venereal diseases are presented as mere inconveniences, the political world is represented by the monarch of an African nation named Buggybooiamcheesetoo, and the romantic liaisons are unabashed and masturbatory fantasies. The most important distinction between *The Ginger Man* and *Schultz* is that in Donleavy's first novel the world was seen as malevolent and in the latter it is seen as benign. In accordance with this movement, the author has shifted from a celebration of gallant but doomed improvised lifestyles to a forthright assertion of their superiority to accepted and inherited modes of behavior.

The style and structure of Donleavy's work continued to evolve: *De Alfonce Tennis, the Superlative Game of Eccentric Champions*, for example, is such a mishmash of story, satire, and whimsy that one would be hard-pressed to categorize it. Despite the negative critical response to *Schultz*, Donleavy's public proved loyal, justifying an even less distinguished sequel, *Are You Listening, Rabbi Löw?* Donleavy's fiction of this period deliberately deprives itself of the emotional conflicts central to his earlier, saintlier protagonists. It represents as well an insolent abrogation of the traditional concerns of "serious" fiction. By contrast, *The Ginger Man* was superior to the bulk of postwar novels about bohemian expatriates in Europe because of its sense of the limitations of that lifestyle as well as its potential. His nonfiction of the same period includes two books about his adoptive country, the largely autobiographical *J. P. Donleavy's Ireland* and *A Singular Country*.

THAT DARCY, THAT DANCER, THAT GENTLEMAN

That Darcy, That Dancer, That Gentleman completes the trilogy of Darcy novels, which collectively provide the high point of Donleavy's later work as a novelist. Although ostensibly set in twentieth century Ireland, the focus is on traditional, even anachronistic Irish rural life and values, which impelled Donleavy to make important stylistic modifications to fit the leisurely milieu, particularly in slowing the pace of events and descriptions to mirror the setting. This well-integrated juxtaposition of plot and characters drawn from the tradition of the eighteenth century novel with Donleavy's distinctively modernist style accounts for much of the freshness of the three works.

Darcy's battle to keep Andromeda Park afloat as his resources run out depends on his finding a wealthy wife, but the only woman he can imagine truly loving, Leila, is lost beyond hope of recovery as a marchioness in Paris. Among the unsuitable matches he considers are his neighbor Felicity Veronica Durrow-Mountmellon and two American heiresses from Bronxville, Florida, and Virginia. Rashers Ronald plays a large role in the book as Darcy's virtually permanent houseguest and best, though most unreliable, friend. The novel's climax is a chaotic grand ball at Darcy's estate, at which virtually every character to have been featured in the trilogy makes an appearance. At the end of the book, Ronald is engaged to Durrow-Mountmellon and Darcy is finally reunited with Leila, providing unusually traditional closure for a Donleavy novel, perhaps by way of winding up the trilogy.

WRONG INFORMATION IS BEING GIVEN OUT AT PRINCETON

Donleavy's next full-length novel, *Wrong Information Is Being Given out at Princeton*, presents the first-person narrative of Alfonso Stephen O'Kelly'O, in some ways a typical Donleavy hero. He is a social outsider with no money and expensive tastes, a problem he thinks he has solved in marrying the daughter of a wealthy family. Stephen differs from most of his predecessors, however, in that he is a dedicated musician, composer of a minuet that has been offered a prestigious opening performance by the book's end. While most of Donleavy's protagonists have artistic sensibilities, Stephen is one of the few who manages to be genuinely productive. His devotion to his work provides him with a moral and ethical center that often outweighs his hedonistic impulses, making him to some extent a principled rebel rather than just another of Donleavy's failed would-be conformists.

John P. Harrington
Updated by William Nelles

OTHER MAJOR WORKS

SHORT FICTION: *Meet My Maker the Mad Molecule*, 1964.

PLAYS: *The Ginger Man*, pr. 1959 (adaptation of his novel; also known as *What They Did in Dublin, with The Ginger Man: A Play*); *Fairy Tales of New York*, pb. 1961 (adaptation of his novel *A Fairy Tale of New York*); *A Singular Man*, pb. 1965; *The Plays of J. P. Donleavy: With a Preface by the Author*, 1972; *The Saddest Summer of Samuel S*, pb. 1972 (adaptation of his novel); *The Beastly Beatitudes of Balthazar B*, pr. 1981 (adaptation of his novel).

NONFICTION: *The Unexpurgated Code: A Complete Manual of Survival and Manners*, 1975; *J. P. Donleavy's Ireland: In All Her Sins and Some of Her Graces*, 1986; *A Singular Country*, 1990; *The History of the Ginger Man*, 1994; *An Author and His Image: The Collected Shorter Pieces*, 1997.

BIBLIOGRAPHY

Contrucci, Lance. "Revisiting *The Ginger Man.*" *Poets and Writers* 31, no. 5 (September/ October, 2003). Profile of Donleavy includes background information on his life, a description of his writing process, and an account of the success of *The Ginger Man*.

Donleavy, J. P. "The Art of Fiction: J. P. Donleavy." Interview by Molly McKaughan. *The Paris Review* 16 (Fall, 1975): 122-166. Lengthy interview includes Donleavy's discussion of the complex publishing history of *The Ginger Man*, the painful process of writing, the differences between his characters and himself, his preference for reading newspapers and magazines rather than novels, his life on his Irish farm, and his attitudes toward critics, New York, and death.

_____. "I Have an Aversion to Literature and Writing." In *Endangered Species: Writers Talk About Their Craft, Their Visions, Their Lives*. Cambridge, Mass.: Da Capo Press, 2001. An interview in which Donleavy addresses a range of topics, including his life as a writer, his writing style, and the influence of other writers on his work.

_____. "Only for the Moment Am I Saying Nothing: An Interview with J. P. Donleavy." Interview by Thomas E. Kennedy. *Literary Review* 40, no. 4 (Summer, 1997): 655-671. In this wide-ranging interview, conducted at Donleavy's mansion in Ireland, the author discusses issues from all periods of his literary career and personal life. Particular attention is afforded to the details of his methods of writing and the status of his manuscripts. Includes a bibliography of Donleavy's works.

Keohan, Joe. "A Man Amuck." *Boston Globe*, February 19, 2006. Revisits *The Ginger*

Man on the occasion of its fiftieth anniversary and provides background about Donleavy's life. Summarizes the novel's plot, and defines the book's theme as "resistance for its own sake. Resistance as a moral virtue."

Lawrence, Seymour. "Adventures with J. P. Donleavy: Or, How I Lost My Job and Made My Way to Greater Glory." *The Paris Review* 33, no. 116 (Fall, 1990): 187-201. Donleavy's first American editor reveals the inside story behind the complicated negotiations, fueled by fears of obscenity prosecution, that plagued the first two novels, *The Ginger Man* and *A Singular Man.* Lawrence eventually had to publish under his own imprint the first unexpurgated American edition of *The Ginger Man,* followed by eleven subsequent Donleavy books.

LeClair, Thomas. "A Case of Death: The Fiction of J. P. Donleavy." *Contemporary Literature* 12 (Summer, 1971): 329-344. Shows how Donleavy's protagonists are both classical rogues in the tradition of Henry Fielding's Tom Jones and modern victims resembling Franz Kafka's Joseph K. One of the best analyses available of Donleavy's obsession with death, which LeClair identifies as the controlling element in his fiction.

Masinton, Charles G. *J. P. Donleavy: The Style of His Sadness and Humor.* Bowling Green, Ohio: Bowling Green State University Popular Press, 1975. Pamphlet-length study of Donleavy's fiction through *A Fairy Tale of New York* places him in the American black humor tradition. Notes that although Donleavy's characters are increasingly morose and withdrawn, the fiction is most notable for its humor and irony. Includes a brief bibliography.

Morse, Donald E. "American Readings of J. P. Donleavy's *The Ginger Man.*" *Eire-Ireland: A Journal of Irish Studies* 26 (Fall, 1991): 128-138. Explores the treatment of the novel in American criticism and discusses reactions in the United States to the use of slang, myth, and Irish values depicted in the novel.

Norstedt, Johann A. "Irishmen and Irish-Americans in the Fiction of J. P. Donleavy." In *Irish-American Fiction: Essays in Criticism,* edited by Daniel J. Casey and Robert E. Rhodes. New York: AMS Press, 1979. Examines Donleavy's attitudes toward his native and adopted countries in *The Ginger Man, The Beastly Beatitudes of Balthazar B,* and other works, and concludes that the author has grown more hostile toward the United States while gradually accepting a romanticized view of Ireland. Presents an excellent discussion of Donleavy's use of Ireland. Includes a bibliography.

RODDY DOYLE

Born: Dublin, Ireland; May 8, 1958

OTHER LITERARY FORMS

In addition to his novels, for which he is best known, Roddy Doyle wrote several highly successful plays, including *Brownbread* (pr. 1987), *War* (pr., pb. 1989), and *The Woman Who Walked into Doors* (pr. 2003), which is based on his 1996 novel. *Family* (1994), a four-part television play, was highly controversial for its treatment of domestic abuse. While the subject of the abusive husband and father was by no means new in Irish literature, the play's widespread distribution through television provoked public debate over the representation of the working-class Irish family.

Doyle also wrote many short stories, including the collection *The Deportees, and Other Stories* (2008), and he wrote several books for children and teenage readers, including *Not Just for Christmas* (1999), *The Giggler Treatment* (2000), *Rover Saves Christmas* (2001), *The Meanwhile Adventures* (2004), and *Wilderness* (2007). He also contributed to the collaborative novels *Finbar's Hotel* (1999, with others) and *Yeats Is Dead!* (2001, with others). In 2002, he published an oral history-memoir about his parents, *Rory and Ita*.

ACHIEVEMENTS

Roddy Doyle's earlier novels are recognized for their unique and original representation of contemporary working-class family life in suburban Dublin. The novels that comprise the Barrytown trilogy (*The Commitments*, *The Snapper*, and *The Van*; all three published later as *The Barrytown Trilogy*) are celebrated for their honest, realistic portrayal of family dynamics and socioeconomic conditions as an antidote to the often romanticized depictions of life in earlier Irish novels. Perhaps as a result of this unique focus, the Barrytown trilogy has enjoyed a rare combination of critical acclaim and popular commercial success. *The Van*, the most serious of the three novels, was nominated for the Booker Prize, which is awarded annually to the best novel in English from the Commonwealth or the Republic of Ireland. All three novels of the Barrytown trilogy have been made into major motion pictures.

Doyle's next novel, *Paddy Clarke, Ha-Ha-Ha*, went on to win the Booker Prize in 1993. With its innovative narrative technique and disturbingly honest portrayal of childhood at the brink of adolescence, *Paddy Clarke, Ha-Ha-Ha* is widely acknowledged to be Doyle's masterpiece. In 1998, Doyle was awarded an honorary doctorate from Dublin City University.

BIOGRAPHY

Roddy Doyle was born May 8, 1958, in Dublin, one of four children born to Rory and Ita Doyle. His father was a printer and his mother worked as a secretary. As a child, Doyle attended schools in the suburbs to the north of the city. He later earned a degree in English and geography from University College, Dublin, and became a teacher. He worked as a schoolteacher from 1979 until 1993, when, after considerable critical and commercial success, he resigned to work full time as a writer.

Doyle seems to have drawn upon the neighbors and neighborhoods of his childhood for his earlier novels, set as they are in Barrytown, a fictional working-class suburb north of Dublin. His interest in portraying the resilience and ingenuity of average people makes this a fertile source of inspiration. Doyle's work with schoolchildren must have been a direct influence on his highly insightful novel *Paddy Clarke, Ha-Ha-Ha*, which portrays the dissolution of a marriage from the point of view of a young boy.

Doyle dabbled in writing for periodicals before seriously attempting to write fiction. His first attempt at a novel was not published, and his second, *The Commitments*, was originally published by a company that Doyle and a friend began just for that purpose. Printed and distributed on borrowed money, *The Commitments* eventually attracted the notice of a major publishing house, which republished the novel for a broad and appreciative audience. Although Doyle is one of Ireland's best-known writers, he has shunned the public limelight and remained a very private person.

ANALYSIS

One of Roddy Doyle's greatest attributes as a writer is his ear for voice and dialogue, and his first five novels in particular display this gift to excellent effect. With minimal third-person narration, Doyle uses realistic dialogue—such as profanities and regional dialect—to achieve vivid characterization. It is not surprising that several of his novels have been adapted effectively for film, since his dialogue-heavy expository technique is essentially dramatic, or cinematic.

Some commentators, however, claim that Doyle's emphasis on dialogue detracts from the novels' plots. Character takes precedence in these novels over author, narrator, and plot. Considered chronologically, Doyle's novels demonstrate an increasingly complex interaction between dialogue and narration. Because his characters do most of their speaking for themselves, there is little evidence of an authoritative, controlling consciousness in his novels. This technique empowers Doyle's characters even as it deprives readers of a comforting narrative guide; whether Doyle is using first-person or third-person narration, there is no concrete, objective perspective with which to compare and measure the perspective of the protagonist.

Doyle's dialogue has attracted much commentary because his characters belong to an economic and social class underrepresented in literature. Prior to Doyle's Barrytown novels, the contemporary, urban, working class of Dublin was an uncommon subject in the Irish novel.

While several of Doyle's novels are notable for their treatment of contemporary Dublin, the past plays a vital role throughout his works. In *The Commitments*, the young protagonist forms a band that plays soul music from the 1960's, hearkening back to an earlier, perhaps more innocent time. *Paddy Clarke, Ha-Ha-Ha* is set in 1968, and young Paddy and his father reflect both on nationalism in Irish history as well as on more contemporary events. The historical novels that comprise the Last Roundup series foreground Doyle's preoccupation with early twentieth century Ireland and with American culture.

THE BARRYTOWN TRILOGY

Doyle's interest in the frank exploration of family dynamics is evident in the three novels that make up the Barrytown trilogy. (The three novels were later published in a single volume under the same title.) While the notion of family values is by no means idealized in these novels, Doyle focuses on the large, resilient Rabbitte family, a family of survivors.

These novels display narrative immediacy because of their emphasis on dialogue and a near absence of intrusive narration. This immediacy is intensified by the pervasive contemporary slang and profanity in the dialogue. In *The Commitments*, young Jimmy Rabbitte, Jr., attempts to bring soul music back to Dublin by bringing together an array of talented musicians (most of them young). He then has to market them as a rhythm-and-blues (R & B) band called the Commitments, to a skeptical public. The trumpet player, an older man who claims friendship with the African American R & B musician Wilson Pickett, is the band's most direct connection to the tradition they are trying to revive. Jimmy understands that the appeal of this genre is not nostalgia, but rather its association with sex and an affinity he perceives between African American culture and the urban, Irish working class. Jimmy's enthusiasm and entrepreneurial skills are impressive but are ultimately not equal to the self-destructive forces that pull the band apart on the eve of its success.

While the Rabbitte family remains in the background through most of *The Commitments*, the family is the focus of *The Snapper*. The book's title refers to Dublin slang for an infant, and the novel centers on the unwanted pregnancy of the eldest daughter, Sharon, and the family's struggle to accept her decision to give birth and to raise the child without revealing the identity of the father, who turns out to be a friend of her own father. Jimmy Rabbitte, Sr., vacillates between disgust, embarrassment at the community's almost tribal reaction to his family's predicament, and, ultimately, acceptance of his daughter's decision. His skirmishes with Sharon form the major conflict of the novel.

The Van tells the story of the business partnership between Jimmy Rabbitte, Sr., and his friend Bimbo after they both lose their jobs. Jimmy has been struggling with unemployment; he takes the opportunity to spend time with his granddaughter but misses the male social interaction provided through work and evenings at the pub. Bimbo buys an old fish-and-chips van, and Jimmy joins him on his new job. At first, all goes well, but business and legal problems strain the friendship and, eventually, Bimbo drives the van into the sea. It is not clear whether the friendship can survive, but it appears Jimmy will with the support of his wife and family.

PADDY CLARKE, HA-HA-HA

While *Paddy Clarke, Ha-Ha-Ha* has earned many critical comparisons to James Joyce's autobiographical novel *A Portrait of the Artist as a Young Man* (1916), it is important to note that Doyle's novel does not seem to draw directly upon his own childhood experiences but rather upon his interactions with his own students and their parents. This novel shares a setting with the Barrytown trilogy as well as a reliance on dialect for character and exposition, and some critics have failed to detect a plot—a criticism levied at Doyle's earlier novels as well. However, there is a story in *Paddy Clarke, Ha-Ha-Ha*, though the narrator, and therefore the reader, becomes aware of it only late in the novel: A marriage dissolves because of economic and other pressures, and children struggle to deal with the consequences during a time (the novel is set in 1968) when broken marriages carried considerable social stigma.

The novel is narrated by ten-year-old Paddy, and the events he describes are those that would likely preoccupy a boy of his age in that time and place. At the beginning of the novel, he is part of the "in" crowd, though not a leader. His hobbies are soccer, picking at scabs, and tormenting his younger brother, Francis, whom he calls Sinbad. His relationship with Sinbad is ambivalent; his younger brother's soccer skills exceed his own, and Paddy is confused by the mixed feelings of pride and hatred this causes him. He tortures Sinbad but defends him from others. Their fellow students are known by their actions: Some are pathetic and to be made fun of, some are strong and to be feared and appeased. The adults in Paddy's life, the ones outside his family, are ancillary for the most part.

Some of the novel's most significant moments are to be found in Paddy's conversations with his father about patriotism and Irish independence, the Cold War, and the Middle East. At the novel's conclusion, Paddy's social status among his peers changes due to his father's departure.

THE WOMAN WHO WALKED INTO DOORS

Doyle's consideration of family dynamics takes a darker turn in *The Woman Who Walked into Doors*. Paula Spencer is abused at the hands of her husband, Charlo. The protagonist demonstrates a complicated mix of denial and inner strength. She recognizes that her situation, raising four children and living in constant fear, is at once very complicated and very simple. Her drinking, at first an apparent solution, eventually becomes a problem in its own right. The novel is ultimately a story of endurance and survival; the protagonist's story of recovery continues in Doyle's novel *Paula Spencer.*

A STAR CALLED HENRY *and* OH, PLAY THAT THING

A Star Called Henry and *Oh, Play That Thing* mark a substantial departure for Doyle; the two novels are works of historical fiction, a challenging mixture of historical fact and invention. The first novel describes the early life of Henry Smart and his experiences and exploits during and after the Easter Uprising of 1916. He encounters many of the famous historical figures who played public roles in the uprising and himself takes active part in the ensuing war for independence, even as he grows increasingly disillusioned over the lack of prospects either side offers for the poor and disenfranchised.

Oh, Play That Thing follows Henry Smart to America, in flight from his former Irish Republican Army associates. He works his way into the world of crime in New York through the gateway of advertising, eventually getting involved with bootlegging and pornography. He then flees to Chicago and befriends Louis Armstrong, whom he assists as a manager and bodyguard.

James S. Brown

OTHER MAJOR WORKS

SHORT FICTION: *The Deportees, and Other Stories*, 2008.

PLAYS: *Brownbread*, pr. 1987; *War*, pr., pb. 1989; *The Woman Who Walked into Doors*, pr. 2003 (adaptation of his novel).

SCREENPLAYS: *The Commitments*, 1991 (adaptation of his novel; with Dick Clement and Ian La Frenais); *The Snapper*, 1993 (adaptation of his novel); *The Van*, 1996 (adaptation of his novel).

TELEPLAY: *Family*, 1994.

CHILDREN'S/YOUNG ADULT LITERATURE: *Not Just for Christmas*, 1999; *The Giggler Treatment*, 2000; *Rover Saves Christmas*, 2001; *The Meanwhile Adventures*, 2004; *Wilderness*, 2007.

BIBLIOGRAPHY

Booker, M. Keith. "Late Capitalism Comes to Dublin: 'American' Popular Culture in the Novels of Roddy Doyle." *Ariel* 28, no. 3 (1997): 27-46. This article examines the portrayal of American popular culture in the novels of Doyle. Examines as well the development of the books around the theme of multinational popular culture.

McCarthy, Dermot. *Roddy Doyle: Raining on the Parade*. Dublin: Liffey Press, 2002. This guide to Doyle's fiction (through *The Woman Who Walked into Doors*) focuses on

Doyle's "counter-mythological" depiction of contemporary urban Ireland and his characters' disengagement with or rejection of traditional Irish nationalism and colonialism.

McGlynn, Mary. "'But I Keep on Thinking and I'll Never Come to a Tidy Ending': Roddy Doyle's Useful Nostalgia." *LIT: Literature Interpretation Theory* 10, no. 1 (July, 1999): 87-105. This article begins by examining Doyle's use of nationalistic color symbolism in *Paddy Clarke, Ha-Ha-Ha* and describes a shift from the insular nationalism of the first part of the twentieth century to an outward-looking construction of nation, focusing on the role of nostalgia.

McGuire, Matt. "Dialect(ic) Nationalism? The Fiction of James Kelman and Roddy Doyle." *Scottish Studies Review* 7, no. 1 (Spring, 2006): 80-94. This article contrasts the use of dialect in the works of Scottish novelist James Kelman and Irish novelist Doyle. Examines their novels in relationship to the respective Scottish and Irish historical contexts of their settings as well as the times in which they were written.

Marsh, Kelly A. "Roddy Doyle's 'Bad Language' and the Limits of Community." *Critique* 45, no. 2. (Winter, 2004): 147-159. This article analyzes self-censorship in Doyle's novels, examining changes in the use of "bad" language from the Barrytown trilogy to the later novels *Paddy Clarke, Ha-Ha-Ha* and *The Woman Who Walked into Doors*. Discusses the significance of censorship and free speech in preserving community.

Mildorf, Jarmila. "Words that Strike and Words that Comfort: Discursive Dynamics of Verbal Abuse in Roddy Doyle's *The Woman Who Walked into Doors*." *Journal of Gender Studies* 14, no. 2 (July, 2005): 107-122. This article uses sociolinguistic and literary analysis to examine characters' use of language in *The Woman Who Walked into Doors*. Studies slang and sexist language and explores how verbal abuse ultimately empowers the novel's protagonist and provides her with a means of retaliation.

Reynolds, Margaret, and Jonathan Noakes. *Roddy Doyle: The Essential Guide*. New York: Vintage, 2004. This book is an interactive reading guide to Doyle's novels, devoting a chapter to each covered novel and including questions for discussion and analysis. Also provides a short interview with Doyle.

MARIA EDGEWORTH

Born: Black Bourton, Oxfordshire, England; January 1, 1768
Died: Edgeworthstown, Ireland; May 22, 1849

OTHER LITERARY FORMS

Like a number of late eighteenth century and early nineteenth century authors, Maria Edgeworth did not intend to become a novelist; rather, she began writing extended prose fiction as an outgrowth of other kinds of literary production. Her first works were children's tales, usually short and always with a clear and forcefully advanced didactic thesis—a few titles suggest the nature of the themes: "Lazy Laurence," "Waste Not, Want Not," "Forgive and Forget." Many of these stories were assembled under the titles *The Parent's Assistant: Or, Stories for Children* (1796, 1800) and *Moral Tales for Young People* (1801), the first of which encompassed six volumes, while the second filled five volumes.

These tales were written largely at the behest of Edgeworth's father, Richard Lovell Edgeworth, who was a deeply committed moralist and is still considered a notable figure in the history of education in England and Ireland. Both father and daughter collaborated on many of the stories, as they did on most of what Maria Edgeworth wrote. As a sort of commentary on the works of short fiction and certainly as an adjunct to them, the essays on education collected in *Essays on Practical Education* (1798) were designed to advance the liberal but moralistic theories on child rearing that the elder Edgeworth had imbibed in part from Jean-Jacques Rousseau and had transmitted to his daughter. Richard Edgeworth's credentials for such a piece of writing were perhaps enhanced by the fact that he fathered no fewer than twenty-two children with four wives.

Apart from further essays (again, chiefly written either in collaboration with her father or under his watchful eye) on education, morals, Ireland, and culture, Edgeworth's primary emphasis was on fiction, usually of novel length (her "novels" range in length from

Maria Edgeworth
(Library of Congress)

the quite short *Castle Rackrent*, merely one hundred pages, to *Belinda*, which extends to almost five hundred pages). The only other form she attempted—one in which, like many nineteenth century authors, she had no publishing success—was the drama. Her plays were composed essentially for the pleasure of the family, as were the first drafts of the majority of her fiction works, and the volume containing the best of the plays, *Comic Dramas in Three Acts* (1817), is now almost universally unread.

ACHIEVEMENTS

During her long lifetime, Maria Edgeworth helped to make possible the Victorian novel. Reared with a rich background in the high achievements of Henry Fielding, Samuel Richardson, and Tobias Smollett, she began to write at a time when female novelists were just beginning to be accepted; a few of them, such as Fanny Burney and Elizabeth Inchbald, managed to attain some popularity. The novel of manners was the prevailing genre produced by these "lady writers." It had affinities with the lachrymose novel of sensibility (the classic example of which, *The Man of Feeling*, was penned in 1771 by a man, Henry Mackenzie), and the tight focus and excessively delicate feelings exhibited in this form limited its appeal and artistic possibilities. It lay to Jane Austen to instill clever and penetrating satire, along with a much greater sense of realism in regard to human behavior, and to Maria Edgeworth to extend its bounds of character depiction, to include persons of the lower classes, and to broaden its range: Men are seen at the hunt, in private conference, and in all manner of vigorous activity unknown in Austen's fiction.

Edgeworth is, of course, bound to be compared with Austen, to the former's derogation; there can be no doubt that the latter is the greater novelist, from an artistic standpoint. This judgment should not blind the reader to Edgeworth's accomplishment, however. As P. N. Newby has observed, although "Jane Austen was so much the better novelist," yet "Maria Edgeworth may be the more important." Her significance rests chiefly on two achievements: She widened the scope of the "female" novel (the emphasis on female sensibility in her work is considerably less than in Austen's novels, though it can be detected), and, as Newby has noted, in her careful and detailed treatment of Ireland and its people she "gave dignity to the regional subject and made the regional novel possible." Today, readers tend to take for granted the insightful historical works of, for example, Sir Walter Scott; they often do not realize that, had it not been for Edgeworth, Scott might not have attempted the monumental effort that he began in *Waverley: Or, 'Tis Sixty Years Since* (1814), in the preface of which he gives Edgeworth full credit for inspiring him to essay the regional fiction in which his work became a landmark. It has also been claimed that such disparate figures as Stendhal and Ivan Turgenev were influenced by Edgeworth's sympathetic treatment of peasants. Some critics and literary historians have gone so far as to claim for her the title of the first intelligent sociological novelist in English literature. More than any author up to her time, Edgeworth revealed human beings as related to, and partially formed by, their environments.

BIOGRAPHY

January 1, 1767, is usually accepted as the birth date of Maria Edgeworth, but, in *Maria Edgeworth: A Literary Biography* (1972), Marilyn Butler asserts that Maria herself "seems to have considered 1768 correct, and the Black Bourton records on the whole support her." This is one of the few uncertainties in a life dedicated to family, friends, and literature. Edgeworth was born in England, the child of Richard Lovell Edgeworth (an Anglo-Irish gentleman with extensive estates in county Longford, about sixty miles from Dublin) and his first wife, Anna Maria Elers Edgeworth, who died when Maria was five years old. By all accounts, Maria got along well with her three siblings, two sisters and a brother (another child died before she was born), and with her father's next three wives and her seventeen half brothers and half sisters, most of whom she helped to rear. The general harmony in the Edgeworth household may be seen as all the more remarkable when one considers that Richard Edgeworth's last wife, Frances Anne Beaufort Edgeworth (with whose family Maria became quite friendly), was a year or two younger than Maria.

Much of this impressive concord can be credited to Richard Lovell Edgeworth, a man of enormous confidence and personal force. He took the not untypical eighteenth century view that, as the father in the household, he was the lord and master in a literal sense. Fortunately, he was a benevolent master. Although he believed firmly that he knew what was best for all his wives and children, what he believed to be best was their relatively free development, confined only by his sense of what was morally right and socially proper. Maria evidently accepted her father's guidance to the point of seeking and welcoming his advice.

Richard Edgeworth had such confidence both in the good sense of his children and in his own principles of education, which were patterned on those of his eccentric friend Thomas Day (author of the once-famous novel of education *The History of Sandford and Merton*, 1783-1789), that he informed his family of the reasons for nearly all of his decisions, and certainly for the important ones. The most important of these was his resolve to settle on his family estate in Ireland (he had been living in England for a number of years, having left Ireland about 1765; and Maria had visited Ireland only briefly, in 1773). One reason for the election to live in Ireland—Edgeworth could have afforded to stay in England, since he received rents from his Irish property—was that Richard Edgeworth was convinced by his reading and by the course of national affairs (one feature of which was the harsh economic treatment of Ireland because of the great expense incurred by England in its war with the American colonies) that Ireland could be one of the best and most productive areas in the British Empire.

To achieve the goal of proper estate management, a subject that was to engage the interest of Maria Edgeworth for the rest of her life, her father had to revolutionize the way in which his lands and tenants were cared for. The salient aspect of the change was a greater concern for genuine productivity and less for high rents. He was quite successful, partly because of the help of his adoring and sensible daughter. The estate and the family survived riots, famines, and the very real threat of a French invasion of Ireland during the Napoleonic campaigns. From the time the Edgeworth family relocated to Edgeworthstown, in 1782, until her death, Maria Edgeworth lived in the family homestead—the constancy of her residence there being broken by only a few trips to England, France, and Scotland and brief visits to other countries on the Continent. During these sojourns, she managed to become acquainted, largely through her father's influence, with some of the leading thinkers and artists of the day, notably Sir Walter Scott, with whom she formed a warm personal friendship and for whom she had a great admiration, which was reciprocated. Edgeworth was one of the first readers to recognize that the anonymously published *Waverley* was the work of "the Wizard of the North."

While visiting France in 1802, Edgeworth met the Chevalier Abraham Niclas Clewberg-Edelcrantz, a Swedish diplomat to whom she was introduced in Paris. For this somewhat shy, very small, not particularly attractive woman, the encounter was extraordinary. Edelcrantz was not handsome, and he was forty-six years old. On the positive side, he was very intelligent and quite well educated, a fact that appealed to Edgeworth. Although evidently astounded and pleased by Edelcrantz's proposal of marriage, she was wise enough to realize that his devotion to Sweden, which he could not think of leaving as his home, and hers to Ireland posed an absolute barrier to any happiness in such a union. Richard Edgeworth was apparently in favor of the marriage, but he did nothing to persuade Maria to accept the Swede, and he received her decision with equanimity.

Apart from helping her father to manage the estate—managing it herself almost single-handedly after his death in 1817—and looking after the family, Edgeworth devoted herself almost exclusively to writing. Some of her novels began as very short tales written (usually on a slate, so that erasures and improvements could be made readily) for the entertainment of the younger members of the family circle. Richard Edgeworth, however, persuaded her to take her writing seriously. This she did for some fifty years, until shortly before her death in 1849, by which time she had become respected and, to a degree seldom achieved by a female author, famous.

ANALYSIS

The novels of Maria Edgeworth are, to the modern reader, an odd combination of strengths and weaknesses. This phenomenon is not really very strange, given the times in which she lived and the progress of fiction writing in the early nineteenth century. The work of all the novelists of that period may be considered strongly flawed and yet often unexpectedly effective (Sir Walter Scott is the obvious example, but the same might even be said of much of the work of Charles Dickens). What is perhaps more surprising is that Edgeworth herself was aware of the defects of her work. She knew, for example, that her writings were didactic to an often annoying degree. Her father, who had a great deal to do with her conviction that fiction should aim to elevate the morals of its readers, even comments on the fact in one of his prefaces to her novels and claims that a severe attempt had been made to subdue the moralistic features. By modern standards, the attempts never fully succeeded in any of Edgeworth's novels.

One reason for the "failure" is simply the prevalence of the late eighteenth century belief that behavior can be modified by edifying reading and that character can be formed and, possibly more important, reformed by acts of the will. Those of Edgeworth's tales titled with the name of the central character, such as *Ormond*, *Belinda*, and *Vivian*, are thus the stories of how these young people come to terms with society and their responsibilities—in short, how they grow up to be worthy citizens. The concept itself is not ludicrous; literature is replete with studies of the ways in which young people come of age successfully. What is distressing in Edgeworth's "moral tales" (and those of many other writers of the era) are the improbable turns of plot such as those by which poor but honest people are suddenly discovered to be heirs to great properties, those believed to be orphans are revealed as the offspring of noble houses, and so forth. This sort of device has a long history in both fiction and drama, but it is especially dismaying in a work that is otherwise, and by clear intention, realistic. The distracting and hardly credible process by which Grace Nugent, in *The Absentee*, is proved legitimate so that Lord Colambre can in good conscience marry her (the moral logic behind his reluctance to wed her, blameless as she is for the situation of her birth, may repel modern readers who are not familiar with the depth of the eighteenth century conviction concerning the influence of a flawed family background) is needlessly detailed. Such a device also intrudes on a story that is otherwise filled with convincing details about estate management (and mismanagement) in Ireland and fairly realistic studies of the lives of the common people.

Richard Edgeworth was blamed, perhaps unjustly, for the excess of didacticism in his daughter's novels (it is surely no accident that the only work lacking such material, *Castle Rackrent*, was her most popular title and is today her only novel still read); some of the tiresome passages of "uplifting" commentary do sound as if they came from his eloquent but ponderous pen, as in Belinda's comment in a letter, "Female wit sometimes depends on the beauty of its possessor for its reputation; and the reign of beauty is proverbially short, and fashion often capriciously deserts her favourites, even before nature withers their charms." To his credit, however, Richard Edgeworth is now known to have done a great deal to provide his daughter with ideas for stories and plot sequences.

Perhaps the most important artistic flaw to which the younger Edgeworth pleaded guilty was a lack of invention, and critics over the decades have noticed that she depends to excess on details and facts, many of which she collected from her own family's records and memoirs. The rest she gathered by direct (and penetrating) observation, as in the realistic farm scenes in the Irish tales and the believable pictures of society gatherings in London and Paris. One of the most obvious indications of Edgeworth's failure to devise plots artfully is her reliance on the retrospective strategy of having a character reveal his or her background by telling it to another. Certainly, the review of her own life that Lady Delacour provides for Belinda is not without interest and is necessary to the story, yet it seems cumbersome, appearing as it does in two chapters that occupy more than thirty pages near the opening of the novel.

The two types of novels that Edgeworth wrote—the Irish tales and, as the title of one collection indicates, the *Tales of Fashionable Life* (1809-1812)—manifest the poles of her thematic interest. She believed, as did her father, that Ireland could benefit and even prosper from a more responsible aristocracy, landowners who lived on their property and saw that it was fairly and efficiently managed. In her three best Irish tales, *Castle Rackrent*, *The Absentee*, and *Ormond*, Edgeworth underlines the virtues of fair play with tenants, caution in dealing with hired estate managers (the wicked Nicholas Garraghty in *The Absentee* should be warning enough for any proprietor), and close attention to details of land and equipment. The years that Edgeworth spent aiding her father at Edgeworthstown bore impressive fruit in her grasp of the problems and difficulties faced by owners of large estates.

Because the sectarian, political, and economic problems that faced Ireland have tended to persist into the present, while the aspects of fashionable life have not, the "society" novels in Irish literature are almost unknown by the reading public today. In any case, Edgeworth was much more intellectually involved in the politics and social problems of her homeland than she was in the vagaries and evils of society life in big cities. Much as she believed that a great deal can be learned about the proper way to live one's life by observing society closely, she was personally never so involved in that topic as she was in such concerns as the injustices created by absentee landlords and the abuse of tenants by land agents hired by the absentees and given enormous power. Thus, while Belinda, Vivian, and Helen do hold some interest for the reader, their problems and challenges are dated. The modern reader has difficulty taking seriously the follies of Vivian, who manages to misjudge nearly everybody in the novel, leading to his not unexpected demise, which is sad but far from tragic. The peculiarities of King Corny in *Ormond*, however, as when it is revealed that he is elevating the roof of his large house so that he can construct attics under it, help to provide the reader with a more substantial grasp of the great power, the tendency toward eccentricity, and the frequent good-heartedness of Irish estate owners.

Edgeworth usually dealt with events and conditions in the fairly recent past; as such, she can be considered a historical novelist. Her emphasis on what can be viewed as an international theme, however (the relationship between English and Irish characters and attitudes), is thought by many to be the most significant aspect of her novels. Critics have even suggested that her treatment of the topic prefigures the more detailed analyses by Henry James.

Edgeworth appeared on the literary scene at the best possible moment for her career and the future of the English novel. Her own records designate the amounts that she was paid by her publishers for each major work, and the list of payments is, by the standards of the time, impressive. For example, the minor novel *Patronage* earned Edgeworth twenty-one hundred pounds, at that time an enormous sum. The influence that she had on the course of the historical and regional novel is proof of her little-known but vital contribution toward the development of the English novel.

CASTLE RACKRENT

In his introduction to the Oxford English Novels edition of *Castle Rackrent* (1964), George Watson claims for this unusual book the distinction of being "the first regional novel in English, and perhaps in all Europe." Certainly, the work is a tour de force, all the more impressive because it was, by most accounts, achieved virtually by accident. Richard Edgeworth had on the estate a steward named John Langan. His opinions and mode of expression so struck Maria Edgeworth that she began to record his comments and became an able mimic of his dialect and turns of speech. Her letters to her father's sister, Mrs. Margaret Edgeworth Ruxton, one of her favorite correspondents, inspired this sympathetic lady to encourage her niece to develop the material into a story. Thus was born Maria Edgeworth's only substantial piece of fiction written during Richard Edgeworth's lifetime in whose composition he evidently did not play a part.

Edgeworth claimed that only the narrator was based on a real-life person, Langan; some scholars have suggested that one or two other characters might have been fashioned after people known to her. An example is the entertaining character Sir Conolly "Condy"

Rackrent, who may have been broadly patterned on Edgeworth's maternal grandfather. However great or small its basis in real life, the novel has the air of reality about it. The actions and the motivations ring true to life. *Castle Rackrent* is often praised for its lack of an obtrusive moral emphasis, but it would be a mistake to read the novel as having no message. The decline and fall of the Rackrent family is the story of irresponsibility and extravagance, an unfortunately common phenomenon in the history of Irish landowners.

The narrator, Thady Quirk, commonly called honest Thady, tells the dismal but occasionally humorous tale of the several masters under whom he has served: Sir Patrick O'Shaughlin, who drinks himself to death early in the story; Sir Murtaugh Rackrent, who dies in a paroxysm of anger over a legalistic contretemps; Sir Kit Rackrent, who dies in a duel over the controversy stemming from his indecision regarding the choice of a new wife, when his first spouse seems on the point of death; and Sir Conolly Rackrent, whose narrative is longer than the tale of the first three owners of Castle Rackrent. Another innovative aspect of the novel, aside from the use of such an authentic narrator, is the consistent employment of dialect. The text is not difficult to read, but many of the expressions are not easily comprehensible to a reader unfamiliar with the Irish speech and mores of that era. Wisely, Edgeworth—with her father's help—appended a glossary that explains, occasionally in needless detail, many of Thady's locutions and references. That Thady opens his memoir on a Monday morning might have little special significance unless the reader is informed by the glossary that "no great undertaking can be auspiciously commenced in Ireland on any morning but *Monday morning.*"

Perhaps the chief appeal of the work to the modern reader lies in the personality of Thady and in the folkways he embodies. On the first page, he tells of his "great coat," which poverty compels him to wear winter and summer but which is "very handy, as I never put my arms into the sleeves, (they are as good as new,) though come Holantide next, I've had it these seven years." The extraordinary loyalty of Thady to a family that seems not to deserve such fidelity is both exasperating and admirable. Thady is not, however, overcome with emotion when unfortunate circumstances arise. Though he cannot recall the drinking habits of Sir Patrick without the brief aside, "God bless him!," he speaks of a shocking event at the funeral with relative calm: "Happy the man who could get but a sight of the hearse!—But who'd have thought it? Just as all was going on right, through his own town they were passing, when the body was seized for debt." Thady is moved enough to call the creditors "villains," but he swiftly moves on with his tale: "So, to be sure, the law must take its course—and little gain had the creditors for their pains." The old man spends more time on the legal implications of the seizure than on the event itself. This passage displays Edgeworth's understanding of the contentious element in the Irish personality and the formidable grasp of the law that even poorly educated people often had. Indeed, lawsuits and legal technicalities abound in Edgeworth's fiction.

Thady's almost eccentric equanimity and generous nature are further revealed when, after Sir Kit has gambled away virtually all the assets of the Rackrent estate, including the goodwill of his wealthy wife, the old retainer remarks, "the Castle Rackrent estate was all mortgaged, and bonds out against him, for he was never cured of his gaming tricks—but that was the only fault he had, God bless him!" Further, Thady seems untroubled by the confinement of Sir Kit's wife for seven years in her apartments (an incident based on the actual imprisonment of a Lady Cathcart, in 1745, who was kept locked up by her husband for a much longer period), apparently lost in admiration of the fierce temper of his master, which not only caused the drastic action but also discouraged anyone from asking him about it.

The first part of *Castle Rackrent* is titled "An Hibernian Tale." It is indeed very "Hibernian," but no more so than the story of Sir Conolly Rackrent, whom Thady refers to as "ever my great favorite, and indeed the most universally beloved man I had ever seen or heard of." Condy's chief attractions are a good nature and a propensity to spend excessively. Both of these qualities contribute to the further impoverishment of the estate, a condition that he does little to alleviate. Even his marriage to the daughter of a wealthy landowner on a nearby estate (who promptly disinherits his offspring as soon as he learns of the wedding, thus frustrating even this halfhearted attempt to repair the Rackrent fortunes) is a matter of chance: Condy, who actually loves Thady's pretty but fortuneless grandniece, Judy M'Quirk, flips a coin to determine whether he will propose to Judy or the moneyed Isabella.

Despite the disinheritance, Sir Condy is fond of Isabella; when financial disaster looms, he attempts to provide her with a generous allotment in his will. The closing of the novel exposes another theme that may be derived from the plot. The villain who buys up Sir Condy's debts and brings on his personal ruin is Thady's own son, the self-serving Jason. Edgeworth possibly had in mind to make some point about the difference between the single-minded loyalty and honesty of the older generation and the selfish heartlessness of the younger. Even the attractive Judy, when Thady suggests that she might become the next mistress of Castle Rackrent (Isabella has had an accident from which Thady believes she will die), tells him there is no point in marrying a poor man; she has evidently set her sights on Jason, much to Thady's dismay.

Typically, the novel ends with a lawsuit. Lady Condy, after her husband's death from drinking, sues for the title to the estate. Thady does not know how the suit will end, and he seems not to care: "For my part, I'm tired wishing for any thing in this world, after all I've seen in it." With this touching close to what is considered Edgeworth's best novel, the reader may well believe that the author has provided the opportunity for a greater understanding of those elements of Irish culture and history that impelled her to devote a lifetime of study to them.

THE ABSENTEE

During Edgeworth's lifetime, *The Absentee* was probably her most influential work. The central problem addressed in the novel is that of the absentee landlords, who left the

management of their often vast Irish estates in the hands of inept and frequently unscrupulous agents. These agents robbed the landlords as well as the tenants, but the indifferent
landowners took little interest in the lands so long as the rents were paid on time. As Edgeworth makes eminently clear by the contrast between the sensible and benevolent Mr.
Burke, one of Lord Clonbrony's agents, and the other, Nicholas Garraghty, who is schem-
ing and dishonest, not all agents were bad; the trouble was that the owners had no accurate
way of knowing, since they were almost never on the scene.

The hero of this novel, Lord Colambre, is the son of Lord and Lady Clonbrony; it is
around this unbelievably virtuous and somewhat stuffy young man that the several sub-
plots and themes are centered. Each subplot is designed to underline an obvious theme,
and Colambre is a vital, if artificial, unifying element in a novel whose general absence of
unity is disquieting. The main plot line has to do with the Clonbronys, who live in London
because Lady Clonbrony believes that high society is indispensable to her happiness (typically, the other members of the "smart set" find her pretensions ridiculous; Edgeworth explores a number of opportunities to satirize the false values of such people). Lord
Clonbrony would not mind returning to the family estate, and he realizes that remaining
away may be ruinous, since he is already in considerable debt. Lord Colambre visits his
father's lands in disguise, where he identifies the problem and recognizes the virtues and
evils of the two agents. After vigorous efforts to repay his father's debts, he saves the
situation and persuades his mother to return to Ireland.

A related theme concerns the actions that Colambre will not take in order to pay the
debts—chiefly, he will not marry for money, a time-honored method of acquiring funds in
a short time. Edgeworth offers several illustrations of the folly of such a practice, though
perhaps to the modern reader her emphasis on the legitimacy of the birth of Grace Nugent,
Colambre's cousin, as a criterion for his proposing to her may seem artificial and even essentially immoral. Interestingly, when Miss Nugent (who has been unaware of the "disgrace") learns of the reason for Colambre's erstwhile restraint, she fully agrees that it
would have been improper for him to offer marriage when her birth seemed under a cloud.
Through an unlikely and tiresome concatenation of circumstances and accidents, the
problem is solved: It is proved that Grace's birth was legitimate, and the marriage is ap-
proved, even by Lady Clonbrony, who for most of the story has been trying to persuade
her son to wed the wealthy Miss Broadhurst.

The Absentee is filled with flat characters created in the heroic mold, most of whom be-
friend Colambre and impress him with a variety of sensible insights: the positive aspects
of life in Ireland; the joys and satisfactions of the quiet country life (the O'Neill family,
tenants on the Clonbrony estate, underline this point; they, too, are so honest and good-
hearted as to be difficult to accept); the emptiness and falseness of "society"; and the great
importance of taking responsibility and performing one's duty well. *The Absentee* emphasizes two aspects of Edgeworth's philosophy of life. She fully accepted the eighteenth
century conviction that the class structure of society was inevitable and proper, and she

wholeheartedly believed in the primacy of duty (a word iterated by her father as the chief element of a worthy life) as everyone's first responsibility. Thus, in *The Absentee* there is an interesting mingling of liberal attitudes toward the rights of the peasants and conservative views regarding the propriety of aristocratic privilege.

At the close of a long and complicated reticulation of plot lines, Edgeworth had the clever notion of ending the story simply and even humorously (there is an unfortunate paucity of humor in this novel) by completing the tale through the device of a letter written by an Irish coach-driver to his brother, who currently lives in England, telling him of the happy return of the Clonbronys to the estate and the upcoming marriage of Colambre and Grace, and urging him to come back to Ireland, since "it's growing the fashion not to be an Absentee." *The Absentee* lacks the humor and directness of *Castle Rackrent*, but it makes its thematic points forcefully, and in Sir Terence O'Fay, Edgeworth has created a revealing, rounded portrait of an interesting Irish type: a good-natured wastrel who is no one's enemy but his own. His function in the plot is minimal, but he displays some of the most engaging features of the Irish personality.

ORMOND

Unlike *The Absentee*, whose title indicates that the subject is a general phenomenon, *Ormond*, as its title suggests, is about the development of a single individual. The novel is based on the view that young people can change their character by learning from their experiences and exerting their will. Although Harry Ormond is not exactly Rousseau's "noble savage," he is clearly intended to be the image of an untutored, raw personality, full of fine possibilities that must be cultivated to be realized. During the long, complex advance of the story, this is just what happens.

The lad has been reared by an old friend of his father, who died in India, a minor aristocrat named Sir Ulick O'Shane, who believes that educating the boy would be a waste of time, since he is destined to be a poor dependent for life. The contrast between Harry Ormond and Ulick's own son, Marcus, a formally educated but weak and ineffective youth, is one of several that give the novel a sense of polarity. Ulick is contrasted with his cousin, Cornelius O'Shane, the King Corny who takes over the care of Harry when he is forced to leave Ulick's estate after a shooting incident; Dora O'Shane, the daughter of Corny, with whom for a while Harry believes himself to be in love, is seen as quite different from the modest and highly moral Florence Annaly, whom he does love and finally marries; White Connal, Dora's first suitor, is, even by his name, contrasted with his brother, Black Connal, who ultimately is the man who marries Dora.

Harry Ormond is placed in the care of a succession of older men, and from each he learns things that help him grow into a responsible and sensitive man. Ulick teaches him some of the complexities of business and helps him to understand the difficulty of judging character in another; King Corny instructs him in the need for bold action and in the excellences to be found in the primitive personality; Dr. Cambray, a clergyman, starts

Harry on his formal education; and, while staying with the Annaly family, Harry perceives the delights of a well-ordered life in a well-regulated family, something he has never before experienced.

The essence of the book, apart from Ormond's development into a mature person, is his ultimate winning of the girl he truly loves. His material dependence is easily (and, again, incredibly) solved by the discovery that his father has left him a fortune. His only real problem, then, is to pass a series of moral tests created by Edgeworth to prove that he is a worthy, responsible man. The novel is marked by a number of traditional devices, such as the timeworn "While Sir Ulick is drinking his cup of cold coffee, we may look back a little into his family history," which is done for some six and a half pages. Frequent references to Ormond as "our hero" remind the reader that this is his story and that Harry is to be thought of as heroic, no matter what mistakes he makes (and he does blunder now and then, usually on the side of excessive credulity). The author does not hesitate to intrude into the story, to proclaim ignorance ("What he said, or what Florence answered, we do not know"), or to move the plot along with phrases such as "We now go on to," or "We now proceed to." *Ormond* is thus in many ways a traditional novel of the period, but it achieves a level of social criticism—of French society (a number of scenes are set in Paris) as well as of English and Irish ways—seldom found before William Makepeace Thackeray in the history of the English novel. This tale, unlike *The Absentee*, is also enlivened by humor.

Edgeworth's novels are unfortunately little read today, except by students of the English novel. Aside from plainly revealing the significant lines of tradition and transition from the eighteenth century to the nineteenth century novel, Edgeworth's work is enjoyable in itself. Nowhere else can one find such a lively and fairly balanced picture of the life and values found in the Ireland and England of the late Georgian period.

Fred B. McEwen

OTHER MAJOR WORKS

SHORT FICTION: *The Modern Griselda*, 1805; *Tales of Fashionable Life*, 1809-1812; *Tales and Miscellaneous Pieces*, 1825; *Garry Owen: Or, The Snow-Woman, and Poor Bob, the Chimney-Sweeper*, 1832; *Orlandino*, 1848; *Classic Tales*, 1883.

PLAYS: *Comic Dramas in Three Acts*, 1817.

NONFICTION: *An Essay on the Noble Science of Self-Justification*, 1795; *Letters for Literary Ladies*, 1795; *Practical Education*, 1798 (with Richard Lovell Edgeworth; also known as *Essays on Practical Education*); *A Rational Primer*, 1799 (with Richard Lovell Edgeworth); *Essay on Irish Bulls*, 1802 (with Richard Lovell Edgeworth); *Essays on Professional Education*, 1809 (with Richard Lovell Edgeworth); *Readings on Poetry*, 1816 (with Richard Lovell Edgeworth); *Memoirs of Richard Lovell Edgeworth Esq.*, 1820 (vol. 2); *Thoughts on Bores*, 1826; *A Memoir of Maria Edgeworth*, 1867 (Francis Edgeworth, editor); *Archibald Constable and His Literary Correspondents*, 1873; *The Life and Letters of Maria Edgeworth*, 1894 (Augustus J. Hare, editor); *Chosen Letters*, 1931 (F. V.

Barry, editor); *Romilly-Edgeworth Letters, 1813-1818*, 1936 (Samuel H. Romilly, editor); *Letters from England, 1813-1844*, 1971 (Christina Colvin, editor).

TRANSLATION: *Adelaide and Theodore*, 1783 (of comtesse de Stephanie Felicite Ducrest de Saint Aubin Genlis's system of education).

CHILDREN'S LITERATURE: *The Parent's Assistant: Or, Stories for Children*, 1796 (3 volumes), 1800 (6 volumes); *Frank, I-IV*, 1801 (with Richard Lovell Edgeworth; this and the two previous titles known as *Early Lessons*); *Harry and Lucy, I and II*, 1801 (with Richard Lovell Edgeworth); *The Mental Thermometer*, 1801; *Moral Tales for Young People*, 1801; *Rosamond, I-III*, 1801 (with Richard Lovell Edgeworth); *Popular Tales*, 1804; *Continuation of Early Lessons*, 1814; *Rosamond: A Sequel to Early Lessons*, 1821; *Frank: A Sequel to Frank in Early Lessons*, 1822; *Harry and Lucy Concluded*, 1825; *Little Plays for Children*, 1827; *The Purple Jar, and Other Stories*, 1931.

MISCELLANEOUS: *Tales and Novels*, 1832-1833 (18 volumes).

BIBLIOGRAPHY

Butler, Marilyn. *Maria Edgeworth: A Literary Biography*. Oxford, England: Clarendon Press, 1972. Standard biography on Edgeworth is strongest when dealing with the complex and voluminously documented Edgeworth family history. Provides a comprehensive sense of the author's immediate family background. The overall social and cultural context of Edgeworth's work receives less detailed treatment, and literary criticism as such is kept to a minimum.

Gilmartin, Sophie. "Oral and Written Genealogies in Edgeworth's *The Absentee*." In *Ancestry and Narrative in Nineteenth-Century British Literature: Blood Relations from Edgeworth to Hardy*. New York: Cambridge University Press, 1998. Chapter on *The Absentee* is included in a volume that explores the importance of the concept of ancestry in Victorian England by examining novels from that era. Includes bibliographical references and an index.

Harden, Elizabeth. *Maria Edgeworth*. Boston: Twayne, 1984. Survey of Edgeworth's life and works is organized around the theme of education. This approach reveals in broad outline the range of Edgeworth's sympathies and activities. Supplemented by an excellent bibliography.

Hollingworth, Brian. *Maria Edgeworth's Irish Writing*. New York: St. Martin's Press, 1997. Focuses on Edgeworth's Irish works, especially the novels *Castle Rackrent* and *Ormond*, to explore the author's attitudes toward language and regionalism. Includes detailed notes and bibliography.

Kaufman, Heidi, and Chris Fauske, eds. *An Uncomfortable Authority: Maria Edgeworth and Her Contexts*. Newark: University of Delaware Press, 2004. Collection of scholarly essays examines Edgeworth's works through attention to various cultural and ideological contexts. Presents analysis of the novels *Ormond, Castle Rockrent, Ennui*, and *Belinda*. Includes bibliography and index.

McCormack, W. J. *Ascendancy and Tradition in Anglo- Irish Literary History from 1789 to 1939*. Oxford, England: Clarendon Press, 1985. Intellectually far-reaching essay in the sociology of Irish literature firmly establishes the ideological lineage of Edgeworth's work, with special reference to the writings of Edmund Burke. Also assesses the role of Edgeworth's work in articulating the outlook of the author's social class.

Manly, Susan. "Maria Edgeworth and 'the Genius of the People.'" In *Language, Custom, and Nation in the 1790's: Locke, Tooke, Wordsworth, Edgeworth*. Burlington, Vt.: Ashgate, 2007. Analyzes Edgeworth's novels, demonstrating how these books, which were written during a period of Irish rebellion, reflect the contemporary political situation by their use of a vernacular language.

Nash, Julie. *Servants and Paternalism in the Works of Maria Edgeworth and Elizabeth Gaskell*. Burlington, Vt.: Ashgate, 2007. Examines the servant characters in Edgeworth's stories and novels, including *Belinda* and *Castle Rockrent*, to show how the author's nostalgia for a traditional ruling class conflicted with her interest in radical new ideas about social equality.

_____, ed. *New Essays on Maria Edgeworth*. Burlington, Vt.: Ashgate, 2006. Collection of essays analyzes Edgeworth's works—including *Belinda, Helen, Castle Rockrent, The Absentee*, and *Ennui*—from a variety of perspectives.

Ó Gallchoir, Clíona. *Maria Edgeworth: Women, Enlightenment, and Nation*. Dublin: University College Dublin Press, 2005. Presents a reassessment of Edgeworth's place in Irish literature, focusing on the author's views on gender and her depiction of Ireland from the 1790's to the aftermath of Catholic emancipation and parliamentary reform.

OLIVER GOLDSMITH

Born: Pallas, County Longford(?), Ireland; November 10, 1728 or 1730
Died: London, England; April 4, 1774

PRINCIPAL LONG FICTION

The Citizen of the World, 1762 (collection of fictional letters first published in
   The Public Ledger, 1760-1761)
The Vicar of Wakefield, 1766

OTHER LITERARY FORMS

Oliver Goldsmith contributed significantly to several literary genres. His works of poetry include *The Traveller: Or, A Prospect of Society* (1764) and *The Deserted Village* (1770), a classic elegiac poem of rural life. He wrote biographies as well, including *The Life of Richard Nash of Bath* (1762), which is especially valuable as a study in the social history of the period, *Life of Henry St. John, Lord Viscount Bolingbroke* (1770), and *Life of Thomas Parnell* (1770). Goldsmith developed principles of literary criticism in *An Enquiry into the Present State of Polite Learning in Europe* (1759), a history of literature in which he laments the decline of letters and morals in his own day. In addition to these publications and works of literary journalism that included humorous studies of London society, Goldsmith wrote two comic plays, *The Good-Natured Man* (pr., pb. 1768) and *She Stoops to Conquer: Or, The Mistakes of a Night* (pr., pb. 1773), a rollicking lampoon of the sentimental comedy then in vogue; *She Stoops to Conquer* is still performed today. In addition, Goldsmith published translations, histories, and even a natural history, *An History of the Earth, and Animated Nature* (1774), containing some quaint descriptions of animals.

ACHIEVEMENTS

Oliver Goldsmith's contemporaries and posterity have been somewhat ambivalent about his literary stature, which is epitomized in English writer Samuel Johnson's estimation of him: "Goldsmith was a man who, whatever he wrote, did it better than any other man could do." Johnson demurred on Goldsmith's *The Vicar of Wakefield*, however, judging it "very faulty." There can be little dispute over critic A. Lytton Sells's judgment that Goldsmith's "versatility was the most remarkable of his gifts."

Although the novel *The Vicar of Wakefield* has usually been considered his best work, Goldsmith despised the novelist's art and regarded himself principally as a poet. His most famous poem is the reflective and melancholic *The Deserted Village*, a serious piece in heroic couplets; however, perhaps his real poetic gift was for humorous verse, such as *The Haunch of Venison: A Poetical Epistle to Lord Clare* (1776) and "Retaliation" (1774). Indeed, humor and wit are conspicuous in all his major works: There is the gentle irony of

Oliver Goldsmith
(Library of Congress)

The Vicar of Wakefield, the comic portraits and satiric observations in *The Citizen of the World*, and the outright farce of *She Stoops to Conquer*.

Goldsmith was not a Romantic but a classicist by temperament, whose taste was molded by the Latin classics, the Augustan poetry of John Dryden and Alexander Pope, and seventeenth century French literature, and for whom the canons of criticism laid down by Nicolas Boileau-Despréaux and Voltaire were authoritative. Reflecting that background, Goldsmith's style is, in Johnson's words, "noble, elegant, and graceful."

BIOGRAPHY

Oliver Goldsmith was born of English stock to Ann Jones and the Reverend Charles Goldsmith, an Anglican curate. He first attended the village school of Lissoy and was taught by Thomas Byrne, a veteran of the War of the Spanish Succession. Byrne, a versifier who regaled his pupils with stories and legends of old Irish heroes, perhaps inspired Goldsmith with his love of poetry, imaginative romance, and adventure. In 1747, Goldsmith attended Patrick Hughes's school at Edgeworthstown, where he received a thorough grounding in the Latin classics. While there he probably first heard Turlogh O'Carolan, "the last of the bards," whose minstrelsy left a lasting impression on him. In 1745, he entered Trinity College, Dublin, as a sizar, a position that required him to do menial work in exchange for room, board, and tuition. Goldsmith earned his B.A. degree in either 1749 or 1750. In 1752, he journeyed to Edinburgh, Scotland, to study medicine, and he continued to pursue his medical studies at the University of Leiden, in the Netherlands, in 1754. The next year he set out on a grand tour of the Continent. In February, 1756, he arrived in London, where he briefly taught in Dr. Milner's school for nonconformists and eked out a living doing hack writing.

A reversal of his fortunes occurred in 1759 with the publication of his first substantial work, *An Enquiry into the Present State of Polite Learning in Europe*. Goldsmith subsequently befriended such luminaries as the great critic and writer Johnson, the Scottish novelist Tobias Smollett, the actor David Garrick, the writer and statesman Sir Edmund Burke, and the aesthetician and portraitist Sir Joshua Reynolds. In 1763, they formed themselves into the famous Literary Club, which is memorialized in James Boswell's great biography of Johnson. Goldsmith died in 1774, possibly of Bright's disease exacerbated by worry over debts, and was buried in Temple Churchyard. Two years later, the Literary Club erected a monument to him in Poet's Corner of Westminster Abbey, for which Johnson wrote an inscription.

ANALYSIS

The themes that run through Oliver Goldsmith's long fiction are his philosophical inquiries into human nature, the problem of evil, the vying of the good and the bad within the human breast, and the conflict between "reason and appetite." His fiction addresses at its deepest level the perennial problem of theodicy, or why God allows the innocent to suffer so grievously. Lien Chi in *The Citizen of the World* exclaims, "Oh, for the reason of our creation; or why we were created to be thus unhappy!" Dr. Primrose in *The Vicar of Wakefield* ruminates, "When I reflect on the distribution of good and evil here below, I find that much has been given man to enjoy, yet still more to suffer." Both come to terms with the conundrum of evil practically, by resolving, in Lien Chi's words, "not to stand unmoved at distress, but endeavour to turn every disaster to our own advantage."

THE CITIZEN OF THE WORLD

The ninety-eight essays that make up *The Citizen of the World* were originally published as the "Chinese Letters" in various issues of *The Public Ledger* from January 24, 1760, to August 14, 1761. They were subsequently collected and published in book form in 1762. These essays purport to be letters from Lien Chi Altangi, a Mandarin philosopher from Peking who is visiting London, to his son Hingpo and to Fum Hoam, first president of the Ceremonial Academy of Peking. This work may be classified as long fiction because of the well-delineated characters it creates and the interwoven stories it relates.

The principal character is Lien Chi, a type made familiar in the eighteenth century by Montesquieu's *Lettres persanes* (1721; *Persian Letters*, 1722). Lien Chi represents the man who, through travel, has overcome provincialism and prejudice and has achieved a cosmopolitan outlook. More specifically, perhaps, he represents the sociable, sanguine, and rational side of Goldsmith, who himself had traveled extensively in Europe.

To reinforce the notion that these are the letters of a Chinese man, Goldsmith studs them with Chinese idioms and makes references throughout to Asian beliefs, manners, and customs. Lien Chi cites the philosopher Confucius, and he compares the enlightenment of the East with the ignorance and folly of the West. *The Citizen of the World* capitalizes on the enthusiasm in eighteenth century England for anything Eastern—particularly Chinese—in the way of literature, fashion, design, and art, a vogue that Goldsmith satirizes through the bemused observations of Lien Chi.

Through the character of Lien Chi, a naïve but philosophically astute observer of the human scene, Goldsmith presents a full-blown satire of English society that is reminiscent of his compatriot Jonathan Swift's *Gulliver's Travels* (1726), but not so savage. In his letters, Lien Chi gives his impressions of the English, particularly of London society—their institutions, traditions, customs, habits, manners, foibles, and follies. He describes for readers a series of charming and funny pictures of London life in the eighteenth century, the literary equivalent of a William Hogarth painting. He shows readers coffeehouses, literary clubs, theaters, parks and pleasure gardens, churches, and private homes. Two scenes are particularly memorable: In one, Lien Chi describes a church service at St. Paul's Cathedral, where he mistakes the organ for an idol and its music for an oracle. In another scene, he attends a dinner for some clergy of the Church of England and is shocked to find that their sole topic of conversation is nothing more spiritual than the merits of the victuals they are intent on devouring. Aside from the entertainment and edification they afford, these letters are a document in social history, much like Samuel Pepys's diary.

While touring Westminster Abbey, Lien Chi meets and befriends the Man in Black, who represents the "melancholy man," a stock character of the Renaissance. He more particularly can be seen to represent Goldsmith's introverted and melancholy side. Through the Man in Black, Lien Chi meets Beau Tibbs, "an important little trifler" who is a rather shabby, snobbish, and pathetic fop who lives by flattering the rich and the famous. In a particularly comic scene, Lien Chi, the Man in Black, the pawnbroker's widow, Beau Tibbs, and his wife make a visit to Vauxhall Gardens. The Tibbses insist on having supper in "a genteel box" where they can both see and be seen. The pawnbroker's widow, the Man in Black's companion, heartily enjoys the meal, but Mrs. Tibbs detests it, comparing it unfavorably to a supper she and her husband lately had with a nobleman. Mrs. Tibbs is asked to sing but coyly declines; however, after repeated entreaties she obliges. During her song, an official announces that the waterworks are about to begin, which the widow is especially bent on seeing. Mrs. Tibbs, however, continues her song, oblivious to the discomfort she is causing, right through to the end of the waterworks. Goldsmith here anticipates Charles Dickens in his comic portrayal of character.

In addition to stories featuring the characters described above, *The Citizen of the World* includes Asian fables interspersed throughout, inspired no doubt by English translations of *The Arabian Nights' Entertainments* (fifteenth century). The *British Magazine* aptly described *The Citizen of the World* as "light, agreeable summer reading, partly original, partly borrowed." A. Lytton Sells regards the work as fundamentally a parody of the genre of satiric letters to which Montesquieu and Jean-Baptiste de Boyer had earlier contributed. It reveals Goldsmith at the top of his form as a humorist, satirist, and ironist.

THE VICAR OF WAKEFIELD

The Vicar of Wakefield, Goldsmith's only true novel, was published in 1766. It is a first-person narrative set in eighteenth century Yorkshire. It is largely autobiographical, with Dr. Primrose modeled on Goldsmith's father and brother and George modeled on Goldsmith himself. Goldsmith likely intended the work to satirize the then-fashionable sentimental novel, particularly Laurence Sterne's *The Life and Opinions of Tristram Shandy, Gent.* (1759-1767). Its style and conventions, such as digressions, charming pastoral scenes, and mistaken identities, are those of the eighteenth century English novel.

Dr. Charles Primrose, the vicar, narrates the story of his family's misfortunes. In addition to his wife, there are six children, among whom George, Olivia, and Sophia figure most prominently in the story. The vicar loses most of his inherited wealth to an unscrupulous banker, necessitating the removal of him and his family to a humbler abode. Their new landlord is Squire Thornhill, a notorious rake, whose uncle is Sir William Thornhill, a legendary benefactor. The family is subsequently befriended by Mr. Burchell and cheated by Ephraim Jenkinson.

Olivia is abducted, and, after a search, her father finds her in an inn, where she informs him that the squire had arranged her abduction and married her, as he had other women, in a false ceremony. The squire visits and invites Olivia to his wedding with Miss Wilmot, assuring Olivia that he will find her a suitable husband. Dr. Primrose is outraged, insisting that he would sanction only the squire's marriage to Olivia. He is subsequently informed of Olivia's death and of Sophia's abduction. Presently Mr. Burchell enters with Sophia, whom he has rescued from her abductor. It is now that Mr. Burchell reveals his true identity as Sir William Thornhill. Witnesses testify that the squire had falsely married Olivia and was complicit in Sophia's abduction. However, on the occasion of the squire's marriage to Olivia, the squire was tricked by Jenkinson with a real priest and marriage license. Jenkinson produces both the valid license and Olivia, having told Dr. Primrose that Olivia was dead in order to induce him to submit to the squire's terms and gain his release from prison.

The Vicar of Wakefield can be read on many levels. First, it is a charming idyll depicting the joys of country life. Second, it dramatizes the practical working-out of virtues such as benevolence and vices such as imprudence. Third, it severely tests seventeenth century German philosopher Gottfried Wilhelm Leibniz's dictum that we live in the best of all possible worlds where all things ultimately work for good. *The Vicar of Wakefield* is thus a philosophical romance, like Voltaire's *Candide: Ou, L'Optimisme* (1759; *Candide: Or, All for the Best*, 1759) and Johnson's *Rasselas, Prince of Abyssinia* (1759), that challenges the shallow optimism of the Enlightenment.

The *Vicar of Wakefield* has been criticized for its overly sentimentalized and idealized picture of English country life, its virtuous characters whose displays of courage in the face of adversity strain credulity, and its villains bereft of any redeeming virtue. Some commentators, however, see these apparent faults as integral to Goldsmith's ironic intention. E. A. Baker was the first to recognize that the work is ironic and comic. Robert Hopkins went further by claiming that Goldsmith intended Dr. Primrose "to satirise the complacency and materialism of a type of clergy."

Richard A. Spurgeon Hall

OTHER MAJOR WORKS

PLAYS: *The Good-Natured Man*, pr., pb. 1768; *She Stoops to Conquer: Or, The Mistakes of a Night*, pr., pb. 1773.

POETRY: "An Elegy on the Glory of Her Sex: Mrs. Mary Blaize," 1759; "The Logicians Refuted," 1759; *The Traveller: Or, A Prospect of Society*, 1764; "Edwin and Angelina," 1765; "An Elegy on the Death of a Mad Dog," 1766; *The Deserted Village*, 1770; "Threnodia Augustalis," 1772; "Retaliation," 1774; *The Haunch of Venison: A Poetical Epistle to Lord Clare*, 1776; "The Captivity: An Oratoria," 1820 (wr. 1764).

NONFICTION: *The Bee*, 1759 (essays); *An Enquiry into the Present State of Polite Learning in Europe*, 1759; *The Life of Richard Nash of Bath*, 1762; *An History of England in a Series of Letters from a Nobleman to His Son*, 1764 (2 volumes); *Life of Henry St. John, Lord Viscount Bolingbroke*, 1770; *Life of Thomas Parnell*, 1770; *An History of the Earth, and Animated Nature*, 1774 (8 volumes; unfinished).

MISCELLANEOUS: *The Collected Works of Oliver Goldsmith*, 1966 (5 volumes; Arthur Friedman, editor).

BIBLIOGRAPHY

Dixon, Peter. *Oliver Goldsmith Revisited*. Boston: Twayne, 1991. Informative introduction to the life and works of Goldsmith presents a discussion of *The Vicar of Wakefield* in chapter 4. Includes bibliography and index.

Donoghue, Frank. *The Fame Machine: Book Reviewing and Eighteenth-Century Literary Careers*. Stanford, Calif.: Stanford University Press, 1996. Examines the careers of Goldsmith and other authors to demonstrate how eighteenth century literary reviewers changed writers' and readers' perceptions of writers and their work.

Flint, Christopher. "'The Family Piece': Oliver Goldsmith and the Politics of the Everyday in Eighteenth-Century Domestic Portraiture." *Eighteenth-Century Studies* 29 (Winter, 1995/1996): 127-152. Argues that the family portrait in *The Vicar of Wakefield* is typical of family in eighteenth century culture, and claims that Goldsmith suggests that both the novel and portraiture are engaged in political acts of domestic regulation free of the corruption often associated with "politics."

Harkin, Maureen. "Goldsmith on Authorship in *The Vicar of Wakefield*." *Eighteenth Cen-*

tury Fiction 14 (April-July, 2002): 325. Analysis of the novel focuses on what Harkin describes as Goldsmith's "uncertainties about what the character and possibilities of his age are, especially for the writer and literary intellectual."

Hopkins, Robert H. *The True Genius of Oliver Goldsmith.* Baltimore: Johns Hopkins University Press, 1969. Interprets Goldsmith's work, not taking the traditional view of the author as a sentimental humanist but examining him as a master of satire and irony. Devotes a chapter each to Goldsmith's crafts of persuasion, satire, and humor, and a chapter titled "Augustanisms and the Moral Basis for Goldsmith's Art" delineates the social, intellectual, and literary contexts in which Goldsmith wrote. Includes a detailed examination of *The Vicar of Wakefield.*

Lucy, Séan, ed. *Goldsmith: The Gentle Master.* Cork, Ireland: Cork University Press, 1984. Brief collection of essays provides interesting biographical material on Goldsmith as well as critical commentary on his works. An essay on *The Vicar of Wakefield* identifies elements of the Irish narrative tradition in the novel.

Quintana, Richard. *Oliver Goldsmith: A Georgian Study.* New York: Macmillan, 1967. Incorporates biography and criticism in a readable account of Goldsmith's colorful life and his development as a writer. Discusses Goldsmith's works in many literary genres in depth, with chapters on his fiction, poetry, drama, and essays. A lengthy appendix offers notes on Goldsmith's lesser writings, such as his biographical and historical works.

Rousseau, G. S., ed. *Goldsmith: The Critical Heritage.* London: Routledge & Kegan Paul, 1974. This collection of critical commentary on Goldsmith is organized by particular works, with an additional section on Goldsmith's life and his works in general. Includes commentary written only up to 1912, but pieces by Goldsmith's contemporaries, such as Sir Joshua Reynolds's sketch of Goldsmith's character, and by later critics, such as William Hazlitt and Washington Irving, offer interesting perspectives on Goldsmith's place in literary history.

Sells, A. Lytton. *Oliver Goldsmith: His Life and Works.* New York: Barnes & Noble Books, 1974. Presents biographical information as well as discussion of the author's works. Individual chapters focus on particular facets of Goldsmith's work (such as "The Critic," "The Journalist," "The Biographer"), whereas others provide more detailed analysis of his major works, including *The Vicar of Wakefield.*

Swarbrick, Andrew, ed. *The Art of Oliver Goldsmith.* New York: Barnes & Noble Books, 1984. Excellent collection of ten essays offers a wide-ranging survey of Goldsmith's works. Essays treat individual works as well as more general topics, such as the literary context in which Goldsmith wrote, the elements of classicism in his works, and his place in the Anglo-Irish literary tradition.

JAMES HANLEY

Born: Dublin, Ireland; September 3, 1901
Died: London, England; November 11, 1985
Also known as: Patric Shone

PRINCIPAL LONG FICTION

Drift, 1930
Boy, 1931 (1990, unexpurgated)
Ebb and Flood, 1932
Captain Bottell, 1933
Resurrexit Dominus, 1934
The Furys, 1935
Stoker Bush, 1935
The Secret Journey, 1936
Hollow Sea, 1938
Our Time Is Gone, 1940
The Ocean, 1941
No Directions, 1943
Sailor's Song, 1943
What Farrar Saw, 1946
Emily, 1948
Winter Song, 1950
The House in the Valley, 1951 (as Patric Shone; also known as *Against the Stream*, 1981)
The Closed Harbour, 1952
The Welsh Sonata: Variations on a Theme, 1954
Levine, 1956
An End and a Beginning, 1958
Say Nothing, 1962
Another World, 1972
A Woman in the Sky, 1973
A Dream Journey, 1976
A Kingdom, 1978
Against the Stream, 1981

OTHER LITERARY FORMS

James Hanley was one of the most prolific of twentieth century writers. Apart from twenty-six novels and many volumes of short stories, he wrote a considerable number of plays for stage, radio, and television. *Say Nothing* (pr. 1961, broadcast) is a successfully produced play based on his novel by the same name. *Plays One* (1968) includes his famous play "The Inner Journey," which was staged at Lincoln Center, New York, to excellent critical reviews.

Hanley's *Broken Water: An Autobiographical Excursion* (1937) provides insights into his early life at sea and his determined efforts to become a writer. *Grey Children: A Study in Humbug and Misery* (1931), is a compassionate study of unemployment among miners in South Wales. *John Cowper Powys: A Man in the Corner* (1969) is a biographical and critical study of the English novelist whose *A Glastonbury Romance* (1932) was Hanley's favorite novel. In *Herman Melville: A Man in the Customs House* (1971), Hanley's own love for the sea enables him to present Melville from a refreshing new perspective. *Don Quixote Drowned* (1953) is a collection of essays, personal and literary. In one of these essays, Hanley includes a passage that describes himself as a "chunky realist and flounderer in off-Dreiserian prose, naïve and touchy about style." The volume also provides valuable information about some of the sources for Hanley's novels.

ACHIEVEMENTS

James Hanley is the neglected giant of modern literature. Around 1940, T. E. Lawrence found in Hanley's novels "a blistering vividness." E. M. Forster called him a novelist of distinction and originality. Henry Green considered him to be superior to Joseph Conrad. Herbert Read commented that Hanley was one of the most vigorous and impressive of contemporary writers. John Cowper Powys called Hanley "a genius." C. P. Snow recognized Hanley's humanity, compassion, and sheer imaginative power. Henry Miller wrote an enthusiastic introduction to the third edition (1946) of Hanley's novel *No Directions*. Yet, in spite of this impressive roster of applause, Hanley has been assessed as "one of the most consistently praised and least-known novelists in the English speaking world."

In the 1930's and early 1940's, Hanley was at the height of his popularity because of his novels about the war and some of the early volumes of the Fury saga. By the 1950's, however, his popularity had declined and his reading public was a small cult group; he was practically unknown in the United States. Hanley is a complex writer who demands from the reader the same undivided attention he devoted to his carefully conceived and crafted novels and plays. Irving Howe points out in his brilliant review of Hanley's *A Dream Journey* that

> Hanley's novels demand to be read slowly, in order to protect oneself from his relentlessness. It's like having your skin rubbed raw by a harsh wind, or like driving yourself to a rare pitch of truth by reflections—honest ones for a change—about the blunders of your life.

Hanley was not unduly concerned about the lack of a wider audience. He pursued his art with dedication and artistic integrity, he was uncompromising and unwilling to change his style to satisfy fluctuating fads and fashions of the literary world, and he survived completely through his writings. Maintaining such an authentic aesthetic individuality over a period of nearly sixty years was in itself a major achievement of James Hanley.

James Hanley was born on September 3, 1901, in Dublin, Ireland. Early in life, he moved with his family to Liverpool, England. Hanley's father, Edward Hanley, gave up a promising career in law for a life at sea, thereby grievously disappointing his mother; James Hanley was strongly counseled by his grandmother not to go to sea. The advice fell on deaf ears, however, and he left school at age fourteen and went to sea as a ship boy. Some of this experience undoubtedly provided him with the raw material for his novel *Boy*.

During Hanley's first transatlantic voyage, war broke out, and for two years he worked on troopships transporting soldiers across the Mediterranean to Salonika, Greece, and Gallipoli, Turkey. *Hollow Sea* draws upon this phase of his life and portrays the intensity of life on troopships during hazardous missions. At age sixteen, Hanley deserted his ship on a stopover in St. John, New Brunswick, Canada. He lied about his age, took on a name randomly selected from a telephone directory, and joined the Canadian army. After training in Canada and in England, he served in France. When he was discharged from the army and returned to England, he settled down with his parents in Liverpool.

In his autobiography, Hanley writes, "I had finished with the sea. I had finished with the army. I had had practically no education." He had seen the ugly and brutal face of war and survived the trauma. In Liverpool, he came across an old sailor friend to whom he had entrusted a letter to his mother with some money. The friend had taken the money and thrown away the letter, an incident that deeply affected Hanley. He made no more friends, and for the next ten years, he kept to himself like a hermit. He found a new personal meaning in the advice "never trust a friend," from August Strindberg's play *Bränea Tomten* (1907; *After the Fire: Or, The Burned Lot*). He took a job as a storeman on the railway and obsessively started on his self-education. He read voraciously during his spare time, studied French and Russian in evening classes, and indulged in his great passion for music as he struggled to play Bach and Beethoven with his small, rough, workingman's hands.

Hanley also wrote short stories and plays with dogged determination and collected a number of rejection slips. He was determined to write "until he was accepted" and completed a book titled *Soldier's Journal of the War*. He was asked to burn it, however, because, as he put it in his autobiographical *Broken Water*, "it went a bit too far as a picture of the war." He completed his first novel, *Drift*, and, after being rejected by eighteen publishers, it was finally published in 1930, with the support of publisher Eric Partridge. Hanley received five pounds and no royalties in payment.

Hanley's next project was to write "the odyssey of a ship" with no human characters. He abandoned that project and instead wrote the controversial novel *Boy*, which proved to be a major success. Hanley then commenced work on his major achievement, a five-volume saga of the Furys, a Liverpool family. The first volume was published in 1935 and the final volume in 1958. After publishing *Say Nothing* in 1962, Hanley abandoned the novel and wrote plays for the next ten years. In these plays, Hanley shows kinship with playwrights such as Harold Pinter, Samuel Beckett, and Strindberg. "I wrote plays for economic reasons," explained Hanley. "I even wrote under a pseudonym Patric Shone, hoping it might change my luck." In 1972, Hanley returned to the novel form with the publication of *Another World*.

Hanley suffered considerable piracy of his works. Notable examples are *A Passion Before Death* (1930), which was reissued in the United States in a limited edition without any remuneration to Hanley, and the play *Say Nothing*, which ran for two months in New York with Hanley receiving no royalties.

When Hanley wrote, he preferred to be in total isolation. He neither read nor talked with people while creating. "It's like a prisoner being a writer," Hanley said, and Wales provided him with a stimulating kind of solitude. As for the writing of the novel itself, to him it was a "series of blind gropings in a dark tunnel." Character in a novel was the most important feature to him. If after the third chapter, the characters took over the telling of the story, Hanley knew that his novel was going well.

Hanley settled in London but always regretted leaving Wales. His loneliness increased after his wife of more than forty years died in 1980 (they had one son, Liam, an artist). Hanley died in London in 1985.

ANALYSIS

Two themes dominate James Hanley's writings. The first concerns humans at sea in ships. Hanley explored, in each succeeding novel, the strange love-hate relationship that men and women have with the sea. The sea, with its violence and tranquillity, its many mysteries and its hypnotic powers over those who live and die by it, is orchestrated by him and becomes "the central experience of his novels." Hanley views the sea from the sailors' viewpoint, unlike Joseph Conrad, who sees the ship from the vantage point of an officer.

Hanley's second theme—often interrelated with the first—concerns men and women imprisoned in the web of poverty from which they have no desire to escape. They have created a world of deprivation for themselves and are terrified to come out of their self-imprisonment; within this confinement, they revolve and eke out their livelihood. Their despair leads them to weave private dreams, and their reluctance to realize their dreams returns them to despair. His characters, for the most part, are marginal people, the remnants of society, the debris of human life: outcasts, hobos, loners, strangers, broken men, women, and children. Hanley is their compassionate chronicler as he conducts a complex investigation into their lives and discovers poetry and drama in their bleak existence. With deep social concern, Hanley reveals how very much these marginal people matter: "the more insignificant a person is in this whirlpool of industrialized and civilized society, the more important he is for me." In making them touch the readers' wellsprings of compassion, Hanley achieved the hallmark of great literature; he moves readers emotionally.

BOY

The novel *Boy* has become a collector's item. In *Broken Water*, Hanley writes about seeing a boy in a Liverpool slum by the docks dragging a heavy cart "like a mule." The dull, vacant look on that boy's face profoundly touched Hanley and became the creative impulse for *Boy*. Also, in an autobiographical sketch titled "Oddfish," from *Don Quixote Drowned*, Hanley reports his sense of shock when he listened to an episode of a ship boy being thrown overboard because he had developed a contagious disease. The memory of that tale remained with him to become an integral part of *Boy*. Furthermore, in the earlier Hanley story *The German Prisoner* (1930), two mentally unbalanced British soldiers rape and brutalize a beautiful German boy. The passionate outrage against mindless violence coupled with a keen sense of social concern expressed in that story are also echoed in the novel.

Boy, because of its graphic descriptions of brutality, sadism, and homosexuality aboard a ship, was banned upon publication. The work became a cause célèbre, and E. M. Forster came to Hanley's defense. William Faulkner called *Boy* "a damn fine job. It springs up like a purifying cyclone, while most contemporary novels sound as if they were written by weaklings."

Boy is the brutal and tragic story of Arthur Fearon, a Liverpool schoolboy who has dreams of becoming a chemist. His sadistic father has more practical plans of having his son work on the docks to help liquidate family debts. He himself had a brutal job as a boy, and he cannot see a better life for his son. At the age of thirteen, Arthur is initiated into physical horrors by the gang on the dock. Arthur flees home and stows away in the coal bunker on a freighter going to Alexandria.

The boy's humiliating experiences, physical and sexual, on the freighter at the hands of almost everyone on board is the theme of *Boy*. A visit to a brothel in Alexandria, his initiation into manhood, is Arthur's one and only experience with beauty. The beauty of the girl soothes him, and "like a dark tapestry it covered his wounded thought, the spoliation, the degradation, the loneliness, the misery of his existence." From the encounter, he contracts syphilis and is shunned by all on the freighter. The ship's doctor wants Arthur to jump overboard and drown himself. Instead, however, the drunken captain gently invites Arthur to come to him by holding up his great coat, and, when Arthur responds unsuspectingly, the captain smothers him to death. The official report: "Boy was lost overboard."

In spite of all the brutality that Arthur faces, he maintains a boyish idealism to the very end. He remains uncorrupted and thereby heightens the sense of tragedy. The novel's strong connotations of sexual urge and clinical descriptions make it a naturalistic work reminiscent of Stephen Crane's *Maggie: A Girl of the Streets* (1893). The epitome of Hanley's technique and style—the use of letters to keep the flow of narrative, the grinding minutiae of financial details, descriptions that often read like stage directions, the longing for the past and the future because the present is so unbearable, prose rising to poetic eloquence when describing ships and sea—*Boy* is a blueprint of the author's craftsmanship and sets the tone for his later novels.

FURY FAMILY CHRONICLE

Comprising 2,295 pages and five volumes, the Fury family chronicle (*The Furys, The Secret Journey, Our Time Is Gone, Winter Song,* and *An End and a Beginning*) is Hanley's magnum opus. Set in Gelton, the fictional counterpart of Liverpool, the sequence of novels chronicles the saga of the Furys, a working-class Liverpool Irish family. Based on references to British and world events, a period of sixteen years from 1911 to 1927 is covered in the novel sequence. In some of the volumes, the period covered is very brief, as in the final volume, *An End and a Beginning,* where the time frame is only three weeks.

Dennis Fury, a seaman, is the main character in the saga. It is his wife, Fanny, however, who is the dominating force in the sequence. One of the most fully realized women in contemporary fiction, she is, as Edward Stokes points out in his study *The Novels of James Hanley* (1964), "both prosaic and legendary, at once middle-aged, dowdy, toil-worn, intensely respectable and bigoted housewife and a creature vital, passionate and a-moral as a heroine of Celtic myth." Fanny Fury holds both the novel and the Fury family together, and Hanley has fused into her something of the obsession of Lady Macbeth. Her son, Peter, whom she wants to be a priest against the wishes of the rest of her family, murders Anna Ragnar, the shrewd moneylender, and so splits the entire Fury family. Fanny uses all her efforts to bring the family together in a semblance of peace. The final novel in the sequence, *An End and a Beginning,* is devoted entirely to Peter Fury, and Hanley skillfully weaves the past and the present to maintain the narrative flow.

In anatomizing the intricacies of the family relationships within the Fury family, Hanley draws upon elements of Lawrentian brutality. Dennis Fury is pitted against his eighty-two-year-old father-in-law, Anthony Mangan, who is incapacitated; Fanny is pitted against her daughter Maureen's husband, John Kilkey, a devout pacifist; the whole family, with the exception of Fanny, is pitted against Peter, who is studying to be a priest at their expense; Fanny and Dennis themselves are locked in ferocious combat concerning a multitude of daily minutiae. Hanley's use of dialogue to reveal these hostilities is crisp, direct, and theatrical in the best sense of the term.

The imagery of a prison dominates the entire saga. To Peter, the seminary is a prison; to Dennis, his home is a prison and the sea is freedom; to Fanny the sea is a steel trap taking away her men, and her very desire to keep the family together imprisons her in her responsibilities; Anthony Mangan, paralyzed and mute, finds that the chair in which he is strapped is his prison, physically and verbally; Peter Fury murders the moneylender and cries out that he is free from debt only to find himself behind prison bars. All the characters in the Fury chronicle are attempting to escape their prisons but find themselves in darker traps for doing so. Hanley has worked out his imagery of frustration, loneliness, and inability to communicate throughout the saga, and an entire study can be made about prison imagery in his novels.

Hanley creates a scene, introduces his characters, gives readers an intense close-up, and reveals his characters through dialogue and intimate conversation. There are always passages of lyrical beauty whenever the sea or a ship is described. Letters, journals, and inner monologues are all used to tell the story and reveal insights into a variety of characters that populate the chronicle. There are a few noteworthy characters among the many found in the novels: John Kilkey, physically repulsive, is a man of deep principles and compassion and a pacifist; Brigid Mangan, Fanny's youngest sister, is a spinster and a devout Catholic strongly feeling her alienation in England and eager to return to her spiritual home, Ireland; Desmond Fury, the eldest son, is ambitious and deeply involved in Labour politics, and his wife, Sheila, has an adulterous affair with Peter Fury; Mrs. Anna Ragner, the sharp moneylender, enjoys having people in her grip and getting rich on poverty; Professor R. H. Titmouse, a self-appointed professor of anthropology, is gay and has a hysterical crush on Peter but acts at times as the voice of sanity when he tells Peter that people are merely sheep ready to be manipulated by politicians. These and a host of other characters give the Fury chronicle a deep richness and diversity of humanity.

The saga of the Furys, however, has not received a great deal of critical attention. It is a work that is original, sustained, and above all, as Edward Stokes maintains, a "compassionate penetration into the dreams and desperations, the illusions and longings of the characters" that move throughout this epic work.

HOLLOW SEA

The years between 1938 and 1943 were a peak period in Hanley's creativity. He wrote three significant novels about ships and sailors, against the backdrop of war: *Hollow Sea*, *The Ocean*, and *Sailor's Song*. The first novel is set within the time frame of a few weeks and is a story of a troopship. A former liner called *Helicon*, the vessel is painted gray and called *A10* and is involved in a war mission to transport fifteen hundred soldiers to a secret destination. To Captain Dunford, *A10* is "the personification of uncontrollable madness"; to the men in overcrowded holds with shortages of food and water, life aboard the *A10* is nasty, brutish, and uncertain. The ship bristles with tensions, and the voyage becomes "a microcosm of a whole world at war." During the voyage, *A10* gets into a violent and bloody skirmish and is compelled to add another two hundred soldiers to its population. Without adequate hospital facilities, the men die, and the ship's captain refuses to bury them without proper authorization. *A10* becomes "a coffin ship" and pressures intensify. Some men capitalize on the tensions and shortages by carrying on a black market in food; others seek escape in fantasy, letting their minds conjure images of reaching home and reunion with their families.

Hanley characterizes vividly the various men on the ship, from the captain who is "imprisoned by his mission," and hence must be totally authoritative, to boatswain Vesuvius with an "eruption of pimples on his face." There is, however, a poetic quality to the novel that echoes the legend of the Flying Dutchman and the eerie atmosphere evoked by Samuel Taylor Coleridge in *The Rime of the Ancient Mariner* (1798). Edwin Muir felicitously noted this in his review of the novel: "*Hollow Sea*'s great virtue is that it is poetically conceived. We are always conscious that the events that Hanley is describing are part of a large pattern." *Hollow Sea* captures the hustle, the bustle, and the ceaseless throb of life aboard a troopship, and had it not been so long, it would have emerged as a great novel.

THE OCEAN

A tight, short, well-structured novel, *The Ocean* is a powerful study in survival. The entire action takes place in an open boat containing five men: Joseph Curtain, the sailor; Father Michaels, a priest; Gaunt, a middle-aged businessman, who worries about his missing wife, Kay; Stone, a middle-aged teacher; and twenty-year-old Benton. These are the survivors from the torpedoed ship *Aurora*. Hanley has endowed a timeless quality to his story by not giving it a local habitation or a specific time. The reader is constantly made aware of the loneliness and helplessness of these men in the middle of the vast empty sea, which is full of beauty and terror.

Joseph Curtain is the key character in the novel. He knows how to deal with the men and can operate on the whole spectrum of human emotions. There is a lean, spare athletic quality to Hanley's prose in *The Ocean*, an economy of word and style that is reminiscent of the best of Ernest Hemingway. It is remarkable that Hanley, who wrote the long, discursive *Hollow Sea*, could also write *The Ocean*: it is one of his very best.

SAILOR'S SONG

The last of Hanley's sea novels, *Sailor's Song*, is set on a raft and concerns four men. The story, told with biblical simplicity and lyrical beauty, is the story of the delirious sailor, Manion, on the raft. Manion's name is a play on "any man." Carefully, through a series of broken images and shuttling back and forth through the corridors of time, Manion's tale—the sailor's song—is unfolded. Manion is the captive of the sea, hypnotized and held by it. Through his life, Hanley distills the strange umbilical feelings that sailors have for the sea and ships. Delirious, Manion remembers his past, particularly the time when he was without a ship and became restless looking for one, believing in a miracle that would result in his signing on another ship. Hanley was also to use this theme—of a sailor desperately looking for a home, a ship on which to sign—in his novel *The Closed Harbour*. After he has sung his song, told his story, John Manion drifts in his sleep to death. *Sailor's Song* is perhaps Hanley's most moving novel.

THE CLOSED HARBOUR

Continuing to master his primary themes of the sea and entrapment, Hanley's creative talents are not exhausted. *The Closed Harbour*, set in Marseilles, is Hanley's only novel with a non-English setting. It is a powerful and intense study of a French merchant captain, Marius, who is under a cloud of suspicion. He wants to get a ship, but none is available. Hanley relentlessly probes Marius's mind, moving back and forth in a fascinating study of a haunted man. George Painter in reviewing the novel rightly pointed out that

Marius "is a figure worthy of Melville, a fallen angel, a monument of man's grandeur in defeat." Felix Levine, of *Levine*, like Marius, is a man without a ship, but Felix is also a man without a country: He is the quintessential displaced person. Felix is a typical Hanley character, who obsessively dreams and weaves fantasies and begins to believe in them so passionately that dreams become his reality. The entire novel itself is a backward dream, and through a series of interior monologues, diaries, and letters, Hanley orchestrates all the subtle nuances that make up the dark despair of loneliness and hunger.

A DREAM JOURNEY

Hanley's 1976 novel, *A Dream Journey*, is the best introduction to Hanley. The story of Clem Stevens, an artist, and his wife, Lena, it is the single novel that distills all of Hanley's themes, styles, concerns, and characterizations. Clem and Lena both appeared earlier in Hanley's short novel *No Directions*. Since Hanley has said that novel writing is a "series of blind gropings in a long dark tunnel," it seems that he looked back at the tunnel where he had left the characters from *No Directions* and found that "they were not so limp" as he had thought they were and so he "gave each character an extra squeeze." In fact, the longest section in *A Dream Journey*, "Yesterday," is the entire text of *No Directions*.

The novel opens in typical Hanley fashion, "a monosyllabic session." The moment a thought appears in the mind of one of the characters, the scene accompanying that thought is conjured in the mind of that character. Everyone is on a dream journey, and dreaming becomes a metaphor for living for both Clem and his wife. They use their dreams to seek tranquillity from the harshness of life by "fondling memories" in their minds.

Clem suffers from depression and has not left his house in more than a year. He has painted a sixty-year-old woman on five canvases, reflecting a whole day in her life, "a whole language of exhaustion." Clem seems to do in painting what Hanley does with words. Yet, Clem is not a successful artist; his paintings sold to the butcher get him "free meat for a month." Lena is his encourager, but the days grind out in sheer monotony, and there is no communication between them. They turn to the past and, in their minds, go on dream journeys. Their small claustrophobic rooms imprison them. Lena thinks of leaving Clem, but "you don't just walk out on a person because he's second rate"; furthermore, "people don't escape from their own illusions, you just live with them." In a way, she enjoys Clem's dependence on her. When the final catastrophe happens—a fire and Clem's death as he attempts to rescue his paintings—it is a logical conclusion based on the characters' "realities." In *A Dream Journey*, Hanley brings to bear the maturity and careful artistry of his talents.

Readers who are familiar with Hanley's works find new meanings and subtle nuances in his writings with each rereading. Those who have the patience to approach and discover his fiction for the first time will be richly rewarded with a satisfying literary and emotional experience. His position as a major literary figure in the twentieth century is firmly established.

K. Bhaskara Rao

OTHER MAJOR WORKS

SHORT FICTION: *The German Prisoner,* 1930; *A Passion Before Death,* 1930; *The Last Voyage,* 1931; *Men in Darkness: Five Stories,* 1931; *Aria and Finale,* 1932; *Stoker Haslett,* 1932; *Quartermaster Clausen,* 1934; *At Bay,* 1935; *Half an Eye: Sea Stories,* 1937; *People Are Curious,* 1938; *At Bay, and Other Stories,* 1944; *Crilley, and Other Stories,* 1945; *Selected Stories,* 1947; *A Walk in the Wilderness,* 1950; *Collected Stories,* 1953; *The Darkness,* 1973; *What Farrar Saw, and Other Stories,* 1984; *The Last Voyage, and Other Stories,* 1997.

PLAYS: *Say Nothing,* pr. 1961 (broadcast); *The Inner Journey,* pb. 1965; *Plays One,* 1968 (collection).

NONFICTION: *Broken Water: An Autobiographical Excursion,* 1937; *Grey Children: A Study in Humbug and Misery,* 1937; *Between the Tides,* 1939; *Don Quixote Drowned,* 1953; *John Cowper Powys: A Man in the Corner,* 1969; *Herman Melville: A Man in the Customs House,* 1971.

BIBLIOGRAPHY

Dentith, Simon. "James Hanley's *The Furys*: The Modernist Subject Goes on Strike." *Literature and History* 12, no. 1 (Spring, 2003): 41-56. Dentith analyzes *The Furys*, discussing the influence of modernism on Hanley's writing, the novel's issues of subjectivism, and its depiction of collective life.

Fordham, John. *James Hanley: Modernism and the Working Class.* Cardiff: University of Wales Press, 2002. Fordham examines Hanley's life and writings, concluding that the author's works, which often have been described as "proletarian realism," should be identified more accurately as modernism. He places Hanley's work within a cultural and social context and examines the author's association with Wales, where Hanley lived for more than thirty years.

Harrington, Frank G. *James Hanley: A Bold and Unique Solitary.* Francestown, N.H.: Typographeum, 1989. A good biographical account, written by a friend of Hanley. Includes a list of Hanley's books.

Mathewson, Ruth. "Hanley's Palimpsest." *New Leader,* January 3, 1977. Reviews *A Dream Journey,* noting that it is a good introduction to Hanley's work. Mathewson also briefly discusses Hanley's earlier novels and comments that *A Dream Journey* is a "palimpsest" of his earlier works.

Vinson, James, ed. *St. James Reference Guide to English Literature.* Chicago: St. James Press, 1985. A critical piece by Edward Stokes cites the importance of Hanley's writing, which has been compared to that of Thomas Hardy and Fyodor Dostoevski. Notes, however, that Hanley's work is uneven and his characters lacking in popular appeal.

Wade, Stephen. "James Hanley: A Case for Reassessment." *Contemporary Review* 274 (June, 1999): 307-310. Wade provides a brief, critical overview of Hanley's fiction, arguing that the author remains relevant and deserves to be reread and reconsidered. While he acknowledges that Hanley's output is uneven, he cites six works that are worthy of special attention, including the novels *Boy*, *The Furys*, *No Directions*, and *The Welsh Sonata*.

Williams, Patrick. "'No Struggle but the Home': James Hanley's *The Furys*." In *Recharting the Thirties*, edited by Patrick J. Quinn. Selinsgrove, Pa.: Susquehanna University Press, 1996. William's essay on Hanley's 1935 novel *The Furys* is included in this essay collection that seeks to refamiliarize readers with British authors who have been largely ignored since their major works first appeared in the 1930's. The essay is preceded by a brief biographical sketch of Hanley.

JAMES JOYCE

Born: Dublin, Ireland; February 2, 1882
Died: Zurich, Switzerland; January 13, 1941
Also known as: James Augustine Aloysius Joyce

PRINCIPAL LONG FICTION

A Portrait of the Artist as a Young Man, 1914-1915 (serial), 1916 (book)
Ulysses, 1922
Finnegans Wake, 1939
Stephen Hero, 1944

OTHER LITERARY FORMS

James Joyce commenced his literary career as a poet, essayist, and dramatist, under the influences of William Butler Yeats and Henrik Ibsen, respectively. His *Collected Poems* (1936) contains *Chamber Music* (1907), thirty-six lyrics written before 1904, and *Pomes Penyeach* (1927), eleven poems written after he had made his commitment to prose fiction. His first published essay, "Ibsen's New Drama" (1900), announced his admiration for the Norwegian dramatist; the same attitude is implied in his only original surviving play, *Exiles* (pb. 1918).

Miscellaneous literary essays, program and lecture notes, reviews, journalism, and two broadsides are collected in *The Critical Writings of James Joyce* (1959). Joyce's correspondence is contained in *Letters of James Joyce* (1957-1966), with some additions in *Selected Letters of James Joyce* (1975).

Through the compilation of fifteen short stories in *Dubliners* (1914), written between 1904 and 1907, Joyce discerned his métier. This apparently random, realistic series was the first announcement of its author's singular genius. While the volume retains a "scrupulously mean" accuracy in regard to naturalistic detail, it also incorporates a multiplicity of complex symbolic patterns. An ephemeral story, "Giacomo Joyce" (1918), was written as he completed *A Portrait of the Artist as a Young Man* and began *Ulysses* in 1914. The collaboration of several editors has produced in facsimile almost the entire Joyce "workshop"—notes, drafts, manuscripts, typescripts, and proofs—in sixty-four volumes (*The James Joyce Archives*, 1977-1979), a project of unprecedented magnitude for any twentieth century author.

ACHIEVEMENTS

From the beginning of his literary career, James Joyce was the most distinctive figure in the renaissance that occurred in Irish cultural life after the death of Charles Stewart Parnell. Despite his early quarrels with Yeats, John Millington Synge, and other leaders of the Irish Literary Revival, and his subsequent permanent exile, he is clearly, with Yeats, its

James Joyce
(Library of Congress)

presiding genius. From the first, he set himself to liberate Ireland, not by returning to Celtic myths or the Gaelic language and folklore, but by Europeanizing its cultural institutions. His early stories are an exorcism of the spirit of paralysis he felt about himself in the Dublin of his youth. As he gained detachment from these obstacles and knowledge of his own capacities as a writer of prose fiction, he produced two of the undisputed masterworks of modern literature, *A Portrait of the Artist as a Young Man* and *Ulysses*, as well as a final work that is perhaps beyond criticism, *Finnegans Wake*.

Throughout this development, Joyce's themes and subjects remain the same, yet his means become more overtly complex: the fabulous comedy, the multivalent language, and the vast design of *Ulysses* and *Finnegans Wake* are strands in the reverse side of the sedulously restrained tapestry of *Dubliners* and *A Portrait of the Artist as a Young Man*.

Joyce's cast of characters is small, his Dublin settings barely change from work to work, he observes repeatedly certain archetypal conflicts beneath the appearances of daily life, and his fiction is marked by certain obsessions of his class, religion, and nationality. Yet his single-mindedness, his wide learning in European literature, his comprehensive grasp of the intellectual currents of the age, his broad comic vision, his vast technical skills, and above all, his unequaled mastery of language, make him at once a Europeanizer of Irish literature, a Hibernicizer of European literature, and a modernizer of world literature.

BIOGRAPHY

James Augustine Aloysius Joyce was born in Dublin, Ireland, on February 2, 1882, the first of John Joyce and Mary Murray's ten children. During the years of Joyce's youth, his father wasted the family's substantial resources based on properties in Cork City; Joyce, at the same time, grew to reject the pious Catholicism of his mother. Except for a brief period, his education was in the hands of the Jesuits: at Clongowes Wood College, the less exclusive Belvedere College, and finally at University College, Dublin, from which he graduated in 1902. Joyce quickly outgrew his mentors, however, so that the early influences of the Maynooth Catechism and Saints Ignatius Loyola and Thomas Aquinas yielded to his own eclectic reading in European literature, especially Dante, Ibsen, Gerhart Hauptmann, and Gustave Flaubert. Politically, he retained his father's Parnellite Irish nationalism, modified by a moderate socialism. Despite his declared abjuration of Catholicism and the Irish political and cultural revivals, he continued to pay to each a proud and private subscription. He considered the professions of music and medicine (briefly attending the École de Medicine in Paris in 1902) before eventually leaving Ireland in October, 1904, for Europe and a literary career. He was accompanied by Nora Barnacle, a Galway-born chambermaid whom he had met the previous June, who became the mother of his two children, Georgio and Lucia, and whom he formally married in 1931.

Between 1904 and the conclusion of World War I, the Joyces lived successively in Trieste, Rome, Pola, and Zurich, where Joyce supported his wife and family by teaching English for the Berlitz schools, bank clerking, and borrowing from his brother Stanislaus, who had joined them in 1905. The *Dubliners* stories, begun shortly before he left Ireland, were finished with "The Dead" in 1907, but it was another seven years of wrangling with Irish and British publishers over details that were considered either libelous or indecent before the volume was published. By then, Joyce had fully rewritten *Stephen Hero*, a loose, naturalistic, and semiautobiographical novel, as the classic of impressionism, *A Portrait of the Artist as a Young Man*. Ezra Pound, then the literary editor of *The Egoist*, recognized the work's permanence, published it in serial form, and recommended its author to the patronage of Harriet Weaver, who anonymously provided Joyce with a handsome annuity for the rest of his life.

Based on this material support and the establishment of his literary reputation, Joyce worked on *Ulysses* in Trieste, Zurich, and Paris, where he moved in 1920. Meanwhile, beginning in March, 1918, Margaret Anderson and Jane Heap's *Little Review* (New York) was publishing the separate episodes of *Ulysses*. The prosecution and conviction in February, 1921, of its two publishers for obscenity gave the novel a wide notoriety that preceded its publication in Paris by Sylvia Beach's Shakespeare and Company on its author's fortieth birthday.

Joyce then became an international celebrity and the center of literary life in Paris during the 1920's. Between 1922 and 1939, he worked on *Finnegans Wake*, which, under the title "Work in Progress," appeared in Eugene Jolas's *transition* and other avant-garde journals. During this period of his life, Joyce contended with the pirating and banning of *Ulysses* in the United States, the worsening condition of his eyes, which required eleven separate operations, his daughter's schizophrenia, and the loss of many of his earlier admirers because of their puzzlement with or hostility toward the experimentation of *Ulysses* and especially of "Work in Progress."

As World War II approached, *Finnegans Wake* was published, and the Joyces moved once again, to neutral Zurich. Following an operation for a duodenal ulcer, Joyce died there on January 13, 1941. With Nora (who died in 1951), he is buried in Flüntern Cemetery, Zurich, beneath Milton Hebald's sprightly statue.

ANALYSIS

The leaders of the Irish Literary Revival were born of the Anglo-Irish aristocracy. Very few were Catholics, and none was from the urban middle class, except James Joyce. The emphasis of the Revival in its early stages on legendary or peasant themes and its subsequent espousal of a vaguely nationalistic and unorthodox religious spirit kept it at a certain distance from popular pieties. It did no more than gesture toward Europe, and it registered very little of the atrophied state of middle- and lower-class city life.

The first to deal with this latter theme realistically, Joyce made a bold show as a "Europeanizer" and openly criticized "patriotic" art. Despite his disdain for contemporary political and literary enthusiasms, his dismissal of Celtic myths as "broken lights," his characterization of the folk imagination as "senile," and his relative ignorance of the Gaelic language, however, his imaginative works are as thoroughly and distinctively Irish as those of William Butler Yeats, John Millington Synge, or Lady Augusta Gregory.

From his earliest childhood, Joyce was aware of the political controversies of the day, observing the conflict between the idealized Charles Stuart Parnell and the ultramontane Church that permanently marked his outlook on Irish public affairs. His faith in Irish nationalist politics and in Catholicism was broken even as it was formed, and soon he launched himself beyond the pales of both, by exile and apostasy, proclaiming that each had betrayed his trust. The supersaturation of his consciousness with the language, attitudes, and myths of Church and State was formative, however, as all of his work documents: *Dubliners*, *A Portrait of the Artist as a Young Man*, *Ulysses*, and *Finnegans Wake* are unparalleled as a record of the "felt history" of Edwardian Dublin, or indeed of any city in modern literature.

From the beginning, Joyce's scrupulous naturalism belied his symbolist tendencies. The revisions of his early stories, and the transformation of *Stephen Hero* into the impressionistic bildungsroman of *A Portrait of the Artist as a Young Man*, indicate that he recognized among his own powers of observation and language a special capacity to decode the socialization process—an aptitude, as he put it, for "epiphany." At certain moments in an otherwise continuous state of paralysis, the truth reveals itself and the spirit is liberated from a conditioned servility. The repeated use of carefully selected words can, without neglecting the obligation to realistic fidelity, have the harmonious and radiant effect of a symbol.

As Joyce's technical skills grew, he extended this principle so that in *Ulysses* the structural symbols become one, while at the same time the demands of realism were superseded. The tendencies implied in this shift have their apotheosis in *Finnegans Wake*. From 1922 to 1939, Joyce was very long removed from the Dublin he had known, and he had come to understand his own genius for language ("I find that I can do anything I like with it"). Drawing on an encyclopedic range of materials, he wrote this final, most challenging work, in which the world of the unconscious, or the sleeping mind, is represented not by realism but by multivalent language and the timeless action of archetypal characters.

In eschewing the narrow confines set by the Irish revival, Joyce turned to the masters of classical and modern European literature for his models: to Homer for his Odysseus, the hero to set against the Christian Savior and the Irish Cuchulain; to Dante for his multiplex realization of Catholic phantasmagoria; to William Shakespeare for his language and his treatment of family relations; and to Henrik Ibsen for his disciplined criticism of modern bourgeois life. Under these influences, Joyce's art developed along highly formalist lines, and mythological antecedents stalk his modern lower-middle-class characters. The effects of such comparisons are, to various ends, ironic; the ordinary Dublin characters lack the remove, heroism, and familiarity with gods or demons of their classic counterparts. Instead, they exhibit various neurotic symptoms associated with modern urban life—repression, anxiety, fetishism, and the confusion of great and small virtue. In these four respects then—in the predilection for formalism, mythologization, irony, and the subject of individual consciousness—Joyce establishes the methods and the subject of literary modernism.

A PORTRAIT OF THE ARTIST AS A YOUNG MAN

A Portrait of the Artist as a Young Man is a semiautobiographical bildungsroman describing the development of the sensibility of Stephen Dedalus from his earliest childhood recollections to the beginnings of manhood. The work evolved from the narrative essay "A Portrait of the Artist" (January, 1904), and its expansion into *Stephen Hero*, an undisguised autobiographical novel in the naturalist tradition. The result of this evolution was a startlingly original composition: a highly structured, symbolic, impressionistic, and ironic treatment of the spiritual formation and reformation of an acutely sensitive young man. Stephen's conscience absorbs the values of his Irish Catholic family; by a progressively more complex use of language and technique through the five chapters of the novel, Joyce portrays that conscience undergoing a process of simultaneous severance and refinement. The conclusion of the process, however, is paradoxical, for as Stephen declares his determination to free himself of the claims of the formative establishments of his family, nation, and religion by setting against them the proud and defiant slogan "silence, exile, and cunning," the terms by which that defiance is made have already been set. Like his language, Stephen's conflicts with the virtues advocated by the three establishments are not different in kind but more profound than those of his fellows. It is one of Joyce's many ironies in *A Portrait of the Artist as a Young Man* that Stephen mistakes these conflicts for a radical independence of spirit. Like Icarus, his mythological antecedent, his destiny is not to escape from the paternal labyrinths, but to fall from the heights of supercilious pride.

One of the signal achievements of the novel is Joyce's management of the distance between reader and protagonist: As Stephen grows older, he becomes less amiable. This distance is achieved by a multiplicity of devices: the subtle weighing of names, the acute selection of sensuous detail, the exaggeration of language, the ironic structure, the counterpointing of incidents, and the elaborate systematizing of all devices. The endearing sensitivity and naïveté of the child slowly yield to the self-absorbed priggishness of the young man.

Chapter 1 is composed of four sections: random sensations of early childhood, Stephen's illness (at approximately seven years) at Clongowes Wood College, the Christmas dinner scene, and Stephen's first victory over injustice—Father Dolan's punishment. Each section gathers materials that dramatize the mysterious interplay of private sensation, communal constraint, and language. Each section culminates in an "epiphany," a metatheological term for "a sudden spiritual manifestation" when a response betrays its socially conditioned origin, and the true feeling or idea radiates forth with the force of a symbol.

The opening section in the language of a preschool child is the kernel out of which the entire work develops. It distinguishes in a rudimentary, purely sensory manner the symbols and themes that will preoccupy Stephen: women, road, rose, paternity, flight, creation, the relationship between experience and the representation of it, his own distinctness, guilt, and the demands of home, religion, and nation.

Stephen's illness at Clongowes Wood College causes him to meditate on the repugnance of physical life and his attraction to mysterious realms of religion and language, an association that is later to prove axial. The Christmas dinner scene, on the other hand, is a brilliant dramatization of the tension between the three establishments and the threats they pose to Parnell and Stephen, heroes alike. In the final section, Stephen successfully protests an unjust school punishment.

Chapter 2 is composed of a series of some dozen epiphanies developing the themes of

Stephen's gradual estrangement from his family, particularly his father, and his perception of sexual identification, leading to his liberation from innocence in the embrace of a prostitute. Among the revelations in this chapter is the news of the Rector's real attitude toward Father Dolan's treatment of Stephen; the jocosity of this attitude deflates the climax of chapter 1. When, in chapter 3, Stephen repents of his sin with the prostitute, the pattern of reversal repeats itself, and the structural irony in the novel is revealed. This chapter falls into three sections—the states of sin, repentance, and grace mediated by the memorable sermon on hell. This terrifying exposition (based on the procedures for spiritual meditation propounded by the *Spiritual Exercises* of Ignatius Loyola) leads Stephen to contrition, confession, and communion, each treated with a certain degree of irony. Not the least of the ironies here is Stephen's dissociated sensibility, as implied in the final page of chapter 3 and expanded in the opening section of chapter 4. The true state of his feelings is elucidated in the course of the succeeding two sections: his consideration and rejection of the priestly vocation and his ecstatic response to the call to the priesthood of the imagination. He rejects the priesthood because of its orderliness and uniformity; the life of community is removed from the risks inherent in secular life, and it denies individual freedom. His response to the muse is, however, heavily overlaid with images of the mysteries of the service of the altar. In this climactic epiphany, Stephen risks loneliness and error to transform in freedom the stuff of ordinary experience into the permanent forms of secular art. In response to the messenger, girl-bird-angel, he accepts a vocation that in the cause of self-expression will set him apart from all institutions.

In the final chapter, Stephen attempts an exorcism of each aspect of the culture that would possess his soul. To this end, he engages in a dialogue with a series of companions who advance three claims: McCann and Davin (international and national politics); Father Darlington and Lynch (servile, practical, or kinetic arts); and Cranly (conventional morality and religion). In the course of the perambulations accompanying *apologia pro futura sua*, Stephen sets forth his aesthetic theory, which in its refusal to grant overt moral purpose to art owes more to Walter Pater than to Aquinas. The pallid "Villanelle of the Temptress" comes as an anticlimax on the heels of such brilliant theorizing and raises the question of Stephen's capacities as a creative artist as opposed to those of an aesthete or poseur. The concluding section, comprising the diary entries from the five weeks preceding Stephen's departure, at once recapitulates the themes of the entire novel and anticipates Stephen's commitment to the proud and lonely life of the committed artist. The impression that this sequence of startling entries makes is of an irony of another kind: Stephen has unknowingly stumbled upon a technique that takes him closer to his creator and to the tenor of twentieth century literature than his self-absorbed and self-conscious villanelle. Thus, at the conclusion of *A Portrait of the Artist as a Young Man*, Stephen has yet to acquire a moral awareness, develop human sympathies, or discern his own voice.

ULYSSES

The Stephen Dedalus of *Ulysses* has returned to Ireland after a brief sojourn in Paris. He has acquired a few new affectations from that experience, is intensely guilt-ridden over his mother's suffering and death, teaches ineffectually at a Dublin boys' school, lives with some companions in a Martello tower, makes desultory efforts at writing poetry, speculates sensitively on a variety of epistemological, theological, and metaphysical questions, theorizes ostentatiously on Shakespeare's psychobiography, delivers himself of cryptic remarks and oblique anecdotes, and wastes his salary on prostitutes and drink. Despite his dissolution and moodiness, however, the Stephen of *Ulysses* is considerably more receptive to the world of ordinary experience that whirls around him than the protagonist of *A Portrait of the Artist as a Young Man*. Leopold Bloom is the personification of that world.

Bloom is a thirty-eight-year-old Irish Jew of Hungarian extraction. A family man, he has a wife, Molly, four years his junior, and a daughter Milly, age fifteen; a son, Rudy, died in infancy. Bloom is observant and intelligent despite his lack of higher education. He lives in Eccles Street and works as an advertising salesman for a daily newspaper. The key event of the day on which the action of *Ulysses* takes place—June 16, 1904—is Molly's infidelity (of which Bloom is aware) with an impresario named Blazes Boylan. During the course of the day, between 8 A.M. and approximately 3 A.M. on June 17, the reader follows Bloom's thoughts and movements as he manages to retain an equilibrium between many demands and disappointments.

Bloom serves his wife breakfast in bed, takes a bath, corresponds with an epistolary lover, attends a funeral, attempts to secure an ad from a firm by the name of Keyes, has lunch, is misunderstood over a horse race, is insulted and almost attacked in a bar, becomes sexually aroused by an exhibitionist girl on the beach, and inquires about a friend at a maternity hospital, where he encounters Stephen Dedalus carousing with sundry dissolutes. Feeling protective of Stephen, he pursues him to a brothel and subsequently rescues him from brawlers and police, taking him home for a hot drink. Bloom retires, noting the signs of Blazes Boylan's recent occupation of the marital bed. Throughout these physical events, Bloom's consciousness plays with myriad impressions and ideas serious and trivial, from his wife's infidelity to imperfectly remembered incidents from his childhood. He also proves himself to be a resilient, considerate, humorous, prudent, and even-tempered man. As the novel progresses, Bloom, certainly one of the most completely realized characters in fiction, grows in the reader's affections and estimation.

Molly, as revealed to the reader in the famous soliloquy of the final chapter, is a substantial embodiment of the anima. Born in Gibraltar of a Spanish mother and an English military father who later took her to Dublin, Molly is a superstitious Catholic, a plainspoken, amoral, fertile, sensual, passive beauty. She is a singer of sentimental concert-stage favorites who, despite her adultery with Boylan, loves and admires her own husband. Throughout *Ulysses*, she is offstage, yet constantly on Leopold's mind.

Each of these three main figures in *Ulysses* is characterized by a distinctly individuated stream of consciousness. Stephen's bespeaks a cultivated sensibility, abounds with intellectual energy, and moves with a varying pace between considerations of language, history, literature, and theology in a private language that is learned, lyrical, morose, and laden throughout with multidirectional allusions. Bloom's stream of consciousness, on the other hand, drifts bemusedly, effortlessly, and with occasional melancholia through a catalog of received ideas, its direction easily swayed by sensual suggestion or opportunities for naïve scientific speculation, yet sometimes revealing a remarkable perspicacity. Molly's, finally, is the least ratiocinative and most fluent and even-paced, an unpunctuated mélange of nostalgia, acidity, and pragmatism.

These three fictional characters share a city with a large cast of figures, some of whom are historical, some based on actual people, and some purely imaginary. All move through the most minutely realized setting in literature. Joyce plotted the action of *Ulysses* so as to conform with the details of the day's news, the typical comings and goings in the city's various institutions, the weather report, and the precise elements of Dublin's "street furniture" on June 16, 1904: the tram schedules, addresses, advertising slogans, theatrical notices, smells and sounds of the city, topics and tone of casual conversation, and so on. At this level, the work is a virtuoso exhibition of realism that challenges the most searching literary sleuths.

On another level, *Ulysses* has an equally astounding system of mythological, historical, literary, and formal superstructures invoked by allusion and analogy. As the title implies, Leopold Bloom is a humble modern counterpart to Odysseus, the archetypal hero of Western civilization. Thus Molly corresponds to Odysseus's faithful wife Penelope, and Stephen to his devoted comrade and son Telemachus. As Joyce first revealed to Stuart Gilbert, his design for *Ulysses* called for the alignment of each of the eighteen chapters of his novel with an episode in Homer's *Odyssey* (c. 725 B.C.E.; English translation, 1614), with a particular location in the city of Dublin, with a particular hour in the day of June 16, 1904, with an organ of the human body, an art or science, a color, and an archetypal symbol. Finally, each of these chapters was to be written in a distinctive style. Two generations of readers have discerned further schemata and elucidated hundreds of ingenious and delicious ironies woven into every chapter, so that critical appreciation of Joyce's technical achievement in the writing of *Ulysses* continues to grow. Bloom's peregrinations through Dublin, his temporary usurpation from his marriage bed, his difficulties with customers and sundry citizens, and his befriending of the fatherless Stephen, under such grand auspices, become objects of simultaneous amusement and admiration. Even the most trivial actions of unremarkable modern citizens gain stature, resonance, and dignity; at the same time, a classic work and its heroic virtues are reinterpreted for this age.

In its broadest sense, *Ulysses* deals with a husband's usurpation from and repossession of his home: Rivals are routed and an ally—a son—found. From another perspective, the plot expounds the relationship of an intellectual abstraction (Stephen) and a sense experience (Bloom). This aspect has its technical analogue in the complex formal structure by which Joyce organizes the myriad material details of the novel. Joyce draws on an impressive range of masterworks from the Western cultural tradition to elaborate these themes and comparisons. Stephen's preoccupation with Shakespeare's *Hamlet* (pr. c. 1600-1601), especially as it is expounded in the ninth episode ("Scylla and Charybdis"), suggests the father-and-son theme in a manner that complements the Homeric. Similarly, the Blazes Boylan-Molly Bloom relationship is orchestrated by reference to Wolfgang Amadeus Mozart's *Don Giovanni* (1787). Among other major organizational devices are the Catholic Mass, Dante's *La divina commedia* (c. 1320; *The Divine Comedy*, 1802), dialectical time-space progressions, Richard Wagner's Ring cycle (1854-1874), and a progression of literary techniques. Thus, for example, as one moves from chapter to chapter under the guidance of a third-person omniscient narrator, one encounters a succession of literary procedures modeled on journalism, classical rhetoric, catechesis, popular romance, musical counterpoint, and expressionist drama.

The fourteenth chapter ("Oxen of the Sun"), for example, narrates Bloom's visit at 10 P.M. to the maternity hospital at Holles Street, the revelry of the medical students and their departure for bar and brothel. The forty-five-page chapter broadly alludes to Ulysses' visit to the Isle of the Sun (*Odyssey*, book 12) and his followers' disobedience of his orders in killing the native oxen, which brings down retribution on them that only the hero survives. Joyce's narrative around the theme of respect for the physical processes of conception, gestation, and childbirth develops as a nine-part episode tracing simultaneously the development of the human embryo and the historical growth of the English language. A complex motif of references to the successive differentiation of organs in the developing human embryo is paralleled by some two score parodies of successive English prose styles from preliteracy and Anglo-Saxon to contemporary slang and a style very like that of *Finnegans Wake*. These progressions are further enhanced by similar motifs alluding to formal evolution, the events of June 16, 1904, and symbolic identifications of Bloom, the hospital, nurse, and Stephen with the sperm, the womb, the ovum, and the embryo, respectively. The cumulative effect of this encyclopedia of procedures is paradoxical: One marvels at the grandeur, the energy, and the variety of the language and the magisterial control of the writer, while at the same time retaining skepticism about the claims of any single perspective.

On almost every aspect of this great novel, the critics are divided: the literary value of such vast systematization, the significance of Bloom's meeting with Stephen, and the very spirit of the work. Nevertheless, its impact on modern literature is immense, from specific literary influences such as that on T. S. Eliot's *The Waste Land* (1922) to all works that mythologize contemporary experience. The themes of *Ulysses*—the dignity of ordinary persons, the values of family and human brotherhood, the consolation of language and the literary tradition, the interrelationships of theological, psychological, and aesthetic language and ideas, the ambiguity of the most profound experiences and the impact of modern revolutions in politics, science, and linguistics on notions of identity—are approached in a manner of unequaled virtuosity.

FINNEGANS WAKE

For all the virtuosity of *Ulysses*, Joyce considered its form inadequate to accommodate the depth and breadth of his vision of human history, experience, and aspiration. Thus, he spent sixteen years of his life composing *Finnegans Wake*, a baffling expedition into the dream of history for which he devised a "night language" composed of scores of languages superimposed on a Hiberno-English base.

Finnegans Wake sets out to express in appropriate form and language the collective unconscious. Thus, it encompasses all of human experience through the millennia in a cycle of recurring forms through a universal language, the language of dreams. The work has five primary dreamers, is divided into four books, and employs a language with simultaneous reference to multiple tongues, expressing the major theme of the cyclical nature of history.

The title derives from the Irish American comic ballad "Finnegan's Wake," in which Tim Finnegan, a hod carrier, has fallen to his apparent death, but under the effect of spilt whiskey, he leaps out of the bed to join the revelry. The fall of this lowly modern Irish laborer recalls previous falls—Lucifer's, Adam's, Newton's, and Humpty Dumpty's—while his resurrection suggests similar parallels, most notably with Christ and, by extension via the implied words *fin* (French for "end"), "again," and "awake," with the myth of the eternal return of all things.

The five primary dreamers are Humphrey Chimpden Earwicker (HCE), a Dublin pub keeper, his wife Anna Livia Plurabelle (ALP), their twin sons Shem and Shaun, and their daughter Issy. HCE (Haveth Childers Everywhere/Here Comes Everybody) is the archetypal husband-father who is burdened with guilt over an obscure indiscretion in the Phoenix Park, an Original Sin, the source of all nightmares in this dreambook of history. News of this sin is carried about by rumors and documents, lectures and arguments, accusations and recriminations. Interrogators appear in fours, and there are twelve onlookers: various jurymen, apostles, mourners, drinkers, and so on. As HCE is identified with the Dublin landscape—from Chapelizod to "Howth Castle and Environs"—his wife is the personification of the River Liffey flowing through that landscape. She is the universal wife-mother, and like all the rivers of the world, constantly in flux. Joyce lavished special care on the section of *Finnegans Wake* (book 1, chapter 8) where she is featured, and he read its conclusion for a phonograph recording. Their warring twin sons, Shem and Shaun, represent the generally opposite character types of introvert and extrovert, subjective and objective, artist and man of affairs, as well as Joyce himself and various antagonists, such as his brother Stanislaus, Eamon de Valera, John McCormack, and Saint Patrick. Issy is the femme fatale, Iseult *rediviva*, the divisive ingenue of *Finnegans Wake*, in contrast with her mother, whose influence is unitive.

The four books of *Finnegans Wake* recount human history according to the four-phase cycle of Giambattista Vico's *Principi di scienza nuova intorno alla natura delle nazioni per la quale si ritruovano i principi di altro sistema del diritto naturale delle genti* (1725;

revised and enlarged as *Principi di scienza nuova d'intorno alla comune natura delle nazioni*, 1744; commonly known as *Scienza nuova*; *The New Science*, 1948): theocratic, aristocratic, democratic, anarchic, and thence via a *ricorso* to the theocratic once again and a new cycle. These four phases of history and the night comprehend the totality of individual and racial development by means of analogies with the four Evangelists of the New Testament, the four Masters of Irish history, the four compass points, and so on. Through a vast elaboration of such correspondences, the Joycean universe of *Finnegans Wake* is populated and structured.

Decades of attempts to explicate *Finnegans Wake* appear to confirm Joyce's prediction that the work would keep the professors busy for centuries. A general opinion among those who take the novel seriously is that as a dreambook and a leading expression of the twentieth century worldview, it is indeterminate, untranslatable, irreducible. It is a work in which every single element has a function: It contains no nonsense yet is finally beyond explication. Critical analyses of *Finnegans Wake* have been either macrocosmic or microcosmic, emphasizing the work's overall design or attempting to gloss particular passages. Since the critics began their attempts, however, neither procedure has progressed very far toward the other.

Finnegans Wake is Joyce's most ambitious literary endeavor. He anticipated, yet underestimated, the difficulties his readers would encounter, and he was disappointed that so many of those who acclaimed *A Portrait of the Artist as a Young Man* and *Ulysses* as supreme expressions of modernity were unprepared to pursue his explorations to the limits of language in *Finnegans Wake*.

Like the great masters in every discipline, Joyce enlarged the possibilities of the forms he inherited. This is indisputably true of the short story, the bildungsroman, and the mythological-psychological novel. In none of these areas has his achievement been superseded, while in the case of *Finnegans Wake*, as Richard Ellmann puts it in the introduction to his classic biography, "we are still learning to be James Joyce's contemporaries, to understand our interpreter."

Cóilín Owens

OTHER MAJOR WORKS

SHORT FICTION: *Dubliners*, 1914.

PLAY: *Exiles*, pb. 1918.

POETRY: *Chamber Music*, 1907; *Pomes Penyeach*, 1927; "Ecce Puer," 1932; *Collected Poems*, 1936.

NONFICTION: *Letters of James Joyce*, 1957-1966 (3 volumes); *The Critical Writings of James Joyce*, 1959; *Selected Letters of James Joyce*, 1975 (Richard Ellmann, editor); *The James Joyce Archives*, 1977-1979 (64 volumes); *On Ibsen*, 1999; *Occasional, Critical, and Political Writing*, 2000.

BIBLIOGRAPHY

Attridge, Derek. *How to Read Joyce.* London: Granta Books, 2007. Analyzes some of Joyce's works to help readers understand this difficult author. Nine of ten chapters are devoted to various elements of Joyce's novels, including the child and the artist in *Portrait of the Artist as a Young Man*, the characters and "musical words" in *Ulysses*, and the parents and the children in *Finnegans Wake*.

_____, ed. *The Cambridge Companion to James Joyce.* New York: Cambridge University Press, 1990. Collection of eleven essays by eminent Joyce scholars provides a valuable aid and stimulus to the study of Joyce's works. Surveys the Joyce phenomenon from cultural, textual, and critical standpoints, devoting a full essay each to *Ulysses* and *Finnegans Wake*. Includes a chronology of Joyce's life and an annotated bibliography.

Bulson, Eric. *The Cambridge Introduction to James Joyce.* New York: Cambridge University Press, 2006. Provides information about Joyce's life and major works, the contexts in which Joyce wrote, and the various critical approaches that have been used to study his writings. An accessible introduction for students and general readers.

Ellmann, Richard. *James Joyce.* 2d ed. New York: Oxford University Press, 1984. The definitive biography, generally regarded as the last word on its subject's life and widely considered one of the greatest literary biographies of the twentieth century. Copiously annotated and well illustrated. Contains informative background on the novels, their characters, and the contexts in which they were written.

Gillespie, Michael Patrick, and Paula F. Gillespie. *Recent Criticism of James Joyce's "Ulysses": An Analytical Review.* Rochester, N.Y.: Camden House, 2000. Survey of *Ulysses* scholarship presents commentary on criticism of the novel since 1970. Organized by topics, such as narrative thread; gender, sex, and sexuality; and cultural identity and the new nationalism.

Jones, Ellen Carol, and Morris Beja, eds. *Twenty-first Joyce.* Gainesville: University Press of Florida, 2004. Useful reference work, intended to be a preview of twenty-first century trends in Joyce studies, collects thirteen scholarly essays written by Joyce experts.

McCourt, John. *James Joyce: A Passionate Exile.* New York: St. Martin's Press, 2001. Photos and sketches embellish this account of the life, times, relationships, and works of Joyce. Excellent introductory text, particularly for its illustrations.

McHugh, Roland. *The Sigla of "Finnegans Wake."* Austin: University of Texas Press, 1976. Informal, refreshing, and valuable guide provides a brief introduction to the compositional character of Joyce's final work.

Potts, Willard. *Joyce and the Two Irelands.* Austin: University of Texas Press, 2001. Aligns Joyce with Catholic nativists, arguing that, while the novelist rejected Catholicism, his treatment of independence and industrialization in his works betrays a sympathy for Irish nationalism.

Schwaber, Paul. *The Cast of Characters: A Reading of "Ulysses."* New Haven, Conn.:

Yale University Press, 1999. A literature professor and a psychoanalyst, Schwaber uses knowledge from both fields in examining characterization in *Ulysses*. Illuminates the psychological depths of Joyce's characters.

Theall, Donald F. *James Joyce's Techno-Poetics.* Toronto, Ont.: University of Toronto Press, 1997. Representative of a new wing of Joyce studies, this volume examines Joyce as a progenitor of modern cyberculture. According to Theall, Joyce saw the artist as an engineer and the artist's works as constructions, and he understood the newly developing technoculture. Includes bibliography and index.

Thornton, Weldon. *Voices and Values in Joyce's "Ulysses."* Gainesville: University Press of Florida, 2000. Attempts to answer a long-standing question about *Ulysses*: Why does Joyce use a different style for each of the novel's last ten episodes?

Tymoczko, Maria. *The Irish "Ulysses."* Berkeley: University of California Press, 1994. Groundbreaking work challenges the conventional wisdom that Joyce rejected Irish mythology in his writing. Describes how Joyce used Irish imagery, myth, genres, and literary modes to create *Ulysses*.

JOSEPH SHERIDAN LE FANU

Born: Dublin, Ireland; August 28, 1814
Died: Dublin, Ireland; February 7, 1873
Also known as: Joseph Thomas Sheridan Le Fanu

PRINCIPAL LONG FICTION

The Cock and Anchor, 1845
The Fortunes of Colonel Torlogh O'Brien, 1847
The House by the Churchyard, 1863
Uncle Silas: A Tale of Bartram-Haugh, 1864
Wylder's Hand, 1864
Guy Deverell, 1865
All in the Dark, 1866
The Tenants of Malory: A Novel, 1867 (3 volumes)
Haunted Lives, 1868
A Lost Name, 1868
The Wyvern Mystery, 1869
Checkmate, 1871
The Rose and the Key, 1871
Willing to Die, 1872-1873 (3 volumes)
Morley Court, 1873

OTHER LITERARY FORMS

Joseph Sheridan Le Fanu (LEHF-uhn-yew) is better known today as a short-story writer than as a novelist. His many tales first appeared in periodicals, later to be combined into collections. In addition to having intrinsic merit, the stories are important to an understanding of Le Fanu the novelist, for in them he perfected the techniques of mood, characterization, and plot construction that make his later novels so obviously superior to his early efforts. Indeed, Le Fanu seems to have recognized little distinctive difference between the novel and the tale; his novels are often expansions of earlier stories, and stories reissued in collections might be loosely linked by a frame created to give them some of the unity of a novel. The major collections, *Ghost Stories and Tales of Mystery* (1851), *Chronicles of Golden Friars* (1871), *In a Glass Darkly* (1872), and *The Purcell Papers* (1880), reveal an artist who ranks with Edgar Allan Poe, Ambrose Bierce, M. R. James, and Algernon Blackwood as one of the masters of supernatural fiction in the English language. One story from *In A Glass Darkly,* "Carmilla," is reprinted in almost every anthology of horror stories and has inspired numerous film versions, the most famous being Carl Theodore Dreyer's *Vampyr* (1932).

Le Fanu wrote verse throughout his literary career. While unknown as a poet to modern audiences, in his own day at least one of his compositions achieved great popularity in both Ireland and the United States. "Shamus O'Brien" (1850) is a fine ballad that relates the adventures of the title character in the uprising of 1798.

ACHIEVEMENTS

In the preface to his most famous novel, *Uncle Silas*, Joseph Sheridan Le Fanu rejects the claim of critics that he is a mere writer of "sensational novels." Pointing out that the great novels of Sir Walter Scott have sensational elements of violence and horror, he denies that his own work, any more than Scott's, should be characterized by the presence of such elements; like Scott, Le Fanu, too, has "moral aims."

To see the truth in this self-appraisal requires familiarity with more than one of Le Fanu's novels. Singly, each of the major works overwhelms the reader with the cleverness of its plot, the depravity of its villain, the suspense evoked by its carefully controlled tone. Several novels together, however, recollected in tranquillity, reveal a unity of theme. Moreover, each novel can then be seen as not merely a variation on the theme but also as a deliberate next logical step toward a more comprehensive and definitive statement. The intricacies of plot, the kinds of evil represented by the villains, the pervasive gothic gloom are to Le Fanu more than story elements; they are themselves his quite serious comment on the nature of human existence, driven by natural and social forces that leave little room for the effective assertion of free will toward any beneficial end.

In Le Fanu's short stories, more often than in his novels, those forces are embodied in tangible supernatural agents. "Carmilla," for example, is the tale of a real female vampire's attack on a young woman, but seen in the context of the larger theme, it is more than a bit of occult fiction calculated to give its readers a scare. With her intense sexuality and lesbian tendencies, the vampire is depicted as nothing less than the embodiment of a basic human drive out of control, and that drive—like the others that move society: self-preservation, physical comfort—can quite unpredictably move toward destruction. Le Fanu's most significant achievement as a novelist was to show how the horror genre could be used for serious purposes—to show that monsters are not as horrible as minds that beget monsters, and that ghosts are not as interesting as people who are haunted.

BIOGRAPHY

Joseph Thomas Sheridan Le Fanu was descended from a Huguenot family that had left France for Ireland in the seventeenth century. Both his grandfather, Joseph, and great uncle, Henry, had married sisters of the famous playwright, Richard Brinsley Sheridan. His father, Philip Le Fanu, was a noted scholar and clergyman who served as rector at the Royal Hibernian School, where Le Fanu was born, and later as dean of Emly. His mother was from all accounts a most charming and gentle person, an essayist on philanthropic subjects and a leader in the movement for humane treatment of animals. With loving and indulgent parents and the excitement of life at the school, where military reviews were frequent, Le Fanu's childhood was a happy one.

In 1826, the family moved to Abington in county Limerick. Le Fanu and his brother, William, were not sent to a formal school but were tutored by their father with the help of an elderly clergyman, who gladly excused the boys from their lessons so he could pursue the passion of his life: fishing. Walking tours through the wild Irish countryside, conversations with friendly peasants, who told of fairies and pookhas and banshees, shaped very early the imagination of the boy who would become the creator of so many tales of the mysterious and supernatural. The Tithe Wars of 1831 and the resulting animosity of the peasants to the Le Fanus, who were seen as representative of the Anglo-Irish establishment, forced the young Le Fanu to examine his own Irishness. On one hand, he was intellectually supportive of the union and convinced that British rule was in the best interests of the Irish people; on the other, the courage and sacrifices of the bold Irish nationalists filled him with admiration and respect.

In 1837, Le Fanu graduated from Trinity College, Dublin. He took honors in classics and was well known for his fine orations before the College Historical Society. Called to the Irish bar in 1839, he never practiced law but entered a productive career in journalism. His first published work, "The Ghost and the Bonesetter," appeared in the *Dublin University Magazine* in January, 1838. That magazine was to publish serially eight of Le Fanu's fourteen novels after he became its owner and editor in 1861. During the early 1840's, Le Fanu became proprietor or part-owner of a number of journals, including *The Warder, The Statesman, The Protestant Guardian*, and the *Evening Mail*.

In 1844, Le Fanu married Susan Bennett. The union was a happy one; the Le Fanus had two sons and two daughters. One son, George, became an artist and illustrated some of his father's works. Le Fanu's novels published in the 1840's, *The Cock and Anchor* and *Torlogh O'Brien*, received poor reviews, and Le Fanu turned from writing fiction to concentrate on his journalistic work. With the death of his beloved wife in 1858, he withdrew from society and became a recluse. Only a few close friends were allowed to visit "the invisible prince" at his elegant home at Merrion Square, Dublin. Emerging only occasionally to visit booksellers for volumes on ghosts and the occult, Le Fanu established a daily routine he was to follow for the remaining years of his life: writing in bed by candlelight from midnight till dawn, rising at noon, and writing all afternoon at a prized, small desk once owned by Richard Brinsley Sheridan. In this manner was produced the greatest share of a literary canon that rivals in quantity the output of the most prolific authors of the Victorian age.

At the end, under treatment for heart disease, troubled by nightmares—especially one recurring scene of a gloomy, old mansion on the verge of collapsing on the terrified dreamer—Le Fanu refused the company of even his closest friends. On the night of February 7, 1873, his doctor found him in bed, his arms flung wide, his unseeing eyes fixed in terror at something that could no longer do him harm. "I feared this," the doctor said; "that house fell at last."

ANALYSIS

After writing two novels that failed to impress the critics, Joseph Sheridan Le Fanu left that genre for approximately fifteen years. In his reclusive later life, he returned to long fiction to produce the fine work for which he is remembered. Le Fanu's career as a novelist reveals a marked change in his perception of humanity and the very nature of the universe itself. The development of the author's major theme can be illustrated by a survey of the major novels in his quite extensive canon.

THE COCK AND ANCHOR

The early works, *The Cock and Anchor* and *Torlogh O'Brien*, are both historical novels dealing with the Ireland of the late seventeenth and early eighteenth centuries, the turbulent time of the Williamite Wars (1689-1691). *The Cock and Anchor* presents a slice of Irish life that cuts across events and persons of real historical significance and the personal misfortunes of one fictional couple, Mary Ashewoode and Edmund O'Connor. The story of these ill-fated lovers has nothing special to recommend it. Mary is kept from Edmund first by her father, Sir Richard, who would marry her for a fortune to Lord Aspenly, a conventional fop, and then by her brother, Henry, who would see her wed to one Nicholas Blarden, a conventional villain. Mary escapes these nefarious designs and flees to the protection of Oliver French, the conventional benevolent uncle. There is, however, no happy ending: Mary dies before Edmund can reach her. The designing Sir Richard suffers a fatal stroke; brother Henry finally finds the destiny for which he was born, the hangman's noose; and even Edmund's unlucky life ends on the battlefield of Denain in 1712.

More interesting to the modern reader are the historical characters. The haughty Lord Warton, Viceroy of Dublin, personifies power and Machiavellian self-interest. Joseph Addison and young Jonathan Swift are also here in well-drawn portraits that demonstrate considerable historical research. Still, the novel is at best uneven, the work of an author with promise who has more to learn about his craft.

The technical obstructions, however, cannot hide Le Fanu's message: The problems of Ireland are profound and rooted deep in a history of conflict. The Anglo-Irish establishment, represented by the Ashewoode family, has lost sight of the values needed to end the strife and move the society toward peace and prosperity, values such as personal responsibility, compassion, and even love within the family. Le Fanu was unwilling to risk clouding his theme by allowing the happy marriage of Mary and Edmund, the conventional ending to which the conventional plot could be expected to lead. They die to prove the point. The Ashewoodes's decay is really Ireland's decay, and the wage is death.

TORLOGH O'BRIEN

Torlogh O'Brien, Le Fanu's second novel and the last he was to write for sixteen years, is set a few years before *The Cock and Anchor*, during the Williamite War. Again, most critics have found little to admire in the work. The historical scenes and characters show that once more Le Fanu thoroughly researched his subject, but the fictional characters reveal little improvement in their creator's art. The plot, except for some unusually violent scenes, would hold no surprises for a reader of romances. The villainous Miles Garret, a traitor to the Protestant cause, wishes to take Glindarragh Castle from Sir Hugh Willoughby, a supporter of William of Orange. Arrested on false charges created by Garret, Sir Hugh and his daughter, Grace, are taken to Dublin for trial. Their escort is Torlogh O'Brien, a soldier in the army of King James II, whose family originally held the estate. O'Brien and Sir Hugh, both honorable men, rise above their political differences to gain mutual respect. Finally, it is O'Brien who intervenes to save the Willoughbys from the designs of Garret, and of course his bravery is rewarded by the love of Grace.

From the first novel to the second, villainy—Nicholas Blarden or Miles Garret—remains a constant, and the agony of a torn Ireland is the common background against which Edmund O'Connor and Torlogh O'Brien act out their parts. The social cancer that blighted the love of Mary and Edmund is, however, allowed a possible cure in *Torlogh O'Brien*. As the deaths of the lovers in the first novel showed Ireland as a sterile wasteland, so the union of the Willoughbys and O'Briens in the second promises restoring rain, but when after the long hiatus Le Fanu returned to novel writing, he chose to let the promise go unfulfilled.

THE HOUSE BY THE CHURCHYARD

Held by many critics to be Le Fanu's finest work, *The House by the Churchyard*, the first novel of his later period, appeared in the *Dublin University Magazine* in 1861; two years later, it was published in London as a book.

The story is set in late eighteenth century Chapelizod, a suburb of Dublin. As in the earlier historical romances, there are villains, lovers, and dispossessed heirs. A major plot concerns the righting of an old wrong. Eighteen years after the death of Lord Dunoran, executed for a murder he did not commit, his son, using the name Mr. Mervyn, returns to the confiscated family lands hoping to establish his father's innocence. The real murderer, Charles Archer, has also returned to Chapelizod under the alias of Paul Dangerfield. He is soon recognized by a former accomplice, Zekiel Irons, and a witness, Dr. Barnaby Sturk. Sturk attempts blackmail, only to have Archer beat him severely. His victim in a coma, Archer plays benefactor and arranges for a surgeon he knows to be incompetent to perform a brain operation, supposedly to restore Sturk to health. To Archer's surprise, the operation gives Sturk a period of consciousness before the expected death. Irons joins Sturk in revealing Archer as the murderer, Lord Dunoran's lands and title are restored to Mervyn, and the family name is cleared at last.

This, however, is only one of several interrelated plots that make *The House by the Churchyard* a marvel of Victorian complexity. To label the Archer mystery as the major story line would be to mislead the reader who has yet to discover the book. More accurately, the novel is about Chapelizod itself. The discovery of a murderer stands out in the plot as, to be sure, it would in any small community, but Le Fanu is reminding his readers that what immediately affects any individual—for example, Mervyn's need to clear his father's name—no matter how urgently, is of limited interest to other individuals, who are in turn preoccupied with their own concerns. Mrs. Nutter has her own problem with protecting her inheritance from wicked Mary Matchwell. Captain Devereux and Lilias Walsingham have their doomed romance to concern them, as, on a more humorous note, Captain Cuffe is preoccupied with his love for Rebecca Chattesworth, who is finally joined with Lieutenant Puddock, the former suitor of Gertrude Chattesworth, who in turn has a secret romance with Mervyn. Indeed, the unsolved murder cannot totally dominate even the life of Lord Dunoran's son.

Some of the characters serve a comic purpose, and with so many complex entanglements, the comic could easily slide into complete farce. Le Fanu avoids caricature, however, by providing each comic figure with some other distinguishing quality—wit, compassion, bravery. In *The House by the Churchyard*, Le Fanu, already a master of description and mood, added the one needed skill so obviously absent in his early novels, the art of characterization.

The characterization of Archer, alias Dangerfield, is by itself sufficient to demonstrate Le Fanu's growth as a novelist. Dangerfield is almost supernatural in his evil; he describes himself as a corpse and a vampire, a werewolf and a ghoul. He is incapable not only of love but also of hate, and he calmly announces before his suicide that he "never yet bore any man the least ill-will." He has had to "remove two or three" merely to ensure his own safety. The occult imagery used to define Dangerfield also links him to the microcosm of Chapelizod, for Mervyn's Tiled House is reputedly haunted; the specter of a ghostly hand has frightened more than one former resident. Le Fanu allows Mervyn, like Torlogh O'Brien, his happy ending, but so powerful is the hold of Dangerfield on the novel that the possibility of colossal evil that he personifies is not totally exorcised even by his death. That he was not really supernatural but was the embodiment of human depravity in no way diminishes the horror.

WYLDER'S HAND

With his fourth novel, *Wylder's Hand*, Le Fanu left historical romances and social panoramas to study evil with a closer eye. The story, certainly Le Fanu's finest mystery, concerns the strange disappearance of young Mark Wylder, a lieutenant in the navy and rival of Captain Stanley Lake for the hand of Dorcas Brandon, a rich heiress. From several locations in Europe, Wylder has sent letters containing instructions for the conduct of his business and releasing Dorcas to marry Lake. The suspicions of Larkin, a family attorney, are aroused by a problem with the dating of certain letters, but then Wylder returns to Brandon Hall, where he is actually seen in conversation with Lake. The very next day, however, Lake is thrown from his horse as the animal is startled by the pointing hand of Mark Wylder's corpse protruding from the ground, exposed by a heavy rain. Dying, Lake confesses to having murdered his rival and arranging for the posting of forged letters. In fact, it was not Wylder who appeared the preceding night at Brandon but one James Dutton, the unwitting accomplice who had posted the letters and who happens to resemble Wylder. Only one person knew of Wylder's fate, having witnessed his midnight burial: Rachel Lake, the murderer's sister. Devotion to her brother and to Dorcas Brandon, who really loves Lake, compelled her silence.

The plot is a masterpiece of suspense, but still more impressive are the characterizations. Each figure is finely drawn and fits into a mosaic of human types that together portrays a species ill equipped to deal with evil. Wylder is a swaggering braggart, crude, unfeeling, with a general air of disreputability that seems to promise some future act of monstrous brutality had not a violent death cut short his career. Like two vicious dogs claiming the same territory, Wylder and Lake cannot exist in the same world without one destroying the other. Lake's evil, however, is of a quite different nature. In many respects, he is Le Fanu's most interesting study. Wylder's is a rather directionless evil; it could as easily manifest itself in one abhorrent action as another. Dangerfield was simply amoral. Born without any sense of restraint, his natural selfishness led to murder for convenience. Lake's evil is weakness. Greed for property and position seems almost an outside force, a part of human society that can compel even murder in those who lack the strength to resist. He experiences guilt and fear and never is able to derive satisfaction from his villainy.

Considering that the murdered man was certainly no credit to the human race, the reader may actually feel sympathy for Lake. In him, Le Fanu presents the criminal as victim, but the consequences of Lake's weakness affect others as well. Rachel's knowledge of the secret and Dorcas's ignorance isolate them from the man they love, much as Lake is himself isolated. Gloom, a sense of a scheme of things not quite right, permeates the texture of the entire novel. There is no happy ending. Years later, Rachel and Dorcas are seen in Venice, sad and alone.

UNCLE SILAS

In *Uncle Silas*, Le Fanu continued his investigation of the terrible yet tragic evil represented by Lake. Two earlier tales, "An Episode in the Secret History of an Irish Countess" (1838) and "The Murdered Cousin" (1851) provided a basic plot structure for the study, and in 1864, the same year that *Wylder's Hand* was published, a bound edition in three volumes with the full title *Uncle Silas: A Tale of Bartram-Haugh* appeared. Considered by most critics Le Fanu's finest novel, it brings all the skill acquired over a productive career to a definitive study of the themes that interested its author most: the nature of evil, and the hereditary aristocracy as a paradigm for the effects of that destructive force. As usual, the study is conducted through carefully drawn characters and a plot filled with mystery and suspense.

In compliance with the will of the deceased Austin Ruthyn, his daughter, Maud, is made the ward of Austin's brother, Silas, a sinister man suspected but never convicted of a past murder. The suspicions are well founded, for Uncle Silas will stop at nothing to gain full ownership of Maud's estate. When an arranged marriage between Maud and Silas's son, Dudley, proves impossible—the scoundrel is discovered to be already married—murder seems the only solution. Dudley botches the job, however, and kills Madame de la Rougierra, another of Silas's agents, by mistake. Maud flees to a kindly relative; Dudley flees to Australia; and Uncle Silas dies that same night from an overdose of opium.

Le Fanu called *Uncle Silas* a "tragic English romance," and indeed the novel does depict a truly tragic situation. The Ruthyns stumble blindly through situations and realities they can hardly perceive, much less understand. Austin Ruthyn, heedless of the suspicions surrounding his brother, sends his daughter into the wolf's lair. Dudley, purposeless and crude, sees only the moment, and this he addresses with instinct rather than intelligent consideration of consequences. Even Maud Ruthyn, the heroine and narrator, is unaware of her perilous situation until it is almost too late. Gothic heroines are expected to be naïve, and Le Fanu uses that trait in his narrator to good advantage. Maud often tells more than she realizes, and the reader sensitive to the unspoken messages that careful diction can convey sees the closing circle of predators before she does. The rhetorical effect is a sense of foreboding, a tension that charges the entire novel.

Despite his avoidance of prosecution for an earlier crime and his careful designs for his niece's downfall, Silas is as blind as any of the lesser characters. His lust for wealth and property is virtually inherited: Similar drives have directed his family for generations. His body a slave to narcotics, his mind to religious fanaticism, he is the aristocracy in decay. Le Fanu surrounds him with appropriate death imagery, and his loutish son, Dudley, married without Silas's knowledge to a barmaid, is final evidence of the collapse of the Ruthyn line. Silas's first murder victim had been a Mr. Charke, to whom he owed gambling debts, but with the planned murder of Maud, the violence turns in upon the Ruthyns themselves. Austin's blind trust puts Maud in harm's way, and Silas's blind greed would destroy her; *Uncle Silas* is ultimately nothing less than a portrait of the aristocratic class cannibalizing itself. Maud survives and eventually marries a young lord, but her concluding words speak more of hope for happiness than happiness realized, and the death of her first child, sorrowfully remembered, strikes at the last the same note sounded throughout the novel.

WILLING TO DIE

That note of futility is heard most clearly in Le Fanu at the end of his career as a novelist. *Willing to Die*, first published serially in *All the Year Round* (1872-1873), is by no means his finest effort. The story, while complex, lacks the gothic excitement of the works for which he is remembered. Still, the novel is important in a thematic study.

Ethel Ware, the heroine, is allowed to sample a full range of life's possibilities. Poverty, loneliness, love, all contribute to the growth of her character; she surmounts all obstacles to achieve great material wealth and an understanding of the meaning of life. This is a new picture; in Ethel, the reader does not meet yet another aristocrat beaten by an ignorance of the forces at work in human society. Ethel wins, in the sense that Silas Ruthyn and Stanley Lake would have liked to win, but the mature vision that comes with the material victory only shows that the quest is pointless and the victory hollow. Isolated in her accomplishment as the protagonists of earlier novels were most often isolated in their failures, Ethel sees that the human struggle is manipulated by forces of society and chance, and whether the struggle culminates in a moment that might be called success or failure is finally irrelevant, for the last force to take part in the struggle, death, affects the Wares and the Ruthyns alike.

The novels of Le Fanu are the record of an artist exploring social structures and individual minds in quest of horrors natural and supernatural. With his final entry in that often brilliant record, *Willing to Die*, he penetrated at last to the very heart of darkness to discover the ultimate horror: the utter futility of it all.

William J. Heim

OTHER MAJOR WORKS

SHORT FICTION: *Ghost Stories and Tales of Mystery*, 1851; *Chronicles of Golden Friars*, 1871; *In a Glass Darkly*, 1872; *The Purcell Papers*, 1880; *The Watcher, and Other Weird Stories*, 1894; *A Chronicle of Golden Friars, and Other Stories*, 1896; *Madam Crowl's Ghost, and Other Tales of Mystery*, 1923 (M. R. James, editor); *Green Tea, and Other Ghost Stories*, 1945; *Best Ghost Stories of J. S. Le Fanu*, 1964; *Ghost Stories and Mysteries*, 1975.

POETRY: *The Poems of Joseph Sheridan Le Fanu*, 1896.

BIBLIOGRAPHY

Begnal, Michael H. *Joseph Sheridan Le Fanu*. Lewisburg, Pa.: Bucknell University Press, 1971. Although this volume is only an essay-length discussion of Le Fanu's works, it is valuable in providing general commentary about Le Fanu's intellectual and artistic interests, especially his sensitive understanding of women.

Browne, Nelson. *Sheridan Le Fanu*. London: Arthur Barker, 1951. This short critical exposition places emphasis on Le Fanu's "essentially Gothick quality." The author believes Le Fanu to be at his best in his short fiction, advancing familiar objections to his novels' prolixity. Dated in tone and attitude, but a pioneering study.

McCormack, William J. *Dissolute Characters: Irish Literary History Through Balzac, Sheridan Le Fanu, Yeats, and Bowen*. New York: Manchester University Press, 1993. The section on Le Fanu discusses his relationship to the English novel, the development of his fiction, his treatment of characters, and his drawing on history. Includes notes but no bibliography.

_____. *Sheridan Le Fanu and Victorian Ireland*. New York: Oxford University Press, 1980. The standard work on Le Fanu. The author's approach is twofold. First, this study is a detailed biography of Le Fanu; second, it locates, with much intellectual sophistication, Le Fanu's life in his times, giving historical significance to its biographical data. A second, enlarged edition of this important work was issued in 1991.

Melada, Ivan. *Sheridan Le Fanu*. Boston: Twayne, 1987. Melada's approach is chronological, proceeding from Le Fanu's early short fiction to the major novels with which his career ends. The critical emphasis sees Le Fanu as a writer of popular fiction, the quality of which entitles him to serious academic consideration. Includes a chronology and bibliography.

Sage, Victor. *Le Fanu's Gothic: The Rhetoric of Darkness*. New York: Palgrave Macmillan, 2004. This work examines Le Fanu's stylistic development and includes extensive analyses of *Uncle Silas* in addition to rarely discussed unpublished romances. Includes a bibliography and an index.

Sullivan, Kevin. "*The House by the Churchyard*: James Joyce and Sheridan Le Fanu." In *Modern Irish Literature: Essays in Honour of William York Tindall*, edited by Raymond J. Porter and James D. Brophy. New Rochelle, N.Y.: Iona College Press, 1972. Le Fanu's novel *The House by the Churchyard* has some of its significant scenes set in the village of Chapelizod, a few miles west of Dublin and at the western end of Phoenix Park. James Joyce's *Finnegans Wake* (1933) contains numerous important allusions to both these Dublin settings. This essay traces the presence of the earlier work in the later. The undertaking is both an academic rehabilitation of Le Fanu's novel and an illustrative instance of Joyce's method in *Finnegans Wake*.

Walton, James. *Vision and Vacancy: The Fictions of J. S. Le Fanu*. Dublin: University College Dublin Press, 2007. An examination of Le Fanu's fiction, discussing his philosophy and literary influences. Walton places Le Fanu's work within the context of Victorian English and Continental novels and shows how his horror writing stands apart from traditional ghost stories of the Victorian era.

PATRICK McGINLEY

Born: Glencolmcille, Donegal, Ireland; February 8, 1937
Also known as: Patrick Anthony McGinley

PRINCIPAL LONG FICTION
Bogmail, 1978
Goosefoot, 1982
Foggage, 1983
Foxprints, 1983
The Trick of the Ga Bolga, 1985
The Red Men, 1987
The Devil's Diary, 1988
The Lost Soldier's Song, 1994

OTHER LITERARY FORMS

Patrick McGinley is known primarily for his long fiction.

ACHIEVEMENTS

From the outset, Patrick McGinley's fiction enjoyed an enthusiastic reception from reviewers, particularly in the United States, where critics, inadequately acquainted with some of his background material, misleadingly drew attention to the work's Irishness. Reviews in England and Ireland, though less generous, were generally favorable, if somewhat resistant to McGinley's prolificity. McGinley's first novel, *Bogmail*, was nominated for several awards, including the prestigious Edgar Award for Best Novel of 1981, an award presented by the Mystery Writers of America.

BIOGRAPHY

Although his books received such popular success, little is known about Patrick Anthony McGinley's life; indeed, at a time when Irish fiction is receiving an increasing amount of academic attention, this author could be called the most anonymous Irish novelist of his generation. McGinley was born to a farming family in a comparatively remote area of county Donegal, Ireland's farthest northwest county. He was educated locally and at University College, Galway, from which he graduated with a bachelor's degree in commerce in 1957. For five years after his graduation he taught secondary school in Ireland before emigrating to England and entering the publishing profession. Apart from a year in Australia (1965-1966), he remained in publishing and became managing director of Europa Publications in 1980. McGinley married Kathleen Frances Cuddy in 1967 and had one son, Myles Peter. His family made its home in Kent, outside London.

ANALYSIS

Because of lack of serious critical attention until the late 1990's, it had been difficult to assess Patrick McGinley's status as a contemporary Irish novelist. Beginning in the early 1960's, Irish writing in all forms underwent major self-interrogation, accompanied by the new thematic and formal considerations. While, unlike many Irish writers, McGinley was anything but vocal in this sustained period of reappraisal, it is instructive to see his work in such a context. Its individuality is arguably its most significant feature and, by a paradox more apparent than real, is the attribute that makes his novels symptomatic of new departures in Irish writing. At the same time, the representations of nature, the sense of the uncanny, the choice of traditional and relatively unchanging rural communities as settings, the focus on death, and the use of the romance form all reveal McGinley as being interestingly related to a long tradition of such preoccupations in Irish writing, from the seventh century writings of Saint Columkille, for whom McGinley's native place is named, to the modern era. More particularly, his fascination with reason's frailty and the fact of death makes his work an intriguing pendant to that of one of the most important Irish novelists of the twentieth century, Flann O'Brien.

Although McGinley is usually classified as a crime novelist, to consider him one in the conventional sense is both accurate and misleading. While it is true that, until the publication of *The Lost Soldier's Song* in 1994, McGinley had not deviated from the path signposted in the opening paragraph of his first published novel, *Bogmail*, where poisonous toadstools are being introduced to a mushroom omelette, and while it is also true that his publishers have tended to emphasize the murderous mysteriousness of his plots, there is both more and less than meets the eye to the convenient classification. This state of affairs is of significance because it draws attention to the fact that it is impossible to approach McGinley's work without drawing attention to its bifocal character.

McGinley's fiction evinces more interest in mystery than in solution—his work has only one detective, McMyler in *Goosefoot*, and the few police officers who crop up in the other novels are somewhat less than a credit to the force and have thoroughly earned their status as minor characters. The works' focus is directed gently but ineluctably toward those areas of existence that may not be brought within stable frameworks of perception. In particular, the unreasonable fact of death is so much more to the fore than is any power to counteract it that it is tempting to attach to the whole of this author's output the quotation from Robert Southey that is the epigraph to *Foggage*: "My name is Death: the last best friend am I."

SETTINGS

For the most part, McGinley's novels are set in the author's native county Donegal. An exception to this general rule is *Foxprints*, which is largely set in the suburban Home Counties of England, a context that the author fails to enliven, perhaps because of its excessively social character. Typically, McGinley feels at home in remoteness, and Donegal settings possess a variety of strategic advantages for a writer of his proclivities. In the first place, by selecting Donegal as the scene of the action, McGinley is clearly presenting settings that he can treat with authority. So faithful is he to the fastidious re-creation of locales clearly maintained in his mind's eye by a deep attachment to his native area that he establishes a very palpable sense of place, and in every McGinley novel there are quietly rapturous descriptive passages that seem to hymn the landscapes they depict.

Situating his plots so squarely in a felt environment—in which the play of light, natural features, the oscillations of the sea, the weather's vagaries, and the presence of wildlife continually recur—seems to enable McGinley to virtually dispense with time. The exigencies of plot naturally require that time pass, but generally speaking there is little specific sense of period. Before *The Lost Soldier's Song*, which is set during the Black and Tan War and focuses on the events of the war itself, as well as its impact on character, long historical perspectives had little or no part to play in the assessing of the characters' problematic destinies. What exceptions there are to this rule—the setting of *The Trick of the Ga Bolga* in the early years of World War II, or the rather boldly stated observations on the spurious development of rural Ireland propounded by the protagonist of *The Devil's Diary*—seem rather to underline how watertight the rule is, since neither note of contemporaneity contributes significantly to the balance of forces at the center of either of these novels.

One effect of McGinley's obviation of cultural conceptions of time, and a general relaxation of time-consciousness, is that it assists in the creation of atmosphere but inhibits in the creation of thrills. Such a result accentuates the all-enveloping quality of the rural setting, while at the same time drawing both the characters' and the readers' attention from event to perception of event. The mystery deepens to the degree that it becomes as much part of the nature of things as the landscape in which it is situated. Any tension that results from the distressingly arbitrary and violent events of the plot—often as much the result of accidents as of articulated intentions—are to be found, unreleased, within the consciousness of McGinley's protagonists, and its psychological repercussions fail, with what the protagonists understandably find to be a maddening consistency, to have an objective correlative in the natural world around them. Remoteness of setting, therefore, is not merely an occasion of picturesqueness for McGinley. On the contrary, it is one of his fundamental means of lending plausibility to the sense of the inscrutable and uncanny that bedevils the mental landscapes of his protagonists, the majority of whom traverse the dual terrains of these novels like lost souls.

By virtue of its very naturalness, setting is experienced by McGinley's protagonists as a primary instance of otherness, of a set of conditions that are not comprehensible, tractable, alterable, or humanly amenable in any particular—conditions that are, strictly speaking, mysterious. Yet it is important to note that McGinley is sufficiently resourceful to prevent his approach from becoming too schematic. The rich farming country of county Tipperary, which provides the setting for *Foggage* and in which its main characters are ostensibly firmly established, engenders as much distress and destruction as county Donegal ever did, revealing unsuspected psychic remoteness. In *Goosefoot*, ungenial Dublin exposes the unsuspecting and vital Patricia Teeling to malevolences that are the antitheses of her winning sense of life.

McGinley's protagonists, settled or unsettled, are peculiarly susceptible to the atmosphere of their environments. For the most part they are unsettled, and it is generally this condition that has brought them to the locale of the story. Once arrived, they seem to believe, however, that they have found a secure haven: To a degree, the enclosed and remote character of their landfall—typified by the Glenkeel in *The Devil's Diary*, which has the same road into it as out—seduces them into thinking that now they are safe, they have come to the end of a particular phase of their lives and are permitted by their new circumstances to live lives that are at once both self-engrossed and detached. In a number of cases—*Foxprints* and *The Trick of the Ga Bolga* are the most significant—the protagonists are on the run from unsatisfactory marriages. The protagonists' status as outsiders, however, gives them novelty value to the locals, and before long they are involved in local affairs, often in a very literal sense, one of the principal means of involvement being that of sexual attraction. The inability to deny the presence of their sexuality has the effect of replicating in more intense form the substance of earlier distressing experiences, with the result that settings that seemed to be escapes end up as terminuses. Aiming for simplicity, McGinley's protagonists find it only to discover its essential mysteriousness.

CHARACTERS

The repetition and duplication of experience, the evidently unforgiving character of one's own nature, are particularly crucial in *The Devil's Diary* and *The Trick of the Ga Bolga*. Yet more important than their presence, and raising their significance beyond that of mere plot devices, is that the protagonists perceive their condition for what it is. The typical McGinley protagonist is well educated and sometimes dauntingly well read.

Not only do repetition and replication feature to a significant degree within each of McGinley's novels, but they are also notably present in his output as a whole. As a result, while resourceful variations in setting and protagonist occur—a female protagonist in *Goosefoot*, three protagonists in *The Red Men*, a suburban never-never land as the setting for *Foxprints*—and while these changes effectively vary the angle of approach from novel to novel, each work's ultimate preoccupations remain essentially unchanged. McGinley's output has a consistency of focus and pliability of approach that are crucially denied its characters. It hardly seems to matter that the English engineer Potter in *Bogmail* is a prototype for Coote, the protagonist of *The Trick of the Ga Bolga*, or that Coote's mistress has a formidable avatar in the insistently incestuous Maureen Hurley of *Foggage*. Story line is more ornament than staple, and while McGinley's plots are richly woven and colorfully peopled, they seem to be considered as no more than edifices of superficial plausibility to an investigation of whose inscrutable foundations the protagonist is, through no fault of his own (McGinley's fiction is resolutely amoral), condemned.

McGinley's sense of setting draws heavily on the elements—the motion of the seasons, the cloudscapes of the often protean Irish sky, the world of crag, pool, bog, and seashore. His sense of protagonist reproduces this concentration on the elemental. These characters seldom have a specific social role, or if they do—as in the case of Father Jerry in *The Devil's Diary*—it produces rather than defends against existential dread. On the other hand, the protagonists, for all the author's concentration on them and his use of them as both embodiments and victims of a unique optic on themselves and their world, are not sufficiently well endowed to render considerations of social role by functioning in a recognizable manner. Deprived of the safeguards that social and literary convention provide, they appear to have no choice but to assume a more fundamental, vulnerable, and elementary condition of selfhood—or rather, the plot lines of McGinley's novels show that fall taking place. In addition, the creation of mysteries without solution and the commissioning of crime without reproducing the social machinery of incrimination that is its normal, or generic, accompaniment, take at face value the genre to which these novels superficially belong, and by doing so subvert it, reducing it to such a bare embodiment of its elements that it only nominally maintains its presence.

THEMES

The unemphatic but omnipresent concentration on a sense of the elemental in McGinley's fiction is nowhere seen to better advantage than in the works' recurring themes. Having brought his unsuspecting protagonists, who without knowing it are at the end of their tether, to what seems like the end of the world, the author subjects them to other experiences of the terminal. The most obvious one of these is death, yet although its literal presence is of prime importance to sustaining these works' fragmentary figment of plot, death is not merely present in a literal sense. It also exists as the pun for sexual climax familiar to students of English Renaissance poetry, where it helps to make a familiar and typically antithetical conjunction for McGinley (the fact of death is frequently deeply implicated in the act of love). In addition, its presence denotes a primary instance of the chaos and nullity to which a protagonist's perception of life may in any case be reduced—a state of perception that is frequently the aftermath of the violent and unexpected deaths that punctuate the duration of the McGinley protagonist's rustication.

Rather than describe McGinley as a writer of mysteries, it seems more appropriate to consider his works as those of a "parablist," who utters in story what cannot be otherwise so readily articulated. At least one McGinley novel, *The Red Men* (commonly taken as a retelling of the parable of the talents in the New Testament), seems to support such a view. More broadly, a strong case may be made for McGinley's novels to be considered as sophisticated romances of consciousness, in which the romantic quest, for all its pastoral trappings, is ironized by succeeding in finding that with which it cannot live.

What the quest locates reveals the philosophical undertow of McGinley's fiction. It would be misleading to consider McGinley a philosophical novelist of the school of, for example, Albert Camus, as is implied by his works' pleasing lightness of tone and deftness of manner. In all McGinley's works prior to *The Lost Soldier's Song*, philosophical themes, however fundamental to the extreme conditions to which action and character are reduced, are treated with no more intensity or deliberation than is any other feature of McGinley's fictional universe, possibly as a result of his having no ideological agenda. At the same time, the clearly existentialist scenarios, the manner in which action preys on the mind to elicit meaning, the emphasis on the mutability of fate as a standby of plot, the frequent epiphanic encounters between humanity and nature, the quietly satirical allusions to mind-body problems, and the impetus toward pattern forming and pattern recognition that initially stimulates and ultimately frustrates the inquirer all suggest works of a speculative, philosophizing, intellectual character.

This omnipresent preoccupation with perception, cognition, and the impossibility of stabilizing or normalizing them that bemuses McGinley's protagonists seems to amuse the author. Not only is his style, for the most part, wry, succinct, and supple, but its tone is also frequently one of comic detachment. A great strength of his work is his ability to create compelling minor characters, all of them gifted talkers, whose presence both diffuses and enhances the works' central preoccupations. In addition, McGinley is not averse to placing the reader in the lexical equivalent of his protagonists' opacity of perception by the inclusion of archaic and unfamiliar terminology. Here again, however, this tactic is employed in a spirit of play rather than one of dogmatism, just as his works as a whole resist to an exemplary degree didacticism and moralizing, preferring to articulate consciousness as a field of forces too vivid to be ignored and too broad to be disciplined. The greatest pleasure to be derived from McGinley's fiction, therefore, is not merely from its undoubtedly attractive and distracting stories, locales, and characters but also from the ruminative cast of mind that sets the various fictive effects in motion.

THE LOST SOLDIER'S SONG

All these elements are present in part or in full before *The Lost Soldier's Song*, and many of them remain important even in this novel, which represents a departure from McGinley's previous fiction. Far from being a crime novel, except perhaps in the sense that the criminality of war is expressed in its pages, this novel focuses on the experiences of Declan Osborne and Maureen Sheehy during the Black and Tan War and the war's repercussions. As in his previous novels, however, McGinley continues his poetic attachment to place with his descriptions of locales such as the enchanted Chalice, his deft creation of minor characters in such figures as the enigmatic Owney Muldowney, his preoccupation with death, and his refusal to moralize.

Some of the most memorable and significant passages in this novel center on what is elemental, and they ably unite place, character, and philosophical concern. After having the prisoners he had taken at Loganboy murdered by McColl, for instance, Declan recalls the bog cotton that had attracted him one summer day with its whiteness from a distance.

However, when viewed closely its corruption was revealed, giving him "a lesson in Irish history," for he had engrossed himself in the middle of something "best viewed from firm ground and from afar." Maureen's tale of the "shadow of redness in the air" left by a passing fox in the rural countryside brings to mind her dead brother, who would have made up a tale to explain the fox's phantom, making her recognize that "what you miss about people is the way they put things. When they've gone, you realise that they've left a little bit of their mind in yours." Declan's own vision of a running fox, "fully and superbly alive," forces him to realize that the courage he showed at Loganboy may never be duplicated; he can never again take anything for granted.

As this example shows and as is true of McGinley's earlier novels, his characters are totally cognizant of their true condition. This is especially true of Declan, who clearly understands his motive for becoming and remaining involved in the war—to find a place for himself in the world, ironically comparable to the safe haven sought by McGinley's characters in previous novels. He unmistakably realizes that luck, not courage, led to his spur-of-the-moment heroism at Fiachra's Well. Like McGinley's other protagonists, Declan is an existential hero who relentlessly follows his course, despite the fact that he is never quite sure he believes in it.

What makes this novel different from McGinley's previous fiction is the necessary importance of the historical perspective, for none of the events would occur without the presence of the war. It is the war that also serves as the philosophical core of the book, as is seen when Declan and Ganly come to realize that they are "fighting high-handed imperialism with high-minded barbarism." Before she drowns herself in the Black Pool, the emotionally wounded Maureen appropriately writes the epitaph for the war: "It was a strange victory. . . . For some it was more like a defeat." Indeed, the final pages of the novel lead the reader to wonder what has improved for the heroes of the war who return to the brickyards or to the farms they had so wanted to escape. Sober, philosophical, poetic, and yet permeated with irony, *The Lost Soldier's Song* lies firmly in the mainstream of Irish fiction, while at the same time continuing to be stylistically and philosophically connected to McGinley's previous fiction.

George O'Brien
Updated by Jaquelyn W. Walsh

BIBLIOGRAPHY

Brown, Richard E. "Patrick McGinley's Novels of Detection." *Colby Quarterly* 33 (September, 1997): 209-222. Brown discusses McGinley's mystery novels as parodies of the traditional detective novel.

Cahalan, James M. *The Irish Novel: A Critical History.* Boston: Twayne, 1988. The concluding chapter of this study is a survey of contemporary Irish fiction, which provides a good sense of McGinley's context. There are also stimulating, though necessarily brief, asides on McGinley's works up to and including *The Red Men.*

Clissmann, Anne. *Flann O'Brien: A Critical Introduction to His Writings*. New York: Barnes & Noble Books, 1975. Chapters 2 and 3 of this work offer a useful means of assessing the imaginative terrain upon which much of McGinley's fiction rests.

Kenner, Hugh. "A Deep and Lasting Mayonnaise." *The New York Times Book Review*, July 21, 1985. A review of *The Trick of the Ga Bolga* by an influential literary critic. Many of McGinley's interests and orientations are succinctly brought to the fore.

Knowles, Nancy. "Empty Rhetoric: Argument by Credibility in Patrick McGinley's *Bogmail*." *English Language Notes* 39 (March, 2002): 79-87. An analysis of the novel, commenting on the postmodern, poststructuralist nature of McGinley's representation of language as "empty," an endless chain of signifiers chasing an elusive signified.

Madden, David W. "Patrick McGinley." In *Critical Survey of Mystery and Detective Fiction*, edited by Carl Rollyson. Rev. ed. Pasadena, Calif.: Salem Press, 2008. Volume 3 of this survey includes an overview of McGinley's life and work, with analyses of *Bogmail, Goosefoot, The Trick of the Ga Bolga, The Red Men*, and *Foxprints* and a discussion about the general character of McGinley's detective fiction.

Patten, Eve. "Contemporary Irish Fiction." In *The Cambridge Companion to the Irish Novel*, edited by John Wilson Foster. New York: Cambridge University Press, 2006. Patten briefly discusses McGinley's novels *Bogmail, Goosefoot*, and *The Trick of the Ga Bolga* in her examination of contemporary Irish fiction, placing McGinley's work in a broader literary context

Shea, Thomas F. "Patrick McGinley's Impressions of Flann O'Brien: *The Devil's Diary* and *At Swim-Two-Birds*." *Twentieth Century Literature* 40 (Summer, 1994): 272-281. Taking a cue from Hugo McSharry, the novelist-character in the work, Shea examines McGinley's novel as a palimpsest, a parchment partially erased yet retaining traces of the original inscriptions, with the echoes of other writers, particularly Flann O'Brien.

CHARLES ROBERT MATURIN

Born: Dublin, Ireland; September 25, 1780
Died: Dublin, Ireland; October 30, 1824
Also known as: Dennis Jasper Murphy

PRINCIPAL LONG FICTION

Fatal Revenge: Or, The Family of Montorio, 1807 (as Dennis Jasper Murphy)
The Wild Irish Boy, 1808 (as Murphy)
The Milesian Chief, 1812 (as Murphy)
Women: Or, Pour et Contre, 1818
Melmoth the Wanderer, 1820
The Albigenses, 1824

OTHER LITERARY FORMS

In addition to his novels, Charles Robert Maturin (MAT-choo-rihn) also wrote plays, three of which were performed and published during his lifetime: *Bertram: Or, The Castle of St. Aldobrand, a Tragedy* (pr., pb. 1816), *Manuel* (pr., pb. 1817), and *Fredolfo* (pr., pb. 1819). A fourth, *Osmyn, the Renegade: Or, The Siege of Salerno, a Tragedy*, written sometime between 1817 and 1821, was produced in Dublin in 1830. It was never published in its entirety; excerpts were printed in *The Edinburgh Literary Journal* (April 24, 1830). Of these plays, only *Bertram* was financially successful. When it first appeared, it was one of the most talked about plays of the season, and today it is noted for being one of the first dramatic portrayals of the brooding, sinned against, and sinning figure who has come to be called the Byronic hero.

Two short fictional pieces were published posthumously: "Leixlip Castle: An Irish Family Legend" appeared in *The Literary Souvenir: Or, Cabinet of Poetry and Romance* of 1825, and "The Sybil's Prophecy: A Dramatic Fragment" was printed in the 1826 edition of the same publication. Both these pieces are in the gothic style.

ACHIEVEMENTS

Charles Robert Maturin is best known for *Melmoth the Wanderer*, the fifth of his six novels. Although, when it first appeared, many critics viewed it merely as an unfortunate attempt to revive the gothic novel, a form earlier made popular by such authors as Ann Radcliffe and Matthew Gregory Lewis, scholars now consider *Melmoth the Wanderer* one of the finest examples of its genre. It is judged to be not only a culmination of the gothic novel but also a forerunner of the psychological novels of such writers as Fyodor Dostoevski and Franz Kafka. Although Maturin's handling of narrative structure is often awkward and confusing, and although he borrowed so closely from the works of others

Charles Robert Maturin
(Library of Congress)

that he can be accused of plagiarism, his novels are original in their depiction of extreme states of mind, especially those engendered by fear.

Maturin himself was aware of his major strength. In the prefatory pages of *The Milesian Chief*, he wrote

> If I possess any talent, it is that of darkening the gloomy, and of deepening the sad; of painting life in extremes, and representing those struggles of passion when the soul trembles on the verge of the unlawful and the unhallowed.

His settings of mazelike madhouses and dungeons lead the reader into the dark places of the human soul. This particular aspect of his novels fascinated and influenced many other authors. Edgar Allan Poe, Robert Louis Stevenson, Oscar Wilde, Christina and Dante Gabriel Rossetti, Honoré de Balzac, and Charles Baudelaire were all impressed by Maturin's attempt to penetrate the mystery of evil.

Critical attention also has been given to Maturin's role in Irish literary history. In such novels as *The Milesian Chief* and *The Wild Irish Boy*, descriptions of Irish settings and character play an important part. More study needs to be done to evaluate fully this contribution to the development of the Irish regional novel; whatever the outcome, Maturin's place among the significant writers of the English gothic novel is assured.

BIOGRAPHY

Charles Robert Maturin was born in 1780, one of several children born to William Maturin and Fidelia Watson. The Maturin family was of French descent. One of their ancestors was a Huguenot priest who was forced to leave France because of religious persecution during the reign of Louis XIV. This aspect of his family history strongly impressed the young Maturin, and throughout his life he was fond of relating how his ancestors had suffered for their faith. He himself was strongly anti-Catholic and especially opposed to the rule of monastic life, which he considered dangerously repressive. His novels contain many scenes and descriptions of monasteries as sadistic places where virtue turns to vice.

When in Ireland, Maturin's family became closely connected with the Anglican Church. Maturin's great-grandfather, Peter Maturin, was dean of Killala from 1724 to 1741, and his grandfather, Gabriel James Maturin, succeeded Jonathan Swift as dean of St. Patrick's in Dublin in 1745. Following this tradition, Maturin entered Trinity College in 1795 to study theology, and in 1803 he took holy orders. In the same year, he married Henrietta Kingsbury, a daughter of the archdeacon of Killala. From all reports, the couple were well suited and happily married. After ordination, Maturin served as curate in Loughrea, Galway, for two years. He then returned to Dublin to become curate of St. Peter's, a position he held for the rest of his life. His small income from this curacy was insufficient to support his family, especially after his father was accused of fraud and dismissed from his position with the Irish post office in 1809. Later, he was cleared and given another position, but for a time, the family struggled in severe poverty. In fact, Maturin was continually troubled by financial difficulties. To supplement his income, he ran a school to prepare boys for college, and later he turned to novel writing.

The prefaces of his novels and the styles of romance he chose to employ indicate that he wanted very much to become a popular writer. Because he realized that many of his parishioners and superiors might not approve of a minister writing novels, he used the pseudonym Dennis Jasper Murphy, publishing three novels under that name. When it was discovered that he was the author of the play *Bertram*, a play involving adultery and an amoral hero, he was for a time in danger of losing his curacy. Apparently, friends intervened to soothe the necessary bishops. After this incident, since his identity was known, he published his next novels and plays under his own name. It is quite possible that his literary activities did prevent his advancement in the clerical profession. There were those who interpreted the beliefs of his characters, some of which were atheistic and heretical, as Maturin's own.

Maturin's novels did gain him one very influential friend, Sir Walter Scott. In 1810, Scott wrote a generally favorable review of *Fatal Revenge* for *The Quarterly Review*. Encouraged, Maturin wrote to him, and a correspondence was begun that lasted until Maturin's death. Although the two never actually met, Scott did assist Maturin with encouragement and advice, and he was instrumental in Maturin's one financial success; he recommended *Bertram* to Lord Byron, who was then responsible for play selection at Drury Lane Theatre. Byron was favorably impressed, and the famous actor Edmund Kean agreed to play the lead. The play's success earned Maturin one thousand pounds, most of which paid a relative's debt. Earlier, Maturin had been able to sell the copyright of his third novel, *The Milesian Chief,* for eighty pounds (the first two novels he had printed at his own expense), and later he was advanced five hundred pounds for *Melmoth the Wanderer,* but his literary efforts never brought the long-sought and often desperately needed financial stability.

Up until his death, Maturin continually tried to write in a style that would sell. *The Albigenses* is a historical romance, a type Scott had established and made quite popular. This novel was the first in what was to be a trilogy depicting European manners in ancient, medieval, and modern times. Soon after *The Albigenses* was completed, Maturin died in his home on October 30, 1824, apparently after a long period of ill health. The exact cause of his death is not known. He left his wife and four children, who were still in desperate need of financial assistance.

ANALYSIS

In his preface to *Fatal Revenge,* Charles Robert Maturin stresses the fear of the unknown as essential in the emotional and spiritual lives of humans:

> It is *not* the weak and trivial impulse of the nursery, to be forgotten and scorned by manhood. It is the aspiration of a spirit; 'it is the passion of immortals,' that dread and desire of their final habitation.

In one of his sermons, he focuses on the same theme:

> The very first sounds of childhood are tales of another life—foolishly are they called tales of superstition; for, however disguised by the vulgarity of narration, and the distortion of fiction, they tell him of those whom he is hastening from the threshold of life to join, the inhabitants of the invisible world, with whom he must soon be, and be for ever.

These quotations indicate a major aspect of Maturin's perception of human existence; the haunted and the sacred are interwoven and share a common ground. Human fascination with the supernatural, the world of demons and ghosts, springs from the same source as the desire to believe in salvation and a return to paradise. In fact, the road to salvation leads through the dark places of the soul where individuals must admit their fallen state, their own guilt.

The theme of guilt is common in all of Maturin's novels. His major characters must struggle with the serpents in their own hearts, their own original sin. In keeping with this theme, the settings of his novels are generally those of a fallen world; dungeons and underground passages are common backgrounds for the action. Even in those novels that contain descriptions of more natural surroundings, storms and earthquakes are common occurrences, always reminding people that they have been exiled from paradise. Harmony with nature, with humanity, and with God has been lost.

Maturin develops this theme of guilt, which brings exile and separation, through his handling of character. The divided nature of humanity is represented by the pairing of characters, especially brothers: Ippolito and Annibal in *Fatal Revenge*, Connal and Desmond in *The Milesian Chief*, Paladour and Amirald in *The Albigenses*. These brothers are described in such a way as to suggest one identity fragmented into two opposing selves. Ippolito is passionate, Annibal rational; Desmond is the soft flower, Connal the proud oak. Often a character is torn in two opposing directions and does not know how to reconcile them: Connal between his Irish pride and his realization that the Irish peasants are not yet ready to govern themselves; Charles in *Women* between his love for Eva, a shy quiet girl, and Zaira, a worldly and more accomplished woman. At times, a character seems pursued by a dark, sinister double: Montorio by Schemoli in *Fatal Revenge*; Alonzo by the parricide in *Melmoth the Wanderer*. By far the most striking and powerful example of this is the character of the wanderer himself. Melmoth represents the potential for evil that can be found in all humans. In developing Melmoth's character, Maturin echoes the warning in Genesis against too much curiosity about the tree of knowledge of good and evil. Melmoth has sold his soul for increased knowledge; his sin is one of "pride and intellectual glorying," the sin of Lucifer and of the first mortals.

As Maturin's characters wander in a fallen world, little guidance is provided. Especially weak and ineffective are the parental figures. In fact, a distinguishing trait of this fallen world is the disintegration of the family. In all of Maturin's six novels, there are parents who are woefully irresponsible. They are often self-centered, putting their own greedy desires before their children's welfare, or they seek to expiate their own guilt by placing the burden of their sin upon their children. This selfish turning inward and transference of guilt to another is also found in Maturin's representations of larger structures of authority, especially the Catholic Church. As the divided soul wanders in a fallen world, parent and church offer little hope.

Maturin reserves the role of spiritual guide for the female characters who either love or are loved by the hero (such love is not always fulfilled or requited). Often his women are idealized creatures who can reconcile within themselves all conflicting opposites: in *Melmoth the Wanderer*, Immalee embodies passion and purity; in *The Albigenses*, Genevieve is a "mixture of strength and purity that is never to be found but in woman." Even if a woman finds herself hurled into a world of experience and corruption, as Zaira is in *Women*, her heart remains pure. At times, Maturin uses his female characters to symbolize self-sacrificing love that, although never placing the beloved before God, does place the beloved before the self. Despite Maturin's emphasis on such redeeming love, however, when domestic happiness is found by his characters it seems contrived and imposed upon them by others. Maturin is undoubtedly at his best when depicting people lost and searching for wholeness, not in actually finding it.

FATAL REVENGE

Maturin titled his first novel *The Family of Montorio*, but the publisher changed the title to *Fatal Revenge*, hoping to attract readers who would be interested in a gothic tale. The novel is definitely written in the style of Radcliffe—one of its central figures, a ghostlike monk who calls himself Schemoli, is clearly patterned on Radcliffe's Schoedoni in 1797's *The Italian*—but Maturin uses what he borrows to develop his own characteristic theme with originality. Although he follows Radcliffe's technique of revealing the supernatural events as merely the result of disguise and charade, his descriptions of aberrant states of mind, to which all are subject, go beyond her handling of evil, and beyond the mere cataloging of grotesque horrors used by those writers who chose to imitate the more sensational style of Matthew Gregory Lewis. Annibal concludes after a brief period of solitary confinement that an "inward acquaintance" delights one not with tranquillity but, on the contrary, with "the grave of the mind." In describing the anguish of his guilt, Montorio cries, "the worm within me never dieth; and every thought and object it converts into its own morbid food." In Maturin, the evil within is quite real.

The plot of this novel is complicated, and Maturin's narrative is at times twisted and confusing. The tale relates the vengeful machinations of Schemoli, the once noble Count Montorio. He is seeking revenge for the wrongs his younger brother committed against him by manipulating Ippolito and Annibal, two young men he believes are his brother's sons, into believing that they are fated to murder their father. In part, the novel's convoluted structure works to Maturin's advantage, for it helps create a nightmare quality that suits this theme of revenge and guilt. By the end of the novel, after several brutal crimes, it is clear that the words of Ippolito to the Inquisition accurately represent human nature as portrayed in the novel:

> There is no human being fully known to another. . . . To his own consciousness and recollection, a man will not dare to reveal every thought that visits his mind; there are some which he almost hopes are concealed from the Deity.

THE WILD IRISH BOY

Maturin's second novel, *The Wild Irish Boy*, although often following the style of the sentimental, regional novel, still has some of the same motifs and themes as those of the gothic *Fatal Revenge*. The novel does have many flaws and is probably Maturin's poorest work: There are long pointless digressions, a decidedly awkward handling of point of view, and an ineffective mixture of literary techniques. Nevertheless, when Maturin touches upon those subjects that most fascinated him, he does so with some success. The novel's most interesting character is Lady Montrevor, a strong, compelling woman who through her own foolish vanity allows herself to be trapped into a loveless marriage, thus sacrificing the sincere love of a good man. She must bear the anguish of her loss and the knowledge of her guilt. She does so grandly, wanting no man's pity. Maturin often alludes to John Milton's fallen angel when describing her: She is "no less than archangel ruined." In many ways, she is a female Byronic hero who knows that evil is more than appearance. This type of female character clearly interested Maturin. Zaira in *Women* and Armida in *The Milesian Chief* are similarly delineated, and all three are quite unlike the sentimental heroines so typical of the other novelists of the day.

THE MILESIAN CHIEF

In Maturin's third novel, *The Milesian Chief*, his interest in the anguish of the proud heart reveals itself in his portrayal of the hero as well as of the heroine. Connal, the Irish rebel, is the once-great angelic chief fallen among lesser spirits, an appropriate male partner for the melancholy Armida, who is shaded by a "proud dejection, like that of an abdicated monarch." The novel is set in Ireland during an uprising against the British in 1798. As the plot unfolds, it becomes clear that Maturin is more successful in handling narrative structure and point of view than in his previous works, and although the final scene, in which the four major characters (Connal, Armida, Desmond, and Ines) all die more or less at the same time in the same place, seems contrived, it is psychologically appropriate. Throughout the novel, these four personalities have been interwoven. Connal and Desmond function as opposites linked in one identity, and each female character both mirrors and complements her male counterpart. Again, even when trying to write a regional novel, Maturin shows that his main interest lies in depicting the individual lost and searching for a way back to some longed-for paradise.

WOMEN

In his preface to *Women*, Maturin writes that he believes his previous novels failed to win popular approval because they lacked reality. He indicates that in this novel he has fashioned his characters to resemble those of "common life." This intention does not, however, cause any significant change in his major theme. Again, through his three central characters, Maturin depicts human nature as torn and guilt ridden. Charles vacillates between his love for Eva, a shy innocent girl, and Zaira, the older, more accomplished woman. He is never able to commit himself fully to loving one or the other until it is too late. Only when Eva is dying of consumption brought on by Charles's abandoning her for Zaira does he desert Zaira to return to Eva.

Throughout the novel, Eva has struggled with her love for Charles, for in her heart it conflicts with her love for God. On her deathbed, she rejects Charles completely, refusing even to see him, and she dies at peace with God. Zaira undergoes a similar ordeal after Charles abandons her. She turns to God, hoping for consolation, yet she continues to see Charles's image before her eyes. After Eva's death, Charles dies from fever and madness. As the novel closes, Zaira becomes the primary figure of guilt. She lives on, always holding her hand to her heart, accusing herself of having murdered her daughter. She has discovered that Eva was the child taken from her at birth, the child she has been trying to find.

This discovery is not made until it is too late to remedy the painful consequences of the mother and daughter loving the same man. Maturin concludes the novel with an image typical of his style: "The serpents that devour us, are generated out of our own vitals."

MELMOTH THE WANDERER

Although Maturin's preface to *Melmoth the Wanderer* suggests that what follows will show the reader the enemy of humankind in the form of Satan, the tales within tales that constitute the novel show instead that this enemy lies within each individual. By combining the qualities of Faust, Mephistopheles, and the Wandering Jew, Maturin fashioned a hero-villain suitable for leading the reader through the maze of tales that takes him into the obscure recesses of the human soul.

Melmoth is Maturin's most compelling and powerful character; he is an embodiment of the dark side of each human being, the shadow that each person casts. Thus, it is particularly appropriate that in the narrative frame of these tales of human malignity, John Melmoth, who bears the same name as the mysterious wanderer, inherits the task of dealing with the molding manuscript that will set him on his own journey into the mystery of evil. His withdrawal at midnight into a closed room, sealed off from society, to read the manuscript, disregarding his uncle's warning that perhaps he should destroy it unread, suggests a type of original sin. Indeed, as he pursues knowledge of the wanderer's life, he learns that all humans are potential agents of Satan. After all, Melmoth the Wanderer did not spring from the fires of hell, but from his own family.

The hope that Maturin offers in his guilty state is to be found in self-sacrificing love; yet to love in this manner one must believe in the potential for goodness in humankind, the possibility of redemption. Melmoth is finally damned not because of his original bargain to sell his soul but because of his own misanthropy. He believes in nothing but the hostility and evil of human nature. Immalee, the island maiden who learns of suffering by loving him, was his hope. If he had chosen to trust in her love, seeing in it the essence of the greater self-sacrificing love of Christ, he might have been saved.

THE ALBIGENSES

Maturin's last work, *The Albigenses*, is a historical novel that focuses on the crusade in 1208 against the Albigenses, a Manichaean sect declared heretical by the Catholic Church. Maturin, however, follows the historical facts only roughly, altering events and chronology to suit plot and character. Again, he portrays two brothers, Paladour and Amirald, and their two loves, Isebelle and Genevieve. Although the theme of the fragmented self is not as predominant as in his previous novels, it is present. Paladour and Amirald were separated at birth, and for most of the novel neither knows the other is his brother; they are characterized in such a way as to suggest differing aspects of one personality. Paladour is associated with iron and Amirald with flowers, yet they are bound together through suffering. In choosing their brides, they also reveal complementary personality traits: Paladour marries the noble Lady Isebelle, and Amirald chooses the simple peasant girl Genevieve. When the novel ends, the reader is left with the impression that all four live together in absolute harmony.

Such an easy resolution does seemed contrived, for *The Albigenses* begins with Paladour's sinister encounter with a seemingly demoniac lady of the lake. He believes there is a curse upon him and that he is fated to murder his bride on their wedding night. When the effects of these dark tones are no longer wanted, Maturin quickly resolves all with rational explanations. Paladour is then free to live as a very natural husband. Part of the dissatisfaction the reader feels with this happy ending may be accounted for by the fact that the novel bristles with gothic motifs that are not smoothly integrated into the historical aspects of the novel.

Despite Maturin's own belief that the day of the gothic novel had already passed when he began writing, and his repeated attempts to use whatever narrative form might suit the reading public, he was continually drawn to the techniques of the gothic tale. Whether it be a mysterious monk haunting underground passages or a madwoman raving prophetic truths, all his novels have gothic elements. The gothic novel provided him with a literary world suitable for the images of evil and suffering that populated his own mind, a mind repeatedly drawn to the problems of human guilt and the divided soul. The body of Maturin's work, although uneven, offers ample proof of his ability to shape these dark themes with power and originality.

Diane D'Amico

OTHER MAJOR WORKS

SHORT FICTION: "Leixlip Castle: An Irish Family Legend," 1825 (in *The Literary Souvenir: Or, Cabinet of Poetry and Romance*); "The Sybil's Prophecy: A Dramatic Fragment" 1826 (in *The Literary Souvenir*).

PLAYS: *Bertram: Or, The Castle of St. Aldobrand, a Tragedy*, pr., pb. 1816; *Manuel*, pr., pb. 1817; *Fredolfo*, pr., pb. 1819; *Osmyn, the Renegade: Or, The Siege of Salerno, a Tragedy*, pr. 1830.

BIBLIOGRAPHY

Bayer-Berenbaum, Linda. *The Gothic Imagination: Expansion in Gothic Literature and Art*. Rutherford, N.J.: Fairleigh Dickinson University Press, 1982. A sympathetic study of gothicism, the essence of which is its confrontation with evil and feelings of doom. Maturin is given considerable attention, including an extensive analysis of *Melmoth the Wanderer*.

Jeffares, A. Norman, and Peter van de Kamp. *Irish Literature: The Nineteenth Century*. Dublin: Irish Academic Press, 2006-2007. A three-volume reference set that contains critical essays about the lives and works of numerous Irish writers. Includes an essay on Maturin in the first volume.

Johnson, Anthony. "Gaps and Gothic Sensibility: Walpole, Lewis, Mary Shelley, and Maturin." In *Exhibited by Candlelight: Sources and Developments in the Gothic Tradition*, edited by Valeria Tinkler-Villani, Peter Davidson, and Jane Stevenson. Amsterdam: Rodopi, 1995. This study of gothic literature includes Johnson's learned and clear discussion of how Maturin handles the gaps in reality that are exploited in gothic fiction.

Kiely, Robert. *The Romantic Novel in England*. Cambridge, Mass.: Harvard University Press, 1972. An important book about Romantic prose fiction, including Maturin's gothic romances, which analyzes twelve Romantic novels. *Melmoth the Wanderer* is covered in detail; this novel is found to be more emotionally involved with Catholicism and rebellion against authoritarian political systems than other gothic fiction.

Kosok, Heinz. "Charles Robert Maturin and Colonialism." In *Literary Inter-Relations: Ireland, Egypt, and the Far East*, edited by Mary Massoud. Gerrards Cross, England: C. Smythe, 1996. Kosok's paper, initially delivered in 1993 at a conference examining Ireland's literary relationships with countries in the Middle and Far East, focuses on Maturin's representation of colonialism.

Kramer, Dale. *Charles Robert Maturin*. New York: Twayne, 1973. Analyzes Maturin's personality, describes the conditions of his life, and indicates his innovations in the gothic tradition. Includes a chronology, notes and references, a selected annotated bibliography, and an index.

Lougy, Robert E. *Charles Robert Maturin*. Lewisburg, Pa.: Bucknell University Press, 1975. An insightful review of Maturin's life and writings, dividing his career into early, middle, and later years. Includes a chronology and a selected bibliography of primary and secondary works.

Moynahan, Julian. "The Politics of Anglo-Irish Gothic: Charles Robert Maturin, Joseph Sheridan Le Fanu, and the Return of the Repressed." In *Anglo-Irish: The Literary Imagination in a Hyphenated Culture*. Princeton, N.J.: Princeton University Press, 1995. Moynahan's analysis of gothic literature by the two authors is included in his study of literary works written by Anglo-Irish authors during the nineteenth century.

Norton, Rictor, ed. *Gothic Readings: The First Wave, 1764-1840*. London: Leicester University Press, 2000. This study of gothic literature includes an excerpt from *Melmoth the Wanderer*, which is defined as belonging to "the German school of horror," and two contemporary reviews of the novel, including one by Sir Walter Scott. Useful for placing Maturin within the larger context of the gothic and Romantic novel.

BRIAN MOORE

Born: Belfast, Northern Ireland; August 25, 1921
Died: Malibu, California; January 11, 1999
Also known as: Michael Bryan; Bernard Mara

PRINCIPAL LONG FICTION

Judith Hearne, 1955 (also known as *The Lonely Passion of Judith Hearne*)
The Feast of Lupercal, 1957
The Luck of Ginger Coffey, 1960
An Answer from Limbo, 1962
The Emperor of Ice-Cream, 1965
I Am Mary Dunne, 1968
Fergus, 1970
Catholics, 1972
The Great Victorian Collection, 1975
The Doctor's Wife, 1976
The Mangan Inheritance, 1979
The Temptation of Eileen Hughes, 1981
Cold Heaven, 1983
Black Robe, 1985
The Colour of Blood, 1987 (also known as *The Color of Blood*)
Lies of Silence, 1990
No Other Life, 1993
The Statement, 1995
The Magician's Wife, 1997

OTHER LITERARY FORMS

In addition to his novels, Brian Moore wrote a travel book, *Canada*, with the editors of *Life* magazine in 1963. A number of his works were regarded by Moore himself as hackwork, written to support his serious fiction; these include romances and mysteries, some published under the pseudonym Michael Bryan. His dozens of short stories appeared in a wide range of periodicals, from *Weekend Review* to *The Atlantic*, and in anthologies including *The Irish Genius*, edited by Devin A. Garrity (1960); *Canadian Writing Today*, edited by Mordecai Richler (1970); and *The Best American Short Stories, 1967* (1967), edited by Martha Foley and David Burnett. Throughout his writing career, he published many articles and reviews. Several of Moore's books have been adapted for films and television, and he wrote screenplays and teleplays produced in the United States, Canada, and Great Britain.

ACHIEVEMENTS

Brian Moore's first novel, published both as *Judith Hearne* and as *The Lonely Passion of Judith Hearne*, established him as a contemporary novelist of the first order. He has appealed to many readers as a novelist who writes without embarrassment in the realistic tradition of the Victorians about distinctively modern topics: spiritual and erotic crises, the reality of the objective world, ethnic conflict, relationships between men and women, and the place of women in the societies of the old world and the new. Modern themes of alienation and estrangement are rooted firmly in Moore's work by a sense of place and of time. His evocation of Montreal in *The Luck of Ginger Coffey* has been compared to James Joyce's portrayal of Dublin on "Bloomsday." The bleak urban environment of Belfast of the earlier works and the windswept Irish coast of *The Mangan Inheritance* strike responsive chords in readers conditioned to the blank landscapes of much modernist literature.

Just as Moore's geographical terrain changes, however, so do his characters and his stylistic formats. From the almost naturalistic treatment of the unfortunate Judith Hearne to the ghostly dialogues of Fergus and the magical creation of *The Great Victorian Collection*, from the Jesuit missionaries in *Black Robe* to the terrorists in *Lies of Silence*, Moore's unpredictable inventiveness and his sure hand in storytelling and character development kept him in the forward ranks of late twentieth century novelists.

Among the honors Moore received were a Guggenheim Fellowship, an award from the American National Institute of Arts and Letters, a Canada Council Fellowship, the Author's Club of Great Britain First Novel Award, the Governor-General Award of Canada for fiction, and honorary literature degrees from Queens University, Belfast (1989) and National University of Ireland, Dublin (1991). He was three times short-listed for the Booker Prize, for *The Doctor's Wife*, *The Color of Blood*, and *Lies of Silence*. *Catholics* won the W. H. Smith Award in 1973, and *The Great Victorian Collection* won the James Tait Black Memorial Prize in 1975. *Black Robe* was given the Heinemann Award from the Royal Society of Literature in 1986.

BIOGRAPHY

The basic facts of Brian Moore's life are familiar to anyone who knows his work, for he has mined heavily his own experiences for his novels. Moore was born in Belfast, in 1921, to James Bernard Moore, a fellow of the Royal College of Surgeons, and Eileen McFadden Moore. His childhood was a stable and fundamentally happy one; the warm and well-ordered O'Neill family in *Judith Hearne* was in fact identified by Moore in an interview as "a sort of facsimile of my own." Although his work reveals a continuing ambivalence about the order and protection of the family, as about other highly ordered forms of community, he clearly finds much to admire in the sort of family structure that provided his early nurturing.

Moore was educated in Catholic schools, leaving St. Malachi's College, Belfast, in 1940 to join the Air Raid Precautions Unit in Belfast. He served with that unit until 1942, when he left Belfast to serve as a civilian employee of the British Ministry of War Transport in North Africa, Italy, and France. Immediately after the war, he served as a port officer in Warsaw, and then remained for some time in Scandinavia, where he was a freelance reporter in Sweden, Finland, and Norway until he emigrated to Canada in 1948. From 1948 to 1952, he continued his career as a journalist in Montreal. His Canadian newspaper career began humbly; he was first a proofreader for the *Montreal Gazette*. He was promoted to reporter, an occupation he continued until he began writing pulp fiction to finance his serious work. Although some of his serious short fiction was published in the early 1950's, Moore was forced to continue to write pulp fiction until the appearance of *Judith Hearne* in 1955, and even after, under the pseudonym Michael Bryan.

The early stages of Moore's life and work essentially came to a close two years after the publication of *Judith Hearne* with the appearance of his second novel, *The Feast of Lupercal*. Shortly thereafter, he moved to the United States from Canada, and in 1959, received the Guggenheim Fellowship that allowed him to complete one of his most highly regarded works, *The Luck of Ginger Coffey* (1960). Between 1960 and the publication of *The Emperor of Ice-Cream* in 1965, he published *An Answer from Limbo*. Moore said, in an interview with Hallvard Dahlie, that a dramatic change in his life occurred in the years between the publication of the latter two novels: "I am much happier now than I was when I was thirty-five or forty. *Emperor* was written at a crucial time in my life—it was the first book after I changed." That change was demonstrated also in his personal life during the year of *The Emperor of Ice-Cream*'s publication. In 1966, Moore married his second wife, Jean Denny, his first marriage having been to Jacqueline Sirois.

From 1966 until his death in 1999, Moore continued to publish at the rate of a novel every one to three years. Although he maintained Canadian citizenship, he continued to live in the United States, in a house overlooking the Pacific Ocean, near Oxnard, California.

ANALYSIS

Although he became increasingly cosmopolitan in his adult life, Brian Moore's work is very much rooted in the place of his origin—Northern Ireland—in his middle-class Irish Catholic upbringing, and in concerns readers have learned to recognize in the work of several generations of Irish writers, from John Millington Synge, William Butler Yeats, and James Joyce to the present. In his earlier work at least, Moore was fettered by the ghost of Evelyn Waugh's Irishman, "dragging everywhere with him his ancient rancours and the melancholy of the bogs." That Irishman, however, is transformed by the multiplicity of thematic and structural interests of the inventive Moore.

Beginning with *Judith Hearne*, the themes that primarily occupied Moore throughout his literary career emerge. There is the struggle with the fathers—fathers embodied in the family, in the Church, in the community, and in Ireland itself, which Moore portrays as a restrictively ordered world isolated from the freer West by Joyce's "dark, mutinous Shannon waves" ("The Dead"). Against the protective but stultifying structures that order life, the individual spirit struggles. On the one side is safety and security, but with the prospect of extended childhood, with its continuing demands for obedience and submission. On the other is adulthood, individual responsibility, the possibility of liberation through the imagination beyond the childish fantasizing that characterizes life within the restricted community—but also on that side is the threat of the void.

The tension between these conflicting choices provides both form and substance to nearly all of Moore's serious fiction. In the earlier works, the struggle is overt and played out in simple correspondences. Judith Hearne, middle-aged, unmarried, and without real personal attachments, except in fantasy, faces literal extinction in her crisis of faith. Diarmud Devine is left sexually and morally powerless as he submits to the hierarchy of the fathers at St. Michan's, and Ginger Coffey is a man without country or community as he severs all ties that bind him to his Irish past.

The tension that characterizes Moore's work is a familiar one, as is the resulting ironic tone that several generations of modern critics since Allen Tate have described. Perhaps in no literature, however, is either the tension or the ironic tone more pervasive than in the Irish tradition to which Moore so clearly belongs. Certainly, the conflict between the desire to identify with and belong to the community on one hand and the need, on the other hand, to define oneself as an individual is nearly universal in Irish literature. Moreover, as Andrew Carpenter has noted, many Irish writers seem to have a double vision that derives "from a view of life that is continually probing the different values which exist in Ireland and testing them one against the other" and from immersion in "interrelationships between values, philosophies and cultures antipathetic if not downright hostile to one another." Irish writers thus come naturally to multiple points of view as well as to the idea that opposing points of view are equally acceptable; they "see two things at once," but "with one eye at a time." This peculiar double vision is manifestly present in Moore's fiction.

JUDITH HEARNE

Explaining the protagonist of the same name of his first novel, *Judith Hearne*, Moore told Hallvard Dahlie that "I wanted my major character to be someone who wasn't me—who could never be mistaken for me. . . . And yet, I was lonely for much of my life, and so I put something of myself into her." This lonely spinster on the brink of middle age with her "chances" all behind her is bedeviled by the same Irish ghosts that confront nearly all of Moore's protagonists, male and female.

Judith Hearne is a true daughter of Catholic Ireland. The "real" world in which she lives is bounded by Church, family—or the idea of family—and sexual mores so restrictive that fantasy life becomes a compelling escape. In Moore's later novels, beginning with *Fergus*, this fantasy life imposed by the Irish past finds an outlet in art; Moore's protagonists become novelists, poets, and even, in *The Great Victorian Collection*, necromancers. For Judith, however, there are only pitiful and predictable adolescent fantasies.

Nearly forty years old, Judith has found herself penniless, without home or family or prospects for either. Wherever she wanders in her penury and displacement after her aunt's death, she anchors herself with two objects: a photograph of her aunt and a picture of the Sacred Heart. Like a child, she ritualistically bids good night to these images of the only protective forces she knows as she turns off the light in her latest bed-sitter, and she is comforted by the knowledge that they are there for her in the darkness.

As her imaginary romance with Madden, the returned emigrant to America, unfolds, the childishness of Judith's fantasy life is revealed. Absorbed in personal ritual, she sits before her glass transforming through her imagination her plain, sallow face and angular figure into the "delightful illusion of beauty." Perhaps legitimately led to believe in Madden's interest in her—an interest later revealed to be motivated by a plan for a joint investment in a hamburger stand—Judith abandons herself to her fantasies. Her arrested sexual development and the debased view she, like nearly all of Moore's characters, has of the possibilities for relationships between men and women are demonstrated in a painful series of encounters with Madden, as in her daydreams about him: "He kissed her," she imagines, "Or, enraged about some silly thing she had done, he struck out with his great fist and sent her reeling, the brute. But, contrite afterwards, he sank to his knees and begged forgiveness."

Sexuality framed in violence, or tied to power struggles, is a hallmark of the identity crises that form the substance of so much of Moore's work. The submission and obedience demanded by religion and family preclude the assertiveness and self-confidence required for adult sexuality, or for any adult relationship. In the early novels, childish sexual fantasies, shaped by cheap romances and shadowed by disapproval of the fathers, are shattered in encounters with real men and women. Spiritual and erotic crises are thus established by Moore as essential to the search for identity in the restrictive world about which he writes.

Judith's passion is sexual, but it is the passion of religious suffering as well. When Judith's frantic search for meaning ends in her challenge to God in the tabernacle, even that door is locked against her. "In the old Irish choice between accepting actuality and retreating from it," Jeanne Flood observes, "the old Irish mistake is choosing the latter alternative." Judith's ultimate fiction at that moment of truth is to transform the scene into a pietà. Her imaginary salvation, like her crisis, is both religious and sexual:

> His mother ran up the altar steps, her painted face still sadly smiling, lifted her as she lay broken on the steps. . . . And He, His fingers uplifted in blessing, bent over her, His bleeding heart held against His white tunic. Lifted her in His arms and His face was close to hers.

In fantasy alone, Judith Hearne is able to have it all—the sheltering arms of family and religion, and the romantic encounter that can exist nowhere but in the adolescent imagination.

THE FEAST OF LUPERCAL

Though more obviously autobiographical, Moore's second novel, *The Feast of Lupercal*, is essentially a variation on the themes established in *Judith Hearne*. Set also in contemporary Belfast, the novel follows the ill-fated adventures of Diarmud Devine, a master at St. Michan's, the same Catholic school that Devine attended as a boy. Devine, now thirty-seven, has spent his entire life within the academic hierarchy of the Church. The family persists as a central force in his life as well, for Diarmud lives in a rented room furnished with the accoutrements of his parents' home. He sleeps in his boyhood bed and is watched over in his daily routines by his dead mother and father posed stiffly in their wedding picture.

The Feast of Lupercal, from which the novel takes its name, was a Roman festival celebrating the god of fertility. Against the ironic backdrop of a study of the festival with his sex-obsessed, leering, adolescent pupils, Diarmud is offered a chance at adult sexuality. The challenge is to abandon childish fantasy and to accept the demands of an adult relationship with its dimensions of sexuality, responsibility, and power. The nearly middle-aged man is unable, however, to bring the moment to its close. At the crucial moment, Dev sees the real Una not as a sinful temptress but as a young girl in a white slip "so unlike his sinful imaginings . . . the sinful imagination which atrophied reality."

The repressive moral world from which Dev has been unable to manage even the slightest distance requires only the simple judgments of childhood, uncluttered by the ambiguities of adult life. So long as Una remained a "hot Protestant," a representative of the sex who were "mockers, character assassins, every single one of them," the simple equations on which Moore's Catholic Ireland rests could be sustained. "Fancy putting yourself in a position where a woman could laugh at you. An intimate moment, a ridiculous posture—a declaration of love, for instance. Or on your wedding night, to hear a girl laugh at you." In the tradition of the early Church Fathers, man is the spirit and woman the body—the defiling physical presence. The sight of a real and vulnerable young woman, however, undoes the myth, and him, in a culturally caused sexual dysfunction suffered by heroes throughout Moore's work.

Dev makes the "Irish choice," retreating from actuality. Afraid of censure from the hierarchy of the fathers, who are embroiled in a power struggle of their own that threatens Dev, he abandons Una to the consequences of the morally compromising position in which he has placed her, and resigns himself to his narrow and deprived existence. The

boy who dreamed of marrying Madeleine Carroll, the film actress, and taking her to the Riviera where they would commit unknown flesh sins the priests warned about in sermons . . . [was] now a man of thirty-seven [who] had not lived a real life; he had been dreaming.

THE LUCK OF GINGER COFFEY

Moore's third novel, *The Luck of Ginger Coffey*, is set in Montreal, and its title character is a man who has nominally extricated himself from the ties of religion, family, and community that bind Judith Hearne and Dev. Still very much a son of Ireland, however, Ginger dreams of success in the New World, just as Judith dreams of love and marriage and Devine fantasizes sexual conquest. The affliction of the "Irish choice" makes Ginger a man for whom, as for Dev, real life is obscured by dreaming.

In Moore's later expatriate novels—and even at the end of *The Emperor of Ice-Cream*, when young Gavin Burke decides to leave Belfast—there is hope of fulfillment for his dreaming Irish men and women. Tierney in *An Answer from Limbo*, and the confused *poète maudit* of *The Mangan Inheritance*, Jamie Mangan, are endowed with the potentially transforming and liberating force of imagination. They are possessed of a creative power denied Ginger Coffey, as it had been denied to Judith and Dev.

Trapped in a series of cheap fictional images of success rooted in his Irish past, Ginger affects a Dublin squire look, and he thinks of himself as being in his soldierly prime, handsomely mustachioed and booted. A Canadian employer to whom he appeals sees him otherwise: "A limely type . . . with his tiny green hat, short bulky car coat and suede boots." Nor is he otherwise successful in adapting to his adopted country. The uniform of a diaper service delivery man is a mockery of his early dreams of military adventure. His dreams of an adventurous career as a journalist shrink in the cellar of the building where he works as a proofreader, and evaporate finally in the words of a dying coworker: "Irish. An immigrant same as you," the dying man tells him. Nearly forty, he looks at his dying compatriot and realizes what he has abandoned, and how little he has gained. Will he so end his days, "his voice nasal and reedy, all accent gone"? Coffey denies such a fate: "Yes, I'm Irish. James Francis Coffey. Fine Irish name."

In the end, though, Coffey is without country or community, and nearly without family, as his wife and daughter yield to the attractions of the vulgar materialism of the country to which he has brought them, in which he has insisted they stay, and where at last he resigns himself to life with them in "humble circs." His marriage to Veronica, née Shannon, whom he calls by a name for Ireland, "Dark Rosaleen," is his only tie to his native land. He must pay a dear price to sustain that tie, his only protection from the chaos that threatened Judith Hearne, and that Dev could not even contemplate. The price is to be what he most feared—an Irish failure, living with a wife he no longer wants, and working at a job worse than the one he left behind in the scorned Ulster.

AN ANSWER FROM LIMBO

Ginger Coffey represents to Moore, as he told Robert Fulford, "what I was terrified would happen to me. I've always felt myself to be a misfit, I still do." By contrast, Brendan Tierney, the protagonist of *An Answer from Limbo*, is the first of Moore's protagonists to possess the creative power that seems to have been Moore's salvation. Curiously, however, Tierney is a less sympathetic character than any of the three doomed and powerless protagonists who precede him in Moore's work. The hapless Judith, who suffers a woman's fate along with the burden of the Irish cross; the tragicomic Dev; and the feckless Ginger, who befriends the lonely child of his landlady in the middle of his troubles—all are caught in the grip of social circumstances, and all struggle to maintain dignity and humanity in spite of those circumstances. That humanity is absent in Brendan Tierney.

The theme of *An Answer from Limbo*, repeated in *Fergus* and in *I Am Mary Dunne*, is a problematic repudiation of the Irish past with its shackles of family, religion, and community in favor of a freer identity, shaped by the personal power of the imagination. Moore's disapproval of Tierney, as of later artist heroes, warns the reader, however, not to expect simple solutions to the conflict.

No childlike victim, no futile fantasizer, Brendan Tierney is a hard-eyed young writer who seems destined to achieve the success and fame for which he hungers. Replete with the self-confidence absent in Judith and Dev, and possessed of talent and purpose lacking in Ginger, Brendan expects his work to find a place among the ranks of "Kierkegaard and Camus, Dostoyevsky and Gide." As John Scanlan has observed, the theme here is Faustian. Tierney is the artist who sacrifices not only his own happiness for his art but also the well-being of those who have loved him or depended on him in the past. He drives his wife, Jane, into miserable infidelity; his rejected mother dies alone, waiting to return to Ireland. Mrs. Tierney is effectively "killed" by Brendan, who rejects her overtly and puts her out of his mind. In his single-minded devotion to his art, Brendan denies his past, the emotional solace and protection offered by Ireland, his family, and his religion. At the novel's end, he is overcome by the self-loathing that even Ginger Coffey was spared. Ginger was able to say at least, as he sought to reconcile himself to his failures, "Life itself is a victory." Brendan, even with the real prospect of attaining his dreams of success, is left with the knowledge that "I have altered beyond all self-recognition. I have lost and sacrificed myself."

I AM MARY DUNNE

I Am Mary Dunne marked a shift in direction for Moore. Having achieved a kind of resolution of his old material with the altered—and happier—perspective of *The Emperor of Ice-Cream*, Moore was ready in this sixth novel to move into new territory. It is significant that the protagonist of the first novel in this less traditional phase is, like that of his first novel, a woman. Just as he wanted to ensure that his first major character "wasn't me—could never be mistaken for me," so *I Am Mary Dunne* is determined to avoid the appearance of autobiography. Despite its innovative style, the novel takes up many of Moore's familiar themes. Mary is an artist—a failed one, perhaps—and an Irish expatriate whose haunted past is full of the old ghosts of religion, a troublesome father, and an identity and community that elude her in both Canada and New York.

Moore, whose insights into female psychology as well as sexual politics were demonstrated in *Judith Hearne*, makes clear the importance of Mary's gender in her search for identity. She has fitted herself to each of her husbands, adopting a new identity with each name change. The novel's epigraph from Yeats is apt: It is no longer possible for Mary to tell the "dancer from the dance." She is threatened by the void that froze the earlier Moore characters into childhood, and drives the quest of the later characters for meaning through acts of the imagination. For Mary, though, the possibilities of the creative imagination have been discarded; her life as an actor is over, her potential as a writer and a painter lie fallow. Her current identity is defined by the successful playwright to whom she is now married. Thus, she tries to find herself by remembering who she once was—her mother's daughter, Mary Dunne.

CATHOLICS

In *Catholics*, Moore's eighth novel and one of his best, the religious commitment that was a major hedge against the void for the victimized early characters regains center stage. For the first time, however, the struggles are sexless. Neither the relationship between men and women nor the exercise of sexual power is at issue here. The confrontation with the empty tabernacle is drawn pure and simple. On a remote rocky island in Kerry, a priest's personal crisis of faith is played out against the clinical relativism of a twenty-first century world, represented by James Kinsella, a young priest sent by Rome to obliterate the last vestiges of the old order to which the priests and parishioners of Muck Abbey still cling.

Unlike Judith Hearne, whose ultimate capacity for childlike fantasy offered her protection against the void, the Abbott has no defenses. He had chosen long ago to forsake all else for his God, and now he has found that "there is no Father in Heaven." When he tries to pray, he "enters null." When the young priest, Kinsella, arrives, the Abbott has not prayed in years. He sees his role as a manager of the Abbey, and also as a human bulwark for others against the void he has confronted. The Abbott knows, just as the behaviorist friend of young Kinsella knows, that "People don't want truth or justice. They want certainties. The old parish priest promised them that." Thus, the Abbott tries to deliver certainty, although it is lost to him. The past, however, is irredeemable. Its loss began long ago with "that righteous prig at Wittenberg nailing his defiance to the church door." The Abbott's attempt to recall it is doomed, as is he.

While those last lines absolve Moore of any suspicion of romanticizing the past of which he once despaired, the earlier faith in the possibilities of the imagination to liberate and to create its own enduring reality seems all but lost here. *The Great Victorian Collection*, Moore's next novel, continues that dark view of the power of the individual spirit and the creative imagination.

THE GREAT VICTORIAN COLLECTION

Moore's increasingly pessimistic vision is expressed in the central conceit of *The Great Victorian Collection*: Anthony Maloney, an undistinguished young professor and student of Victorian life, dreams into existence an authentic and unprecedented collection of Victoriana, an opportunity for the creative synthesis of past and present, of tradition and the imagination, that would resolve the fundamental conflict Moore presents. Significantly, however, the Collection is dreamed into existence in California, a land of hollow dreams. Moreover, it appears in a motel parking lot in that precious California tourist mecca, Carmel-by-the-Sea, with its "galleries filled with local paintings, arcade shops selling homemade candles, and bookstores displaying the complete works of Kahil Gibran."

The California tourist town becomes, in this most imaginative of Moore's novels, a world that, however far in form and principle from Belfast, has an equivalent capacity to thwart the individual spirit and to stultify the creative process. Tony is trapped by the Collection, which begins to deteriorate as he allows his attention to waver from it. Trapped in the dilemma of the successful artist, he must involve other people in his work. Other people include, notably, a commercial agent whose efforts to "market" the Collection lead to great commercial success, but the real "success" is a facsimile of the Collection at a place and in a form more palatable to the public. Tony's own investment in his creation becomes increasingly detached, until the pieces of it become artificial, and his caretaking is mechanistic. His dreams are reduced to soul-deadening surveillance by a black-and-white television camera. Finally, he tries to destroy his deteriorated creation, but it has assumed a life of its own and is indestructible.

This parable of the failure of the imagination to liberate or to sustain the spirit includes Moore's familiar erotic crisis. The creation of The Great Victorian Collection seems to be connected with Maloney's relationship with the beautiful young girl who comes into his life almost immediately after the Collection appears. A Dutch clairvoyant warns him that she is important to what has happened, and indeed, Mary Ann McKelvey soon emerges as Tony's anchor to reality in the feverish life of the imagination in which he finds himself. In a scene highly reminiscent of Moore's early works, their first and only sexual encounter ends in disaster, with Mary Ann thinking she has "failed" Tony. In fact, as with Dev, the apprehension of Mary Ann as a real woman "undid him." Tony "was, and always would be, a dreamer. . . . No longer a man and maid in those far-off wicked times, they were now equals, contestants, almost enemies." Unable to live with the human challenges of the real world or with women who are real people, and faced in his life as an artist with a choice between commercial exploitation of his gifts or the caretaking of deteriorating museum pieces, Maloney chooses to end his own life.

THE MANGAN INHERITANCE

The connection between Moore's concern with a particular male inability to form adult sexual relationships and the failure of the imagination to craft a synthesis of tradition and the individual creative spirit is treated most directly in *The Mangan Inheritance*. In this novel the connection, at least in outline, is simplistic. Jamie Mangan, failed poet, failed husband, perhaps even failed son, uses the windfall from his wife's sudden death to try to bury his failures in a return to a romanticized past. His search in the Irish village of his ancestors for confirmation of his relationship to the nineteenth century *poète maudit* James Clarence Mangan is a search for validation by the past, and is as doomed to failure as that of the Abbott in *Catholics*.

Unlike some of Moore's previous protagonists, however, Jamie is able to acknowledge his failures and learn from them. He refuses to succumb to the romantic fantasies that have spoiled the lives of past and present members of his Irish family. The excesses of the *poète maudit* are revealed to him in their sordid reality in the lives of his Irish cousins. He even comes to see his sexual infatuation with the beautiful but slovenly teenage Kathleen for the destructive fantasy it is in the light of the story of incest and sexual abuse he hears from his Irish doppelgänger, Michael Mangan. In the end, Jamie is able to repudiate his fantasies, literary and sexual, and return to his dying father and to responsibility to a future generation. In the daguerreotype of James Clarence Mangan lying smashed beyond repair against the stones of a ruined Irish castle, Jamie sees the features of his dying father and "wished that those features were his own." Implicit is the promise that his father's unborn child, whom he has promised to protect, will be welcomed into a family free of romantic illusion about itself, and that Jamie has a chance at fulfillment in the real world. The resolution is not unshadowed, however, for Jamie was a poet, and apparently will be no longer.

THE TEMPTATION OF EILEEN HUGHES

The note of guarded optimism on which *The Mangan Inheritance* ends is not repeated in Moore's next novel, *The Temptation of Eileen Hughes*. Bernard McAuley, the novel's "artist," is a strange admixture of Moore's earlier protagonists. Sexually paralyzed, though married to Mona, a beautiful woman who loves him, Bernard searches for identity and meaning in his life, ranging from "offering [himself] to God" as a priest and finding he "wasn't wanted," through studies of history, art, music, and business, and finally to his bizarre attempt to force his strangely celibate relationship with young Eileen Hughes into his sordid household.

The themes of sexual power and the act of the imagination attain a distorted unity in this novel. Bernard enacts an evolution into decadence, and in a confirmation of Moore's recurrent tendency to find healthy self-knowledge in women targeted as victims by male identity-seekers, Eileen ultimately understands the manipulative and powerful McAuleys: "It was not she who had been in their power but they in hers. She had escaped them. Would they escape her?" Like Mary Ann McKelvey, or Diarmud Devine's Una, Eileen is anchored in a reality to which men such as Bernard (and the women whose lives they steal) will be forever denied admission.

The four novels that followed *The Temptation of Eileen Hughes* are diverse in setting and character, yet they are linked both stylistically and thematically; together they mark a new phase in Moore's work. In three of the four—*Cold Heaven*, *The Color of Blood*, and *Lies of Silence*—Moore adopts the plot-scaffolding and many of the generic conventions of the thriller, while in *Black Robe*, set in the 1630's in the Canadian wilderness, he adopts the conventions of the historical adventure novel.

Some reviewers have seen in this shift an attempt on Moore's part to win a larger audience. If that is the case, the attempt must be judged a failure, for while these works have been well received by critics, they did not make Moore a best-selling author. It seems just as likely, though, that Moore turned to the thriller for other reasons. In *Black Robe*, which centers on the physical hardships and spiritual conflicts of a Jesuit missionary to the Indians, in *The Color of Blood*, a pre-glasnost novel set in Eastern Europe and focusing on a Roman Catholic cardinal and the prime minister of an unnamed nation closely resembling Poland, and in *Lies of Silence*, about a man who is inadvertently drawn into a plot by Irish Republican Army terrorists, Moore grounds individual moral conflicts in the context of larger social and political struggles.

THE STATEMENT

Moore's concern with history is evident in his last two novels, *The Statement* and *The Magician's Wife*. In the first of these he chooses as his subject the French government and Catholic Church's protection of and complicity with Nazi war criminals. The protagonist, Pierre Broussard, is based on Paul Touvier, a functionary of the Vichy government who was found guilty of war crimes and who spends twenty-five years hiding in monasteries and avoiding Jewish agents hired to assassinate him. To save the government embarrassment, he is eventually betrayed by a former police commissioner who has been aiding him in his flight.

Once again Moore finds a way to use the conventions of a popular thriller to present probing moral and political observations. However, the most compelling and challenging aspect of the novel is its concentration on the thoughts and torment of a monstrous individual. Broussard was an adroitly expert killing machine during the war, and he remains one after, as he eludes captors and assassins. In these ways the novel is oddly Dostoevskian in presenting a despicable person, in all his turpitude, yet showing him to be deeply pathetic.

Moore long wrestled with his own conflicted feelings about the Catholic Church, feelings he candidly expressed in interviews, and his books often represent oscillations in his attitudes toward issues of faith and dogma. *Cold Heaven* is a perfect example of literary agnosticism, wherein a woman is forced to deal with rationally inexplicable phenomena that priests and nuns have no trouble accepting as signs of divine intervention. *The Statement*, however, offers a bleaker vision of religion; here the Church, the putative exemplar of moral authority, is run by self-serving hypocrites bent on protecting their own political power before all else.

THE MAGICIAN'S WIFE

The Magician's Wife extends Moore's concerns with history, and once again he seizes on a tiny incident to reveal the workings of power and coercion. The setting is 1856 at Napoleon III's winter palace. The foremost magician of the day, Henri Lambert, and his wife, Emmeline, have been called for mysterious but presumably high purposes. The emperor informs him that he is to travel to Algiers, dazzle and terrify the local authorities with his illusions, and aid France in its conquest of this foreign territory. When the magician's assistant dies of cholera, his wife assumes that role; she becomes fascinated with the local Muslim leader, eventually seeking a clandestine audience and convincing him to forestall a planned jihad. Although he is successful, the magician is permanently injured when an outraged spectator shoots and paralyzes him.

Once again Moore's concerns with religion and faith are paramount, and the novel offers numerous comparisons between Christianity and Islam, with the deck stacked squarely in favor of the latter. When Emmeline contemplates these differences, she comes to profound personal realizations about cultures, politics, her marriage, and most sweepingly, the place of women in her world. She realizes that she is the sum of everyone else's projection of who she should be, and her experience emboldens her to begin defining herself in her own terms.

Moore wrote with grace, felicity, and remarkable insight; his novels do not obviously pontificate. He was deeply concerned with moral conflicts and the individual's search for identity and authenticity, and his characters are typically figures who endure profound crises. Moore manipulates otherwise humble forms, such as the thriller and the historical novel, to reach an audience and then to interrogate assumptions subtly.

Michele Wender Zak
Updated by David W. Madden

OTHER MAJOR WORKS

SCREENPLAYS: *The Luck of Ginger Coffey*, 1963 (adaptation of his novel); *Torn Curtain*, 1966; *The Slave*, 1967; *Catholics*, 1973 (adaptation of his novel); *Black Robe*, 1991 (adaptation of his novel).

NONFICTION: *Canada*, 1963; *The Revolution Script*, 1971.

BIBLIOGRAPHY

Craig, Patricia. *Brian Moore: A Biography*. London: Bloomsbury, 2002. An authorized biography of Moore, which recounts the events and influences in his life that led him to create his fiction.

Dahlie, Hallvard. *Brian Moore*. Boston: Twayne, 1981. This comprehensive study of Moore discusses his short stories and nonfiction as well as his novels. Dahlie addresses the metaphysical dilemmas presented in some of Moore's characters who struggle for identity and meaning. Selected bibliography and chronology.

Flood, Jeanne A. *Brian Moore*. Lewisburg, Pa.: Bucknell University Press, 1974. Covers Moore's work until 1973, with some emphasis on *Catholics*. Each chapter looks at a different position taken by the novelist. This slim volume is a solid piece of criticism and contains much insight into Moore's narrative technique and purpose. Includes a chronology and bibliography.

Gearon, Liam. *Landscapes of Encounter: The Portrayal of Catholicism in the Novels of Brian Moore.* Calgary, Alta.: University of Calgary Press, 2002. Gearon analyzes Moore's novels to examine his treatment of Catholicism, showing how this depiction was altered after the Church initiated its Vatican II reforms. This study also includes a discussion of Moore's portrayal of the Catholic Church in the modern world.

O'Donoghue, Jo. *Brian Moore: A Critical Study.* Montreal: McGill-Queen's University Press, 1991. Examines sixteen novels in terms of Moore's spiritual questioning and the personal search for freedom. Although the study examines each novel, particular emphasis is given to his novels dealing with female protagonists.

Sampson, Denis. *Brian Moore: The Chameleon Novelist.* Dublin: Marino Books, 1998. Sampson interviewed Moore and members of his family, as well as friends and colleagues, to write this biography, which chronicles Moore's life and discusses his literary works.

Sullivan, Robert. *A Matter of Faith: The Fiction of Brian Moore.* Westport, Conn.: Greenwood Press, 1996. An extensive and detailed treatment of Moore's fiction, examining novels up to *No Other Life.* Concentrates on the themes of love and faith and suggests that the writer's oeuvre is a cohesive master narrative. Sullivan is equally concerned with issues of craft and reveals the author's dedication to the art of fiction.

GEORGE MOORE

Born: Moore Hall, County Mayo, Ireland; February 24, 1852
Died: London, England; January 21, 1933
Also known as: George Augustus Moore

PRINCIPAL LONG FICTION

A Modern Lover, 1883
A Mummer's Wife, 1884
A Drama in Muslin, 1886
A Mere Accident, 1887
Spring Days, 1888
Mike Fletcher, 1889
Vain Fortune, 1891
Esther Waters, 1894
Evelyn Innes, 1898
Sister Teresa, 1901
The Lake, 1905
Muslin, 1915
The Brook Kerith, 1916
Lewis Seymour and Some Women, 1917
Héloise and Abélard, 1921
Ulick and Soracha, 1926
Aphrodite in Aulis, 1930

OTHER LITERARY FORMS

George Moore was a man of letters rather than purely a novelist. He published seven collections of short fiction, and all but the first of his eight plays were produced in London or Dublin. He published two volumes of poetry in 1877 and 1881. Moore published numerous nonfictional works, and more than one thousand of his periodical writings have been located in English, Irish, French, and American journals. In addition, he published a notable translation of Longus's *Daphnis and Chloë* in 1924.

ACHIEVEMENTS

George Moore's fiction was at all times innovative and influential. Amid much controversy in the early 1880's, he adapted the methods of French realism to the English novel. His earliest goals were to liberate the novel from Victorian conventions of subject and treatment and from commercial constraints imposed by a monopolistic book trade.

By the middle 1880's, Moore began to turn from realism to aestheticism. Under the influence of his friend Walter Pater and the rising Symbolist poets of France, Moore antici-

George Moore
(Library of Congress)

pated the "decadence" of the 1890's by eschewing the conflict between realism and popular Romanticism that had formerly absorbed him. He realized that these schools of writing were generally organized and evaluated on moral and social grounds. In regard to prose narrative, Moore's increasing and then sole preoccupation became literary art.

As an aesthete in the early 1890's, he composed his masterpiece *Esther Waters*. He also wrote some of the short stories that later contributed to his reputation as an inventor of modern Irish fiction. The large income generated by his books allowed him to quit his second career as one of England's leading art critics. He cofounded the Independent Theatre and Irish Literary Theatre and by the turn of the century he became a leading polemicist of the Irish revival.

The major achievement of Moore's Irish involvement was the composition of *Hail and Farewell: A Trilogy* (1911-1914). In the tradition of Laurence Sterne, Thomas De Quincey, and George Borrow, Moore wrote the story of his life using the conceptual framework of fiction rather than history. The trilogy contains an account of artistic movements of the late Victorian era, but attention is concentrated on the intellectual life of Dublin in the early years of the twentieth century.

During the 1910's and 1920's, Moore retreated from the popular literary market to the composition of prose epics. Biblical history in *The Brook Kerith*, medieval history in *Héloise and Abélard*, and classical history in *Aphrodite in Aulis* offered structural premises for a new exploration of human problems and for the development of a modern, rarefied aestheticism. Reviewers greeted the novels as exemplars of composition and elevated Moore to the status of Ireland's senior man of letters.

BIOGRAPHY

The Moores of Moore Hall were a prominent Catholic family in the west of Ireland. Their home, a large, gray, stone mansion presiding over 12,500 acres, was built in 1795 by George Moore, the novelist's great-grandfather. The founder of Moore Hall was a businessman. His eldest son, Peter, was certified insane for most of his life; the second son, John, was martyred in the 1798 rebellion (see Thomas Flanagan's novel *The Year of the French*, 1979); the youngest son, George, the novelist's grandfather, was a scholarly historian. George inherited the estate and through marriage established an intimate connection with the Brownes of Westport. His eldest son was George Henry Moore (1810-1870), a keeper of excellent racing stables and member of Parliament for the nationalist cause. In 1851, he married Mary Blake (1829-1895), daughter of a neighboring landlord.

George Augustus Moore, the eldest of G. H. Moore's five children, was born at Moore Hall on February 24, 1852. He was a robust but rather backward child: a late talker, then an endearing but poor pupil under a succession of governesses. Beginning in 1861, he attended Oscott College, Birmingham, a famous preparatory school designed as the Catholic complement of Eton or Harrow. He remained at Oscott until 1868, when his learning disabilities finally convinced the headmaster that further attempts at instruction would be futile.

After leaving Oscott, Moore lived with his parents in London while Parliament was in session. His time was divided between military tutors and amusements, including betting shops, music halls, and painting studios. When his father died suddenly in 1870, the quest for an army commission was dropped, and soon Moore was devoting most of his energy to the study of painting.

From 1873 until 1879, he lived mostly in Paris, first as a student painter at the École des Beaux Arts and Académie Julian. Before setting aside his brushes in 1875, he had received instruction from James Whistler, John Millais, Alexandre Cabanel, and several less famous painters in France and England. Education did not make a painter of him, but it did help make him a sensitive art critic later in life. His first steps in literature during the later 1870's were likewise tentative. He was enraptured with French Romantic drama and Parnassian poetry. By the time the income from his property suddenly failed and he was forced to leave France, he had published two volumes of exotic juvenile verse and a large Romantic drama that was intended for but declined by Henry Irving.

Moore's literary career properly began in London in 1881. He was then settled in inexpensive rooms near the Strand and determined to make a living by his pen. While developing the plan of a naturalistic novel, he contributed paragraphs and reviews to the weekly press. Among his friends he numbered several poets and critics of the Pre-Raphaelite circle, but these receded as his friendship with Émile Zola became a discipleship. "When I attacked the Philistine," Algernon Charles Swinburne commented after reading *A Mummer's Wife*, "it was not with a chamber pot for a buckler and a dung fork for a spear." Moore's first two novels and his early journalism, although consonant with the ideals of the French avant-garde, drew charges of indecency from English readers. Although he moderated his style as his aestheticism changed, the reputation he earned at the start of his career remained with him, and all of his fiction until the turn of the century was banned from the circulating libraries.

Moore continued to live in the vicinity of the Strand until 1886, when he moved to a village near Brighton and afterward to a house atop the Sussex downs. In the English countryside he found an almost idyllic refuge from the distractions of London. His fiction of the period shows an increasing tolerance of ordinary life, and his literary theories, which he collected for *Confessions of a Young Man* (1888), reveal a firmer, more self-reliant mind than was evident before. He returned to London in 1889, engaged to write art criticism for his brother's magazine *The Hawk* and, more important, with the plan for a novel that became *Esther Waters*.

From 1889 until 1895, Moore contributed columns of art criticism briefly to *The Hawk* and then to *The Speaker*, both weekly reviews of politics and the arts. He was the first Impressionist art critic in England. Aside from writing fiction and criticism, he became deeply involved in theater reform and in 1890 cofounded the Independent Theatre, where Henrik Ibsen and George Bernard Shaw had their London premieres. With the publication of *Esther Waters*, Moore was soon able to leave the staff of *The Speaker*.

During the rest of the 1890's, Moore was prominent among the aesthetes and Decadents generally associated with *The Yellow Book*. He also took a publicized interest in the revival of early music, begun by his friend Arnold Dolmetsch, and in Wagnerism. His annual pilgrimage to Bayreuth began at this time, and his last novel of the century is permeated with musical theory. Drawn by the ideas of William Butler Yeats and others concerning the artistic possibilities of Gaelic, he also became involved in the Irish revival. With Yeats and Edward Martyn he founded the Irish Literary Theatre (precursor of the Abbey). In 1901, enamored of the "new Ireland" and bitterly depressed by British conduct of the Boer War, Moore leased a house in Upper Ely Place, near St. Stephen's Green in Dublin. He remained there until 1911.

Owing mainly to aesthetic and religious convictions, Moore's return to Ireland was characterized more by frustration than success. Having learned his profession in Paris and

London, he could feel little sympathy for the relatively parochial challenges that writers of the movement faced. His advocacy of intellectual freedom for the artist was inappropriate to prevailing ideology. Worse, his notion that a politically free Ireland was one that would disown both Westminster and the Vatican virtually exiled him from the cause he tried to embrace. Though he made several friends among literary Dubliners, wrote polemics in the Irish press, and published important fiction, his greatest achievement was the comic indictment of the movement that appeared, after he left Dublin, in *Hail and Farewell*.

From 1911 until his death, Moore lived in Ebury Street, London. For the first time he was associated with no movement but instead practiced his art purely as an individual. His fiction and books of theory were welcomed by an elite readership of a few thousand. His best friends were the English Impressionist painters who lived in nearby Chelsea. Turning about-face on the six-shilling format he had invented with publisher Henry Vizetelly in 1884, he issued his books in limited, sometimes elegantly illustrated editions that took him entirely out of the popular market. He died in his home on January 21, 1933, and was buried on an island in Lough Carra, in front of Moore Hall. Because the rites of burial were pagan, a police guard was called to protect the funeral. George Russell composed the oration and the epitaph of George Moore: "He forsook his family and friends for his art. But because he was faithful to his art his family and friends reclaimed his ashes for Ireland. VALE."

ANALYSIS

Thirty of George Moore's fifty years as a novelist postdate the Victorian era, yet he is not generally remembered as a modern writer. To some extent this is because his aestheticism was the outcome of inspiration rather than experiment. "I desire above all things," he wrote in 1892, "to tell the story of life in grave simple phrases, so grave and simple that the method, the execution would disappear, and the reader, with bating breath, would remain a prey to an absorbing emotion."

Complexity and diversity are striking characteristics of the Moore corpus. He told "the story of life" ranging from classical Greece (*Aphrodite in Aulis*) to industrial England (*A Mummer's Wife*). His changing style reflected the influence of diverse writers, including Gustave Flaubert, Ivan Turgenev, and Walter Pater. Confused by such diversity, Arthur Symons reached the conclusion that Moore had no style, and James Whistler believed that he had no conscience. In a curious way this is true. He achieved not style, but expression. As an artist he avoided moral judgments and ceased his endeavors after discovering the soul in the body, the idea in action. The nature of his critical theories and the evolution of his fiction confirm that he was not a modernist, but a classicist.

A MODERN LOVER

Moore's first novel, *A Modern Lover*, like his last, is a study of artistic temperament. The chief protagonist is Lewis Seymour, a young painter of middling talent whose problem is to advance his career. He is attracted to a fraternity of avant-garde artists called the moderns, who advocate a radical departure from academic painting. However, he realizes that to achieve success in the sense of worldly recognition, he must be conventional and flatter the tastes of an ignorant public. The narrative traces Lewis's development as a painter with a "market" that expands in proportion to the distance between himself and personal integrity.

A Modern Lover represents the first conscious attempt to write a naturalistic novel in English. Reviewers noticed its power. In addition to its literary qualities, the novel offers an account of conflicting trends in art: The moderns are painters modeled on the French Impressionists; the medievalists are modeled on the Pre-Raphaelites; the Royal Academy appears as a copy of the original. Through the character of John Harding, Moore expounded his own views as a critic of Victorian culture and advocated reforms that prepared the way for a new definition of modern art.

Susan Mitchell noted in her study of Moore that he had an uncanny ability to understand women. *A Mummer's Wife* and *A Drama in Muslin* may be regarded as portraits of women: the first novel rather sinister and tragic, the second almost feminist and deeply encouraging.

A MUMMER'S WIFE

Kate Ede is introduced in *A Mummer's Wife* as the wife of a shopkeeper living in the industrial town of Hanley. She is a young woman of sober character and dry religious convictions. Dick Lennox, the actor-manager of a touring company, rents lodgings in her house and seduces her. She is persuaded to leave her unhappy marriage and to accompany Dick on his travels. In Moravia, Kate's self-discipline gives way to a sensuous dreaminess. After becoming an actor, she marries Dick and has a baby by him, but her course runs steadily downward. As the moral underpinnings of her life are loosened, she slips almost unawares into depravity and dies in the end, an alcoholic among prostitutes.

A DRAMA IN MUSLIN

Alice Barton, the heroine of *A Drama in Muslin*, is the daughter of an Irish landlord. She is an intellectual girl and rather homely; consequently she is unfitted for the grotesque "marriage market" of the Castle season in Dublin. Her sister and acquaintances spend their energy and sometimes dignity in preparing for the most important event of their lives: the entrapment of a moneyed young man in matrimony. All the innocence, loveliness, and promise of girlhood are publicly and somewhat brutally bartered for the passing illusions of title and fortune. Alice remains aloof, quietly preparing herself for a literary career. In the end, because of her intelligence and self-reliance, she alone makes a happy marriage.

Apart from many distinguishing features, the one shared by Kate Ede and Alice Barton is a departure from the common rut of experience. When Kate becomes the mummer's mistress, she breaks free from the paralyzing control of her husband and mother-in-law. During the months before conscience prods her to become the mummer's wife, she achieves sexual and emotional fulfillment and finds herself on the verge of a career and independence. Kate's is not a social tragedy: The opportunity to change her life was offered, but for personal reasons she neglected it. Alice's success is likewise of her own making. The reader finds soon after beginning *A Drama in Muslin* that the heroine is set apart less by her lack of beauty than by her strength of character. By virtue of a correct perception of Vanity Fair, Alice disentangles herself from the fatal bonds of family, class, and background to secure a hopeful future.

ESTHER WATERS

Esther Waters, properly regarded as one of the greater novels in English literature, is also one of the least understood. From the year of its publication, reviewers and scholars have persisted in classing it as a realistic novel, using "realism" to mean an imitation of nature.

Esther Waters has been bound in its reputation of realism because Moore's choice of a subject from nature was powerful enough to be blinding. His protagonists were servants, characters whose place in English fiction had been confined to doing odd jobs and providing comic entertainment. Now they were comprehended as full human beings and their vast subculture moved from the periphery to the center of consciousness. The force of Moore's decision to write about servants was increased by the novel's central problem: the struggle of an unmarried mother to rear her child. By making Esther Waters his heroine, Moore overturned an array of Victorian sexual mores and political assumptions.

It is not surprising that the controversy that greeted publication of the novel distracted readers from its artistic merits. It must be emphasized, however, that Moore was no champion of the working class; he was neither a sociologist nor a philanthropist. He was only what he claimed to be: an artist. Essentially, he was no more interested in servant girls than his friend Edgar Degas was interested in ballerinas: They merely represented new opportunities for artistic expression. To think otherwise is to obscure the development of Moore's fiction and to ignore his many explanations of his aestheticism.

The quality of beauty Moore captured in *Esther Waters* may be summarized in its theme: the drama of motherhood, the presence in human nature of maternal instincts that create and protect life in a threatening environment. Rising from numerous realistic scenes in mansion, tenement, hospital, and public house, at racecourses and in the streets of London, the ineffable mystery of human love and self-sacrifice irradiates the text. At the conclusion of the novel Esther does not inherit a fortune; her son does not grow up to be prime minister; the villains are not punished and the heroes are not rewarded. A life of dedicated struggle is simply allowed to come to rest with a mild sense of achievement. In so doing, this ordinary life becomes a thing of extraordinary beauty.

EVELYN INNES

Evelyn Innes is another study of a woman seeking independence from stifling conventions and expectations. Evelyn, the daughter of a musicologist, carries on relationships with two men, each representing a principle of her life. Sir Owen Asher, the patron of her opera singing career, is the carnal. Ulick Dean, a musician and mystic, is the intellectual. The contradictory emotions these men inspire make her anxious about personal morality. The narrative traces her meditations until they reach a logical though drastic conclusion: religious vocation. Evelyn abandons love, career, and society, entering a convent in a desperate attempt to reconcile her life with her conscience. The novel concludes with a statement of her mature beliefs, which might be characterized as a somewhat secularized Christianity.

Moore did not explain why an author who cherished personal freedom, did not believe in God, and hated Catholicism should feel compelled to write the story of Evelyn Innes. Compelled by his imagination he certainly was, for he continued to revise the work for ten years until putting it aside, unsatisfied. It is possible that the trappings of Catholicism and musical theory were as incidental to his purpose as the kitchen and garret were in *Esther Waters*. He was essentially concerned about the problem posed by a woman's liberation from traditional restraint and the use to which she puts her freedom. Kate Ede in *A Mummer's Wife* shared Evelyn's dilemma, though in a different setting.

During the last twenty-five years of Moore's career, his longer fiction was historical. Ancient and medieval landscapes of Greece, Palestine, and France were more capable of supporting his literary ideas, though he continued to view the twentieth century in Great Britain through the media of essay and autobiography.

Moore's turn from modern subjects was accompanied by a turn from modern spoken English. In regard to both subject and treatment, he wished to emulate Pater, whose pure literary English was free of associations carried over from worldly usage and whose setting, in the much admired *Marius the Epicurean* (1885), was remote enough from mundane reality to assume more easily the aura of myth.

THE BROOK KERITH

The Brook Kerith retells the story of Christ in accordance with the Synoptic Gospels and later histories but adds an enormous new dimension by allowing him to survive the crucifixion and live, in thoughtful retirement, at an Essene monastery. Christ in the Bible struck Moore as an unfinished man, a visionary glimpsed only in his immaturity. As Christ matures he develops a more generous and sympathetic morality as part of a better understanding of humanity. At the conclusion of the novel, St. Paul comes to the monastery. Messiah and apostle are brought face-to-face. When Christ hears about the founding of the bellicose Christian tradition, he is horrified. When Paul learns the identity of his auditor, he rages and strikes Christ to the ground. Their paths soon part, Paul to carry his dogma to Europe and Christ to carry the truth to Jerusalem.

HÉLOISE AND ABÉLARD

The process of humanizing religious history and of faulting dogma in favor of free intelligence is continued in *Héloise and Abélard*. The figure of Abélard as perhaps the first Renaissance man was profoundly attractive to Moore, but he was equally moved by his conception of Héloise, who is his chief protagonist. The novel pits intellectual freedom and its complement, wholesome sexual love, against the rigors of doctrine and medieval customs of chastity and celibacy. In its blending of landscape and character, idea and expression, *Héloise and Abélard* might well be ranked the most nearly perfect "aesthetic novel" ever written.

APHRODITE IN AULIS

In order to strengthen his sense of place in *The Brook Kerith* and *Héloise and Abélard*, Moore had traveled over Palestine and France and "assimilated" culture. By the time he had the plan for *Aphrodite in Aulis*, however, he was too old and frail to make a tour of Greece. Illness for the first time settled in his body, and, though his mind remained vigorous, he was forced to live with a great deal of pain. Despite these obstacles, he achieved a final novel of abundant mystery and flawed but engrossing beauty.

The story is set in Greece of the fifth century B.C.E. Kebren, a young Athenian actor and rhapsodist, settles in Aulis as the husband of Biote and business partner of her father, Otanes. Biote gives birth to two sons, Rhesos the sculptor and Thrasillos the architect. After a period of training under Phidias in Athens, the brothers return to Aulis and marry their cousins Earine and Melissa. Earine is the inspiration for the figure of Aphrodite that Rhesos carves for a temple in Aulis. Following her role of inspiration, at the conclusion of the novel she embraces a new role as the mother of his children.

The book may be read as an act of devotion to art and thus a fitting conclusion to Moore's career. Throughout the narrative, art and life are almost hypnotically counterpointed. Each recovers the continuing theme from the other, seeming for a moment to frustrate the other's aims. In the end an exquisite harmony occurs: Art is animated by life, while life is beautified and ennobled by art. That harmony characterizes the oeuvre of George Moore.

Robert Becker

OTHER MAJOR WORKS

SHORT FICTION: *Parnell and His Island*, 1887; *Celibates*, 1895; *The Untilled Field*, 1903; *Memoirs of My Dead Life*, 1906; *A Story-Teller's Holiday*, 1918; *In Single Strictness*, 1922; *Peronnik the Fool*, 1924; *Celibate Lives*, 1927; *A Flood*, 1930; *In Minor Keys: The Uncollected Short Stories of George Moore*, 1985 (David B. Eakin and Helmut E. Gerber, editors).

PLAYS: *Martin Luther*, pb. 1879 (with Bernard Lopez); *The Strike at Arlingford*, pr., pb. 1893; *The Bending of the Bough*, pr., pb. 1900; *Diarmuid and Grania*, pr. 1901 (with William Butler Yeats); *Esther Waters*, pr. 1911; *The Apostle*, pb. 1911; *Elizabeth Cooper*, pr., pb. 1913; *The Making of Immortal*, pb. 1927; *The Passing of the Essenes*, pr., pb. 1930 (revision of *The Apostle*).

POETRY: *Flowers of Passion*, 1878; *Pagan Poems*, 1881.

NONFICTION: *Confessions of a Young Man*, 1888; *Impressions and Opinions*, 1891; *Modern Painting*, 1893; *Hail and Farewell: A Trilogy*, 1911-1914 (*Ave*, 1911; *Salve*, 1912; *Vale*, 1914); *Avowals*, 1919; *Conversations in Ebury Street*, 1924; *Letters from George Moore to Edouard Dujardin, 1886-1922*, 1929; *The Talking Pine*, 1931; *A Communication to My Friends*, 1933; *Letters of George Moore*, 1942; *Letters to Lady Cunard*, 1957 (Rupert Hart-Davis, editor); *George Moore in Transition: Letters to T. Fisher Unwin and Lena Milman, 1894-1910*, 1968 (Gerber, editor).

TRANSLATION: *Daphnis and Chloë*, 1924 (of Longus).

BIBLIOGRAPHY

Dorré, Gina M. "Reading and Riding: Late-Century Aesthetics and the Cultural Economy of the Turf in George Moore's *Esther Waters*." In *Victorian Fiction and the Cult of the Horse*. Burlington, Vt.: Ashgate, 2006. Dorré analyzes *Esther Waters* and other Victorian-age novels to describe their inclusion of horses to reflect Victorian society during a period of massive technological, economic, and social change.

Dunleavy, Janet Egleson. *George Moore: The Artist's Vision, the Storyteller's Art*. Lewisburg, Pa.: Bucknell University Press, 1973. A review of Moore's writings, presented in chronological form, with particularly useful commentary on his earlier novels. Dunleavy describes the societal influences on Moore's work and his changing ideas about literary form, style, theme, and characterization.

_____, ed. *George Moore in Perspective*. New York: Barnes & Noble Books, 1983. A compilation of critical essays on Moore that discuss his Irish background and the Irish Literary Renaissance, his connections with Samuel Beckett, and his relationship to James Joyce. The appendix includes a bibliographical essay by Edwin Gilcher.

Fratantaro, Sal. *The Methodology of G. E. Moore*. Brookfield, Vt.: Ashgate, 1998. Part of the Avebury series in philosophy, this volume presents a comprehensive description of Moore's complex philosophy and the methodology he used in his fiction.

Frazier, Adrian. *George Moore, 1852-1933*. New Haven, Conn.: Yale University Press, 2000. A thorough biography, drawing on much previously unpublished material and emphasizing Moore's historical and cultural context. This is not a critical examination of his works but a narrative of his life, including his time in Paris during the era of Impressionism and in Dublin during the Irish Literary Renaissance.

Gray, Tony. *A Peculiar Man: A Life of George Moore*. London: Sinclair-Stevenson, 1996. A good, updated biography of Moore, which takes into account his different vocations, such as art critic and landowner. Includes a short bibliography and an index.

Grubgeld, Elizabeth. *George Moore and the Autogenous Self: The Autobiography and*

Fiction. Syracuse, N.Y.: Syracuse University Press, 1994. As Grubgeld's title suggests, she explores the interdependence of Moore's fiction and autobiography; her discussion of narrating and remembering is especially good. Includes detailed notes and an extensive bibliography.

Jeffares, A. Norman. *George Moore.* London: Longmans, 1965. Part of the British Council series and one of the best short introductions to the author and his work. Jeffares devotes a chapter to Moore's life and another to a discussion of his novels.

Pierse, Mary, ed. *George Moore: Artistic Visions and Literary Worlds.* Newcastle, England: Cambridge Scholars Press, 2006. A collection of papers delivered at a 2005 international conference on Moore. The papers analyze Moore's works, discussing, among other topics, his literary innovations, avant-garde feminism, and his literary significance and legacy.

Swafford, Kevin. "Reification and Respectability in Thomas Hardy's *Tess of the D'urbervilles* and George Moore's *Esther Waters.*" In *Class in Late-Victorian Britain: The Narrative Concern with Social Hierarchy and Its Representation.* Youngstown, N.Y.: Cambria Press, 2007. Swafford's study of how social-class distinctions were depicted by late nineteenth century British authors includes this comparison of *Esther Waters* with a famous novel by Thomas Hardy.

EDNA O'BRIEN

Born: Tuamgraney, county Clare, Ireland; December 15, 1930
Also known as: Josephine Edna O'Brien

OTHER LITERARY FORMS

In addition to her novels, Edna O'Brien has published short fiction, plays and screenplays, poetry, children's books, and works of nonfiction. Her short stories have appeared regularly in magazines such as *The New Yorker*, *The Atlantic Monthly*, and *Cosmopolitan*; collections of her stories include *The Love Object* (1968), *A Scandalous Woman, and Other Stories* (1974), and *Lantern Slides* (1990). Chief among O'Brien's stage plays are *A Cheap Bunch of Nice Flowers* (pr. 1962), *A Pagan Place* (pr. 1972), *Virginia* (pr. 1980), *Triptych* (pr., pb. 2003), and *Iphigenia* (pr., pb. 2003). Her works for film and television include the screenplays *Time Lost and Time Remembered* (1966), *Three into Two Won't Go* (1969), and *X, Y, and Zee* (1971) and the teleplays *The Wedding Dress* (1963), *Mrs. Reinhardt* (1981), and *The Country Girls* (1983). Among her works of nonfiction are the autobiographical *Mother Ireland* (1976); *Arabian Days* (1977), a travel book; *Vanishing Ireland* (1987), a pictorial; and *James Joyce* (1999), a biography.

ACHIEVEMENTS

After moving to London from Dublin, Ireland, in 1959, Edna O'Brien published at a furious pace, mining her early experiences in Ireland and then as a single parent with two sons to rear in England. There was something of a lull in her long fiction, however, from 1977 to 1986. Nearly always from a female narrator's point of view, O'Brien has brilliantly transmuted her personal experiences into art. Her recall and selection of the tiny details that make up the texture of life, particularly in her Irish scenes (*The Country Girls, The Lonely Girl, A Pagan Place*) are most dazzling. Impressive, too, is her evident love and savoring of words—sometimes clearly in a fashion reminiscent of James Joyce—for their own sake, and often in good dialogue. Perhaps because of the speed with which she works, the vivacity and brilliance of her prolific output is frequently marred by awkward grammar, punctuation, and syntax. Apparently, her editors have felt these stylistic lapses are all part of her Irish use of the language and have accordingly let them stand.

O'Brien was a feminist before the term became fashionable, but her works also affirm a wider humanistic sympathy for all people. Early, she took up the topics of women's attitudes toward their bodies, their sexuality, and their roles as mothers and daughters. In Ireland, several of her books have been banned because of their negative commentary on the Roman Catholic Church, more common in her early work, and her frequent use of graphic sexual terms and scenes. Outside Ireland, O'Brien's reputation as a writer of fiction seems assured, although reviewer Marianne Wiggins, writing in *The Nation*, observed that "to the English [she is] a minor self-promoting legend." Despite conflicting critical responses to her work, O'Brien has received numerous awards, including the Kingsley Amis Award in 1962, the Yorkshire Post Award in 1970 for *A Pagan Place*, the Los Angeles Times Book Prize in 1990 for *Lantern Slides* and again in 1992 for *Time and Tide*, the Writers' Guild of Great Britain's Prize for Fiction in 1993, and the European Prize for Literature in 1995; the last of these was presented to O'Brien in tribute to her entire oeuvre.

BIOGRAPHY

Josephine Edna O'Brien was born to Michael and Lena (Cleary) O'Brien in Tuamgraney, county Clare, Ireland, on December 15, 1930. She has one brother and two sisters. Her father was an impractical man who bred horses and squandered his wealth; her mother worked in the United States for eight years, returning to Ireland to marry. O'Brien has characterized her mother as an ambitious, frustrated woman who mistrusted books and was unsympathetic to her daughter's emerging literary interests. (Although O'Brien dedicated her first novel to her mother, she later found her mother's copy with the inscription page torn out and angry comments written throughout.) O'Brien first attended Scarriff National School in 1936, then boarded at the Convent of Mercy, Loughrea, county Galway, in 1941 before going off to the Pharmaceutical College of Ireland in Dublin in 1946, where she worked in a chemist's shop, or drugstore, during the day and attended lectures at night. One of her first purchases in Dublin was a secondhand copy of *Introduc-*

ing James Joyce (1944), edited by T. S. Eliot, which first exposed her to the influence of that Irish literary giant. In 1948, she began to write short pieces for the *Irish Press*.

In 1951, O'Brien married novelist Ernest Gebler and lived for a time in rural county Wicklow (the marriage ended in 1964). Two sons, Carlos and Sasha, were born, in 1952 and 1954. In 1959, the family moved to London, and O'Brien's career as a published writer was quickly launched. In three weeks, far from county Clare, she wrote *The Country Girls*, tracing the development of fourteen-year-old Caithleen Brady. The trilogy begun with that first novel was continued in *The Lonely Girl* and *Girls in Their Married Bliss* (the three novels were published together, appended with *Epilogue*, in 1986). O'Brien composed a second trilogy in the 1990's, made up of *House of Splendid Isolation, Down By the River*, and *Wild Decembers*. In these later works, O'Brien focused on modern Irish life and problems as they affect both men and women. In addition to her prolific career as a writer, O'Brien teaches her craft. She has lectured in numerous countries and has taught creative writing at City College in New York. In 2006, she was appointed adjunct professor of English literature at University College, Dublin, returning home after her self-imposed exile of many years.

ANALYSIS

Edna O'Brien's early years in Ireland profoundly affected her view of the world, and particularly of women's relationships and their place in society. Being Irish, she says in *Mother Ireland*, gives one a unique view of pleasure and punishment, life and death. O'Brien's work is lyrical and lively. Her memory for people and places, for the minutiae of daily living, is prodigious; her zest for language is Joycean. She is frequently on the attack, but at her best, which is often, she transcends her immediate cause to encourage, with a grain of humor, those who still dream of love achieved through kindness and decency—common virtues still no more common than they ever were.

O'Brien's concerns are most readily accessible in her very eccentric travel/autobiography *Mother Ireland*. Her Irishness is something of which O'Brien is proud: "It's a state of mind." She is not, however, blind to Ireland's faults, appreciating that there must be something "secretly catastrophic" about a country that so many people leave. After an iconoclastic opening chapter on Irish history, with its uncanonized patron saint and its paunchy Firbogs, follow six chapters in which are sketched O'Brien's dominant themes: loneliness, the longing for adventure (often sexual), the repressive Irish Roman Catholic Church, family ties (the martyred mother and the rollicking father), and the courageous hopelessness with which life at best must be lived.

It would be a melancholy picture if it were not for O'Brien's saving, ironic sense of humor and the skill with which she roots her observations in the sensual details of the actual world. Her readers share vividly with her a world of wet batteries for radios, ink powder, walls with fragments of bottles embedded in their tops, Fox's (Glacier) Mints, orange-boxes, and lice combed from a child's head onto a newspaper. O'Brien's recurring themes, her experiments with form, and the feeling she succeeds in communicating that this Irish microcosm has its universal significance are all clearly present in *Mother Ireland*.

THE COUNTRY GIRLS

From its detailed, evocative opening page, redolent of genteel poverty, *The Country Girls*, O'Brien's first novel, serves notice of an unusual voice. The shy and sensitive Caithleen tells her first-person story and shares the action with her alter ego, the volatile and malicious Baba. It is a world divided into two warring camps, male and female, where Caithleen's aspirations toward romantic love are doomed to failure. Mr. Gentleman is the first in a long line of rotters (the drunken, brutal father; Eugene Gaillard; Herod; Dr. Flaggler), far outnumbering the few men with decent inclinations (Hickey, Auro); in such a world women stand little chance, single, married in the usual sense, or brides of Christ.

The repressive effects of poverty and a patriarchal society are hardly alleviated by the Church and its proscriptions. Her mother drowned, Caithleen spends her mid-teen years boarding in a strict convent school from which Baba contrives their expulsion for writing a ribald note. In their late teens, joyously, they come up to Dublin, Baba to take a commercial course, Caithleen to work as a grocer's assistant until she can take the civil service examinations. Loneliness, however, follows them: Baba contracts tuberculosis; Caithleen's Mr. Gentleman lets her down. With the resilience of youth, however, her last line in this novel is, "I was almost certain that I wouldn't sleep that night."

THE LONELY GIRL

The Lonely Girl continues the saga two years later, with Baba healthy again. It is, however, largely Caithleen's story; again she is the narrator. The repressive effects of her family, her village community, and her convent education are again in evidence. O'Brien has her heroine involved romantically with Eugene Gaillard, whose face reminds her of a saint and who is about the same height as her father; he is a cultivated snob, and in an often cold fashion he begins the further education of his naïve, prudish "student," both in bed and in the salon. (As Grace Eckley has pointed out, Caithleen's stiff tutor and O'Brien's former husband, Ernest Gebler, share the same initials.) At the novel's conclusion, Caithleen, wild and debased "because of some damned man," is learning, is changing; she is, as she says, finding her feet, "and when I'm able to talk I imagine that I won't be alone." Still seeking their connection, she and Baba sail on the *Hibernia* from Dublin to Liverpool and London.

GIRLS IN THEIR MARRIED BLISS

Girls in Their Married Bliss continues the story of the two in London, where, for the first time, Baba assumes the first-person narration, alternating with an omniscient voice distancing O'Brien and the reader from Caithleen's role—a process O'Brien will carry even further with her protagonist in *A Pagan Place*. The women, now about twenty-five years old, have not left their Irish baggage behind in Dublin; there is a splendid, blustery Celtic quality to the scapegrace Baba's style. Kate (as Caithleen is called), too, has her share of one-liners, word associations, epigrams, and zany metaphors: "Self-interest," she observes on one occasion, "was a common crime"; on another, at a party, she is amused by a girl wearing a strawberry punnet on her head to make herself taller.

In these early novels, O'Brien, like her leading characters, is learning and developing her skills. In *Girls in Their Married Bliss*, the topic is still the female search for love and connection. The novel is a precisely observed account of a marriage failing. People rub exquisitely on one another's nerves in the larger context of women's role in society; in the smaller context of bedroom politics, "Men are pure fools." Marriage, at least on the grounds on which the women enter it here, is evidently no end to the quest. Baba makes a calculated move for comfort; Kate sees that her interest in people is generated solely by her own needs. They have matured to the point where they no longer believe much in romantic plans. Kate's answer to the biological unfairness of God's scheme for women, as Baba sees it, is to have herself sterilized; she will not make the same mistake again: No other child of hers will be abducted by its father; no further child of hers will in its turn become a parent.

In the edition of the complete trilogy that was published in one volume in 1986, O'Brien includes a brief *Epilogue* in the form of a monologue delivered by Baba. Here the ebullient Baba brings the reader up to date: The despairing Kate is dead; she drowned, perhaps deliberately.

AUGUST IS A WICKED MONTH

In O'Brien's next novel, *August Is a Wicked Month*, an omniscient narrator describes the protagonist's abortive attempts at self-liberation, largely through sexual activity. Ellen is something like Kate of the earlier trilogy—a superstitious, convent-bred, twenty-eight-year-old Irish magazine writer, formerly a nurse, living in London when the novel begins. She takes a trip to France when the husband from whom she is separated and their eight-year-old son, Mark, who lives with her, go on a camping holiday together. Her "pathetic struggles towards wickedness" involve rejecting the first sexual invitations she encounters. Eventually, however, when Ellen does become intimately involved with a high-living group, O'Brien subjects her to two catastrophic accidents: She receives a call from her husband, who tells her that her son has been killed by a car in a roadside accident, and she fears, wrongly as it turns out, that she has contracted a venereal disease. The guilt and the judgment are clear; perhaps they are too clear to make this novel an artistic success. Ellen finally finds an uneasy autumnal peace, unlike the women in O'Brien's next novel, who have a genuine joy ripped away from them.

CASUALTIES OF PEACE

In *Casualties of Peace*, Willa McCord, artist in glass, and her earthy domestic, Patsy Wiley, are the protagonists, exemplary victims of male violence. An omniscient narrator views the two unhappy women—Willa having escaped from a nightmarish marriage to the sadistic Herod, Patsy currently suffering her husband Tom's blows. Both have their dreams of happiness outside marriage shattered. There was a chance for peace for them, but accidents prevented them from knowing joy. Patsy blabs to Willa about leaving Tom rather than doing it immediately, as planned, and her lover, Ron, believes she has let him down. Willa, just when a loving connection with Auro seems possible, is murdered by Tom, who mistakes her for Patsy.

Casualties of Peace is second only to *Night*, which it anticipates to some extent, among O'Brien's most Joycean novels. Patsy's love letters to Ron are reminiscent of the earthiest of James Joyce and Nora Barnacle's correspondence; Patsy indeed is a kind of Molly Bloom figure (more clearly developed in *Night*). Willa's letters to Auro, delivered posthumously, share the same stream-of-consciousness qualities: Words pile up into lists; associations trigger other more graphic associations; "memory is the bugger." At times lyrical, at times humorous, O'Brien develops here the Celtic flair with words that is associated with Joyce or Dylan Thomas. Her theme is loneliness and its myriad causes; her characters search to alleviate their pain, to make connections, to overcome their feelings of guilt for being themselves.

A PAGAN PLACE

A Pagan Place is a very odd novel; it is largely a sophisticated rewrite of *The Country Girls*, as O'Brien perhaps would have written that work had she had ten more years of reading, writing, and living behind her at the time. Baba is dropped in favor of one unnamed, preadolescent girl whose sexual arousal when her father beats her accomplishes her move toward adolescence. Getting away from her Irish family and Irish community, with their hereditary guilt, will, it is suggested, take her yet a stage further. At the end of the novel she leaves to the accompaniment of an eerie Hibernian howl.

Throughout the work an omniscient narrator, who sometimes uses dialect forms and sometimes very erudite words, and who is clearly unreliable in matters of fact (putting an English "general" on Nelson's pillar), places the reader at the center of the action by using the second-person narrative. No one but "you," then, is at the center of the action; the narrator and the writer are similarly distanced from the action.

Perhaps in this novel O'Brien exorcised the worst of her Irishness; certainly, very violent feelings surface, all in the consciousness of a young girl. O'Brien, in contrast to her contemporaries among Irish writers of fiction, such as Brian Friel or Benedict Kiely, really seems to dislike her Celtic community. Here is a very bitter indictment of the Church, and perhaps its ultimate rejection in the priest's attempt to seduce "you," masturbating and ejaculating on "you." Here, too, is a savage, repressive, guilt-ridden world of so-called

Christians where unwed mothers receive no *caritas*, and where legally wed mothers and fathers show no love either. It is a world where holy water is sprinkled on thoroughbred foals, where a black dog, chasing a frog that jumps out of the ashes at Della's wake, is seen as one and the same with the devil. All in all, it is, with few exceptions, a nightmarish community, especially for a child. For "you" as a child at the center of this world, deserted even by "your" mother at one period, a thing "you" thought would never happen, the only certainty is that "you" want to escape, whatever the burden of guilt "you" carry.

ZEE AND CO.

The theme of escape is continued in *Zee and Co.*, where O'Brien's heroines are back in London, and again a pair. Zee moves increasingly aggressively and ruthlessly to hold her man, Robert, while dominating Stella, her rival. She succeeds in both endeavors. As the war of the sexes heats up, Zee refuses to be a victim; she is no patsy. O'Brien's long preoccupation with the defensive role of women in society appears to be shifting to the offensive in her later works as her heroines themselves become less fragmented. A person needs to be integrated psychically to withstand not only sexual partners and spouses but also all manifestations of phantoms, prejudice, repression, guilt, and loneliness. This new positive attitude is well illustrated in the rambunctious Mary Hooligan, whose nightlong monologue forms O'Brien's next work, *Night*.

NIGHT

In form and style, *Night* is O'Brien's most Joycean novel. In a harangue from her bed in England, Mary Hooligan—Irish, abused, divorced—delivers herself of an aggressive, courageous, independent, first-person autobiographical statement. Beginning with an Anglo-Saxon monosyllable in the opening paragraph, the nonconciliatory tone of her monologue is established. "I am a woman," Mary affirms, and proceeds to weave, in time and place, the story of her connection with her father and mother, her former husband— "the original Prince of Darkness"—and her son. It is an exuberant linguistic spree: From a "trepidation" of gelatin-like dessert to the welcome "tap o' the mornin'," metaphors and apt words are savored and invented. The pervasive humor is wry; the aggressive tone and confident technique perfectly match the content of a work whose burden is rebellion against loveless unions and ignorance.

Mary Hooligan is another in O'Brien's procession of outsiders, an Irish woman in England, merely house-sitting, so even less important in the community. O'Brien, however, establishes Mary as a force on her own: Mary rejects her friend Madge—Mary needs no Kate figure to complement her being; she is complete on her own. The theme under review remains the eternal search for love in its myriad manifestations; what is new here is the heroine's joyful attack as she continues her pilgrimage to "the higher shores of love." Family, community, and marriage settings are again explored. Many of the details are familiar: the vicious father, the ignoramuses who could not tell cheese from soap, the cold-fish husband. Constant and familiar in O'Brien's work is the warm regard for children, particularly mothers' regard for their sons. This aspect of love leads O'Brien to flirt with incest in her most violent work, *I Hardly Knew You*, in which the narrator has an affair with and then murders her son's friend.

I HARDLY KNEW YOU

Nora, the protagonist of *I Hardly Knew You*, tells her story in yet another night monologue, from her prison cell, as she awaits trial for the murder of Hart, her young lover. Again, O'Brien's narrator is an Irish exile in England, divorced from an overly frugal husband, with a son, and literally in prison, isolated from all society. Loneliness is at the core of her existence, as it is, she remarks, at the core of Celtic songs. Her monologue shuffles time and space more formally than Mary Hooligan's in *Night* and reveals a world of increasing violence. Details and incidents from O'Brien's previous works, as far back even as *The Country Girls*, show up: the drunken father taking the cure, the child-abduction threat, the child scraping the toilet-seat paint, the kicking match engaged in by brutish relatives.

The world has become an increasingly violent place, and the response of O'Brien's narrator matches it. Like Mary's, Nora's personality is integrated, but toward the Kate side. She engages in an explicitly lesbian encounter, but she needs no other woman to complement her. Indeed, she acts increasingly like the worst stereotype of the sadistic male predator, who uses and abuses other people, particularly women and especially wives. This is a chilling picture of a person driven to violence, to kill without regret. Here is a woman who has lost her balance and whose sweeping indictment of men must surely be viewed as just as reprehensible as male chauvinism. "I am proud . . . to have killed one of the breed to whom I owe nothing but cruelty, deceit, and the asp's emission," she avers, ignoring absolutely O'Brien's often-stated support for "human decency" and kindness among people of whatever sex.

THE HIGH ROAD

The graph of O'Brien's fictional split personalities is by no means a straight line. A clearly differentiated pair in the early trilogy, each "Kate" and "Baba" is subsequently given an alternating fictional forum. The *Epilogue* may have seemed to clear the way for Baba and zesty Baba types, but *The High Road*, published two years later, has readers once again seeing a sophisticated society through the moist eyes of a Kate type.

Anna, the narrator of *The High Road*, like many of the women in O'Brien's short stories as well, has come on Easter Sunday to a Mediterranean paradise to get over a London love doomed from its inception. In this exotic setting, she encounters eccentric members of the international set: the superannuated debutante, Portia; the grotesques who make up a German fashion-magazine staff on location; the fading jet-setter, Iris; the itinerant Irish painter, D'Arcy, with the Joycean language flair; and Catalina, the hotel chambermaid, with whom she has an affair. It all ends in murder; D'Arcy, to buy some time, paints

"Lesbos" on a multitude of walls, not merely on Catalina's gable, where the word first appeared, but to no avail. Clutching a scarf full of Catalina's blood-soaked hair, in what in its accumulation of similes seems at times a parody of the gothic romance, Anna sets out, she says, for the last time, for home. Whether she has left behind her the purgatory of motherhood, in its various manifestations, remains to be read.

TIME AND TIDE

O'Brien continues her focus on Irish women's lives and social roles in *Time and Tide*. The title of the work refers to linear progression and cyclical repetition, devices that she incorporates not only thematically (the changeability and sameness of women's lives) but stylistically. The story develops episodically, providing vignettes from the narrator's life. The protagonist, Nell, following a failed marriage to an abusive spouse, has raised two sons independently. Early in the novel it is revealed that her eldest son, Paddy, is enmeshed in drug use. Ironically, it is not an overdose but a boating accident that claims his life. The novel then reverses time to recount earlier family events, contributory tragedies that lead up to and culminate in the loss of Nell's firstborn son.

A powerful image in the novel is that of a barge colliding with a tourist boat on the Thames. That Paddy should be aboard the latter and this random accident claims his life not only reveals the unpredictability of events but also highlights the young man's chosen and quick route through life. Rejecting the misery he associates with his long-suffering mother, he embraces the thrills of drugs and holidays, but his pleasure-seeking life, prematurely ended, only intensifies his family's despair. For O'Brien's characters, there is no respite from the barges of life, from the inevitable hardships that destroy any illusion of happiness.

Despite the desolate events recounted—Nell herself has indulged in narcotics and sexual liaisons, finding solace in neither—the novel ends with a measure of optimism. When her surviving son, Tristan, leaves home to join Paddy's girlfriend (who is pregnant with Paddy's child), Nell is dejected at first by his departure. Eventually, she finds respite in her now quiet home. Having borne the worst, the death of a child, she must accept what is to come, life in all its myriad sorrows and momentary pleasures.

HOUSE OF SPLENDID ISOLATION

O'Brien returns to her native territory with a trilogy of novels set in modern Ireland. The first, *House of Splendid Isolation*, is a stunning book, quite different from her previous work. It reveals a microcosm of divided Ireland, embodied by the patriot-terrorist McGreevy and the widow Josie O'Meara. McGreevy, seeking to free Northern Ireland from British rule, has been sent to the complacent South to murder a prominent English visitor. He plans to hide in Josie's decaying mansion, which he believes is empty. Feared as a coldly efficient terrorist, McGreevy emerges as a surprisingly kind, ordinary man who has been honed to a thin edge by violence.

Josie, ill with pneumonia and high blood pressure, has just been released from a nursing home to her house of isolation. She seems pluckier than most O'Brien heroines, perhaps because she is elderly, although flashbacks illuminate the early life that formed her. The collision of the revolutionary and the antiterrorist, and their gradual sympathy and understanding, defines the conflict of the novel and the hunt that follows. Josie can be seen as the *Shan Van Vocht*, the Poor Old Woman, a historical symbol of Ireland, exemplifying the domestic life of her people. McGreevy represents the bitter fruit of the country's troubled political history. The inevitable conclusion proceeds as well-meaning, patriotic volunteers from both factions struggle with duty, guilt, and grief.

Surprisingly, O'Brien avoids her usual male stereotypes in this novel; she presents imperfect men, both law-abiding and lawless, who are racked by ambivalence. She remains neutral, revealing with rueful detachment the human damage caused by centuries of conflict. *House of Splendid Isolation* offers a portrait of Ireland in all its complexity, with its intense people and its bloody and heartbreaking history.

DOWN BY THE RIVER

The second installment in the trilogy, *Down by the River*, is a less objective book than *House of Splendid Isolation*. The novel was inspired by a controversial incident that took place in Ireland in 1992, when a pregnant fourteen-year-old girl fled to England for an abortion but was brought back and made a ward of the court. O'Brien has changed some details of the case; in her version, Mary MacNamara is impulsively raped by her father as they are picking berries. Mary's dying mother and a female doctor suspect the truth, as do others, but no one acts.

Here again is the world familiar to O'Brien's readers, a world of repression and guilt, in which people do not look directly at each other or say what needs to be said. In a tacit conspiracy of avoidance, everyone knows that Mary is pregnant as a result of the rape, but no one will confront the problem. Worse is the hypocrisy of those quick to judge without mercy. Self-righteous adulterers preen in antiabortion meetings while a shrill speaker waves bloody photographs, even as a retired midwife recalls the dead babies she has found stuffed in drawers and toilets. Other folks are genuinely troubled, torn between religious conviction and pity for the girl. Although a sympathetic neighbor finally agrees to help Mary escape to London to obtain an abortion, the plan is thwarted. People on both sides of the issue exploit Mary for their own purposes, and the novel's ending is tense and melodramatic, though not entirely convincing.

WILD DECEMBERS

Wild Decembers completes the political trilogy begun with *House of Splendid Isolation*. Each of the three novels explores a social issue that has plagued Ireland in its recent history but the origins of which stretch back in time. Whereas the first novel in the series focuses on sectarian violence and the second on abortion rights, the third and final work tills Ireland's very soil. Set in the fictional rural parish of Cloontha, *Wild Decembers* chronicles a series of seemingly petty land disagreements between two farmers: longtime resident Joseph Brennan and his immigrant neighbor, Michael Bugler. Further complications arise from Bugler's growing interest in Brennan's younger sister, Breege, and the unexpected arrival of Bugler's Australian fiancé. By novel's end, one farmer is dead and the other in prison, the land and the women who remain behind abandoned by the men. O'Brien layers the text with numerous references, Irish (the Great Famine), mythological (stories of Greek gods and mortals), and biblical (the struggle between Cain and Abel), thus expanding the significance of this tale of two Irish farmers who feud over territory.

IN THE FOREST

In the Forest explores the childhood trauma and mental frailty that eventually lead a deranged young Irishman to take the lives of three innocent people, including a single mother and her child. As she has in previous novels, notably *House of Splendid Isolation* and *Wild Decembers*, O'Brien incorporates elements of Irish and Greek mythology to imbue her story with universal qualities. Michael O'Kane, whose name (literally "of Cain") carries biblical import, is either a monster or an emotionally disturbed young man. His victims try to relate to him as the latter in a failed attempt to avoid their fates and in an effort to understand the source of his psychosis. As they learn from their captor, O'Kane's childhood was marked by abuse, abandonment, and confinement.

In his youth, Michael O'Kane was identified by his community as an individual capable of great cruelty. His adolescent nickname, *Kinderschreck* (German for "one who scares children"), connotes his designation by society as a monster. Institutionalized and drugged for much of his life, including a final stint in an English facility, Michael is allowed by British authorities to return to Ireland. The multiple murders he commits on his home soil verify that his release was premature and imprudent. In this portrait of a serial killer, O'Brien raises disturbing questions that remain with readers. To what extent does society contribute to the making of its monsters, its sociopaths and violent criminals? Once these dangerous outsiders have been identified, where should society place them? Most pointedly, after such individuals have been labeled *Kinderschrecken*, how should society expect them to behave?

THE LIGHT OF EVENING

In *The Light of Evening*, O'Brien returns to the subject matter of earlier novels: an examination of the troubled and changing lives of Irish women. She also mines biographical material as she depicts the tense relationship between a traditional Irish mother and her less traditional daughter, an emerging writer. Perhaps as a sign of her own maturity as an author and a woman, O'Brien allows the aged Dilly to reminisce about the past from her hospital bed as she awaits the arrival of her adult daughter Eleanora. Recalled in Dilly's mind are events from her life that are similar to episodes in O'Brien's mother's life, including an emigration to America that is followed by a return to Ireland and marriage.

Most revealing of their troubled relationship is Dilly's maternal disappointment when Eleanora marries a foreigner, an act that for a time severs familial and national ties. When Eleanora finally arrives at her bedside, Dilly's anticipated encounter with her daughter proves disappointing; the two women remain estranged. Left behind as counterevidence to Dilly's more positive remembrances is Eleanora's personal journal, which houses a far different and darker perspective on the events of the women's lives.

Archibald E. Irwin; Joanne McCarthy
Updated by Dorothy Dodge Robbins

OTHER MAJOR WORKS

SHORT FICTION: *The Love Object*, 1968; *A Scandalous Woman, and Other Stories*, 1974; *Mrs. Reinhardt*, 1978 (also known as *A Rose in the Heart*, 1979); *Returning*, 1982; *A Fanatic Heart*, 1984; *Lantern Slides*, 1990.

PLAYS: *A Cheap Bunch of Nice Flowers*, pr. 1962; *A Pagan Place*, pr. 1972 (adaptation of her novel); *The Gathering*, pr. 1974; *Virginia*, pr. 1980; *Flesh and Blood*, pr. 1985; *Iphigenia*, pr., pb. 2003 (adaptation of Euripides' play); *Triptych*, pr., pb. 2003.

POETRY: *On the Bone*, 1989.

SCREENPLAYS: *Girl with Green Eyes*, 1964 (adaptation of her novel); *Time Lost and Time Remembered*, 1966 (with Desmond Davis; also known as *I Was Happy Here*); *Three into Two Won't Go*, 1969; *X, Y, and Zee*, 1971 (also known as *Zee and Company*; adaptation of her novel).

TELEPLAYS: *The Wedding Dress*, 1963; *Nothing's Ever Over*, 1968; *Mrs. Reinhardt*, 1981 (adaptation of her short story); *The Country Girls*, 1983 (adaptation of her novel).

NONFICTION: *Mother Ireland*, 1976; *Arabian Days*, 1977; *James and Nora: A Portrait of Joyce's Marriage*, 1981; *Vanishing Ireland*, 1986; *James Joyce*, 1999.

CHILDREN'S LITERATURE: *The Dazzle*, 1981; *A Christmas Treat*, 1982; *The Expedition*, 1982; *The Rescue*, 1983; *Tales for the Telling: Irish Folk and Fairy Stories*, 1986.

EDITED TEXT: *Some Irish Loving*, 1979.

BIBLIOGRAPHY

Byron, Kristine. "'In the Name of the Mother . . . ': The Epilogue of Edna O'Brien's Country Girls Trilogy." *Women's Studies* 31 (July/August, 2002): 447-465. Analyzes the function of O'Brien's epilogue and contrasts it with more traditional literary uses of epilogues in general. Argues that the epilogue does not provide closure to the saga of Kate and Baba, but rather disclosure, allowing for a rereading of the entire trilogy.

Colletta, Lisa, and Maureen O'Connor, eds. *Wild Colonial Girl: Essays on Edna O'Brien*. Madison: University of Wisconsin Press, 2006. Collection of critical essays examines O'Brien's works, assessing the manner in which O'Brien both responds to and undermines traditional Irish literature and figureheads while simultaneously charting a decisively feminist literary course for her native tongue.

Eckley, Grace. *Edna O'Brien*. Lewisburg, Pa.: Bucknell University Press, 1974. Excellent brief study was the first such examination of O'Brien's fiction. Among the themes in O'Brien's extremely personal work discussed are those of love and loss.

Gillespie, Michael Patrick. "(S)he Was Too Scrupulous Always." In *The Comic Tradition in Irish Women Writers*, edited by Theresa O'Connor. Gainesville: University Press of Florida, 1996. Discusses how O'Brien's humor is distinguished from that of Irish male writers; shows the relationship between her humor and that of James Joyce, particularly the relationship between her short stories and those in Joyce's *Dubliners* (1914).

Harris, Michael. "Outside History: Edna O'Brien's *House of Splendid Isolation*." *New Hibernia Review* 10 (March 3, 2006): 111-122. Examines the novel in the context of postmodernism, including the author's use of pastiche, decentering, and fragmentation.

Hooper, Brad. Review of *In the Forest*, by Edna O'Brien. *Booklist*, January 1-15, 2002, 776. Observes that this psychological thriller breaks with previous O'Brien works by exposing a dark side to the human condition that is universal as opposed to uniquely Irish—in this case, the communal fear generated by a killer at large.

Mara, Miriam. "The Geography of Body: Borders in Edna O'Brien's *Down by the River* and Colum McCann's 'Sisters.'" In *The Current Debate About the Irish Literary Canon: Essays Reassessing the Field Day Anthology of Irish Writing*, edited by Helen Thompson. Lewiston: N.Y.: Edwin Mellen Press, 2006. Explores borders as a metaphor for both bodily and national boundaries and notes O'Brien's ability to trespass on and transcend barriers in *Down by the River.*

O'Brien, Edna. "Edna O'Brien." Interview by Caitriona Moloney and Helen Thompson. In *Irish Women Writers Speak Out: Voices from the Field.* Syracuse, N.Y.: Syracuse University Press, 2003. O'Brien discusses her intertwined identities as writer, woman, and postcolonialist.

Quintelli-Neary, Margaret. "Retelling the Sorrows in Edna O'Brien's Country Girls Trilogy." *Nua: Studies in Contemporary Irish Writing* 4, nos. 1/2 (2003): 65-76. Examines O'Brien's treatment of female experiences in relationship to tragedy.

FLANN O'BRIEN
Brian O'Nolan

Born: Strabane, Ireland; October 5, 1911
Died: Dublin, Ireland; April 1, 1966
Also known as: Brian O'Nuallain; Brother Barnabus; George Knowall; Myles na Gopaleen; Great Count O'Blather; John James Doe

OTHER LITERARY FORMS

Flann O'Brien was the pen name used by Brian O'Nolan for the four novels he wrote in English, and so it is used here, although his work in other forms appeared under other names. He was a talented and prolific journalist as well as a novelist. He began to write satiric essays for student publications at University College, Dublin; a sampling of this student work was reprinted in the "Flann O'Brien Number" published by the *Journal of Irish Studies* in 1974. Although a civil servant by profession, O'Brien also wrote a famous column for *The Irish Times* under the name Myles na Gopaleen. This column continued on a regular basis for twenty-five years; selections were reprinted in *Cruiskeen Lawn* (1943), *The Best of Myles* (1968), and *The Various Lives of Keats and Chapman and the Brother* (1976).

Throughout his career, O'Brien sporadically produced skits for theater, essays other than journalism, and short stories. These are most conveniently located in two posthumous collections. *Stories and Plays* (1973) reprints two dramatic skits, two short stories, an essay on James Joyce called "A Bash in the Tunnel," and the seven existing chapters of an unfinished novel called *Slattery's Sago Saga. A Flann O'Brien Reader* (1978) includes examples of his journalism, short fiction, and essays, along with excerpts from his five novels.

ACHIEVEMENTS

Flann O'Brien's contemporary reputation rests on the rediscovery of his first novel, *At Swim-Two-Birds*, an event that occurred about twenty years after the novel was published. The novel had received praise from Joyce, Dylan Thomas, and Graham Greene, among others, but its possibilities for broad critical and popular success were thwarted by the onset of World War II. His next novel, *The Third Policeman*, could find no publisher until after his death, and his third novel, *The Poor Mouth*, was written in Gaelic and thus limited to an extremely small audience. These three novels are now considered to be O'Brien's most important works.

About 1960, O'Brien's work was rediscovered by American writers S. J. Perelman and William Saroyan. Their praise, principally of his journalism, led to a reissue of *At Swim-Two-Birds* and critical recognition of it as an important novel. In response to this renewal of interest in his fiction, O'Brien wrote *The Hard Life* and *The Dalkey Archive*, but neither of these later novels is as interesting nor as important as his three earlier novels. O'Brien's journalism, in posthumous collections, is the source of most of his popular appeal today, particularly in Ireland. The focus of almost all critical interest in his work, however, is on his novels, especially *At Swim-Two-Birds* and *The Third Policeman*. O'Brien is now universally recognized as the most significant Irish novelist of his generation.

BIOGRAPHY

Flann O'Brien was born Brian O'Nolan on October 5, 1911, in Strabane, county Tyrone, Ireland. He was the third of twelve children of Michael Victor O'Nolan, a customs officer, and Agnes Gormlet O'Nolan. O'Brien's family was frequently relocated in the course of his father's profession, and this postponed his early formal education. His family was extremely literate, however, and in the home O'Brien developed early fluency in Irish Gaelic as well as English and also some familiarity with Latin and Greek classics. It was only in 1923, when his father was transferred to Dublin, that O'Brien was enrolled, at the age of twelve, in the Synge Street School run by the Christian Brothers. In 1925, his father was appointed a revenue commissioner in Dublin Castle, and this advancement permitted the family to settle permanently in Blackrock, a southern suburb of Dublin, in 1927. In that year, O'Brien was enrolled in Blackrock College, a preparatory school. In 1929, he entered University College, Dublin.

At University College, O'Brien was a success in his studies and in extracurricular literary activities. In 1933, he earned a bachelor of arts degree in English, Irish, and German; won the school's gold medal for debate; and was awarded a scholarship for study at the University of Cologne. After a year in Germany, he returned to University College and earned his master of arts degree in 1935 with a thesis on Irish poetry in Gaelic. The early intimations of his literary career, however, were more apparent in his nonscholarly activities. In 1931, he invented the persona Brother Barnabas for the student magazine *Comhthrom Féinne*. A subsequent series of articles under this name was brought to a close in 1934 by a "posthumous" piece called "Scenes from a Novel" that anticipates the metafictional premise of *At Swim-Two-Birds*. In 1934, O'Brien also invented the persona Count O'Blather for his own short-lived magazine in English called *Blather.*

Following the conclusion of his graduate work, O'Brien joined the Irish civil service in

1935; he would continue in its employ until 1953. In 1935 he also began work on *At Swim-Two-Birds*, which was published in 1939 but commercially undone by the decimation of English book sales by World War II. By 1940, he had completed *The Third Policeman*, which was not published until after his death. In subsequent years, O'Brien told friends that he had lost this manuscript, but he nevertheless reworked it into the much more superficial novel *The Dalkey Archive* two decades later.

These discouraging setbacks were offset to some extent by the success of an outrageous literary scam. Under a series of fictitious names, O'Brien and Niall Sheridan began an attack on Dublin's presiding literary deities in the pages of *The Irish Times*, and, during the exchange of heated letters to the newspaper that followed, they began to attack their own original position under new fictitious names. When the scheme came to light, *The Irish Times* editor R. M. Smyllie had the goodwill and foresight to hire O'Brien to write a regular column. First in Irish and then in English, these columns of Myles na Gopaleen appeared at a rate of approximately three per week from October 4, 1940, until his final illness in 1966. As an outgrowth of his first columns in Irish, O'Brien wrote *The Poor Mouth* in Irish as Myles na Gopaleen in 1941.

O'Brien had thus completed his three important novels by the age of thirty; one was generally ignored, one remained in manuscript, and one was published in a language inaccessible even to most Irish citizens. A combination of cynicism and absorption in journalism effectively ended his career as a novelist at that point. By the time of the rediscovery of *At Swim-Two-Birds*, O'Brien was already suffering from the effects of lifelong heavy drinking. He managed to respond to interest in his past work with *The Hard Life* and *The Dalkey Archive*, but these works lack the textual complexities of his earlier and more important novels. It is a final, appropriate irony that O'Brien, inventor of fictional disguises and elaborate literary conceits, died of alcohol-related maladies on April Fools' Day of 1966.

ANALYSIS

Flann O'Brien's first and most important novel, *At Swim-Two-Birds*, was published the year that William Butler Yeats died. The coincidence is notable because the novel was a parodistic melange of styles spawned by the Irish Literary Revival championed by Yeats and because all of O'Brien's important novels critique literary fabrications akin to those of the revival. The Irish Literary Revival was based on the rediscovery of the special identity of Ireland, especially as this was apparent in the literature of the Celtic legends. In popularizing these legends, the participants in the revival, many of whom—unlike O'Brien—had no fluency in the Gaelic language, were prone to literary extravagance and inflated notions of Celtic nobility. The literature of the revival was instrumental in arousing political energies that led to the creation of the Irish Free State, but after this goal of political independence had been realized, many of the revival's own literary excesses became apparent. Modern problems such as economic recession, entanglements of church and state, and the entrenched conservatism of an emerging middle class made the essential artifice of the inspiring revival literature especially visible for the first time.

O'Brien wrote none of the important fiction about the Irish Republic of his own day; instead, his major works look back to the earlier mythologizing of Celtic identity and modern Irish culture. *At Swim-Two-Birds*, *The Third Policeman*, and *The Poor Mouth* all ridicule the pretensions of literature by emphasizing its artificiality. O'Brien's work is satiric in effect because it implicitly corrects notions of literary authority, cultural privilege, and innate national aristocracy. Its primary mode is parody, adoption, and exaggeration of a variety of recognizable literary styles to demonstrate their essential mendacity.

The salient quality of O'Brien's career is ambiguity concerning his name and identity. He took the pen name Flann O'Brien from Gerald Griffin's 1829 novel *The Collegians*, while the name Myles na Gopaleen came from Dion Boucicault's play *The Colleen Bawn* (1860), based on Griffin's novel. Both of these pseudonyms recall stage Irishmen, a stereotype of nineteenth century English fiction. In the revival, a new domestic stereotype of the Irish prevailed, one as falsely noble as the earlier English one was debased. Thus, these names attached to O'Brien's novels challenged the new literary identity of Ireland as a sheer fabrication.

O'Brien's first three novels are relentless in their scrutiny of fabricated literary identities; his later two novels are less successful because that scrutiny is limited, and because some assumptions about identity are allowed to stand unchallenged. Ultimately, his finest works have affinities with that strain of modern literature that asserts the reality of a metaphysical void, a senseless core of anonymity beneath the guises, literary and otherwise, protectively adopted to give life a semblance of meaning. This is especially true of *The Third Policeman*, which is freer of provincial references than O'Brien's other novels. The relish for parodying things Irish, most apparent in *At Swim-Two-Birds* and *The Poor Mouth*, however, suggests that the primary frame of reference for O'Brien's novels will always be the cultural history of early twentieth century Ireland.

AT SWIM-TWO-BIRDS

At Swim-Two-Birds, which takes its name from the literal translation of a Gaelic placename, is the most complete critique in novel form of the excesses of the Irish Literary Revival. O'Brien was fluent in Gaelic and a talented parodist, and in this novel he exploits the essential artifice of revival literature by placing its various literary styles in collision with one another. Here Finn MacCool, evoked in all his epic splendor, meets the hack writer Dermot Trellis; the mad bard Sweeny, whose verses are included in hilarious literal translations into English, meets Jem Casey, poet of porter; the Good Fairy, taken from the most sentimental of Irish tourist literature, sits down to cards with urban characters taken from the bleak world of Joyce's *Dubliners* (1914). The product is a novel about the unreality of various kinds of fictions, an exercise in style whose only subject is the extravagance of the styles it exploits by parody.

At Swim-Two-Birds is a collection of brief fragments organized only by the desire to express the multiple contrasts of their incompatible styles. The thread that links these fragments is situational rather than narrative: A university student is attempting to write a novel whose three possible openings and four possible conclusions frame *At Swim-Two-Birds*; among the characters in his novel is Dermot Trellis, himself a novelist with a work in progress; the characters in Trellis's novel are dissatisfied with their treatment and so wreak revenge by writing their own novel about Trellis, whose authorial control lapses when he sleeps. This conceit allows O'Brien to include in his novel a plethora of styles from imaginary authors, especially rich in ironies for readers knowledgeable about Irish literature from the Celtic legends to modern writers such as Yeats.

As many of its commentators have pointed out, *At Swim-Two-Birds* has far more appeal and significance than most metafictional novels about a novel in progress. It is, above all else, exuberantly comic rather than pretentious.

THE THIRD POLICEMAN

Although it was not published until after O'Brien's death, *The Third Policeman* was written immediately after *At Swim-Two-Birds*, and it should be considered beside that novel, despite its publication date. Like *At Swim-Two-Birds*, it is a very modernist exercise in the novel as a self-contained and self-generating literary text. In this case, however, O'Brien is less concerned with the identifiable styles of the Irish revival than with the ways any style creates an identity in narrative fiction, the ways style is a source of authority and control in fiction. It is crucial to this novel that the narrator be nameless; without the identity provided by a name, he must create a persona for himself by appropriating styles of expression.

The novel opens with the robbery and murder of a businessman named Mathers by the narrator and his accomplice, John Diviney. The fantastic events that ensue concern the narrator's attempts to recover the stolen money and to hide his complicity in the crime from an omniscient but apparently uninterested pair of police officers. The appearance of Fox, the third police officer, seems to promise the release of the narrator from his predicament, but in fact it presages the realization that the narrator has been dead since the opening pages, betrayed and himself murdered by Diviney.

Released from even the faintest restraints of realism by setting his novel in the afterlife, O'Brien is free in *The Third Policeman* to allow language and rhetoric, rather than cause and effect, to determine the direction of his tale. The most prominent style and source of authority in the novel is an academic one related to the narrator's interest in a fictional philosopher named de Selby, whose works are evoked for the sake of clarification, summarized, and cited in scholarly footnotes throughout the novel. Elsewhere, *The Third Policeman* sporadically adopts the style of the modern murder mystery, a pretentious opera review, scientific analysis, Eastern mysticism, and gothic romance. These intrusive styles color the events of the novel for the reader, much as the alien laws of the afterlife color the experiences of the narrator: They are oblique, intriguing, and ultimately baffling.

The Third Policeman lacks the dimension of cultural commentary provided by evocation of local literary styles in At Swim-Two-Birds. This same generalized environment, however, makes O'Brien's second novel an even richer contemplation on the nature of identity than his first, one that is capable of generalizations about definitions of self that rise above provincial contexts. It is also fully self-contained by a cyclic conclusion that returns the narrator, now accompanied by Diviney, to the earliest situations in the novel. It is precisely this degree of absorption in the interior logic of its own conceits that distinguishes The Third Policeman from O'Brien's later, less interesting reworking of these ideas in The Dalkey Archive.

THE POOR MOUTH

In a letter to Sean O'Casey quoted in The Flann O'Brien Reader, the author described The Poor Mouth, in its original Gaelic version, as "an honest attempt to get under the skin of a certain type of 'Gael,' which I find the most nauseating phenomenon in Europe." This kind of Gael was in fact more a creation of the literary revival than a significant social group. The Poor Mouth, as translated by Patrick C. Power after O'Brien's death, is a parody of a literary genre rather than a parody of life in Gaeltachts, the remote Irish-speaking areas of Ireland that continue to erode in character despite well-intentioned government subsidies. The primary targets of the parody are the enormously popular autobiographies of Gaeltacht life such as Twenty Years A-Growing (1933) by Maurice O'Sullivan, but O'Brien's more general object of parody is all fictionalized versions of peasantry, from the folktales of Standish Hayes O'Grady to the plays of Lady Gregory and J. M. Synge.

The title of the novel evokes the idiom of "poormouthing," or inventing poverty for self-serving purposes, and The Poor Mouth is about the discovery by enthusiastic outsiders of a Gaeltacht in the middle of truly astonishing poverty. The wretched cohabitation of these peasants with their pigs in leaky shacks is a source of some tall-tale humor in the novel, although this poverty does have its darker side, as indicated by casual references to disease and death from starvation, alcoholism, and fighting. O'Brien's real focus here, however, is on the willful self-degradation of the peasants at the feet of their enlightened English-speaking visitors, who gauge the merit of Gaelic tales by the poverty of the teller and limit their own charity lest they spoil the purity of the peasants' profound misery.

The great irony of The Poor Mouth, and an essential component of its publication in Gaelic, is that these visitors are, rather than actual Englishmen, anglicized Irishmen enamored of the peasantry. The pure bile of the novel, which is well preserved in its English translation, derives from this image of Ireland foisting a factitious stereotype on itself, of romanticizing a peasantry in such rigid ways that all males in this Gaeltacht are called James O'Donnell. The use of this collective name is only the most obvious indication of the novel's relevance to O'Brien's governing interest in the theme of identity. Rather than a parody of multiple identities, however, The Poor Mouth is a portrait of surrender after limited resistance to a bleak and uniform identity. It has a special importance in O'Brien's work for this pessimism, for its publication in Gaelic, for his refusal to permit a translation, and for the fact that he would not write another novel until twenty years later.

THE HARD LIFE

The Hard Life lacks the literary frames of reference that give O'Brien's first three novels their focus and energy. Published in the wake of the rediscovery of *At Swim-Two-Birds*, it is a charming rather than derisory treatment of characteristically Irish forms of naïveté and provinciality, one that panders to audience expectations about Irish writing that were ridiculed by the ironies of O'Brien's earlier novels. It is harsh in its criticisms of the Jesuit father, Kurt Fahrt; the misguided Dubliner, Mr. Collopy; and his slatternly daughter, Annie. These satiric elements, however, are rendered benign by the time frame of the novel, written in 1961 but set in the years preceding 1910. The most attractive qualities of the novel—its digressive narration, bitter account of lower-class Dublin propriety, and the extravagantly misinformed conversations of Father Fahrt and Collopy—are facile if skillful entertainments never qualified by the shrewd ironies surrounding such mannerisms in O'Brien's earlier novels.

In all of O'Brien's novels, narrative structure is incidental to stylistic preoccupations, but in *The Hard Life* there is no literary focus to compensate for the lack of narrative structure. The comedy of the Fahrt-Collopy conversations and of several of the improbable events in the novel is brilliant, but the lack of an informing literary perspective renders them isolated exercises in caricature, resembling in tone and length the best of O'Brien's newspaper columns.

THE DALKEY ARCHIVE

In reworking some of the central conceits, notably the de Selby material, from *The Third Policeman*, O'Brien made *The Dalkey Archive* his only novel narrated in the third person. This alteration eliminates many of the ambiguities and complications found in his earlier novels because of their limited narrators. In other respects, too, *The Dalkey Archive* turns away from the most imaginative conceits of O'Brien's earlier work. As such, it represents a distinctly regressive coda in the works of O'Brien.

The novel individually treats the imaginative constructions of three personages. St. Augustine appears and reveals that neither his youthful sins nor his religious conversion were as complete as have been supposed. Sergeant Fottrell reveals his theory that the molecules of men and bicycles mix during riding, with predictable results. Finally, Joyce, discovered living in retirement in the seaside resort called the Skerries, denounces *Ulysses* as a scam perpetrated by Parisian intellectuals and reveals that his true vocation is writing pamphlets for the Catholic Truth Society. These three are joined by their shared intellectual pride, a characteristic that the novel condemns even as it luxuriates in the pleasures of intricate shams.

O'Brien's first three novels were entirely enclosed within their literary conceits. In *The Dalkey Archive*, however, the elaborate shams and crazed logic are dispersed and corrected by the omniscient narrator on surprisingly moralistic grounds. In O'Brien's first three novels, no assumptions about identity were exempt from scrutiny, but *The Dalkey Archive* ends with an extremely complacent announcement of betrothal by its lackluster central characters Mick and Mary. With this gesture, O'Brien's last novel relinquishes the imaginative explorations of self and the elaborate metafictional elements of his finest novels.

Brian O'Nolan adopted the pseudonyms Flann O'Brien and Myles na Gopaleen with a characteristically ironic purpose: He would, under the names of one literary fabrication about Ireland and the Irish, expose the fabulous nature of a later image of the country and the people. At the end of his life, he wrote two novels, *The Hard Life* and *The Dalkey Archive*, deficient in the ironic intent of his important novels. It was as if at this point in his career he actually became Flann O'Brien, the stage Irishman, content with the identity foisted upon him. In *At Swim-Two-Birds*, *The Third Policeman*, and *The Poor Mouth*, however, the ironies surrounding his choice of pseudonyms were in full operation. The complexities and opacities of those novels represent a break from the mainstream of modern Irish literature and the most probing examination of the new national literature's roots in the mythologies of the Irish Literary Revival.

John P. Harrington

OTHER MAJOR WORKS

NONFICTION: *Cruiskeen Lawn*, 1943; *The Best of Myles*, 1968; *The Various Lives of Keats and Chapman and the Brother*, 1976; *Myles Away from Dublin*, 1985 (selected essays from journal columns).

MISCELLANEOUS: *Stories and Plays*, 1973; *A Flann O'Brien Reader*, 1978 (Stephen Jones, editor).

BIBLIOGRAPHY

Asbee, Sue. *Flann O'Brien*. Boston: Twayne, 1991. This overview of O'Brien's life and work contains a solid discussion of his major prose fiction. Includes A chronology, notes, and an annotated bibliography.

Brooker, Joseph. *Flann O'Brien*. Tavistock, England: Northcote House, 2005. An appraisal of all of O'Brien's (and Brian O'Nolan's) writings, including his early attempts at public satire. Examines these works in light of current debates about modernism.

Clissmann, Anne. *Flann O'Brien: A Critical Introduction to His Writings*. New York: Barnes & Noble Books, 1975. An exhaustive discussion of the author's writings in English, with lengthy chapters on the major novels. Includes a bibliography and an index.

Clune, Anne, and Tess Hurson, eds. *Conjuring Complexities: Essays on Flann O'Brien*.

Belfast: Institute of Irish Studies, Queen's University of Belfast, 1997. A solid volume of critical papers analyzing O'Brien's work that were initially delivered at a conference in Dublin in 1986. Includes bibliographical references and an index.

Cronin, Anthony. *No Laughing Matter: The Life and Times of Flann O'Brien.* London: Grafton, 1989. A biography of the complex and somewhat reclusive O'Brien. Cronin's focus is on O'Brien himself, rather than on his work. Little-known personal details illustrate the narrative. A thorough treatment of a difficult subject.

Donohue, Keith. *The Irish Anatomist: A Study of Flann O'Brien.* Dublin: Maunsel, 2002. Donohue assesses O'Brien's entire oeuvre, including works in Irish, his college writings, and letters to the editor, and draws upon biographies of the author to trace O'Brien's development as a postmodernist writer.

Hopper, Keith. *Flann O'Brien: A Portrait of the Artist as a Young Post-Modernist.* Cork, Ireland: Cork University Press, 1995. A study focusing on the narrative structure, style, and other elements of *The Third Policeman*. Hopper argues that the novel is one of the earliest works of postmodernist fiction.

O'Keeffe, Timothy, ed. *Myles: Portraits of Brian O'Nolan.* London: Martin Brian and O'Keeffe, 1973. An invaluable biographical source and critical commentary on O'Brien. Contains reminiscences by friends, colleagues, and one of the author's brothers. Among the critical commentaries, the essay by J. C. C. Mays, "Flann O'Brien: Literalist of the Imagination," stands out.

Shea, Thomas F. *Flann O'Brien's Exorbitant Novels.* Lewisburg, Pa.: Bucknell University Press, 1992. Shea analyzes O'Brien's early experimental fiction, two unpublished manuscripts of *At Swim-Two-Birds*, and unpublished letters in order to better understand his novels. Includes four chapters devoted to the novels, notes, a select bibliography, and an index.

Taaffe, Carol. *Ireland Through the Looking-Glass: Flann O'Brien, Myles na Gopaleen and Irish Cultural Debate.* Cork, Ireland: Cork University Press, 2008. Taaffe explores how the cultural climate of Ireland influenced O'Brien's fiction and journalism, maintaining that his humor and preoccupation with the role of the author were as much influenced by the position of the writer in 1930's and 1940's Ireland as it was by postmodernism.

KATE O'BRIEN

Born: Limerick, Ireland; December 3, 1897
Died: Canterbury, England; August 13, 1974

PRINCIPAL LONG FICTION

Without My Cloak, 1931
Mary Lavelle, 1936
Pray for the Wanderer, 1938
The Land of Spices, 1941
The Last of Summer, 1943
That Lady, 1946 (also known as *For One Sweet Grape*)
The Flower of May, 1953
As Music and Splendour, 1958

OTHER LITERARY FORMS

Kate O'Brien's first success was a play, *Distinguished Villa*, which had a three-month run in London's West End in 1926. She successfully dramatized her novel *That Lady* for a Broadway production (1949) in which Katherine Cornell played the title role. O'Brien was also the author of two travel books, *Farewell, Spain* (1937) and *My Ireland* (1962). Her *English Diaries and Journals* was published in 1943 and a biography, *Teresa of Avila*, in 1951. Her last major published work was a book of reminiscences, *Presentation Parlour* (1963).

ACHIEVEMENTS

While Kate O'Brien's first novel, *Without My Cloak*, received two of the English literary establishment's most prestigious awards, the Hawthornden Prize and the James Tait Black Memorial Prize, her most notable achievement may best be assessed in the context of contemporary Irish literature. In this context, she remains—together with, though in a much more culturally significant manner than, her perhaps better-known contemporary Elizabeth Bowen—an exemplary representative not only of women's writing but also, through her works and career, of women's potential, broadly considered. Partial recognition of her achievement came in 1947 with her election to the Irish Academy of Letters.

BIOGRAPHY

Kate O'Brien was born in the city of Limerick, Ireland, on December 3, 1897, to a comfortable, middle-class family. Educated at a local convent, she went on to attend University College, Dublin, at a time when Ireland's capital was witnessing the consolidation of the Irish Literary Revival, though the cultural enthusiasm of the time left little or no mark either on O'Brien's student days or on her writing.

Kate O'Brien
(Library of Congress)

The years immediately following graduation seem to have been marked by a degree of uncertainty. She first worked in England as a journalist for the (then) *Manchester Guardian* and as a teacher. A brief period in Washington, D.C., as a diplomatic aide was followed by a sojourn in Bilbao, Spain, as a governess. Returning to London in 1924, she married Gustav Renier; the marriage was not a success. Spain soon became her second home, though for more than ten years after the completion of her World War II service at the ministry of information in London she was refused admission to Spain, her depiction of King Philip II in *That Lady* having rendered her persona non grata.

By this time, O'Brien was no stranger to controversy arising out of her fiction: Her 1941 novel, *The Land of Spices*, was notoriously banned by the Irish censorship board for alleged sexual impropriety. In 1950, she took up residence again in Ireland and lived there until 1961, when she returned to England. She died on August 13, 1974.

ANALYSIS

Kate O'Brien's career emerged and developed during a difficult time for Irish writing; indeed, models of Irish women novelists who might have provided her with beneficial influence and nurturing were virtually nonexistent. Despite these unpromising cultural origins, and despite the obvious struggle O'Brien experienced in order to express herself and command a responsive and sustaining audience, her career can be seen in historical retrospect to be marked with notable integrity, independence of mind and action, and devotion to her art.

In a literary culture where women have not always received sufficient critical attention and have not had their works readily incorporated into the canon of a given generation's achievements, critical responses to O'Brien's life and work have belatedly been seen as manifestations of unwarranted narrowness. The belatedness of this view is perhaps a result of the author's long years of exile, along with the fact that her one major popular success, *That Lady*, published when a fresh audience was ready for her work, is a historical romance rather than another in her sequence of novels about Irish family life. Yet the republication of many of her works during the 1980's not only facilitated a reappraisal of her literary achievements but also had the effect of redrawing the map of Irish literary culture at a crucial period in its development.

The generation of Irish writers to which O'Brien belongs had the unenviable task of following in the pathbreaking footsteps of the principal artists of the Irish Literary Revival—the novelist George Moore, the poet William Butler Yeats, and the playwright John Millington Synge. O'Brien's generation was as different in background and outlook from these three illustrious avatars as it is possible to be. Provincial in upbringing, nationalist in politics, unexperimental in art, and Catholic in cultural formation, this generation had at once a greater intimacy with the actual life of its fellow citizens and a more actively critical perception of the society in whose name it had elected to speak. It also had the not inconsiderable disadvantage of attempting to assert its cultural and artistic validity and viability while the star of the revival had not yet entirely waned, and while Yeats, for example, was willing to co-opt new voices to articulate the agenda of his cultural politics.

The most important writers of this generation—those who went on to establish a somewhat more populist orientation for Irish literature, or at least a more populist role for the Irish writer—have long been considered to be Seán O'Faoláin, Frank O'Connor, and Liam O'Flaherty. The different orientation that they represent may be initially discerned in the fact that they each espoused a form largely neglected by the revival—namely, prose fiction, in particular the short story—and implicitly rejected the formal and ideological explorations of their more modernist forebears. O'Brien is a member of this generation not merely by virtue of her provincial background and conventional education but also because her works reflect this generation's concerns, a reflection that receives added point and importance from the fact of its feminist—or, to be historically accurate, protofeminist—perspectives.

The disillusion and disorientation that emerge as a resonant theme in Irish fiction during the 1930's, the problematized rendering of the independence that the country secured in the late twentieth century in juridical and political terms, and the conflicts between tradition and individuality as the culture seeks not merely aesthetic but moral renewal, far from being neglected by O'Brien, are all the more authentically present in her work through being presented from the standpoint of already marginalized female protagonists. (With the exception of *Pray for the Wanderer*, with its protagonist Matt Costello, all of O'Brien's works feature female protagonists.)

WITHOUT MY CLOAK

O'Brien's first novel, *Without My Cloak*, rehearses a number of the problems that arise from her heritage and anticipates the most important of her fiction's preoccupations. A family saga, it brings to awareness, through the use of an essentially nineteenth century model, the social and psychological forces that gave cultural and moral legitimacy to O'Brien's own class and ideological background. The novel traces the development of the Considine family through three generations from the late eighteenth century, plausibly detailing its establishment in an urban, mercantile setting, for which the author uses her native Limerick.

A major motif in the work is the question of security. The Considine ethos consists of a sublimation of development in consolidation, and the emotional claustrophobia that results from this mode of behavior within the family circle is memorably detailed. The security motif is tensely related to its obverse, a quest for independence; the dynamics of the novel enact the struggle familiar from nineteenth century fiction between individual and society, between the assertion of selfhood and institutional constraints, with the emphasis in this instance falling on the power of institutions.

In particular, the social and moral function of the Catholic Church receives special attention in *Without My Cloak* and retains a particularly important place throughout O'Brien's fiction. Because of its status in her first novel, it is possible to refer to the Considine family as embodying an ethos, since the Church operates as a source of moral and social identity, and alternative sources of such security and self-awareness are nowhere to be found. The power of the Church to authorize selfhood as a tissue of constraints makes of it a second, larger, more absolute family, and the matter of the effect of its power on the individual conscience and consciousness, rather than being resolved in *Without My Cloak*, becomes an increasingly emphatic preoccupation in O'Brien's fiction prior to the publication of *That Lady*. (The fact that O'Brien herself seems to have considered the conflicts of her first novel unresolved may be inferred from their reenactment in condensed and more artistically disciplined form in her next work, *The Anteroom*.)

The role and power of the Church is so central to her work that O'Brien has frequently been thought of as a Catholic, more than as an Irish, novelist. Like most Irish writers, however, she is concerned with the culture of Catholicism; its social, personal, and interpersonal influence; and its significance as a generator of a politics of the spirit rather than as a spiritual convalescent home. Indeed, one of her most fundamental fictional preoccupations is with the difficulty of dealing with impersonal authority, whether conceived as institutional or, as in the portrait of Philip II in *That Lady*, monarchical.

MARY LAVELLE

The fact that O'Brien perceived her preoccupations as continuing difficulty rather than as eventual solution is suggested by the regularity with which her protagonists, for all the author's sympathetic dramatization of their intensity of their struggles, typically fail to attain the independence they desire. An exception to this general outcome is the eponymous heroine of *Mary Lavelle*. This novel, which draws more directly on immediate personal experience than does *Without My Cloak*, tells of a young Irish woman working as a governess for a bourgeois Spanish family. In some sense an account of an innocent abroad—Mary seems to be innocence itself—the novel is also a narrative of conflicting loyalties. The heroine is in many respects an ideal employee, fitting into the Areavaga family with the ease of somebody familiar with a culture in which people know their places. It is Mary's very compliance, however, that is responsible for the novel's central drama.

Mary involuntarily falls for Juanito, the married son of the house, a state of affairs that brings her into conflict not only with the outlook in which she had been rigorously brought up in Ireland but also with its powerfully reinforced presence in Doña Consuelo, the commanding head of the household. The conflict between duty and freedom, between individual desire and ethical obligation, in addition to the novelist's welcome transposition of her concerns to a non-Irish locale and the development of a sexual dimension to Mary's struggle for authentic womanhood, contributes to an impressive sense of the novelist's development. Nevertheless, it is not clear what the overall effect of Mary's experiences has been, whether she accepts or rejects the conflict-laden nature of her experiences. "Anguish and anger for everyone and only one little, fantastic, impossible hope," read the closing lines of *Mary Lavelle*, "was the fruit of her journey to Spain." An unexpected fruit of the publication of *Mary Lavelle*, however, was its banning by Irish censors, an act that may be read now as an unintended tribute to O'Brien's insightful presentation of her heroine's moral authenticity but that, at the time, deepened the alienation from her background that her works articulated with increasing conviction.

THE LAND OF SPICES

This alienation reached its highest level when O'Brien's next novel, *The Land of Spices*, met with a similar fate to that of *Mary Lavelle* at the hands of the censors, as a result of which the novel achieved unjust notoriety—and subsequently, when censorship was relaxed in the early 1970's, a certain amount of popular success. The banning of *The Land of Spices* proved instrumental in calling the censorship board's procedures into question and led indirectly to a revision of its mode of operation. It might be argued that the board's very existence was in itself strongly illustrative of the cultural conflicts and repressions that, from a broader, nonbureaucratic, social perspective, form the core of O'Brien's fictional concerns. The pretext for banning *The Land of Spices* was so slender—consisting of a mere handful of words with potentially homosexual implications—that it came to be seen as a paradigm of the narrow-minded, prurient, and often antifeminist orientation of the official guardians of Irish literary culture.

The Land of Spices can be read as a redeployment and intensification of the mother-and-governess relationship in *Mary Lavelle*, a relationship that is emblematic of relationships conceived throughout O'Brien's work as exercises in power. On this occasion, foreignness of setting and the enclosed nature of the immediate environment are combined to attain a new level of intensity: The action takes place within an Irish convent of a French order of nuns. In addition, this work's animating relationship now has the intimacy of teacher, Mère Marie-Hélène Archer, and pupil, Anna Murphy, with all of its reverberations of nurturing and mastery, the source of which is the overarching presence of Mother Church. The pressures Mary Lavelle felt with regard to her moral development and sense of autonomy are here articulated more dramatically, given how much more difficult it is to escape them, and the sexual component of *Mary Lavelle* is similarly intensified.

The novel, however, has a more meditative than critical tone. Taking its title from the English metaphysical poet George Herbert's "Prayer (1)" ("Church bells beyond the stars heard, the soul's blood,/ The land of spices, something understood"), the emphasis falls on the ritualistic and selfless aspects of the vocational life, on the complexities of agape rather than the challenge of eros, on the willingness to serve rather than the urge to escape, while at the same time remaining crucially sensitive to the urgent presence of humanity and its needs. *The Land of Spices* will seem to many O'Brien's most satisfying production, in which she attains more objective possession of her psychological and spiritual preoccupations without running the risk of compromising them.

THAT LADY

O'Brien's characterization of a woman's fate in the context of power relationships receives its most lavish treatment in her greatest popular success, *That Lady*. As well as being adapted for the stage, *That Lady* was filmed with Olivia de Havilland in the title role in 1955. Set in sixteenth century Spain, the novel tells the story of Ana de Mendoza y de la Cerda, princess of Eboli and duchess of Pastrana; clearly, despite O'Brien's strong Spanish interests, it is an entirely new departure for her as a novelist. Instead of concentrating on the various stages of Ana's life as a woman in an attempt to reconstruct a novel of historical verisimilitude, O'Brien concentrates instead on the years of Ana's unlikely liberation into an experience of womanhood that had hitherto been hidden from her. The reader is explicitly informed in a foreword that this "is not a historical novel"; instead, the imaginative treatment of the material dwells centrally on a dramatization of the psychological and emotional conflicts of the case. Thus, despite a certain amount of costumery, inevitable under the circumstances, *That Lady* achieves an internal consistency with O'Brien's other novels.

That Lady covers the years spent by Ana, now widowed, in state service. To some extent, her work for the Spanish Crown during this brief period recapitulates her early years, when by virtue of her noble birth and excellent marriage she became intimate with affairs of state. Together with the old intimacy, however, there now comes a new, and this development of an additional dimension in Ana's life is at once enhancing and destructive, enriching her personal existence while risking a scandal that would entail the king's serious displeasure. Because of the character of the prevailing power structure, the most significant experience in Ana's personal life—the affair with Don Antonio Pérez—becomes the occasion of her banishment and confinement. The novel's heightened courtly context accentuates rather than dilutes its emphasis on tensions familiar from O'Brien's earlier novels—between passion and form, between desire and responsibility, between a woman's external role and her internal needs. To these tensions and conflicts her work returns again and again, and it is in her identification and negotiation of them that O'Brien's fiction is worthy of the critical attention that, beginning in the late 1980's, it has at length come to receive.

O'Brien's work is noteworthy on two levels. In the first place, it represents significant additions to the history of anglophone women's writing in the period between the two world wars. Her location of her female protagonists in conditions of moral difficulty, emotional complexity, cultural unfamiliarity, and even geographical estrangement provides a comprehensive method of dramatizing women's experience as problematic and unamenable to tidying away by the powers that be. O'Brien's own willingness to live a life as autonomous as that sought by her protagonists testifies to her steadfastness, courage, and integrity. The fact that so much of her writing life was spent in exile is a tribute to both her singularity and her perseverance.

In addition, however, O'Brien's accomplishments become all the more significant when seen in an Irish context. While her novels do not articulate the concerns of her generation as explicitly as the critiques of nationalism and assumption of embattled cultural and ideological positions favored by many of her contemporaries, her work belongs with theirs as part of a concerted effort to render more authentically—that is, with greater respect for individuality and its internal realities—the life of her time. O'Brien's original contributions to this effort make her the first significant female writer of independent Ireland.

George O'Brien

OTHER MAJOR WORKS

PLAYS: *Distinguished Villa*, pr. 1926; *The Bridge*, pr. 1927; *The Schoolroom Window*, pr. 1937; *That Lady*, pr. 1949.

NONFICTION: *Farewell, Spain*, 1937; *English Diaries and Journals*, 1943; *Teresa of Avila*, 1951; *My Ireland*, 1962 (travel); *Presentation Parlour*, 1963 (reminiscence).

BIBLIOGRAPHY
Bloom, Harold, ed. *British Women Fiction Writers, 1900-1960*. 2 vols. Philadelphia: Chelsea House, 1997-1998. Volume 2 includes brief biographies of O'Brien and

twelve other authors and critical essays about their work, including analyses of individual books and broader discussions of the authors' place in literary history

Dalsimer, Adele. *Kate O'Brien: A Critical Study.* Dublin: Gill and Macmillan, 1990. The first comprehensive study of O'Brien's entire literary output, with an emphasis on the feminist dimension of her works. Includes a biographical sketch, a bibliography, and an index.

Kiberd, Declan. "Kate O'Brien: *The Ante-Room.*" In *Irish Classics.* Cambridge, Mass.: Harvard University Press, 2001. O'Brien's novel is one of the thirty-five greatest works of Irish literature that Kiberd discusses in her book on the classics of the Irish literary tradition.

Kiely, Benedict. "Love and Pain and Parting: The Novels of Kate O'Brien." In *A Raid into Dark Corners: And Other Essays.* Cork, Ireland: Cork University Press, 1999. Kiely, a popular Irish literary critic and a writer for more than fifty years, includes an analysis of O'Brien's novels in this collection of his essays.

O'Brien, Kate. "The Art of Writing." *University Review* 3 (1965): 6-14. Provides valuable insights into the author's thoughts about the writing process.

Reynolds, Lorna. *Kate O'Brien: A Literary Portrait.* Totowa, N.J.: Barnes & Noble Books, 1987. This study is divided into two parts, the first dealing with the major fiction in chronological order and the second surveying O'Brien's treatment of various major themes. Also contains a valuable treatment of O'Brien's family background.

Walshe, Eibhear. *Kate O'Brien: A Writing Life.* Dublin: Irish Academic Press, 2006. A comprehensive chronicle of O'Brien's life. Walshe maintains that O'Brien was a pioneering writer whose novels depicted independent female protagonists and created a literary identity for the Irish middle class.

———, ed. *Ordinary People Dancing: Essays on Kate O'Brien.* Cork, Ireland: Cork University Press, 1993. This selection of critical essays examines O'Brien's heritage and feminism, describing how her works challenged the religious and social restrictions of the new Irish republic.

JONATHAN SWIFT

Born: Dublin, Ireland; November 30, 1667
Died: Dublin, Ireland; October 19, 1745

A Tale of a Tub, 1704
Gulliver's Travels, 1726 (originally titled *Travels into Several Remote Nations of the World, in Four Parts, by Lemuel Gulliver, First a Surgeon, and Then a Captain of Several Ships*)

OTHER LITERARY FORMS
Jonathan Swift's oeuvre includes a large and important body of verse, best assembled in *The Poems of Jonathan Swift* (1937, 1958), edited by Harold Williams. His letters may be found in *The Correspondence of Jonathan Swift* (1963-1965), also edited by Williams. Outstanding among a variety of political writings are Swift's contributions to *The Examiner* (1710-1711), the treatise called *The Conduct of the Allies and of the Late Ministry, in Beginning and Carrying on the Present War* (1711), and the important *The Drapier's Letters to the People of Ireland* (1735).

His prose writings have been published together in *The Prose Works of Jonathan Swift* (1939-1968), a fourteen-volume collection edited by Herbert Davis.

ACHIEVEMENTS
It is generally conceded that Jonathan Swift is the greatest satirist among English-language writers, possibly the most brilliant ironist and acerb wit in any language. The force of his satiric barbs has rendered him controversial, however, and many critics have retaliated against his potent quill by claiming that Swift is reckless, uncontrolled, spiteful, insensate, heathenish, and insane. Such rash responses merely demonstrate the powerful effects of his writing.

Swift is not an overt lampooner, diatribe-monger, or name-caller. Curiously, he never utilizes the direct approach; he almost always speaks through a defective mouthpiece, a flawed, self-incriminating persona who forges a case against himself. Indeed, Swift is to be remembered as a grand satiric mimic, finely shaping and generating the voices of knaves and fools alike (the "modern" hack writer in *A Tale of a Tub*, the ignorant serving-woman Frances Harris, the idiot astrologer Isaac Bickerstaff, the callous and mathematical Modest Proposer, the proud but demented simpleton Lemuel Gulliver).

Swift's ear for clichés and inflections of dullness is almost perfect, and authors such as Herbert Read (in *English Prose Style*, 1928) have hailed Swift as the inevitable and clear master of "pure prose" style. Swift is, without doubt, the major satirist in prose, yet he is also a first-rate light poet (in the manner of Horace and the coarser Samuel "Hudibras"

Jonathan Swift
(Library of Congress)

Butler), and, if anything, his reputation as a poet is rising. Furthermore, Swift wrote political pamphlets with ruthless force, and his prose in sermons, letters, and treatises is virile and direct. Finally, Swift should not be forgotten as wit and jester. He invented a child-language when corresponding with Stella, wrote mock-Latin sayings, devised wicked epigrams, created paraphrases of Vergil and Ovid, and could even toy with versifying when devising invitations to dinner. In a word, Swift is the all-around expert in English in straightforward exposition—especially when it is bent to provoke savage mockery and the *jeu d'esprit.*

BIOGRAPHY

Jonathan Swift was born in Dublin, Ireland, on November 30, 1667, after the death of his father, a lower-middle class Anglo-Irishman. His grandfather, the Reverend Thomas Swift, had been a vicar in Herefordshire. His father, also named Jonathan, had settled in Ireland to work as a steward of the King's Inns in Dublin. His mother was Abigail Erick, the daughter of a Leicestershire clergyman. Swift's mother entrusted her young son to a nurse, who spirited the infant Swift away from Ireland for several years; he was eventually returned, and he was peculiarly linked with Ireland throughout his life. In any case, it was his fancy to picture himself a lonely outcast amid barbarians.

Swift attended Kilkenny School in his youth and Trinity College, Dublin, obtaining a bachelor's degree in 1686. He spent most of the following decade at Moor Park, Surrey, in the household of Sir William Temple, the distinguished Whig statesman. It was at Moor Park that Swift met, in 1689, the child of Esther Johnson (whom Swift later immortalized as "Stella"), the daughter of Temple's widowed housekeeper. Swift helped in supervising her education and inaugurated a lifelong (and little understood) relationship, for Stella later immigrated to Dublin and spent her life near the Anglican Dean Swift. Naturally, under Temple's aegis, Swift hoped for introductions and advancement, but little came of promises and possibilities, and in 1694 he returned to Dublin long enough to be ordained an Anglican priest (in 1695). He subsequently was reunited with Temple until the latter's death in 1699. Thereafter, he returned to Ireland as chaplain to the Earl of Berkeley. His reputation for talent and wit was rapidly growing.

Swift's great political period took place in London from 1708 to 1714. He became the chief spokesman, apologist, and pamphleteer for the powerful Tory leaders then in power, Robert Harley and Henry St. John, first Viscount Bolingbroke. Their fall and disgrace ushered in a lengthy era of Whig dominance that permanently drove Swift back to what he must have considered exile in Ireland. Swift had been finally rewarded (although he would have perceived it as a paltry recognition) with the deanery of St. Patrick's Cathedral in Dublin, where he served for the remainder of his life. His powerful satires had earned him powerful enemies, and significant advancement in the Anglican Church or in England was never permitted to him.

In any event, Swift served with precision, justness, and rectitude as a clergyman and continued throughout his career to be an admirable satirist and wit. He even elected to champion the rights of the maltreated Irish, and he came to be admired as their avatar and protector, a "Hibernian Patriot." In his last years, Swift suffered increasingly from deafness and vertigo (the results of a lifelong affliction by Ménière's syndrome, a disease of the inner ear), which resulted in senility and, most likely, a stroke. Guardians were appointed to oversee his affairs in his last years, and he died in 1745, shortly before his seventy-eighth birthday.

Swift played his last ironic jest on humankind in his will, which committed the bulk of his estate to the founding of a "hospital" for fools and madmen, just as he had pronounced the plan in his *Verses on the Death of Dr. Swift, D.S.P.D.* (1739):

> He gave the little Wealth he had,
> To build a House for Fools and Mad;
> And shew'd by one satyric Touch,
> No Nation wanted it so much

ANALYSIS

It must be noted that Jonathan Swift's "fictions" are nothing like conventional novels. They seldom detail the "adventures" of a hero or even a protagonist and never conclude with a character's romantic achievement of goals or fulfillment of desires. Indeed, Swift is the great master of fictionalizing nonfiction. His satires always purport to be something factual, humdrum, diurnal, unimaginative: a treatise, a travel diary, an annotated edition, a laborious oration, a tendentious allegory, a puffed-out "letter to a friend." Extremist Protestant sects condemned fiction, and "projectors" and would-be investigators in the dawning age of science extolled the prosaic, the plodding, the scholarly, the methodical, and the factual. At the same time, urban population growth and the rise of the middle class created a growing new audience, and printing presses multiplied in accordance with demand. Many "popular" and best-seller art forms flourished: sermons, true confessions, retellings (and second parts) of hot-selling tales and political harangues, news items, hearsay gossip, and science all became jumbled together for public consumption, much of which led to spates of yellow journalism. Throughout his life Swift rebelled against such indelicacies and depravities, and his satiric procedure included the extremist parody of tasteless forms—*reductio ad absurdum*. It was by such means that Swift secured his fame as an author.

A TALE OF A TUB

Doubtless his most dazzling prose performance of this kind was his earliest, *A Tale of a Tub*, which appeared anonymously in 1704. (Swift, in fact, published most of his satires anonymously, although his work was usually instantly recognized and acclaimed.) *A Tale of a Tub* is actually a "medley" of pieces imitating the penchant for an author's combining fiction, essays, letters, verse, fragments, or anything else to enable him to amass a book-length manuscript. It contains "The Battle of the Books," a wooden allegorical piece in the manner of *Aesop's Fables*, detailing the "quarrel of ancients versus moderns," and a fragmentary treatise titled "The Mechanical Operation of the Spirit," trussed up in the inept form of a casual letter to a friend.

The treatise mocks the new "scientific" trend of reducing all things to some species of Cartesian (or Newtonian) materialism. Rather comically, it deploys in a blasé manner the language of ancient Greek and Roman atomists—Democritus and Epicurus—as if they were contemporary modernists. Indeed, one pervasive theme throughout this volume is the ridiculousness of the modernist position of "independence"—although the moderns might be ignorant of the past, the ideas and genres of classical antiquity keep recurring in their works, a fact that belies their supposed originality (even while demonstrating that, as a result of solipsism, their form and control disintegrate into chaos).

Clearly, the titular piece, "A Tale of a Tub," is Swift's early masterpiece and one of the great (and most difficult) satires in any language. In its pages, an avowed fanatic "modern" aspires to "get off" an edition, to tout and sell himself, to make money, to demonstrate his uniqueness and, however evanescently, tyrannically to be "the latest modern." He seeks to reedit an old tale of three brothers and their adventures. Naturally, he decorates and updates such a version to give it the latest cut and fashion, the style and wit and jargon of the moment. (It is perhaps an accident that this tale of the dissensions of Peter, Martin, and Jack parallels the vicissitudes of the history of Christianity, as it splinters into differing and quarreling religious sects. The modern appears ignorant of historical sense.)

The new version of the old story, however, is fragmented: Every time the modern's imagination or his fancy supplies him with a spark, he promptly follows his rather meandering muse and travels into an elaboration, an annotation, or a digression. In fact, the opening fifty pages of the work are cluttered with the paraphernalia of "modern" publishing: dedications, publisher's comments, introductions, apologies, notes to the second edition, acknowledgments, prefaces, and forewords. Thereafter, when such a cloud of ephemeral formalities would seem to have been dispensed with, the author still manages to interject a plethora of digressions—afterthoughts, asides, cute remarks apropos of nothing, commentary, snipings at critics, obsequious snivelings for the reader, canting pseudophilosophy for the learned, and pity and adoration for himself. In no time at all, the entire tale is awash in detours, perambulations, and divagations.

This modern storyteller is nothing if not effervescent, boorish, and chronically self-indulgent. He claims that his pipe dreams and diversions are in essence planned excursions and in fact deliberately philosophical meditations, rich with allegorical meanings. The opposite is also true, and the modern's tub is like an empty cart—rattling around most furiously in its vacuity, making the most noise. Furthermore, the digressions become unwieldy. The tale is disrupted more and more frequently, and the digressions become longer and longer. The modern is his most penetrating in the trenchant section IX—a digression in praise of madness—as he coyly confesses that his reason has been overturned, his intellect rattled, and that he has been but recently confined. The continued multiplication of digressions (until they subvert sections of the tale) and the finale, when the modern loses his notes and his ramblings give out entirely, are easily understood as the wanderings of a madman—a modern who suppresses the past, memory, reason, and self-control. If Swift's warning about the growing taste for newness, modernity, and things-of-the-moment appears madcap and farcical, it is nevertheless a painfully close nightmare preview of future fashions, fantasms, and fallacies that subsequently came to be real.

A Tale of a Tub clearly demonstrates several of Swift's most common fictional ploys and motifs. Some representative of the depraved "moderns" is usually present, always crass, irreligious, ignorant, arrogant, proud, self-adulatory, concerned with the events of the moment. Indeed, Swift was fond of scrupulously celebrating every April 1 as All Fools' Day, but he also recognized April 2: All Knaves' Day. He doubtless felt that both halves of humankind deserved some token of official recognition. Swift also favored mixing the two, however: He frequently shows readers that a man who is manipulator, con man, and knave in one set of circumstances is himself conned, befooled, and gulled in another. As such, the modern reveals an unexpected complexity in his makeup; he also illustrates the era (as Swift imagines it) that he inhabits—a period overfull of bad taste and poor writing, which are the broad marks of cultural decadence.

   In the work of a satirist, the world is regularly depicted as cyclic in historic periods, and usually in decline. Swift and Sir William Temple both stressed some trend toward decay in the modern era and spoke often of barbarians and invasions; it was a type of satiric myth suitable to the disruptive fictions that the satirist envisions. In section IX of *A Tale of a Tub*, the modern vacillates between viewing all humankind as "curious" or "credulous," as busy probers, analysts, and excavators or as superficial and inert: knaves versus fools. As is typical of Swift, the fool and knave personas are infused with enough familiar traits to suggest that all people partake of either. Further, Swift entraps his reader by implying that there are no other categories: One is either fool or knave or both. His irony is corrosive and inclusive, capturing the reader in its toils. In that sense, Swift is deliberately disruptive; he seeks to startle and to embroil the reader in his fictions about stupidity and depravity. To such an end, he tampers with logic to make his case appear substantial and manipulates paradox to keep his readers off balance. Such techniques lend Swift his volatile force.

   These strategies are to be found in Swift's best verse; the same may be said for his two great ironic short-prose pieces: *Argument Against Abolishing Christianity* (1708) and *A Modest Proposal for Preventing the Children of Poor People of Ireland from Being a Burden to Their Parents or the Country, and for Making Them Beneficial to the Public* (1729). Both of these works seek to shock the reader and to propose the discomforting, the alarming, the untenable.

GULLIVER'S TRAVELS

   Swift's undisputed masterpiece is *Gulliver's Travels*, originally titled *Travels into Several Remote Nations of the World, in Four Parts, by Lemuel Gulliver, First a Surgeon, and Then a Captain of Several Ships*. This fictional work accommodates all of Swift's perennial themes and does so effectually. First, the work is perhaps the definitive study of new middle-class values, specifically the preoccupation with slang, cash, smug self-righteousness, self-assertion, and self-congratulation. Second, it might not be considered a "novel" in the conventional sense of the term, but it is a delightfully fact-filled simulation of adventure fiction, and it stems assuredly from the satiric picaresque tradition (in Spain and France) that greatly contributed to the formulation of modern novelistic techniques and themes.

   Swift's Lemuel Gulliver (a mulish gull) is a model representative of the fool and the knave: He aspires to befool others but nevertheless befuddles himself. His medium is the very popular literary genre of the travelogue, or record of a "voyage of discovery." The genre grew popular through its Cartesian emphasis on an inductive observer-self and the Romantic subject of adventures in far-off lands. Such a travelogue format allows the narrator to take his readers on a vicarious journey of adventure and concludes by suggesting that the traveler has fulfilled the pattern of the bildungsroman and has attained education, growth, experience, and Aristotelian *cognitio* (insight, maturation, the acquisition of new knowledge). As might be expected in an exemplary case manipulated by Swift, Gulliver is anything but the apt learner. He is a crass materialist for whom experiences consist of precise measurements of objects observed, a tedious cataloging of dress, diet, and customs, and an infinite variety of pains in note taking, recording, transcribing, and translating. He is superficiality and rank objectivity incarnate. Naturally, therefore, his everyday mean density prevents his acquisition of any true understanding.

Gulliver is a minor physician, the mediocre little man, anxious, like Daniel Defoe's Robinson Crusoe, to make sightseeing tours and to acquire cash. His first of four voyages carries him to the land of six-inch mites, the Lilliputians, and his second voyage to the land of gargantuan giants, the Brobdingnagians. Gulliver remains myopic in both locations, for he can hardly consider that tiny creatures can (and do) perpetuate monstrous deeds, and, once he perceives that the giants are rather tame, he leaps to the conclusion that they are infinitely superior to other human types (even though their political and social institutions are no better than they should be, given the quirks and flaws of human nature). In sum, the tour from very small to very large merely stimulates in Gulliver a sense of wondrous contrast: He expects in these different worlds wondrous differences.

Amusingly, what the reader finds is much the same—that is, the uneven and imperfect human nature. Equally amusing, Gulliver behaves much the same himself in his attempts to ingratiate himself with his "superiors": He aspires to become a successful competitor in all worlds as a "titled" nobleman, a "nardac," a "courtier" with "connections" at court. Like many middle-class people, he is a man in the middle, aspiring above all for upward mobility, mouthing the commonplaces of the day, utterly incapable of judging people and events. He is also the worst sort of traveler; he is a man who sees no further than his own predilections and preconceptions and who imitates all the manners that he sees around him. Actually, the realms of big and little are merely distortions of the real world. Here, one of the work's central ironies is found in the fact that Gulliver could have learned as much, or as little, if he had stayed at home.

The world of sizes is replaced in Gulliver's third voyage by the world of concepts: The muddled peoples he visits are victims of mathomania and abstraction-worship. At the same time, it is revealed that the world of the past, like the world of the present, has been tainted and corrupt. Even the potentially ideal Struldbruggs, who live forever, are exposed as being far from lucky. They are, rather, especially accursed by the afflictions of impotence, depression, and senility. Swift has, with cartoon facility, carted Gulliver all around the world, showing him the corrosive face of fallen humanity, even among the various robbers, cowards, pirates, and mutineers that had beset him as he traveled in European ships—but Gulliver does not see.

The stage is properly set for the fourth voyage. Utilizing his favorite ploys of reversal and entrapment, Swift puts Gulliver into a land of learned and rational horses (the

Houyhnhnms) and debauched hairy, monkeylike beasts (the Yahoos). Once again, there is no middle ground: All in this world is rational horse or wolfish (and oafish) bestiality. Obviously, Gulliver chooses the equestrian gentlemen as his leaders and masters. (Indeed, throughout all the voyages, Gulliver the conformist is in quest of a staid position and "masters" who will tell him what to do and grant him praise and sustenance for his slavish adulation.)

Slowly it is revealed, however, that the Yahoos are men: Gulliver *is* a debased, gross, and deformed member of the Yahoo tribe; as Swift sweetly and confoundingly phrases it, Gulliver is a "perfect yahoo." The horses themselves rebuff this upstart, and Gulliver, who has undergone every other sort of ignominy in the course of his travels, is finally evicted as an undesirable alien from the horsey paradise. At last, Gulliver thinks he has learned a lesson; he aspires to be a horse, and, back in Europe, he shuns the human species and favors the environs of straw and stables. He has hardly acquired the rationality of his leaders and appears quite mad. Swift's ultimate paradox seems to imply that people can "know" about reason and ideals but can never master or practice them. Even here, however, Swift cruelly twists the knife at the last moment, for Gulliver, several years later, is revealed as slowly forgetting his intense (and irrational) devotion to the Houyhnhnms and slowly beginning to be able to tolerate and accept the lowly human race that he had earlier so intransigently spurned. Gulliver cannot even stick to a lesson painfully and rudely learned during many years; he lacks the brains, drive, ambition, and consistency necessary to keep him on any course. Gulliver's travels eventually get him nowhere.

In sum, *Gulliver's Travels* makes a huge tragicomical case for the absurdity of pretentious humankind. Gulliver is fool enough to believe that he is progressing and knave enough to boast about it and to hope to gain some position and affluence from the event. At his proudest moments, however, he is little more than a driveler, a gibbering idiot who is raveningly insane. Gulliver's painful experiences and the brute instruction his readers acquire are a caustic finale to much of the heady and bold idealism of the Renaissance and a cautionary plea for restraint in an era launched on celebrating reason, science, optimism, and enlightenment. Time has shown that Swift was largely right: Blithe superconfidence in people, their sciences, and their so-called progress is very likely to come enormously to grief. *Gulliver's Travels* speaks to everyone because it addresses crucial issues about the human condition itself.

John R. Clark

OTHER MAJOR WORKS

POETRY: *Cadenus and Vanessa*, 1726; *On Poetry: A Rapsody*, 1733; *Verses on the Death of Dr. Swift, D.S.P.D.*, 1739; *The Poems of Jonathan Swift*, 1937, 1958 (3 volumes; Harold Williams, editor).

NONFICTION: *A Discourse of the Contests and Dissensions Between the Nobles and the Commons in Athens and Rome*, 1701; *The Battle of the Books*, 1704; *The Accomplishment of the First of Mr. Bickerstaff's Predictions*, 1708; *Argument Against Abolishing Christianity*, 1708 (first published as *An Argument to Prove That the Abolishing of Christianity in England May, as Things Now Stand, Be Attended with Some Inconveniences, and Perhaps Not Produce Those Many Good Effects Proposed Thereby*); *Predictions for the Year 1708*, 1708; *A Project for the Advancement of Religion, and the Reformation of Manners by a Person of Quality*, 1709; *A Vindication of Isaac Bickerstaff, Esq.*, 1709; *The Conduct of the Allies and of the Late Ministry, in Beginning and Carrying on the Present War*, 1711; *A Proposal for Correcting, Improving, and Ascertaining the English Tongue, in a Letter to the Most Honourable Robert Earl of Oxford and Mortimer, Lord High Treasurer of Great Britain*, 1712; *The Public Spirit of the Whigs, Set Forth in Their Generous Encouragement of the Author of the Crisis*, 1714; *A Letter from a Lay-Patron to a Gentleman, Designing for Holy Orders*, 1720; *A Proposal for the Universal Use of Irish Manufacture*, 1720; *A Modest Proposal for Preventing the Children of Poor People of Ireland from Being a Burden to Their Parents or the Country, and for Making Them Beneficial to the Public*, 1729; *The Drapier's Letters to the People of Ireland*, 1735; *A Complete Collection of Genteel and Ingenious Conversation, According to the Most Polite Mode and Method Now Used at Court, and in the Best Companies of England, in Three Dialogues*, 1738; *Directions to Servants in General . . .* , 1745; *The History of the Four Last Years of the Queen, by the Late Jonathan Swift DD, DSPD*, 1758; *Journal to Stella*, 1766, 1768; *Letter to a Very Young Lady on Her Marriage*, 1797; *The Correspondence of Jonathan Swift*, 1963-1965 (5 volumes; Harold Williams, editor).

MISCELLANEOUS: *Miscellanies in Prose and Verse*, 1711; *Miscellanies*, 1727-1733 (4 volumes; with Alexander Pope and other members of the Scriblerus Club); *The Prose Works of Jonathan Swift*, 1939-1968 (14 volumes; Herbert Davis, editor).

BIBLIOGRAPHY

Barnett, Louise. *Jonathan Swift in the Company of Women*. New York: Oxford University Press, 2007. Focuses on Swift's relationships with the women in his life and his attitudes toward the fictional women in his texts. Explores Swift's contradictory views and illustrates how he respected and admired individual women yet loathed the female sex in general. Offers a critical, nonjudgmental discussion of the misogynistic attitude Swift displays in his writing when he expresses contempt and disgust for the female body.

Connery, Brian A., ed. *Representations of Swift*. Newark: University of Delaware Press, 2002. Collection of essays examines, among other topics, Swift's treatments of gender, class, and Ireland. Includes an analysis of *A Tale of a Tub*.

Ehrenpreis, Irvin. *Swift: The Man, His Works, and the Age*. 3 vols. Cambridge, Mass.: Harvard University Press, 1962-1983. Monumental biography rejects long-held myths about Swift and provides much previously unavailable information about the author and his works. Relates Swift to the intellectual and political currents of his age.

Fox, Christopher, ed. *The Cambridge Companion to Jonathan Swift*. New York: Cambridge University Press, 2003. Collection of essays about Swift's life and work includes analysis of *A Tale of a Tub* and *Gulliver's Travels* and discussions of Swift's religion, the language and style of his works, and his representation of women.

Fox, Christopher, and Brenda Tooley, eds. *Walking Naboth's Vineyard: New Studies of Swift*. Notre Dame, Ind.: University of Notre Dame Press, 1995. Collection of essays opens with an introduction that discusses Swift in relation to Irish studies, and the subsequent essays all consider aspects of Swift as an Irish writer.

Glendinning, Victoria. *Jonathan Swift: A Portrait*. New York: Henry Holt, 1998. Biography serves to illuminate Swift's nature as a proud and intractable man. Investigates the main events and relationships of Swift's life, which may be viewed as a tapestry of controversy and paradox.

Hunting, Robert. *Jonathan Swift*. Boston: Twayne, 1989. Good source of biographical information as well as insightful, if general, analysis of Swift's art. Devotes one chapter to *Gulliver's Travels*. Includes chronology, notes and references, bibliography, and index.

Kelly, Ann Cline. *Jonathan Swift and Popular Culture: Myth, Media, and the Man*. New York: Palgrave, 2002. Chronicles the creation of Swift's literary legend in his own time and in succeeding generations. Swift realized that in "a print-contracted world, texts create authors, not the other way around," and Kelly demonstrates how the writer constructed a print persona that differed from the "real" individual.

Nokes, David. *Jonathan Swift, A Hypocrite Reversed: A Critical Biography*. New York: Oxford University Press, 1985. Offers a good introduction for the general reader seeking information about Swift's life and works, drawing heavily on Swift's writings. Nokes views Swift as a conservative humanist.

Palmieri, Frank, ed. *Critical Essays on Jonathan Swift*. New York: G. K. Hall, 1993. Collection of essays is divided into sections on Swift's life and writings, *Gulliver's Travels*, *A Tale of a Tub* and eighteenth century literature, and his poetry and nonfiction prose. Includes index.

Quintana, Ricardo. *The Mind and Art of Jonathan Swift*. 1936. Reprint. New York: Oxford University Press, 1953. One of the standards of Swift criticism, concentrating on the public Swift. Examines his political activities and writings, tracing the intellectual sources of his thought. Includes synopses of his major works and provides historical background.

Rawson, Claude. *The Character of Swift's Satire: A Revised Focus*. Newark: University of Delaware Press, 1983. Presents eleven essays by Swift scholars, including John Traugatt's excellent reading of *A Tale of a Tub*, Irvin Ehrenpreis on Swift as a letter writer, and F. P. Lock on Swift's role in the political affairs of Queen Anne's reign.

WILLIAM TREVOR

Born: Mitchelstown, county Cork, Ireland; May 24, 1928
Also known as: William Trevor Cox

<small>PRINCIPAL LONG FICTION</small>
A Standard of Behaviour, 1958
The Old Boys, 1964
The Boarding-House, 1965
The Love Department, 1966
Mrs. Eckdorf in O'Neil's Hotel, 1969
Miss Gomez and the Brethren, 1971
Elizabeth Alone, 1973
The Children of Dynmouth, 1976
Other People's Worlds, 1980
Fools of Fortune, 1983
Nights at the Alexandra, 1987
The Silence in the Garden, 1988
Juliet's Story, 1991
Two Lives, 1991
Felicia's Journey, 1994
Death in Summer, 1998
The Story of Lucy Gault, 2002
My House in Umbria, 2003

<small>OTHER LITERARY FORMS</small>

In addition to novels, William Trevor has written numerous short stories, many of which have appeared in collections such as *The Day We Got Drunk on Cake, and Other Stories* (1967), *Angels at the Ritz, and Other Stories* (1975), *The News from Ireland, and Other Stories* (1986), and *Outside Ireland: Selected Stories* (1995); his short fiction has also been published in *The New Yorker* and other periodicals. Most critics recognize Trevor as a master of both the short story and the novel. His works of nonfiction include his memoir *Excursions in the Real World* (1993), and he has also written many plays for the stage, radio, and television. Several of his television plays have been based on his short stories.

<small>ACHIEVEMENTS</small>

Considered one of the most important storytellers in the English-speaking world, William Trevor is a member of the Irish Academy of Letters. His books have won numerous awards: *The Children of Dynmouth*, *Fools of Fortune*, and *Felicia's Journey* each won the

Whitbread Award; *The Silence in the Garden* won the *Yorkshire Post*'s Book of the Year Award; *Reading Turgenev* (a novella included in *Two Lives*) was short-listed for the Booker Prize; *My House in Umbria* (the other novella included in *Two Lives*) was short-listed for the Sunday Express Prize; and *The Story of Lucy Gault* was short-listed for both the Booker Prize and the Whitbread Award. Trevor has received the O. Henry Award for four of his short stories: "Sacred Statues" (2003), "The Dressmaker's Child" (2006), "The Room" (2007), and "Folie à Deux" (2008). In 2008, he was awarded the Bob Hughes Lifetime Achievement Award in Irish Literature. In addition, a bronze sculpture of Trevor's image by Liam Lavery and Eithne Ring was unveiled in his hometown, Mitchelstown, in 2004. Always aware of a moral vision, Trevor is known for his ability to combine this vision with sometimes chilling stories, usually about the psychology of eccentrics and outcasts of society.

BIOGRAPHY

Born William Trevor Cox in Mitchelstown, county Cork, Trevor spent his childhood in provincial Ireland. After attending a number of Irish schools, and later Trinity College in Dublin, he began his career as an instructor and sculptor, teaching history and art in Northern Ireland and England. He married Jane Ryan in 1952, and in 1960 they moved to London, where Trevor worked as an advertising copywriter. In describing this period of his life (1960-1965), he has noted the boredom he experienced as well as the rewards of the job: The company had given him a typewriter to work on, thus offering him the impetus to start writing stories.

Trevor then moved to Devon, England, to write full time in his home, an old mill surrounded by forty acres. Often described as an Anglo-Irish writer, Trevor actually transcends that label, having once said that the advantage of living in England is that "it is sometimes easier to write about your own people from a foreign country," and having developed the pattern of spending half the year traveling in Italy or in Ticino, the nub of Switzerland that juts down into Italy, and visiting Ireland during the other half of the year.

ANALYSIS

William Trevor began to write fiction in his thirties and soon became one of the most revered and prolific writers in the English language. Influenced by the popular Irish writer James Joyce and the English writer Charles Dickens—writers from the two countries in which Trevor has lived—he is known for his lyrical and psychologically rich fiction, in which a moral vision shines through with unusual clarity. With a wry and often macabre sense of humor, he develops characters who are social outsiders and eccentrics, putting them into situations in which they must make decisions that irreversibly affect their lives and the lives of others. The story is always at the heart of Trevor's work, for he is a consummate narrator who weaves tales that capture readers in his fictional webs.

THE OLD BOYS

The Old Boys, Trevor's second novel, opens with the meeting of a group of "old boys," a committee of an alumni association of an English public school that is five hundred years old. As it is a tradition of the association that members do not serve on the committee until they are very senior and that all members of the committee during a two-year term of office should have been at the school at the same time, these individuals are indeed appropriately described as "old boys." This small group of men, all between seventy and seventy-five years old, includes Mr. Turtle, Mr. Nox, Mr. Swabey-Boyns, Mr. Jaraby, General Sanctuary, Sir George Ponders, Mr. Sold, and Mr. Cridley. United by their memories, jealousies, anecdotes, and dislikes, they are holding an important meeting to decide the next chairman of the Old Boys' Association. The setting is contemporary London.

Mr. Jaraby wants the job. Mr. Nox does not want Jaraby to have it, and to prevent him from getting the position, he hires a detective to watch Jaraby, whom he suspects of frequenting prostitutes, and then gets a prostitute to approach Jaraby. Meanwhile the other old boys meet, talk, and reminisce. A number of events complicate the election process, including a visit that the committee makes to the school for Old Boys Day, and Turtle dies there. This death does not perturb the others, however, since they have become accustomed to the deaths of their old friends. While the plot line of the novel is not completely unexpected—Jaraby is clearly an unpleasant character who gets what he deserves—the development of the characters is a rare accomplishment. Eccentric geriatrics, they offer Trevor the opportunity to explore old age with the skills that have become his trademarks: humor and compassion. The story is written largely in stylized dialogue, which some have criticized as artificial; however, it is consistent with the satiric tone of this novel as well as with its message about the persistence of smug, insular, superficial—and perhaps artificial—groups of old boys at every level of society and within every country.

THE CHILDREN OF DYNMOUTH

At the heart of *The Children of Dynmouth* is an aimless, sadistic fifteen-year-old named Timothy Gedge, a virtual orphan who wanders about the seaside town of Dynmouth trying to connect himself with other people. In his desperate quest for connections, he goes to funerals, knocks on people's doors, and greets everyone he meets on the street. To fulfill his dream of participating in a talent show, and thus launching a career as a comic impersonator, he enlists the assistance of several people, all of whom he tries to blackmail: an aging homosexual whose marriage he almost destroys, an adulterer who has been having an affair with Timothy's mother, and a twelve-year-old boy and his stepsister. Timothy is unmasked at the end of the novel, and he surrenders his hope of becoming a famous comedian. He does not surrender everything, however; instead, he takes on the fantasy of being the son of a couple more attractive than his own parents.

As in other Trevor novels, the characters are the focus of *The Children of Dynmouth*. United in a town that is a veritable failure, they likewise share another unity: a dislike of

Timothy, whose menacing omnipresence is unnerving and ominous. Although nothing is neatly resolved at the conclusion of the novel, there is the suggestion of redemption insofar as the vicar's wife, unable to have a son, sees Timothy as that son. In his characteristic way, Trevor leaves a trail of memorable characters and unanswered questions, both developed with humor and compassion.

TWO LIVES

The title of *Two Lives*, which contains two novellas, seems straightforward and simple. In fact, this book does trace the lives of two women, both captives of their own lives and both attempting to find escape through literature. The first, *Reading Turgenev*, is a sorrowful love story about a woman trapped in Ireland; the second, *My House in Umbria*, is a kind of thriller about a woman trapped in Italy. Though different in style and setting, the two stories have thematic similarities, including the complexity of being human and the ways in which humanity can encourage or discourage love and life.

Mary Louise Quarry is the heroine of *Reading Turgenev*, which opens with the following understated description:

> A woman, not yet fifty-seven, slight and seeming frail, eats carefully at a table in a corner. Her slices of buttered bread have been halved for her, her fried egg mashed, her bacon cut. . . . She's privileged, the others say, being permitted to occupy on her own the bare-topped table in the corner. She has her own salt and pepper.

This apparently "privileged" woman, who has been institutionalized for more than half her life, is preparing to leave the institution that has been both her confinement and her security. The authorities have decided that the patients currently in the institution will be better off in the community, and thus Mary Louise is facing a return to her husband, Elmer, and his two maiden sisters, Matilda and Rose. This trio has been getting along quite nicely without Mary Louise—just as they had before Elmer courted this unwanted intruder.

Moving back and forth in time, Trevor tells the story of Mary Louise Dallon, the twenty-one-year-old daughter of a poor Irish Protestant farmer, who tries to escape the boredom of country life by marrying tradesman Elmer Quarry, almost twice her age. He also tells the story of Mary Louise Quarry, the anguished wife whose husband is unable to consummate their marriage and whose sisters-in-law make daily life a living hell for her. Elmer retreats into alcoholism, and Mary Louise retreats into books. She enters into a chaste relationship with her invalid cousin Robert, who reads to her from the novels of nineteenth century Russian writer Ivan Turgenev. This dual relationship—with Robert and with Turgenev—allows her to escape the harsh reality of life with Elmer and his sisters. When Robert dies, Mary Louise plunges deep into herself and into literature, eventually to be institutionalized and, as described in the opening lines, eventually to be released. Past and present, as well as reality and fantasy, converge in Mary Louise's life until they create a blurry universe within which she survives.

Her counterpart in Italy and in *My House in Umbria* also deals with this blurry convergence and, like Mary Louise Quarry, holds on to literature as a ballast amid the storms of memory and reality. Emily Delahunty, also in her mid-fifties, has lived a life that is even more fantastic than the formulaic romances she has begun to write in her middle age. Sold at birth by her natural parents, she was sexually abused at an early age by her adoptive father, and eventually she becomes a prostitute in Africa, where she saves enough money to buy a villa in Italy and begin writing her novels. On a trip to Milan, she travels in a railway carriage in which a terrorist bomb has been planted. She is not harmed by the explosion, but nonetheless she is hurt in another way, for she develops writer's block, which prevents her from continuing her next novel, a work she has planned to call *Ceaseless Tears*.

Deciding to offer shelter to the other victims of the bombing, Emily also chooses to write about these survivors, intending to write about reality instead of romance. Just as the distinction between these two views of life is a literary blur, however, so it becomes ambiguous for Emily. As she narrates her story, and as she tries to write the stories of the others, she layers numerous scenes: from her past, her dreams, her romances, films, biblical stories, her fan mail from readers. The result is what she describes as the writer's challenge—and her own: "pieces of a jigsaw jumbled together on a table . . . that higgledy-piggledy mass of jagged shapes." Trying to assemble this mass, trying to write the story of her life and the lives around her, compels Emily to state what may be the moral of all of Trevor's fictions: "Survival's a complicated business."

The complications within these two novellas are testimony to Trevor's insistence that there are no neat resolutions to messy situations, no neat conclusions to fictions that resound with the complexities of human behavior. Even the obvious similarities between the novellas, including the focus on two middle-aged women who escape into literature, are deceptively complicated, for Trevor has said that he did not plan to write a book comprising a pair of novellas about two women. In his words, "They just seemed to belong together. They seemed instinctively to contain echoes and reflections of each other. Most things in art of any kind happen by accident, and this is a case in point." That two lives should intersect by accident, and that two novellas should complement each other by accident, is just one more mystery to add to the numerous other inexplicable dimensions of Trevor's fiction in general and *Two Lives* in particular.

DEATH IN SUMMER

Three deaths occur in the summer of *Death in Summer*. Like many of Trevor's novels, including *Felicia's Journey*, which immediately precedes *Death in Summer*, this novel reads like a thriller, a mystery story that begins with one premature demise and ends with another. In between, Trevor explores the complex psychology of characters, some of whom live on the fringes of society, others of whom appear to be privileged but who are nonetheless also disconnected internally and externally.

At the heart of *Death in Summer* is Thaddeus Davenant, an emotional cripple who is scarred by a lonely childhood. His short-lived marriage was for money, and it leaves him with a daughter to care for, a mother-in-law who moves in to help with this care, and potential nannies who apply for a position within the household. One rejected applicant, Pettie, reveals herself as a person as troubled and lonely as Thaddeus, and their two social classes—his the privileged elite and hers the economically deprived—clash and collide. This collision course is complicated by still other factors: an older woman with whom Thaddeus had a brief affair and who reenters his life, seeking financial help; the kidnapping of Thaddeus's daughter; and minor characters who are intriguing and critical to the ultimate outcome of the novel.

The novel's ending does not provide solutions to all the mysteries in this fiction. Indeed, Trevor concludes this book characteristically—with unanswered questions as chilling as the events he chronicles. Like Emily Delahunty in *My House in Umbria*, Thaddeus Davenant and the other survivors in *Death in Summer* learn that survival is a complicated business, one that is dependent on connections with others while at the same time threatened by those connections.

THE STORY OF LUCY GAULT

In the heartrending novel *The Story of Lucy Gault* Trevor recounts the tale of a young girl whose Protestant family is forced to leave turbulent Catholic Ireland in 1921. Lahardane is the name of the house where the eight-year-old Lucy, an only child, lives in edenic happiness with her adoring mother and British army captain father until one night when an attempt is made to burn it down. Lucy does not want to leave her idyllic life next to the sea, so before moving day she runs away in an effort to make her parents change their minds. A piece of Lucy's clothing is found on the beach, and her heartbroken parents, believing Lucy to be dead, leave Ireland for the Continent in the hope of forgetting the past.

Lucy is not dead, however. After breaking her leg, she manages to crawl to a derelict cottage and is almost dead when a servant discovers her and returns her to Lahardane. Now a pariah in the village, Lucy spends her lonely childhood in the company of childless servants, waiting for her parents to return. Meanwhile, the boy who attempted to set the fire that caused Lucy's parents to want to leave Ireland is filled with guilt and sinks into madness. Unable even to talk about the life they lived in Ireland, Lucy's parents move disconsolately from place to place, attempting to forget their daughter. As in many of Trevor's other novels, the characters go to grave lengths to avoid the truth and manage, despite unfathomable odds, to achieve forgiveness.

Marjorie Smelstor
Updated by M. Casey Diana

OTHER MAJOR WORKS

SHORT FICTION: *The Day We Got Drunk on Cake, and Other Stories*, 1967; *The Ballroom of Romance, and Other Stories*, 1972; *The Last Lunch of the Season*, 1973; *Angels at* the Ritz, and Other Stories, 1975; *Lovers of Their Time, and Other Stories*, 1978; *Beyond the Pale, and Other Stories*, 1981; *The Stories of William Trevor*, 1983; *The News from Ireland, and Other Stories*, 1986; *Family Sins, and Other Stories*, 1990; *Collected Stories*, 1992; *Ireland: Selected Stories*, 1995; *Marrying Damian*, 1995 (limited edition); *Outside Ireland: Selected Stories*, 1995; *After Rain*, 1996; *The Hill Bachelors*, 2000; *A Bit on the Side*, 2004; *The Dressmaker's Child*, 2005; *Cheating at Canasta*, 2007.

PLAYS: *The Elephant's Foot*, pr. 1965; *The Girl*, pr. 1967 (televised), pr., pb. 1968 (staged); *A Night Mrs. da Tanka*, pr. 1968 (televised), pr., pb. 1972 (staged); *Going Home*, pr. 1970 (radio play), pr., pb. 1972 (staged); *The Old Boys*, pr., pb. 1971; *A Perfect Relationship*, pr. 1973; *Marriages*, pr. 1973; *The Fifty-seventh Saturday*, pr. 1973; *Scenes from an Album*, pr. 1975 (radio play), pr., pb. 1981 (staged).

RADIO PLAYS: *Beyond the Pale*, 1980; *Autumn Sunshine*, 1982.

NONFICTION: *A Writer's Ireland: Landscape in Literature*, 1984; *Excursions in the Real World*, 1993.

EDITED TEXT: *The Oxford Book of Irish Short Stories*, 1989.

BIBLIOGRAPHY

Bloom, Jonathan. *The Art of Revision in the Short Stories of V. S. Pritchett and William Trevor*. New York: Palgrave Macmillan, 2006. Focuses on Trevor's short fiction (and that of Pritchett) but provides fascinating insights into Trevor's method of transforming actual events and people into fiction and the critical role of fantasy in all of Trevor's fiction.

Bonaccorso, Richard. "William Trevor's Martyrs for Truth." *Studies in Short Fiction* 34 (Winter, 1997): 113-118. Discusses two types of Trevor characters: those who try to evade the truth and those who gravitate, often in spite of themselves, toward it. Argues that the best indicators of the consistency of Trevor's moral vision may be his significant minority, those characters who find themselves pursuing rather than fleeing truth.

Fitzgerald-Hoyt, Mary. *William Trevor: Re-imagining Ireland*. Dublin: Liffey Press, 2003. Examines Trevor's fiction in the light of the great social and economic changes that have taken place in Ireland, including its growing cultural diversity. Discusses all of Trevor's major works, including *The Story of Lucy Gault*.

MacKenna, Dolores. *William Trevor: The Writer and His Work*. Dublin: New Island, 1999. Offers interesting biographical details that help explain the influences on Trevor's fiction. Includes bibliography and index.

Morrison, Kristin. *William Trevor*. New York: Twayne, 1993. Presents a good general introduction to Trevor's work, focusing on a conceptual "system of correspondences" often manifested in the fiction by a rhetorical strategy of "significant simultaneity" and a central metaphor of the Edenic garden. Examines the overall unity of Trevor's fiction through close readings of his major works.

Schirmer, Gregory A. *William Trevor: A Study in His Fiction*. New York: Routledge,

1990. Excellent study, one of the first book-length examinations of Trevor's fictional writings, notes the tension in Trevor's works between morality and the elements in contemporary society that make morality almost an impossibility, with lonely alienation the result. Discusses Trevor as an outsider, both in Ireland and in England. Includes bibliographical references.

OSCAR WILDE

Born: Dublin, Ireland; October 16, 1854
Died: Paris, France; November 30, 1900
Also known as: Oscar Fingal O'Flahertie Wills Wilde

PRINCIPAL LONG FICTION

The Picture of Dorian Gray, 1890 (serial), 1891 (expanded)

OTHER LITERARY FORMS

Oscar Wilde wrote in a number of literary forms. His earliest works were poems published in various journals and collected in a volume titled *Poems* in 1881. His later and longer poems, including *The Sphinx* (1894), were occasionally overwrought or contrived, but his final published poem, *The Ballad of Reading Gaol* (1898), is regarded by many as a masterpiece. Wilde wrote two collections of fairy tales, *The Happy Prince, and Other Tales* (1888) and *A House of Pomegranates* (1891). He wrote several plays, most notably the comedies *Lady Windermere's Fan* (pr. 1892), *A Woman of No Importance* (pr. 1893), the successful farce *The Importance of Being Earnest: A Trivial Comedy for Serious People* (pr. 1895), and the controversial and temporarily banned *Salomé* (pb. 1893 in French; pb. 1894 in English). Finally, Wilde wrote a few short stories, including "The Canterville Ghost" (1887) and "Lord Arthur Savile's Crime" (1887).

ACHIEVEMENTS

Oscar Wilde's works remain popular more than a century after his death. This is due in part to the enduring beauty of Wilde's poetry and prose as well as to the timeless insights the works offer about art and morality. Wilde's conclusions are presented with such easy elegance and wit that readers enjoy the seduction of the narrative. No doubt Wilde's provocative statements and iconoclastic poses, as well as the notoriety of his trial, helped to immortalize him and thus to sustain interest in his writings for generations. Wilde received Trinity College's Berkeley Gold Medal for Greek in 1874, and he won the Newdigate Prize for Poetry in 1878.

BIOGRAPHY

Oscar Fingal O'Flahertie Wills Wilde was born to ambitious, successful Irish parents in Dublin in 1854. As a young man he attended Trinity College, and in 1874 (at age twenty) he entered Magdalen College, Oxford, on a scholarship. Wilde was drawn to art criticism and literature in his studies, and he was strongly influenced by several mentors, most notably writers John Ruskin and Walter Pater. At college Wilde discovered, developed, and began to refine his extraordinary gifts of creativity, analysis, and expression. These he pressed into the service of aestheticism, an iconoclastic artistic movement, pro-

Oscar Wilde
(Library of Congress)

moted by Pater, that advocated art for art's sake. Wilde would come to personify aestheticism, with all its intellectual refinement, provocative posing, and hedonistic excess.

Wilde married Constance Lloyd in 1884 and with her had two sons. Although throughout his short life Wilde evinced great love and devotion to his wife and sons, he grew increasingly involved in sexual liaisons with men. Most notably and tragically, Wilde became engrossed in an obsessive and rocky gay friendship with Lord Alfred Douglas, the son of the marquis of Queensberry. Douglas helped to lead Wilde deeper into London's gay underworld. While Douglas at times seemed to love Wilde genuinely, he periodically became impatient, selfish, and abusive toward his older friend. Still, Wilde remained, with increasing recklessness, committed to Douglas.

During the second half of the 1880's Wilde wrote poems, plays, and stories with increasing success. To a large extent, however, it was the provocative and radical remarks he made at public lectures and at the social functions he so frequently attended that gained for him sustained public attention. Wilde was a gifted speaker with a keen sense of timing and an ability to lampoon societal standards with his humorous remarks.

The Victorian public's amusement with Wilde's contrarianism turned to contempt in 1895. In that year the marquis of Queensberry, furious over the writer's continuing relationship with his son, accused Wilde of being a "sodomite." Wilde ill-advisedly sued for libel, maintaining that he was not, in fact, gay. The marquis, to support his claim about Wilde's homosexuality, entered into court various letters and other pieces of evidence. When Queensberry's lawyer was about to produce as witnesses young male prostitutes who had had sexual relations with Wilde, Wilde's lawyer withdrew from the suit. Queensberry was acquitted by the jury, and almost immediately after the trial, Wilde was arrested for violation of England's sodomy laws. By now the public had all but deserted Wilde, and after his conviction even most of his friends disavowed him. Wilde spent two years in prison for his offenses.

Upon his release from prison in 1897, Wilde left England to live in exile, finally locating in Paris. He lived under the alias Sebastian Melmoth, attempting to expunge his notoriety as the humiliated Oscar Wilde. His spirits and his health had been broken by his prison sentence, however, and Wilde died within three years, at age forty-six.

ANALYSIS

Oscar Wilde began his literary efforts with poetry, which was a common approach in his day. He published *Ravenna* in 1878. He would write little poetry after the release of *Poems* in 1881. For the next several years he gave lectures in Europe and the United States, establishing his name on both sides of the Atlantic. He also assumed the editorship of a monthly magazine, *The Lady's World*, which was rechristened *The Woman's World*.

In the late 1880's Wilde wrote two collections of fairy tales as well as a number of short stories, essays, and book reviews. He steadily gained attention as a writer, social critic, and, most of all, aesthete. Literary critics frequently were unenthusiastic, or even hostile, toward his works, finding them to be overly contrived or recklessly immoral. There is no doubt that Wilde's characteristic indolence (which he exaggerated for show) constrained his ability to see his works through to the final stages of editing and polishing. It is true also that Wilde's writing frequently ridiculed social conventions, mores, and morals. Wilde was, however, indisputably an ingenious analyst of art and culture, possessing a mastery of prose and verse and equipped with a keen sense of paradox.

THE PICTURE OF DORIAN GRAY

Oscar Wilde's only novel was published in its complete form in 1891. It is not a long book, and some of its features reflect the writer's haste or carelessness. However, the story is a fascinating and engaging one, at once depicting basic elements of human nature and conjuring fantastic, almost gothic images. Its plot is rather simple, but the ideas and issues that the narrative presents are complex and even profound. Perhaps for this reason the book has stood the test of time.

The story centers on three figures: an artist (Basil Hallward), his clever but impudent friend (Lord Henry Wotton), and a young, attractive, and impressionable man (Dorian Gray). Basil paints a full-length portrait of young Dorian and presents it to him as a gift. Lord Henry, who meets Dorian for the first time at Basil's studio, talks at length about the supreme value, but transience, of youth. Immediately drawn to Lord Henry's theories, Dorian observes the just-completed portrait of himself and remarks on "how sad it is" that he "shall grow old, and horrible, and dreadful. But this picture will remain always young. . . . If it were only the other way!" In the first section of the book, therefore, Wilde sets up a framework to examine some fundamental ideas about art and beauty: the transience of beauty, the inevitability of aging and death, the goal of the artist to "capture" beauty in art, and the corruptive influence of ideas, among others.

Wilde uses Lord Henry—whom Wilde later declared to be a depiction of how the public perceived Wilde—to provide the corruptive theories and ideas. Throughout the book Lord Henry utters clever aphorisms and paradoxes in Wilde's celebrated wordplay. Dorian is infatuated by Lord Henry and appears receptive to his theories and values. Readers soon see evidence of the corruptive influence of those theories and values in Dorian's behavior. Dorian becomes smitten by a young actress in a seedy theater. He returns with Basil and Lord Henry to watch her perform, but this time he is disappointed by her acting. After the performance the actress declares to Dorian that he has helped her see how false is her world of acting—the false world of the stage—and she declares her love for him. Dorian, however, spitefully dismisses her, claiming that she had thrown away her artistic genius and poetic intellect. Now, she "simply produce(s) no effect."

Upon returning home, Dorian observes a slight change in the portrait Basil had painted of him. Dorian notes a "touch of cruelty in the mouth." It becomes evident that the painting shows the outward signs of sin and of aging, while Dorian himself does not change appearance. Although first horrified by this, Dorian eventually learns to take advantage of the situation. The narrative traces an ever-worsening degradation of Dorian Gray's soul. He lives for sensations and self-gratification, without regard for the consequences of his actions for others. He is seemingly unbound by any sense of morality—indeed, the very notion of violating moral strictures seems to be an attractive prospect for him. Near the climax of the story Dorian goes so far as to murder Basil.

The story thus raises provocative questions about morality and self-imposed restraint. If a person could be assured that any indulgences, including gluttony, sexual abandon, and avarice, would have no effects on his or her earthly body, would self-control survive? What opportunities and temptations are imposed on a person who possesses unusual and eternal beauty? What is the relationship between virtue and constraint? What are the consequences of unexposed moral degradation? Indeed, what are the causes of immorality?

The Picture of Dorian Gray aroused enormous indignation in Wilde's contemporaries, and it was treated especially harshly by most critics. There seemed to be a consensus that the book itself was immoral, that it could corrupt readers, and that it somehow promoted decadent behavior. One can easily arrive at the opposite conclusion, however. The story clearly emphasizes the costs of self-indulgent, immoral behavior. It literally shows this in the changes that appear in the painting, which is understood to portray the condition of Dorian's soul. The story also makes a point of noting the harm done to others by Dorian's misbehavior: reputations ruined, hearts broken, suicides induced, murders committed. In no way does the book portray the corruption of Dorian Gray in a glamorous or seductive way. Instead, the effect is to repulse the reader.

The book might be somewhat corruptive in its suggestion that immorality may be less a choice than simply a product of circumstances. We have no reason to believe that Dorian Gray is intrinsically evil; rather, if the book's basic premise is that one's soul is normally reflected in one's appearance, then the introduction of Dorian as possessing "youth's passionate purity" conveys the idea that he is especially innocent. Ironically, Wilde himself was accused of corrupting a young man (Lord Alfred Douglas), and his writings (including *The Picture of Dorian Gray*) were held up as evidence of his dangerous ideas. That Wilde responded that he believed there was no such thing as an immoral book, only a badly written one, compounds the irony.

The fatalistic view of sin (which might be consistent with Wilde's religious upbringing, such as it was) is further evidenced when Dorian is unable to change his course toward the end of the book. He feels his past starting to catch up with him as people he has wronged, or their defenders, begin to identify him and his actions. Resolving to abandon his ways, Dorian decides to do a good deed; he cancels an arranged plan to go off with (and undoubtedly take advantage of) a young female acquaintance. When he subsequently examines the portrait for evidence of his good deed, however, he detects only a smirk of hypocrisy.

In a conclusion laden with symbolism, Dorian considers his situation hopeless. He reflects that "there [is] a God who called upon men to tell their sins to earth as well as to heaven." He cannot fathom how he could ever confess his sins, however, and he recognizes that even his attempt to do good sprung from a hypocritical desire to experience new sensations. In desperation, he decides to drive a knife into the loathsome painting, which reflects all his sins. The servants downstairs hear a scream, and when they enter the room they see the portrait, restored to its original beauty, hanging on the wall. Dorian Gray lies on the floor with a knife in his heart, looking just as the figure in the loathsome portrait had moments earlier.

The conclusion creates a striking and stark symmetry, although how it answers the questions raised earlier is unclear. Still, the ending is satisfying in that it allows reality finally to come out of hiding. The parallels to Wilde's life are exceptional. While Wilde noted that the character of the languid iconoclast Lord Henry reflected how people viewed Wilde, he also asserted that it was the artist, Basil, whom Wilde actually resembled, and that it was Dorian himself whom Wilde wanted to be.

Steve D. Boilard

OTHER MAJOR WORKS

SHORT FICTION: "The Canterville Ghost," 1887; *The Happy Prince, and Other Tales*, 1888; *A House of Pomegranates*, 1891; *Lord Arthur Savile's Crime, and Other Stories*, 1891.

PLAYS: *Vera: Or, The Nihilists*, pb. 1880; *The Duchess of Padua*, pb. 1883; *Lady Windermere's Fan*, pr. 1892; *Salomé*, pb. 1893 (in French; pb. 1894 in English); *A Woman of No Importance*, pr. 1893; *An Ideal Husband*, pr. 1895; *The Importance of Being Earnest: A Trivial Comedy for Serious People*, pr. 1895; *A Florentine Tragedy*, pr. 1906 (one act; completed by T. Sturge More); *La Sainte Courtisane*, pb. 1908.

POETRY: *Ravenna*, 1878; *Poems*, 1881; *Poems in Prose*, 1894; *The Sphinx*, 1894; *The Ballad of Reading Gaol*, 1898.

NONFICTION: *Intentions*, 1891; *De Profundis*, 1905; *The Letters of Oscar Wilde*, 1962 (Rupert Hart-Davis, editor); *The Complete Letters of Oscar Wilde*, 2000 (Merlin Holland and Hart-Davis, editors).

MISCELLANEOUS: *Works*, 1908; *Complete Works of Oscar Wilde*, 1948 (Vyvyan Holland, editor); *Plays, Prose Writings, and Poems*, 1960.

BIBLIOGRAPHY

Beckson, Karl E. *The Oscar Wilde Encyclopedia*. New York: AMS Press, 1998. Comprehensive compendium of useful information on Wilde and his times. One of the entries is a lengthy and thorough analysis of *The Picture of Dorian Gray*.

Ellmann, Richard. *Oscar Wilde*. New York: Alfred A. Knopf, 1988. Standard biography draws much insight from Wilde's published works and makes use of many of Wilde's writings and recorded conversations. Extensively documented; includes bibliography and informative appendixes.

Eriksen, Donald H. *Oscar Wilde*. Boston: Twayne, 1977. Brief work provides a corrective to studies of Wilde that see him and his work as anomalies of literature and history. Eriksen assesses his poetry, fiction, essays, and drama. Chronology, notes and references, annotated bibliography, and index supplement the text.

Gillespie, Michael Patrick. *"The Picture of Dorian Gray": "What the World Thinks Me."* New York: Twayne, 1995. Maintains that the novel is a fictional model of the moral contradictions in late Victorian society. Includes information about the historical and literary contexts in which the novel was published and the book's critical reception.

Holland, Merlin. *The Wilde Album*. New York: Henry Holt, 1998. Holland, Wilde's grandson, supplements a biographical narrative with various artifacts—including photographs, press clippings, and political cartoons—that document Wilde's emergence as a media celebrity and show how Wilde consciously created his own fame. Includes rare family photographs and all twenty-eight of the publicity portraits made for Wilde's 1882 U.S. tour. This book is a useful complement to the weightier biography by Ellmann (cited above).

Kileen, Jarlath. *The Faiths of Oscar Wilde: Catholicism, Folklore, and Ireland*. New York: Palgrave Macmillan, 2005. Examination of Wilde's work focuses on his lifelong attraction to Catholicism and explores the influence of his Protestant background on his work. Devotes a chapter, "Body and Soul: Nature, the Host, and Folklore in *The Picture of Dorian Gray*," to an analysis of the novel.

Kohl, Norbert. *Oscar Wilde: The Works of a Conformist Rebel*. Translated by David Henry Wilson. New York: Cambridge University Press, 1989. Interprets Wilde's works mainly through textual analysis, although the study includes discussions of the society in which Wilde lived and to which he responded. Argues that Wilde was not the imitator he is often accused of being but a creative adapter of the literary traditions he inherited. Supplemented by detailed notes, a lengthy bibliography, and an index.

McCormack, Jerusha Hull. *The Man Who Was Dorian Gray*. New York: St. Martin's Press, 2000. John Gray, the supposed model for Wilde's most famous character, is profiled in this examination of the life of a decadent poet turned priest. This work reveals much about early twentieth century literary society and the emerging gay culture.

McKenna, Neil. *The Secret Life of Oscar Wilde*. London: Century, 2003. Controversial and groundbreaking biography focuses on how Wilde's sexuality, and homosexuality in the Victorian era, influenced the writer's life and work. Includes illustrations, bibliography, and index.

Pearce, Joseph. *The Unmasking of Oscar Wilde*. London: HarperCollins, 2000. Avoids lingering on the actions that brought Wilde notoriety and instead explores Wilde's emotional and spiritual search. Discusses *The Picture of Dorian Gray* and other works and traces Wilde's fascination with Catholicism.

Varty, Anne. *A Preface to Oscar Wilde*. New York: Longman, 1998. Provides an introduction to Wilde's life and works, particularly the period from 1890 to 1895. Some discussion of the author's earlier work gives some insight into the motivating forces behind Wilde's output. Includes index.

BIBLIOGRAPHY

SELECTION

Every effort has been made to include studies published in 2000 and later. Most items in this bibliography contain a listing of secondary sources, making it easier to identify other critical commentary on novelists, movements, and themes.

THEORETICAL, THEMATIC, AND HISTORICAL STUDIES

Altman, Janet Gurkin. *Epistolarity: Approaches to a Form.* Columbus: Ohio State University Press, 1982. Examines the epistolary novel, explaining how novelists use the letter form to develop characterization, further their plots, and develop meaning.

Beaumont, Matthew, ed. *Adventures in Realism.* Malden, Mass.: Blackwell, 2007. Fifteen essays explore facets of realism, which was critical to the development of the novel. Provides a theoretical framework for understanding how novelists attempt to represent the real and the common in fiction.

Brink, André. *The Novel: Language and Narrative from Cervantes to Calvino.* New York: New York University Press, 1998. Uses contemporary theories of semiotics and narratology to establish a continuum between early novelists and those of the postmodern era in their conscious use of language to achieve certain effects. Ranges across national boundaries to illustrate the theory of the development of the novel since the seventeenth century.

Brownstein, Rachel. *Becoming a Heroine: Reading About Women in Novels.* New York: Viking Press, 1982. Feminist survey of novels from the eighteenth century through the latter half of the twentieth century. Examines how "becoming a heroine" defines for women a sense of value in their lives. Considers novels by both men and women, and discusses the importance of the traditional marriage plot.

Bruzelius, Margaret. *Romancing the Novel: Adventure from Scott to Sebald.* Lewisburg, Pa.: Bucknell University Press, 2007. Examines the development of the adventure novel, linking it with the medieval romance tradition and exploring readers' continuing fascination with the genre.

Cavallaro, Dani. *The Gothic Vision: Three Centuries of Horror, Terror, and Fear.* New York: Continuum, 2005. Study of the gothic novel from its earliest manifestations in the eighteenth century to the early twenty-first century. Through the lenses of contemporary cultural theories, examines readers' fascination with novels that invoke horror, terror, and fright.

Doody, Margaret Anne. *The True Story of the Novel.* New Brunswick, N.J.: Rutgers University Press, 1996. Traces the roots of the novel, traditionally thought to have been developed in the seventeenth century, to classical Greek and Latin texts that exhibit characteristics of modern fiction.

Hale, Dorothy J., ed. *The Novel: An Anthology of Criticism and Theory, 1900-2000.* Malden, Mass.: Blackwell, 2006. Collection of essays by theorists and novelists. Includes commentary on the novel form from the perspective of formalism, structuralism, poststructuralism, Marxism, and reader response theory. Essays also address the novel through the lenses of sociology, gender studies, and feminist theory.

_____. *Social Formalism: The Novel in Theory from Henry James to the Present.* Stanford, Calif.: Stanford University Press, 1998. Emphasizes the novel's special ability to define a social world for readers. Relies heavily on the works of contemporary literary and cultural theorists. Provides a summary of twentieth century efforts to identify a theory of fiction that encompasses novels of many kinds.

Hart, Stephen M., and Wen-chin Ouyang, eds. *A Companion to Magical Realism.* London: Tamesis, 2005. Essays outlining the development of Magical Realism, tracing its roots from Europe through Latin America to other regions of the world. Explores the political dimensions of the genre.

Hoffman, Michael J., and Patrick D. Murphy, eds. *Essentials of the Theory of Fiction.* 2d ed. Durham, N.C.: Duke University Press, 1996. Collection of essays by influential critics from the late nineteenth century through the twentieth century. Focuses on the essential elements of fiction and the novel's relationship to the world it depicts.

Lodge, David. *The Art of Fiction: Illustrated from Classic and Modern Texts.* New York: Viking Press, 1993. Short commentaries on the technical aspects of fiction. Examples from important and minor novelists illustrate literary principles and techniques such as point of view, suspense, character introduction, irony, motivation, and ending.

Lynch, Deirdre, and William B. Walker, eds. *Cultural Institutions of the Novel.* Durham, N.C.: Duke University Press, 1996. Fifteen essays examine aspects of long fiction produced around the world. Encourages a redefinition of the genre and argues for inclusion of texts not historically considered novels.

Moretti, Franco, ed. *The Novel.* 2 vols. Princeton, N.J.: Princeton University Press, 2006. Compendium exploring the novel from multiple perspectives, including as an anthropological, historical, and sociological document; a function of the national tradition from which it emerges; and a work of art subject to examination using various critical approaches.

Priestman, Martin, ed. *The Cambridge Companion to Crime Fiction.* New York: Cambridge University Press, 2003. Essays examine the nature and development of the genre, explore works by writers (including women and ethnic minorities) from several countries, and establish links between crime fiction and other literary genres. Includes a chronology.

Scaggs, John. *Crime Fiction.* New York: Routledge, 2005. Provides a history of crime fiction, explores key subgenres, and identifies recurring themes that suggest the wider social and historical context in which these works are written. Suggests critical approaches that open crime fiction to serious study.

Shiach, Morag, ed. *The Cambridge Companion to the Modernist Novel.* New York: Cambridge University Press, 2007. Essays explaining the concept of modernism and its influence on the novel. Detailed examination of works by writers from various countries, all influenced by the modernist movement. Includes a detailed chronology.

Vice, Sue. *Holocaust Fiction.* New York: Routledge, 2000. Examines controversies generated by novels about the Holocaust. Focuses on eight important works, but also offers observations on the polemics surrounding publication of books on this topic.

Zunshine, Lisa. *Why We Read Fiction: Theory of Mind and the Novel.* Columbus: Ohio State University Press, 2006. Applies theories of cognitive psychology to novel reading, explaining how experience and human nature lead readers to constrain their interpretations of a given text. Provides numerous examples from well-known novels to illustrate how and why readers find pleasure in fiction.

British fiction
(including Australian, Canadian, Scottish, and Irish fiction)

Ahern, Stephen. *Affected Sensibilities: Romantic Excess and the Genealogy of the Novel, 1680-1810.* New York: AMS Press, 2007. Explores the rise and rapid demise of various forms of fiction that feature excessive sensibility. Considers amatory fiction, sentimental fiction, and gothic narratives produced during the eighteenth century.

Crowe, Marian E. *Aiming at Heaven, Getting the Earth: The English Catholic Novel Today.* Lanham, Md.: Rowman & Littlefield, 2007. Surveys works of four twentieth century Catholic novelists. Introductory chapters provide detailed examination of the theory of the English Catholic novel, its history, and practices current in the last half of the twentieth century.

Damrosch, Leopold, Jr., ed. *Modern Essays on Eighteenth-Century Literature.* New York: Oxford University Press, 1988. Overview of critical commentary on important eighteenth century figures and literary works. Selections represent critical approaches popular during the 1970's and 1980's.

David, Deirdre, ed. *The Cambridge Companion to the Victorian Novel.* New York: Cambridge University Press, 2001. Eleven essays offer thematic analyses of issues important for understanding Victorian fiction. Discusses Victorian publishing practices and examines issues of gender, sexuality, race, aesthetics, religion, and science.

Eagleton, Terry. *The English Novel: An Introduction.* Malden, Mass.: Blackwell, 2005. Surveys English fiction by concentrating on the work of major authors. Considers novels from various theoretical perspectives, giving primacy to Marxist readings that stress the historical and sociological aspects of fiction.

ECW's Biographical Guide to Canadian Novelists. Oakville, Ont.: ECW Press, 1993. Brief sketches of the careers of forty-nine Canadian novelists, providing information on major works and principal literary interests.

James, Louis. *The Victorian Novel.* Malden, Mass.: Blackwell, 2006. Overview of the historical and social context in which Victorian novels were written. Also examines this fiction in relationship to historical, religious, and biographical works produced contemporaneously. Includes a chronology.

Kenyon, Olga. *Women Novelists Today: A Survey of English Writing in the Seventies and Eighties.* New York: St. Martin's Press, 1988. Extensive critical commentary on six important English women novelists. Introductory chapter examines the effect of the feminist movement on women novelists and reviews the importance of techniques such as realism in English fiction.

Levine, George. *The Realistic Imagination: English Fiction from Frankenstein to Lady Chatterley.* Chicago: University of Chicago Press, 1981. Examines the concept of realism and its application in important nineteenth century novels. Provides an overview of the development of fiction during this period.

McKeon, Michael. *The Origins of the English Novel, 1600-1740.* New ed. Baltimore: Johns Hopkins University Press, 2001. Theoretically based assessment of the cultural, political, and philosophical conditions in England that gave rise to the novel in the eighteenth century. Considers a number of important precursors to novelists Samuel Richardson and Henry Fielding.

MacLulich, Thomas D. *Between Europe and America: The Canadian Tradition in Fiction.* Toronto, Ont.: ECW Press, 1988. Explores the sources of Canadian fiction to identify its unique characteristics. Traces the development of that lineage from the nineteenth century through the twentieth century.

Nolan, Emer. *Catholic Emancipations: Irish Fiction from Thomas Moore to James Joyce.* Syracuse, N.Y.: Syracuse University Press, 2007. Traces the development of the Irish novel from 1820 into the twentieth century, concentrating on the influence of Catholicism on the production of fiction.

Norton, Rictor, ed. *Gothic Readings: The First Wave, 1764-1840.* London: Leicester University Press, 2000. Sketches the careers of important Gothic novelists, provides samples from their works, and discusses the development of the genre. Includes commentary on Gothic fiction from eighteenth and nineteenth century critics and readers.

O'Gorman, Francis, ed. *The Victorian Novel.* Malden, Mass.: Blackwell, 2002. Excerpts from dozens of influential twentieth century studies of Victorian fiction. Organized thematically; includes materials on formalist approaches, feminist readings, issues involving realism, historical approaches to fiction, postcolonial readings, discussions focusing on language and form, the impact of science on the novel, and the importance of publication practices.

Parrinder, Patrick. *Nation and Novel: The English Novel from Its Origins to the Present Day.* New York: Oxford University Press, 2006. Historical account of English fiction as a representation of the concept of nationhood and character. Organized chronologically. Includes significant critical commentary on important novels and novelists. Heavily reliant on theoretical studies of fiction and culture.

Peters, Joan Douglas. *Feminist Metafiction and the Evolution of the British Novel.* Gainesville: University Press of Florida, 2002. Uses feminist theory to reexamine the development of English fiction, demonstrating the key role women writers played in shaping the genre. Also discusses novels written by men that feature female protagonists.

Powell, Kersi Tarien. *Irish Fiction: An Introduction.* New York: Continuum, 2004. Handbook designed to introduce readers to Irish fiction. Explores themes common among most Irish writers and examines key novels that have shaped the genre.

Pykett, Lyn, ed. *Reading Fin de Siècle Fictions.* London: Longman, 1996. Twelve essays on writers who flourished between 1880 and 1910, applying contemporary critical theories to analyze individual works. Attempts to explore changes that transformed the novel during this period in English literary history.

Reed, Walter L. *An Exemplary History of the Novel: The Quixotic Versus the Picaresque.* Chicago: University of Chicago Press, 1981. Systematic study of the novel that examines its unique qualities and contrasts it with older forms of discourse. Offers close readings of several texts, explaining how the English novel fits within the larger developments in European fiction.

Richetti, John, ed. *The Cambridge Companion to the Eighteenth Century Novel.* New York: Cambridge University Press, 1996. Focuses on the cultural and historical context in which the novel developed. Chapters explore the work of major figures, the role of women writers, and the rise of gothic fiction.

_____, et al., eds. *The Columbia History of the British Novel.* New York: Columbia University Press, 1994. Collection of essays tracing the development of English fiction from the seventeenth century through the twentieth century. Explores important recurring themes and also writers not normally identified as the most notable. Contains brief biographies of one hundred novelists.

Ter Horst, Robert. *The Fortunes of the Novel: A Study in the Transposition of a Genre.* New York: Peter Lang, 2003. Reviews the rise of the English novel from its roots in early Spanish prose fiction, especially the work of Miguel de Cervantes, through the novels of Daniel Defoe, Sir Walter Scott, and Charles Dickens. Focuses on the preoccupation of novelists with economic issues, broadly defined.

Van Sant, Ann Jessie. *Eighteenth-Century Sensibility and the Novel.* New York: Cambridge University Press, 1993. Thematic analysis of eighteenth century fiction, focusing on the concept of sensibility and the use of the sensual (both visual and tactile) as a technique in novels.

Willmott, Glenn. *Unreal Country: Modernity in the Canadian Novel in English.* Montreal: McGill-Queen's University Press, 2002. Attempts to identify the critical and cultural dimensions of a specifically Canadian literature. Relies on theories of modernism for establishing the theoretical framework in which individual novels are examined.

Laurence W. Mazzeno

GLOSSARY OF LITERARY TERMS

absurdism: A philosophical attitude, pervading much of modern drama and fiction, that underlines the isolation and alienation that humans experience, having been thrown into what absurdists see as a godless universe devoid of religious, spiritual, or metaphysical meaning. Conspicuous in its lack of logic, consistency, coherence, intelligibility, and realism, the literature of the absurd depicts the anguish, forlornness, and despair inherent in the human condition. Counter to the rationalist assumptions of traditional humanism, absurdism denies the existence of universal truth or value.

allegory: A literary mode in which a second level of meaning, wherein characters, events, and settings represent abstractions, is encoded within the surface narrative. The allegorical mode may dominate an entire work, in which case the encoded message is the work's primary reason for being, or it may be an element in a work otherwise interesting and meaningful for its surface story alone. Elements of allegory may be found in Jonathan Swift's *Gulliver's Travels* (1726) and Thomas Mann's *Der Zauberberg* (1924; *The Magic Mountain*, 1927).

anatomy: Literally the term means the "cutting up" or "dissection" of a subject into its constituent parts for closer examination. Northrop Frye, in his *Anatomy of Criticism* (1957), uses the term to refer to a narrative that deals with mental attitudes rather than people. As opposed to the novel, the anatomy features stylized figures who are mouthpieces for the ideas they represent.

antagonist: The character in fiction who stands as a rival or opponent to the *protagonist*.

antihero: Defined by Seán O'Faoláin as a fictional figure who, deprived of social sanctions and definitions, is always trying to define himself and to establish his own codes. Ahab may be seen as the antihero of Herman Melville's *Moby Dick* (1851).

archetype: The term "archetype" entered literary criticism from the psychology of Carl Jung, who defined archetypes as "primordial images" from the "collective unconscious" of humankind. Jung believed that works of art derive much of their power from the unconscious appeal of these images to ancestral memories. In his extremely influential *Anatomy of Criticism* (1957), Northrop Frye gave another sense of the term wide currency, defining the archetype as "a symbol, usually an image, which recurs often enough in literature to be recognizable as an element of one's literary experience as a whole."

atmosphere: The general mood or tone of a work; atmosphere is often associated with setting but can also be established by action or dialogue. A classic example of atmosphere is the primitive, fatalistic tone created in the opening description of Egdon Heath in Thomas Hardy's *The Return of the Native* (1878).

bildungsroman: Sometimes called the "novel of education," the bildungsroman focuses on the growth of a young *protagonist* who is learning about the world and finding his or her place in life; typical examples are James Joyce's *A Portrait of the Artist as a*

Young Man (1914-1915, serial; 1916, book) and Thomas Wolfe's *Look Homeward, Angel* (1929).

biographical criticism: Criticism that attempts to determine how the events and experiences of an author's life influence his or her work.

bourgeois novel: A novel in which the values, preoccupations, and accoutrements of middle-class or bourgeois life are given particular prominence. The heyday of the bourgeois novel was the nineteenth century, when novelists as varied as Jane Austen, Honoré de Balzac, and Anthony Trollope both criticized and unreflectingly transmitted the assumptions of the rising middle class.

canon: An authorized or accepted list of books. In modern parlance, the literary canon comprehends the privileged texts, classics, or great books that are thought to belong permanently on university reading lists. Recent theory—especially feminist, Marxist, and poststructuralist—critically examines the process of canon formation and questions the hegemony of white male writers. Such theory sees canon formation as the ideological act of a dominant institution and seeks to undermine the notion of canonicity itself, thereby preventing the exclusion of works by women, minorities, and oppressed peoples.

character: Characters in fiction can be presented as if they were real people or as stylized functions of the plot. Usually characters are a combination of both factors.

classicism: A literary stance or value system consciously based on the example of classical Greek and Roman literature. While the term is applied to an enormous diversity of artists in many different periods and in many different national literatures, "classicism" generally denotes a cluster of values including formal discipline, restrained expression, reverence for tradition, and an objective rather than a subjective orientation. As a literary tendency, classicism is often opposed to *Romanticism*, although many writers combine classical and romantic elements.

climax/crisis: The term "climax" refers to the moment of the reader's highest emotional response, whereas "crisis" refers to a structural element of plot, a turning point at which a resolution must take place.

complication: The point in a novel when the *conflict* is developed or when the already existing conflict is further intensified.

conflict: The struggle that develops as a result of the opposition between the *protagonist* and another person, the natural world, society, or some force within the self.

contextualist criticism: A further extension of *formalist criticism*, which assumes that the language of art is constitutive. Rather than referring to preexistent values, the artwork creates values only inchoately realized before. The most important advocates of this position are Eliseo Vivas (*The Artistic Transaction*, 1963) and Murray Krieger (*The Play and Place of Criticism*, 1967).

conventions: All those devices of stylization, compression, and selection that constitute the necessary differences between art and life. According to the Russian Formalists, these conventions constitute the "literariness" of literature and are the only proper concern of the literary critic.

deconstruction: An extremely influential contemporary school of criticism based on the works of the French philosopher Jacques Derrida. Deconstruction treats literary works as unconscious reflections of the reigning myths of Western culture. The primary myth is that there is a meaningful world that language signifies or represents. The deconstructionist critic is most often concerned with showing how a literary text tacitly subverts the very assumptions or myths on which it ostensibly rests.

defamiliarization: Coined by Viktor Shklovsky in 1917, this term denotes a basic principle of Russian Formalism. Poetic language (by which the Formalists meant artful language, in prose as well as in poetry) defamiliarizes or "makes strange" familiar experiences. The technique of art, says Shklovsky, is to "make objects unfamiliar, to make forms difficult, to increase the difficulty and length of perception. . . . Art is a way of experiencing the artfulness of an object; the object is not important."

detective story: The so-called classic detective story (or mystery) is a highly formalized and logically structured mode of fiction in which the focus is on a crime solved by a detective through interpretation of evidence and ratiocination; the most famous detective in this mode is Arthur Conan Doyle's Sherlock Holmes. Many modern practitioners of the genre, however, such as Dashiell Hammett, Raymond Chandler, and Ross Macdonald, have de-emphasized the puzzlelike qualities of the detective story, stressing instead characterization, theme, and other elements of mainstream fiction.

determinism: The belief that an individual's actions are essentially determined by biological and environmental factors, with free will playing a negligible role. (See *naturalism.*)

dialogue: The similitude of conversation in fiction, dialogue serves to characterize, to further the *plot*, to establish *conflict*, and to express thematic ideas.

displacement: Popularized in criticism by Northrop Frye, this term refers to the author's attempt to make his or her story psychologically motivated and realistic, even as the latent structure of the mythical motivation moves relentlessly forward.

dominant: A term coined by Roman Jakobson to refer to that which "rules, determines, and transforms the remaining components in the work of a single artist, in a poetic canon, or in the work of an epoch." The shifting of the dominant in a *genre* accounts for the creation of new generic forms and new poetic epochs. For example, the rise of *realism* in the mid-nineteenth century indicates realistic conventions becoming dominant and *romance* or fantasy conventions becoming secondary.

doppelgänger: A double or counterpart of a person, sometimes endowed with ghostly qualities. A fictional character's doppelgänger often reflects a suppressed side of his or her personality. One of the classic examples of the doppelgänger motif is found in

Fyodor Dostoevski's novella *Dvoynik* (1846; *The Double*, 1917); Isaac Bashevis Singer and Jorge Luis Borges, among others, offer striking modern treatments of the doppelgänger.

epic: Although this term usually refers to a long narrative poem that presents the exploits of a central figure of high position, the term is also used to designate a long novel that has the style or structure usually associated with an epic. In this sense, for example, Herman Melville's *Moby Dick* (1851) and James Joyce's *Ulysses* (1922) may be called epics.

episodic narrative: A work that is held together primarily by a loose connection of self-sufficient episodes. *Picaresque novels* often have episodic structure.

epistolary novel: A novel made up of letters by one or more fictional characters. Samuel Richardson's *Pamela: Or, Virtue Rewarded* (1740-1741) is a well-known eighteenth century example. In the nineteenth century, Bram Stoker's *Dracula* (1897) is largely epistolary. The technique allows for several different points of view to be presented.

euphuism: A style of writing characterized by ornate language that is highly contrived, alliterative, and repetitious. Euphuism was developed by John Lyly in his *Euphues, the Anatomy of Wit* (1578) and was emulated frequently by writers of the Elizabethan Age.

existentialism: A philosophical, religious, and literary term, emerging from World War II, for a group of attitudes surrounding the pivotal notion that existence precedes essence. According to Jean-Paul Sartre, "Man is nothing else but what he makes himself." Forlornness arises from the death of God and the concomitant death of universal values, of any source of ultimate or a priori standards. Despair arises from the fact that an individual can reckon only with what depends on his or her will, and the sphere of that will is severely limited; the number of things on which he or she can have an impact is pathetically small. Existentialist literature is antideterministic in the extreme and rejects the idea that heredity and environment shape and determine human motivation and behavior.

exposition: The part or parts of a fiction that provide necessary background information. Exposition not only provides the time and place of the action but also introduces readers to the fictive world of the story, acquainting them with the ground rules of the work.

fantastic: In his study *The Fantastic* (1970), Tzvetan Todorov defines the fantastic as a *genre* that lies between the "uncanny" and the "marvelous." All three genres embody the familiar world but present an event that cannot be explained by the laws of the familiar world. Todorov says that the fantastic occupies a twilight zone between the uncanny (when the reader knows that the peculiar event is merely the result of an illusion) and the marvelous (when the reader understands that the event is supposed to take place in a realm controlled by laws unknown to humankind). The fantastic is thus essentially unsettling, provocative, even subversive.

feminist criticism: A criticism advocating equal rights for women in political, economic, social, psychological, personal, and aesthetic senses. On the thematic level, the feminist reader should identify with female characters and their concerns. The object is to provide a critique of phallocentric assumptions and an analysis of patriarchal ideologies inscribed in a literature that is male-centered and male-dominated. On the ideological level, feminist critics see gender, as well as the stereotypes that go along with it, as a cultural construct. They strive to define a particularly feminine content and to extend the *canon* so that it might include works by lesbians, feminists, and women writers in general.

flashback: A scene in a fiction that depicts an earlier event; it may be presented as a reminiscence by a character in the story or may simply be inserted into the narrative.

foreshadowing: A device to create suspense or dramatic irony in fiction by indicating through suggestion what will take place in the future.

formalist criticism: Two particularly influential formalist schools of criticism arose in the twentieth century: the Russian Formalists and the American New Critics. The Russian Formalists were concerned with the conventional devices used in literature to defamiliarize that which habit has made familiar. The New Critics believed that literary criticism is a description and evaluation of its object and that the primary concern of the critic is with the work's unity. Both schools of criticism, at their most extreme, treated literary works as artifacts or constructs divorced from their biographical and social contexts.

genre: In its most general sense, this term refers to a group of literary works defined by a common form, style, or purpose. In practice, the term is used in a wide variety of overlapping and, to a degree, contradictory senses. Tragedy and comedy are thus described as distinct genres; the novel (a form that includes both tragic and comic works) is a genre; and various subspecies of the novel, such as the *gothic* and the *picaresque*, are themselves frequently treated as distinct genres. Finally, the term "genre fiction" refers to forms of popular fiction in which the writer is bound by more or less rigid conventions. Indeed, all these diverse usages have in common an emphasis on the manner in which individual literary works are shaped by particular expectations and conventions; this is the subject of genre criticism.

genre fiction: Categories of popular fiction in which the writers are bound by more or less rigid conventions, such as in the *detective story*, the *romance*, and the *Western*. Although the term can be used in a neutral sense, it is often used dismissively.

gothic novel: A form of fiction developed in the eighteenth century that focuses on horror and the supernatural. In his preface to *The Castle of Otranto* (1765), the first gothic novel in English, Horace Walpole claimed that he was trying to combine two kinds of fiction, with events and story typical of the medieval romance and character delineation typical of the realistic novel. Other examples of the form are Matthew Gregory

Lewis's *The Monk: A Romance* (1796; also known as *Ambrosio: Or, The Monk*) and Mary Wollstonecraft Shelley's *Frankenstein: Or, The Modern Prometheus* (1818).

grotesque: According to Wolfgang Kayser (*The Grotesque in Art and Literature*, 1963), the grotesque is an embodiment in literature of the estranged world. Characterized by a breakup of the everyday world by mysterious forces, the form differs from fantasy in that the reader is not sure whether to react with humor or with horror and in that the exaggeration manifested exists in the familiar world rather than in a purely imaginative world.

Hebraic/Homeric styles: Terms coined by Erich Auerbach in *Mimesis: The Representation of Reality in Western Literature* (1953) to designate two basic fictional styles. The Hebraic style focuses only on the decisive points of narrative and leaves all else obscure, mysterious, and "fraught with background"; the Homeric style places the narrative in a definite time and place and externalizes everything in a perpetual foreground.

historical criticism: In contrast to *formalist criticism*, which treats literary works to a great extent as self-contained artifacts, historical criticism emphasizes the historical context of literature; the two approaches, however, need not be mutually exclusive. Ernst Robert Curtius's *European Literature and the Latin Middle Ages* (1940) is a prominent example of historical criticism.

historical novel: A novel that depicts past historical events, usually public in nature, and features real as well as fictional people. Sir Walter Scott's Waverley novels established the basic type, but the relationship between fiction and history in the form varies greatly depending on the practitioner.

implied author: According to Wayne Booth (*The Rhetoric of Fiction*, 1961), the novel often creates a kind of second self who tells the story—a self who is wiser, more sensitive, and more perceptive than any real person could be.

interior monologue: Defined by Édouard Dujardin as the speech of a character designed to introduce the reader directly to the character's internal life, the form differs from other kinds of monologue in that it attempts to reproduce thought before any logical organization is imposed on it. See, for example, Molly Bloom's long interior monologue at the conclusion of James Joyce's *Ulysses* (1922).

irrealism: A term often used to refer to modern or postmodern fiction that is presented self-consciously as a fiction or a fabulation rather than a mimesis of external reality. The best-known practitioners of irrealism are John Barth, Robert Coover, and Donald Barthelme.

local colorists: A loose movement of late nineteenth century American writers whose fiction emphasizes the distinctive folkways, landscapes, and dialects of various regions. Important local colorists include Bret Harte, Mark Twain, George Washington Cable, Kate Chopin, and Sarah Orne Jewett. (See *regional novel*.)

Marxist criticism: Based on the nineteenth century writings of Karl Marx and Friedrich Engels, Marxist criticism views literature as a product of ideological forces determined by the dominant class. However, many Marxists believe that literature operates according to its own autonomous standards of production and reception: It is both a product of ideology and able to determine ideology. As such, literature may overcome the dominant paradigms of its age and play a revolutionary role in society.

metafiction: This term refers to fiction that manifests a reflexive tendency, such as Vladimir Nabokov's *Pale Fire* (1962) and John Fowles's *The French Lieutenant's Woman* (1969). The emphasis is on the loosening of the work's illusion of reality to expose the reality of its illusion. Other terms used to refer to this type of fiction include "irrealism," "postmodernist fiction," "antifiction," and "surfiction."

modernism: An international movement in the arts that began in the early years of the twentieth century. Although the term is used to describe artists of widely varying persuasions, modernism in general was characterized by its international idiom, by its interest in cultures distant in space or time, by its emphasis on formal experimentation, and by its sense of dislocation and radical change.

motif: A conventional incident or situation in a fiction that may serve as the basis for the structure of the narrative itself. The Russian Formalist critic Boris Tomashevsky uses the term to refer to the smallest particle of thematic material in a work.

motivation: Although this term is usually used in reference to the convention of justifying the action of a character from his or her psychological makeup, the Russian Formalists use the term to refer to the network of devices that justify the introduction of individual *motifs* or groups of motifs in a work. For example, "compositional motivation" refers to the principle that every single property in a work contributes to its overall effect; "realistic motivation" refers to the realistic devices used to make a work plausible and lifelike.

multiculturalism: The tendency to recognize the perspectives of those traditionally excluded from the canon of Western art and literature. In order to promote multiculturalism, publishers and educators have revised textbooks and school curricula to incorporate material by and about women, members of minority groups, persons from non-Western cultures, and homosexuals.

myth: Anonymous traditional stories dealing with basic human concepts and antinomies. According to Claude Lévi-Strauss, myth is that part of language where the "formula *tradutore, traditore* reaches its lowest truth value. . . . Its substance does not lie in its style, its original music, or its syntax, but in the story which it tells."

myth criticism: Northrop Frye says that in myth "we see the structural principles of literature isolated." Myth criticism is concerned with these basic principles of literature; it is not to be confused with mythological criticism, which is primarily concerned with finding mythological parallels in the surface action of the *narrative*.

narrative: Robert Scholes and Robert Kellogg, in *The Nature of Narrative* (1966), say that by "narrative" they mean literary works that include both a story and a storyteller. The term "narrative" usually implies a contrast to "enacted" fiction such as drama.

narratology: The study of the form and functioning of *narratives*; it attempts to examine what all narratives have in common and what makes individual narratives different from one another.

narrator: The *character* who recounts the *narrative*, or story. Wayne Booth describes various dramatized narrators in *The Rhetoric of Fiction* (1961): unacknowledged centers of consciousness, observers, narrator-agents, and self-conscious narrators. Booth suggests that the important elements to consider in narration are the relationships among the narrator, the author, the characters, and the reader.

naturalism: As developed by Émile Zola in the late nineteenth century, naturalism is the application of the principles of scientific *determinism* to fiction. Although it usually refers more to the choice of subject matter than to technical conventions, those conventions associated with the movement center on the author's attempt to be precise and scientifically objective in description and detail, regardless of whether the events described are sordid or shocking.

New Criticism: See *formalist criticism.*

novel: Perhaps the most difficult of all fictional forms to define because of its multiplicity of modes. Edouard, in André Gide's *Les Faux-monnayeurs* (1925; *The Counterfeiters*, 1927), says the novel is the freest and most lawless of all *genres*; he wonders if fear of that liberty is the reason the novel has so timidly clung to reality. Most critics seem to agree that the novel's primary area of concern is the social world. Ian Watt (*The Rise of the Novel*, 2001) says that the novel can be distinguished from other fictional forms by the attention it pays to individual characterization and detailed presentation of the environment. Moreover, says Watt, the novel, more than any other fictional form, is interested in the "development of its characters in the course of time."

novel of manners: The classic examples of this form might be the novels of Jane Austen, wherein the customs and conventions of a social group of a particular time and place are realistically, and often satirically, portrayed.

novella, novelle, nouvelle, novelette, novela: Although these terms often refer to the short European tale, especially the Renaissance form employed by Giovanni Boccaccio, the terms often refer to that form of fiction that is said to be longer than a short story and shorter than a novel. "Novelette" is the term usually preferred by the British, whereas "novella" is the term usually used to refer to American works in this *genre*. Henry James claimed that the main merit of the form is the "effort to do the complicated thing with a strong brevity and lucidity."

phenomenological criticism: Although best known as a European school of criticism practiced by Georges Poulet and others, this so-called criticism of consciousness is also propounded in the United States by such critics as J. Hillis Miller. The focus is less on individual works and *genres* than it is on literature as an act; the work is not seen as an object but rather as part of a strand of latent impulses in the work of a single author or an epoch.

picaresque novel: A form of fiction that centers on a central rogue figure, or picaro, who usually tells his or her own story. The plot structure is normally *episodic*, and the episodes usually focus on how the picaro lives by his or her wits. Classic examples of the mode are Henry Fielding's *The History of Tom Jones, a Foundling* (1749; commonly known as *Tom Jones*) and Mark Twain's *Adventures of Huckleberry Finn* (1884).

plot/story: "Story" refers to the full *narrative* of *character* and action, whereas "plot" generally refers to action with little reference to character. A more precise and helpful distinction is made by the Russian Formalists, who suggest that "plot" refers to the events of a narrative as they have been artfully arranged in the literary work, subject to chronological displacement, ellipses, and other devices, while "story" refers to the sum of the same events arranged in simple, causal-chronological order. Thus story is the raw material for plot. By comparing the two in a given work, the reader is encouraged to see the narrative as an artifact.

point of view: The means by which the story is presented to the reader, or, as Percy Lubbock says in *The Craft of Fiction* (1921), "the relation in which the narrator stands to the story"—a relation that Lubbock claims governs the craft of fiction. Some of the questions the critical reader should ask concerning point of view are the following: Who talks to the reader? From what position does the narrator tell the story? At what distance does he or she place the reader from the story? What kind of person is he or she? How fully is he or she characterized? How reliable is he or she? For further discussion, see Wayne Booth, *The Rhetoric of Fiction* (1961).

postcolonialism: Postcolonial literature emerged in the mid-twentieth century when colonies in Asia, Africa, and the Caribbean began gaining their independence from the European nations that had long controlled them. Postcolonial authors, such as Salman Rushdie and V. S. Naipaul, tend to focus on both the freedom and the conflict inherent in living in a postcolonial state.

postmodernism: A ubiquitous but elusive term in contemporary criticism, "postmodernism" is loosely applied to the various artistic movements that followed the era of so-called high modernism, represented by such giants as James Joyce and Pablo Picasso. In critical discussions of contemporary fiction, the term "postmodernism" is frequently applied to the works of writers such as Thomas Pynchon, John Barth, and Donald Barthelme, who exhibit a self-conscious awareness of their modernist predecessors as well as a reflexive treatment of fictional form.

protagonist: The central *character* in a fiction, the character whose fortunes most concern the reader.

psychological criticism: While much modern literary criticism reflects to some degree the impacts of Sigmund Freud, Carl Jung, Jacques Lacan, and other psychological theorists, the term "psychological criticism" suggests a strong emphasis on a causal relation between the writer's psychological state, variously interpreted, and his or her works. A notable example of psychological criticism is Norman Fruman's *Coleridge, the Damaged Archangel* (1971).

psychological novel: A form of fiction in which *character,* especially the inner lives of characters, is the primary focus. This form, which has been of primary importance at least since Henry James, characterizes much of the work of James Joyce, Virginia Woolf, and William Faulkner. For a detailed discussion, see *The Modern Psychological Novel* (1955) by Leon Edel.

realism: A literary technique in which the primary convention is to render an illusion of fidelity to external reality. Realism is often identified as the primary method of the novel form: It focuses on surface details, maintains a fidelity to the everyday experiences of middle-class society, and strives for a one-to-one relationship between the fiction and the action imitated. The realist movement in the late nineteenth century coincides with the full development of the novel form.

reception aesthetics: The best-known American practitioner of reception aesthetics is Stanley Fish. For the reception critic, meaning is an event or process; rather than being embedded in the work, it is created through particular acts of reading. The best-known European practitioner of this criticism, Wolfgang Iser, argues that indeterminacy is the basic characteristic of literary texts; the reader must "normalize" the text either by projecting his or her standards into it or by revising his or her standards to "fit" the text.

regional novel: Any novel in which the character of a given geographical region plays a decisive role. Although regional differences persist across the United States, a considerable leveling in speech and customs has taken place, so that the sharp regional distinctions evident in nineteenth century American fiction have all but disappeared. Only in the South has a strong regional tradition persisted to the present. (See *local colorists.*)

rhetorical criticism: The rhetorical critic is concerned with the literary work as a means of communicating ideas and the means by which the work affects or controls the reader. Such criticism seems best suited to didactic works such as satire.

roman à clef: A fiction wherein actual people, often celebrities of some sort, are thinly disguised.

romance: The romance usually differs from the novel form in that the focus is on symbolic events and representational characters rather than on "as-if-real" characters and events. Richard Chase says that in the romance, character is depicted as highly stylized, a function of the plot rather than as someone complexly related to society. The romancer is more likely to be concerned with dreamworlds than with the familiar world, believing that reality cannot be grasped by the traditional novel.

Romanticism: A widespread cultural movement in the late eighteenth and early nineteenth centuries, the influence of which is still felt. As a general literary tendency, Romanticism is frequently contrasted with *classicism*. Although many varieties of Romanticism are indigenous to various national literatures, the term generally suggests an assertion of the preeminence of the imagination. Other values associated with various schools of Romanticism include primitivism, an interest in folklore, a reverence for nature, and a fascination with the demoniac and the macabre.

scene: The central element of *narration*; specific actions are narrated or depicted that make the reader feel he or she is participating directly in the action.

science fiction: Fiction in which certain givens (physical laws, psychological principles, social conditions—any one or all of these) form the basis of an imaginative projection into the future or, less commonly, an extrapolation in the present or even into the past.

semiotics: The science of signs and sign systems in communication. According to Roman Jakobson, semiotics deals with the principles that underlie the structure of signs, their use in language of all kinds, and the specific nature of various sign systems.

sentimental novel: A form of fiction popular in the eighteenth century in which emotionalism and optimism are the primary characteristics. The best-known examples are Samuel Richardson's *Pamela: Or, Virtue Rewarded* (1740-1741) and Oliver Goldsmith's *The Vicar of Wakefield* (1766).

setting: The circumstances and environment, both temporal and spatial, of a *narrative*.

spatial form: An author's attempt to make the reader apprehend a work spatially in a moment of time rather than sequentially. To achieve this effect, the author breaks up the *narrative* into interspersed fragments. Beginning with James Joyce, Marcel Proust, and Djuna Barnes, the movement toward spatial form is concomitant with the *modernist* effort to supplant historical time in fiction with mythic time. For the seminal discussion of this technique, see Joseph Frank, *The Widening Gyre* (1963).

stream of consciousness: The depiction of the thought processes of a *character*, insofar as this is possible, without any mediating structures. The metaphor of consciousness as a "stream" suggests a rush of thoughts and images governed by free association rather than by strictly rational development. The term "stream of consciousness" is often used loosely as a synonym for *interior monologue*. The most celebrated example of stream of consciousness in fiction is the monologue of Molly Bloom in James Joyce's *Ulysses* (1922); other notable practitioners of the stream-of-consciousness technique include Dorothy Richardson, Virginia Woolf, and William Faulkner.

structuralism: As a movement of thought, structuralism is based on the idea of intrinsic, self-sufficient structures that do not require reference to external elements. A structure is a system of transformations that involves the interplay of laws inherent in the system itself. The study of language is the primary model for contemporary structuralism. The structuralist literary critic attempts to define structural principles that operate intertextually throughout the whole of literature as well as principles that operate in *genres* and in individual works. One of the most accessible surveys of structuralism and litera-ture available is Jonathan Culler's *Structuralist Poetics* (1975).

summary: Those parts of a fiction that do not need to be detailed. In *Tom Jones* (1749), Henry Fielding says, "If whole years should pass without producing anything worthy of ... notice ... we shall hasten on to matters of consequence."

thematics: According to Northrop Frye, when a work of fiction is written or interpreted thematically, it becomes an illustrative fable. Murray Krieger defines thematics as "the study of the experiential tensions which, dramatically entangled in the literary work, become an existential reflection of that work's aesthetic complexity."

tone: The dominant mood of a work of fiction. (See *atmosphere.*)

unreliable narrator: A narrator whose account of the events of the story cannot be trusted, obliging readers to reconstruct—if possible—the true state of affairs themselves. Once an innovative technique, the use of the unreliable narrator has become commonplace among contemporary writers who wish to suggest the impossibility of a truly "reli-able" account of any event. Notable examples of the unreliable narrator can be found in Ford Madox Ford's *The Good Soldier* (1915) and Vladimir Nabokov's *Lolita* (1955).

Victorian novel: Although the Victorian period extended from 1837 to 1901, the term "Victorian novel" does not include the later decades of Queen Victoria's reign. The term loosely refers to the sprawling works of novelists such as Charles Dickens and William Makepeace Thackeray—works that frequently appeared first in serial form and are characterized by a broad social canvas.

vraisemblance/verisimilitude: Tzvetan Todorov defines vraisemblance as "the mask which conceals the text's own laws, but which we are supposed to take for a relation to reality." Verisimilitude refers to a work's attempts to make the reader believe that it conforms to reality rather than to its own laws.

Western novel: Like all varieties of *genre fiction*, the Western novel—generally known simply as the Western—is defined by a relatively predictable combination of *conven-tions, motifs*, and recurring themes. These predictable elements, familiar from many Western films and television series, differentiate the Western from *historical novels* and idiosyncratic works such as Thomas Berger's *Little Big Man* (1964) that are also set in the Old West. Conversely, some novels set in the contemporary West are re-garded as Westerns because they deal with modern cowboys and with the land itself in the manner characteristic of the *genre.*

Charles E. May

GUIDE TO ONLINE RESOURCES

American Literature on the Web
http://www.nagasaki-gaigo.ac.jp/ishikawa/amlit

Among this site's features are several pages providing links to Web sites about specific genres and literary movements, southern and southwestern American literature, minority literature, literary theory, and women writers, as well as an extensive index of links to electronic text collections and archives. Users also can access information for five specific time periods: 1620-1820, 1820-1865, 1865-1914, 1914-1945, and since 1945. A range of information is available for each period, including alphabetical lists of authors that link to more specific information about each writer, time lines of historical and literary events, and links to related additional Web sites.

Books and Writers
http://www.kirjasto.sci.fi/indeksi.htm

This broad, comprehensive, and easy-to-use resource provides access to information about hundreds of authors throughout the world, extending from 70 B.C.E to the twenty-first century. Links take users from an alphabetical list of authors to pages featuring biographical material, lists of works, and recommendations for further reading about individual authors; each writer's page also includes links to related pages on the site. Although brief, the biographical essays provide solid overviews of the authors' careers, their contributions to literature, and their literary influences.

The Canadian Literature Archive
http://www.umanitoba.ca/canlit

Created and maintained by the English Department at the University of Manitoba, this site is a comprehensive collection of materials for and about Canadian writers. It includes an alphabetical listing of authors with links to additional Web-based information. Users also can retrieve electronic texts, announcements of literary events, and videocasts of author interviews and readings.

A Celebration of Women Writers

http://digital.library.upenn.edu/women

This site presents an extensive compendium of information about the contributions of women writers throughout history. The "Local Editions by Authors" and "Local Editions by Category" pages include access to electronic texts of the works of numerous writers, including Louisa May Alcott, Djuna Barnes, Grazia Deledda, Edith Wharton, and Virginia Woolf. Users can also access biographical and bibliographical information by browsing lists arranged by writers' names, countries of origin, ethnicities, and the centuries in which they lived.

Contemporary Writers

http://www.contemporarywriters.com/authors

Created by the British Council, this site offers "up-to-date profiles of some of the U.K. and Commonwealth's most important living writers (plus writers from the Republic of Ireland that we've worked with)." The available information includes biographies, bibliographies, critical reviews, news about literary prizes, and photographs. Users can search the site by author, genre, nationality, gender, publisher, book title, date of publication, and prize name and date.

Internet Public Library: Native American Authors

http://www.ipl.org/div/natam

Internet Public Library, a Web-based collection of materials, includes this index to resources about writers of Native American heritage. An alphabetical list of authors enables users to link to biographies, lists of works, electronic texts, tribal Web sites, and other online resources. The majority of the writers covered are contemporary Indian authors, but some historical authors also are featured. Users also can retrieve information by browsing lists of titles and tribes. In addition, the site contains a bibliography of print and online materials about Native American literature.

LiteraryHistory.com

http://www.literaryhistory.com

This site is an excellent source of academic, scholarly, and critical literature about eighteenth, nineteenth, and twentieth century American and English writers. It provides numerous pages about specific eras and genres, including individual pages for eighteenth, nineteenth, and twentieth century literature and for African American and postcolonial literature. These pages contain alphabetical lists of authors that link to articles, reviews, overviews, excerpts of works, teaching guides, podcast interviews, and other materials. The eighteenth century literature page also provides access to information about the eighteenth century novel.

Literary Resources on the Net

http://andromeda.rutgers.edu/~jlynch/Lit

 Jack Lynch of Rutgers University maintains this extensive collection of links to Internet sites that are useful to academics, including numerous Web sites about American and English literature. This collection is a good place to begin online research about the novel, as it links to hundreds of other sites with broad ranges of literary topics. The site is organized chronically, with separate pages for information about the Middle Ages, the Renaissance, the eighteenth century, the Romantic and Victorian eras, and twentieth century British and Irish literature. It also has separate pages providing links to Web sites about American literature and to women's literature and feminism.

LitWeb

http://litweb.net

 LitWeb provides biographies of more than five hundred world authors throughout history that can be accessed through an alphabetical listing. The pages about each writer contain a list of his or her works, suggestions for further reading, and illustrations. The site also offers information about past and present winners of major literary prizes.

The Modern Word: Authors of the Libyrinth

http://www.themodernword.com/authors.html

 The Modern Word site, although somewhat haphazard in its organization, provides a great deal of critical information about writers. The "Authors of the Libyrinth" page is very useful, linking author names to essays about them and other resources. The section of the page headed "The Scriptorium" presents "an index of pages featuring writers who have pushed the edges of their medium, combining literary talent with a sense of experimentation to produce some remarkable works of modern literature." The site also includes sections devoted to Samuel Beckett, Umberto Eco, Gabriel García Márquez, James Joyce, Franz Kafka, and Thomas Pynchon.

Novels

http://www.nvcc.edu/home/ataormina/novels/default.htm

 This overview of American and English novels was prepared by Agatha Taormina, a professor at Northern Virginia Community College. It contains three sections: "History" provides a definition of the novel genre, a discussion of its origins in eighteenth century England, and separate pages with information about genres and authors of nineteenth century, twentieth century, and postmodern novels. "Approaches" suggests how to read a novel critically for greater appreciation, and "Resources" provides a list of books about the novel.

Outline of American Literature

http://www.america.gov/publications/books/outline-of-american-literature.html

This page of the America.gov site provides access to an electronic version of the ten-chapter volume *Outline of American Literature*, a historical overview of prose and poetry from colonial times to the present published by the U.S. Department of State. The work's author is Kathryn VanSpanckeren, professor of English at the University of Tampa. The site offers links to abbreviated versions of each chapter as well as access to the entire publication in PDF format.

Voice of the Shuttle

http://vos.ucsb.edu

One of the most complete and authoritative places for online information about literature, Voice of the Shuttle is maintained by professors and students in the English Department at the University of California, Santa Barbara. The site provides thousands of links to electronic books, academic journals, association Web sites, sites created by university professors, and many, many other resources about the humanities. Its "Literature in English" page provides links to separate pages about the literature of the Anglo-Saxon era, the Middle Ages, the Renaissance and seventeenth century, the Restoration and eighteenth century, the Romantic age, the Victorian age, and modern and contemporary periods in Britain and the United States, as well as a page focused on minority literature. Another page on the site, "Literatures Other than English," offers a gateway to information about the literature of numerous countries and world regions.

ELECTRONIC DATABASES

Electronic databases usually do not have their own URLs. Instead, public, college, and university libraries subscribe to these databases, provide links to them on their Web sites, and make them available to library card holders or other specified patrons. Readers can visit library Web sites or ask reference librarians to check on availability.

Canadian Literary Centre

Produced by EBSCO, the Canadian Literary Centre database contains full-text content from ECW Press, a Toronto-based publisher, including the titles in the publisher's Canadian fiction studies, Canadian biography, and Canadian writers and their works series, *ECW's Biographical Guide to Canadian Novelists*, and *George Woodcock's Introduction to Canadian Fiction*. Author biographies, essays and literary criticism, and book reviews are among the database's offerings.

Literary Reference Center

EBSCO's Literary Reference Center (LRC) is a comprehensive full-text database designed primarily to help high school and undergraduate students in English and the humanities with homework and research assignments about literature. The database contains massive amounts of information from reference works, books, literary journals, and other materials, including more than 31,000 plot summaries, synopses, and overviews of literary works; almost 100,000 essays and articles of literary criticism; about 140,000 author biographies; more than 605,000 book reviews; and more than 5,200 author interviews. It also contains the entire contents of Salem Press's MagillOnLiterature Plus. Users can retrieve information by browsing a list of authors' names or titles of literary works; they can also use an advanced search engine to access information by numerous categories, including author name, gender, cultural identity, national identity, and the years in which he or she lived, or by literary title, character, locale, genre, and publication date. The Literary Reference Center also features a literary-historical time line, an encyclopedia of literature, and a glossary of literary terms.

MagillOnLiterature Plus

MagillOnLiterature Plus is a comprehensive, integrated literature database produced by Salem Press and available on the EBSCO*host* platform. The database contains the full text of essays in Salem's many literature-related reference works, including *Masterplots*, *Cyclopedia of World Authors*, *Cyclopedia of Literary Characters*, *Cyclopedia of Literary Places*, *Critical Survey of Long Fiction*, *Critical Survey of Short Fiction*, *World Philosophers and Their Works*, *Magill's Literary Annual*, and *Magill's Book Reviews*. Among its contents are articles on more than 35,000 literary works and more than 8,500 writers, poets, dramatists, essays, and philosophers, more than 1,000 images, and a glossary of more than 1,300 literary terms. The biographical essays include lists of authors' works and secondary bibliographies, and almost four hundred overview essays offer information about literary genres, time periods, and national literatures.

NoveList

NoveList is a readers' advisory service produced by EBSCO. The database provides access to 155,000 titles of both adult and juvenile fiction as well information about literary awards, book discussion guides, feature articles about a range of literary genres, and "recommended reads." Users can search by author name, book title, or series title or can describe the plot to retrieve the name of a book, information about the author, and book reviews; another search engine enables users to find titles similar to books they have enjoyed reading.

Rebecca Kuzins

CATEGORY INDEX

SUBJECT INDEX